Shakespeare

A LIFE

PARK HONAN

OXFORD
UNIVERSITY PRESS

This book has been printed digitally and produced in a standard specification in order to ensure its continuing availability

OXFORD
UNIVERSITY PRESS

Great Clarendon Street, Oxford OX2 6DP
United Kingdom

Oxford University Press is a department of the University of Oxford.
It furthers the University's objective of excellence in research, scholarship,
and education by publishing worldwide. Oxford is a registered trade mark of
Oxford University Press in the UK and in certain other countries

© Park Honan 1999

The moral rights of the authors have been asserted
Database right Oxford University Press (maker)

Reprinted 2012

British Library Cataloguing in Publication Data
Data available

Library of Congress Cataloging in Publication Data
Data available

ISBN 978-0-19-282527-8

Jacket illustration by Scott Graham based on a portrait of William
Shakespeare c.1610. Photo: Hulton Getty.

SHAKESPEARE
A Life

To Jeannette

CONTENTS

I. A STRATFORD YOUTH

II. ACTOR AND POET OF THE LONDON STAGE

LIST OF ILLUSTRATIONS

(between pp. 240 and 241)

I should like to acknowledge the following sources of facsimile illustrations:

Colgate University Library, Hamilton, New York (plate 10); Dulwich Picture Gallery, London, by permission of the Trustees (plate 23); Folger Shakespeare Library, by permission (plates 1, 4, 13, 14, 16, 17, 19, 20, 24, 25, 26, 27, 33, 34); Edgar I. Fripp, *Shakespeare: Man and Artist* (1964) vol. i, facing p. 81 (plate 6); The Huntington Library, San Marino, California, by permission (plates 8, 9); John Rylands University Library of Manchester, reproduced by courtesy of the Director and University Librarian (plate 12); National Portrait Gallery, London, by courtesy (plates 15, 21); Mary A. Porter, by kind permission (plate 22); Public Record Office (plate 28); Shakespeare Birthplace Trust Records Office, Stratford-upon-Avon, by permission (plates 2, 3, 5, 7, 11, 29, 30, 31, 32).

INTRODUCTION

Research into the Elizabethans is of such quality today that new material about Shakespeare, his town, his parents, his schooling, his friendships, or his career comes to light continually. My aim in this book is to show in an accurate narrative all that can be known of Shakespeare's life, at present, and to offer some account of his writing in relation to his life.

I have tried to supply a dispassionate, up-to-date report on the available facts, and to add new and relevant material. I write for the general public, but think that scholars will find fresh details about Shakespeare here.

This book differs from those biographies which imagine for him political roles, sexual relationships, or colourful intrigues not in the factual record. Imaginative reconstructions and elaborate psychological theories about him can be amusing; but, for me, they strain credulity. The attempt to understand his life is not new—a start was made with Nicholas Rowe's forty-page sketch in 1709. Since then, a major effort of biographers has been to collect what is known about the playwright, to synthesize it, and in a sense to clean the bones of the 'Shakespeare documents' or to separate facts from myths and errors. That effort continues today. Our knowledge of him is refined in new editions of his plays or in searching performances of them, as well as in discoveries at Stratford's Birthplace Records Office, at the Public Record Office or county record offices, or at the great collections of Renaissance books and manuscripts at the British, Huntington, or Folger Shakespeare libraries. As data accumulates, so do myths. But what, surprisingly, emerges is that the factual truth as we piece it together is more exciting, suggestive, and tantalizing than anything so far dreamed up about him. What do the facts reveal of Shakespeare's relations with Marie Mountjoy or Jennet Davenant? Or about the murders connected with his house, and the brutal killing of a family friend? If we grant that not all of his work was miraculous, how did he come to write *Hamlet*? I find such questions more intriguing than the suppositions of popular mythology, in which he is involved with so many Dark Ladies, poor boys, conspiracies, and meetings in taverns that only a miracle could explain how he found time for the stage.

One cannot escape from documentary facts. Yet it must be said that biographical forms have had to evolve so as not to distort the historical record. A whole variety of recent views of history by those whose approaches have been linked with Fernand Braudel and the Annales school in France, or with Renaissance studies in Britain and America, for example, point to the reality of social contexts. And this is the essential new insight that applies to Shakespeare biography: the historical document with its pinpoints of light, its 'facts', is an illusory thing, unless the document is used in conjunction with other facts in the continuum of its own time. The *only* way any data from the Tudor past can validly be used to show what an individual was like is as the context for a well-researched and more or less linked or continuous account. It follows that an accurate life of Shakespeare may require more research today than was thought necessary even twenty or thirty years ago. Inevitably, a wary piecing together of a factual Tudor and Jacobean 'historical present' has its own pitfalls. But only in a contextualized, pertinent, and more or less continuous narrative will there be a chance to separate fact from supposition.

What is most at stake is the matter of being accurate, or at least not woefully wrong, about individuals. I comment further on the Shakespeare biographical tradition in Appendix C, but here—for a moment—let me focus on lapses into untruthfulness. It may seem a trivial error of a recent writer to state that one day, in the 1570s, John Shakespeare took his small son William by the hand and led him over to Coventry to see the Queen's entertainments. But in inventing that incident (no record supports it) and supposing the father behaved as modern fathers might, the writer loses his chance to be accurate about a Tudor family. It is a more serious lapse, in an otherwise valuable documentary life, to establish almost no historical context for Shakespeare's schooling, his acting company, or his visits at Stratford. My point is that the form of a traditional 'documentary life' only poorly accommodates research into milieux, into changes over a span of time, or into facts about any process or development in the life being described. Even E. K. Chambers, whose syntheses of the factual record are admirable, can plunge into the Sonnets for 'glimpses of a soul-side of Shakespeare' and conclude in part that the poet was 'tired of life before his time'. Now, I do not know that the creator of Falstaff and Rosalind was especially 'tired of life', though no remark by Chambers is to be quickly dismissed. But how are we to judge the validity of Chambers's intuition without an account of context and change in Shakespeare's developing life to support it?

Cleaning one's teeth at Henley Street

It is one thing to ask for a continuous factual account of Shakespeare, and another to give it. Any new synthesis will have hundreds of gaps. One must fail again and again to find out all one would like to know about a problem, but it is not impossible to learn about Tudor social milieux. The question, I think, is whether what we can know is susceptible to delicate and accurate use. Thus, for example, we know something of John Shakespeare's double house at Henley Street, but we can only say that it was normal in households of the country bourgeois, in the 1570s, for a boy to rise at one hour in the summer, at a later hour in winter, and to clean his teeth with a sweetish paste and a cloth. We cannot say that John's son, young William Shakespeare, did just that. But to cite a norm in this case is not trivial, irrelevant, or unfactual. Cleanliness in houses of skilled craftsmen and leading aldermen in the 1570s is related to notions of 'decorum', and of respect for the self, the family, and the crafts, which Shakespeare at an early point unmistakably imbibed. Again, it cannot factually be said that *this* boy knelt before his father for a morning blessing, but until we grasp what would have been normal in many households roughly similar to his own, we can have no context for his youth and little understanding of anything unique in his development. In Chapter 5, I have used a method of 'alternative narrative' to show some of the conditions he may have found if he worked briefly for Hoghton and Hesketh, and if the best-authenticated report about his youth is true. The evidence, to date, relating to his possible stay in Lancashire is neither dismissible nor certain, and I have tried to show what has come to light about the matter after 400 years.

What is new?

Nothing that is 'new' in the present book is more central than the complex evolution in Shakespeare's mind and being that it tries to show. In ten years of work, I have examined every known source for his life, and though I use manuscripts I have not hesitated to draw on past studies of the Shakespeare documents and a wide range of other works. For their relevance to his life, I begin with sudden changes at Tudor Stratford after its more or less sedate and secure 400 years of civic life. Similarly, I have tried to relate later developments in the Midlands town, in London, and in the varying fortunes of Shakespeare's main acting company (the Chamberlain's or King's men) to documentary facts about himself. Fresh details about his youth show that he did not leave home unprepared for his career. Evidence of his mother's quick intelligence and familiarity with a quill pen, new light on his father's managerial work and troubles and on schooling at the time, neglected evidence about the social revolution of the 1570s, and fresh details about the Hathaways of Shottery all give us a fuller picture. New, or recently discovered, information about the house where he was born, the illegal activities of acquaintances such as Sturley and Quiney, about Shakespeare's investments, and about his relations with his own relatives sharpen our picture.

Further, we know more about his milieu and working conditions in London than formerly, as well as about theatres such as the Rose, the Globe, and Blackfriars, and Shakespeare's reactions to the children's companies. In a continuous narrative one has a chance to see what he learned and how he thrived, whom he imitated and at least some of the factors that set him apart as a person. The inner theatre of his development is a deep, wonderful story, of which his colleagues, his rivals, his company, his Ovidian poems, his plays, and even Stratford grain-speculators give us varying glimpses. That development occurred in an England in which communal instincts and divisions of social rank were almost unimaginably stronger than today, and where terms such as 'homosexual' and 'bisexual' and certain other modern categories did not exist. I have tried to sketch briefly the homoerotic world of his patron Southampton's friends, some attitudes expressed in the sonnet vogue, and to say what Shakespeare's sonnets may suggest about him. I include material on Hunsdon and Howard's theatrical plan, also on Shakespeare's access to books, on his reactions to changing modes in plays and to dilemmas of his company, and again on his relations with individual actors, poets, or the Revels Office so far as these can be known.

The plays

In a biography one may only touch upon great, textually unstable, works which have elaborate stage histories and critical histories of their own, and which will surely evolve or seem fresh in many new ways in the future. Without distortion, I hope, I have 'used' the plays to suggest, for example, what is known today of Shakespeare's processes of writing: of his imitativeness or response to rivals, his awareness of a troupe's needs at particular times, and his self-mockery, limited satire, and topicality. I offer no separate sections of 'literary criticism', but have not eschewed interpretation. Having read dozens of articles, books, and reviews of the dramas for thirty-five years, I make no plea for my originality, but I criticize in my own right and have tried to signal a debt when I can recall the creditor. I look into Shakespeare's apparent uses of memory and of locales that he knew, his reflection of changing theatrical conditions and of implicit criticisms of his work (as in the Poetomachia, or Poets' War), his varying attitudes to history and to sources, and some of his deepest exploratory interests in life.

As for the topic of Shakespeare's personality, I have meant it to be the implicit subject of every chapter, and yet he is to be no more fully defined and categorized, finally, than any of his sonnets or plays. At the end of the book I have offered a family tree for central figures appearing in this narrative, a tree for descendants of the poet's sister Joan Hart who are alluded to in Chapter 18, and a sketch of the Shakespeare biographical tradition and useful and relevant sources.

The notes and the third appendix will signal my chief debts to persons and sources. Yet notes many times as lengthy could not acknowledge what I have learned from others about Shakespeare. My interest began even before I brashly proposed, fresh out of the army, to write a thesis on his tragedies, decades ago, at University College London. Before a supervisor sent me on to my friend Paul Turner, James Sutherland told me, over sherry, to look into other writers 'first'. Cause and effect in a life are less neatly related than one may think, but, for a few decades, I looked into biographical problems involved with Browning, Arnold, and Jane Austen, and have not regretted that experience, as oddly preparatory as it may seem. Colleagues invited me to lecture at Birmingham's Shakespeare Institute off and on, over fifteen years, before my teaching in Renaissance literature began at Leeds.

I owe a large debt to modern Shakespeare scholarship, criticism, and performance. I gladly acknowledge fellowships at the Huntington Library and at the Folger Shakespeare Library, and grants from the Leeds English School and the International Shakespeare Association. I have been especially helped at the Huntington, the Newberry, and the Folger, at the Birthplace Records Office in Stratford, at Worcester, Tewkesbury, and the archives of Birmingham, Edinburgh, Leeds, and at those county record offices mentioned in the notes. Stanley Wells asked to read this work in draft, and I am deeply grateful for his and Ernst Honigmann's comments on the manuscript, and to Martin Banham, Inga-Stina Ewbank, David Hopkinson, and Douglas Jefferson for comments on parts of it. Kathleen Tillotson and Paul Turner helped in many ways; I have turned repeatedly to Andrew Gurr for generous advice and debate, and to Gerald and Moira Habberjam in matters of genealogy and palaeography. I am also glad to acknowledge the help of Robert Bearman, J. W. Binns, Michael Brennan, Susan Brock, Martin Butler, H. Neville Davies, R. A. Foakes, Donald Foster, Levi Fox, G. K. Hunter, Jeanne E. Jones, D. P. Kirby, Sir Ian McKellen, Tom Matheson, Peter Meredith, Richard Pennington, Roger Pringle, Elizabeth Williams, Ian Wilson, and Laetitia Yeandle. The late Fredson Bowers, Kenneth Muir, Lawrence Ragan, and Samuel Schoenbaum advised me more than once, and I am grateful for a note from the late A. L. Rowse. None of these persons can be held responsible for any of my blunders. The largest debt is to my family, all of them, including my elder daughter Corinna Honan and my brother W. H. Honan who enhanced my clarity, and my wife Jeannette, who made the task possible over ten years and who encouraged my researches long before.

P.H.

A NOTE ON CONVENTIONS USED IN THE TEXT

In Shakespeare's time, the year began on 25 March (or Lady Day), but in this book it is assumed that the year starts on 1 January.

My citations from Shakespeare are normally to the texts and line numbers in *The Complete Works*, ed. Stanley Wells, Gary Taylor, *et al.* (Oxford, 1986). In a few cases, I have quoted from the companion volume of Shakespeare, *The Complete Works: Original-Spelling Edition* (Oxford, 1986) (*O-S*).

It has seemed wise to respect the original spelling of historical documents when the sense of the quoted words is clear; but the older form of a letter (such as 'v' for 'u', or 'i' for 'j') is changed in some instances. Italicized letters within a quoted word ('her majestie') and [bracketed] words signify modern additions, such as a spelling out in full. For clarity, with longer extracts dating from after Shakespeare's early years, I have sometimes used modern spelling.

I have used M^r and M^{rs} to signify 'Master' and 'Mistress' as distinct from the modern 'Mr' and 'Mrs'. In Shakespeare's day the rank (or title) of Master usually conveyed a special degree of social distinction or gentlehood.

I

A STRATFORD
YOUTH

I
BIRTH

the cruel times before

(John Foxe)

Stratford

*S*hakespeare's life began near the reflecting, gleaming river Avon, which today flows past Stratford's Church of the Holy Trinity where he lies buried, and past a theatre where his dramas are seen and heard by visitors from all nations. In rare flood times, the river was wild and destructive, sweeping away bridges and much in its path, but normally it was hospitable to truant boys or patient fishermen, and no guttered rocks or congregated sands imperilled any large keel here. The river arises in grassy highland in the east of England near Naseby, and for miles hardly deserves the name Avon, or 'river', which has echoes all over Celtic Europe: the Avon or Aven in Brittany, the Avenza in Italy, and the Avona in Spain. This Avon is at first only a runnel and then a willow-bordered stream, but below the old city of Warwick it is slow and stately as it divides Warwickshire and cuts the middle of England.

To the north is the Arden region, where the Forest of Arden was more thinly wooded in Shakespeare's day than in medieval times. Here were irregular fields, meadows, moated farmsteads, and groups of cottages, but few villages. South and west lay the Feldon, with new ornamental parks at Clopton and Goldicote, Ettington and Charlecote. Round about were fields cultivated in narrow strips, as well as tithe barns, villages, and black and white half-timbered cottages.

Stratford-upon-Avon, between Arden and Feldon, was a market town where goods from the two regions could be exchanged. Protected because it lay in the rain-shadow of Welsh hills to the west, it had a mild climate. Farmers found the Avon valley fertile and took

3

advantage of a bridge built by the town's benefactor Sir Hugh Clopton in the reign of Henry VII to take goods to market. John Leland, the antiquary, saw Stratford's bridge with its fourteen stone arches around 1540, and noted the well-laid-out town. A parish church rose to the south at Old Stratford, and from here one walked north into good streets, partly paved, to see the Pedagogue's House accommodating a grammar school, a range of almshouses, and the Gild hall and Gild chapel. Besides back lanes the town 'hath 2. or 3. very lardge stretes', Leland wrote. 'One of the principall stretes ledithe from est to west, anothar from southe to northe.' Houses of two and three storeys were of timber, and he was struck by the 'right goodly chappell' in Church Street.[1]

The land on which Stratford was built had belonged to bishops of Worcester after Ethelhard, a Saxon king, granted it to the third bishop (AD 693–714). From then until fifteen years before Shakespeare's birth Stratford had been a *manerium* of Worcester bishops.[2] Once the town had been a small group of farms called Straetford, meaning a Roman approach to a ford, and it stood on a Roman road. But in 1196 there had been a change: a bishop purchased the right to hold a weekly market at the Avon, and his plan avoided the existing village. Land north of Straetford, some 109 acres, was laid out into six streets, forming a grid which is still visible in the town's pattern today. Three streets ran roughly parallel to the river, intersected by three more, and the land within this grid was marked into 'burgage' plots, each of which was 12 perches in length and $3\frac{1}{2}$ perches in breadth (198 feet by 57 feet 9 inches). The plots would be subdivided in various ways in the years ahead, but they allowed for ample buildings and convenient neighbourhoods. The Roman road was worked into the grid to form an open area, and hence Bridge Street is wide today. Craftsmen and merchants were attracted to settle in this well-planned town, and the 'Manerium de novo Stratford' began to thrive. It had tall inns and some 240 built-up plots (besides other tenements, shops, and stalls) in the thirteenth century, and would have been no larger in Shakespeare's day.

The medieval town of Stratford was known for one of its social features, its lay religious Gild. Membership in the Gild of the Holy

Cross was open to all men and women—and the fame of this organization spread beyond the county. Members elected their own aldermen, and a woman's vote counted as equal to a man's; the Gild provided jurors for the manorial courts, looked after the sick and the poor, prayed for the dead (even admitting departed souls to the membership), and founded a school. The Gild nearly absorbed the local government and gave continuity to local life.

Indeed, the Gild not only linked the generations, and gave common religious and social purposes to the people of Stratford, but it had too the effect of stimulating at least a few men of exceptional talent. Robert de Stratford (taking his surname from the town) probably founded the chapel of the Gild in 1296. John de Stratford, his son, rose to be Bishop of Winchester and three times Chancellor of England, before returning to found, in 1331, a chantry in honour of Thomas à Becket and a college of five priests who were bidden to pray for his family, himself, the bishops of Worcester, and kings of England. When Henry V (Shakespeare's most heroic king) confirmed the college, Stratford's church came to be called the Collegiate Church of the Holy Trinity.[3]

Civic pride—and the long traditions of the Gild—were nevertheless affected by a convulsion. Until the sixteenth century, little had unsettled the town's religious life. But new Protestant reforms struck hard at Stratford—when the College was forced to close. Then after the Gild was dissolved and its properties were confiscated, in 1547, the town government collapsed.

Worried merchants petitioned the Crown. They received a charter of 28 June 1553, which incorporated the town as a royal borough. Yet no sooner was the Corporation of Stratford-upon-Avon in being than Mary Tudor returned the nation to Roman Catholicism. Under Henry VIII, her father, few people had known from day to day which opinions were orthodox and which heretical; but Queen Mary was clearer. A woman of inflexible honesty with a dim, obstinate mind, she pressed ahead with heresy trials, supported by her bureaucracy. Stratford became the eye of a circle of martyr fires at Coventry, Lichfield, Gloucester, Wotton-under-Edge, Banbury, Oxford, Northampton, and Leicester. Women and tradesmen were burned—and a baby born in Coventry's fire was thrown back onto the hard, burning faggots. Lest anyone forget these events John Foxe, in his 'Book of Martyrs' or *Actes and Monuments*, published a year before Shakespeare's birth, was to describe them in lurid detail. One effect was that people living under the reign of Mary's successor were often reticent on points of faith. Shocking and violent as it was, doctrinal controversy had torn at the normal fabric of social connections in the Midlands, and proved bad for trade. As late as the 1590s Stratford's wardens were to be lax or restrained in reporting on non-attendance at church; Shakespeare's father and Shakespeare himself, at different times, were to camouflage their religious commitments and feelings with a caution that seems typical of all but an outspoken few at Stratford. Foxe had meant his martyrs to be remembered—and had excelled himself in an account of Bishop Hooper, who when burning had cried out to 'Lord Jesus'. When 'blacke in the mouth, and his tonge swollen, that he could not speak' he struck off an arm into the fire and 'knocked still with the other, what time the fat, water, and bloud dropped out at his fingers endes, until by renewing the fire, his strength was gone, and his hand did cleave fast in knocking to the yron on his brest'.[4]

Mary's martyrs, of course, gave immense authority to the Protestant cause, and her marriage with her cousin Philip II of Spain led to a ruinous war. When her half-sister, the Lady Elizabeth, came to the throne in 1558, French troops were in Scotland with nothing between them and England but an ill-manned fortess at Berwick. Coinage was debased, and the religious problem festered at Stratford, where a town constable had been assaulted by Alderman Perrott. If blood flew even among the council, merchants might well worry. After the Catholic vicar left in 1558, Stratford's people lived in an odd limbo with no regular vicar at all.

Master Bretchgirdle's arrival

When a sound Protestant, John Bretchgirdle, became Stratford's new vicar in 1561, Catholics were then still in the town council and Catholic frescos in the Gild chapel—but the new vicar waited. A native of Baguley near Manchester with his MA degree from Christ Church, Oxford,

Master Bretchgirdle wrote in Latin in the town's registers (whereas the Catholic vicar had used English) and settled down as a bachelor on Church Street, where as 'vicar perpetuall' he unpacked a library.

Few clergymen—outside London and the universities—could have matched it. He had a Horace, a Sallust and a Virgil, Aesop's fables, two or three books by Erasmus, with *Acts of the Apostles translated into English Metre*[5]—and his books took a long view of those forces that helped to form Shakespeare's mind. Once the Roman empire had held sway over Europe, to be replaced by the order of an imperial papacy; now the collapse of the Catholic Church in England was releasing the full effect of the European Renaissance and Reformation, so that gusto, freedom, and energy were in the English air. At the vicar's Oxford, medieval logic had given way to the humanist study of rhetoric, but everywhere an older, calmer temper of life was also passing—or was locked up in London with the 'caged wolves', the Marian bishops, six of whom Queen Elizabeth kept imprisoned. People were to know incipient doubt, a loss of calm certainty about human destiny, and sharp changes in the nation's mood. Shakespeare was born when things began to seem badly out of date. Lost with the 'old faith' were Catholic dirges and trentals, or the sets of thirty requiem services, and the *De Profundis*, shrines, pilgrimages and incense, as well as candles and torches and old ceremonies, extreme unction and purgatory and satisfactory masses. Holy days had been cut in number from over a hundred to twenty-seven, and a vicar was now exalted. The Catholic priestly function had never depended on the moral worth of the priest. Now, a vicar had to be exemplary as a teacher of God's will, and so a deep change, in each community, was helping to foster a new interest in the person—in behaviour and character.

Yet—at Stratford—one thing was unchanged. Into the fourth year of a Protestant reign the council had not removed Catholic traces in the Gild chapel; their caution was in keeping with Elizabeth's wish not to have any 'image in glass windows' broken nor to leave 'the place of prayers desolate' in chapels and churches.[6] Indeed, the Queen wisely avoided enquiry into Catholic consciences—and Bretchgirdle, in his correct Anglican 'square cap', did not purge the town of papists. He had to placate the council—and he was more articulate than many clergymen. An outcry was loud in the land against non-residency, pluralism (the holding of two or more benefices at the same time), and the horrors of 'lay patronage' which sent men to pulpits from which they never preached.[7] The power of appointment to five-sixths of the church livings in south Warwickshire was in lay hands—but Stratford's council were confident of the new vicar. In 1563 they decided at last to expunge the Catholic decor of the old Gild chapel, and in that sense the town's past was to be removed.

The Chamberlain's first son

Sitting on Stratford's governing council were trusted local men, including a bailiff or mayor (elected by themselves for a year), thirteen other aldermen, and fourteen capital burgesses. They had many rules to enforce. Bretchgirdle was responsible to the council, but he did not have to desecrate the chapel *himself*—or record the deed. The aldermen had other help, and no one helped them more in seven years than John Shakespeare.

Stratford's records tell us more about this man than appears in any biography of his son, and we see him at first as a yeoman farmer from nearby Snitterfield, who had set up as a craftsman and merchant. He had become a glover and whittawer (a dresser of soft, white-coloured leather) on Henley Street, and he would have had other interests. In the hand of a clerk, his name appears typically as 'Jhon shacksper' or 'John Shaxpere', once in a London record as John 'Shakespeare',[8] and we find it beneath terse, efficient reports.

In September 1556 John was chosen as one of the council's two tasters of ale and bread, a job for an able and 'discreet' man. He was burly enough to be a constable who had to deprive 'single-men' of weapons, and astute enough to be an affeeror, or assessor of fines. On 3 October 1561, he was sworn in as one of the two chamberlains in charge of the borough's property and finances.[9]

We have no example of his writing—though he drew his mark as a cross or as a pair of glover's compasses (an instrument used for making designs on the back of gloves); one of his marks resembles a glover's stitching clamp, or 'donkey'. Men such as John Shakespeare could often read, but not write, as writing was an advanced, fairly spe-cialized, skill, and Tudor people learned to write only after getting the basic skill of reading; he probably would not have kept the borough's accounts, as he did for over three years, if he had been unable to read sums. His wife had given birth so far to infants who died—her first child, Joan, evidently died in infancy,[10] and a second child, Margaret, was baptized on 2 December 1562 and buried four months later.

During the period when John Shakespeare was keeping the accounts, the Gild chapel was defaced. Near its orchard border of sun-dried clay, workmen moved into the chapel to see its painted walls with legends—the town's old Catholic poetry:

WHEN ERTH UPON ERTH HATH BYLDED HIS BOWERS
THEN SHALL ERTH FOR ERTH SUFFER MANY HARD SHOWERS

Over the chancel arch was a Doom, or Last Judgement, with the Vir-gin in blue and St John in bright brown. Heaven was a palace with St Peter in a red alb and green cope, and burning souls fell through a hell-mouth into a cauldron. A crucifixion rose on the south wall, and on jambs for the tower arch were Thomas à Becket and the names of his murderers.[11] After the Doom had been whitewashed, for which the workmen were paid 2s., but before the rood-loft was taken down and seats were installed for the vicar and his clerk, the acting cham-berlain's account noted on 10 January 1564:

Item payd for defasyng ymages in yᵉ chappell   ijˢ

The altar may have been removed then—but otherwise the chapel was mainly untouched. The council replaced stained glass with 'quar-rells', or glass panels, yet kept forbidden 'George' armour for their Catholic St George festival well scoured. No one knew if the old faith would return; and there were more dire problems. A plague had rav-aged London—where a fifth of the population died—and Spaniards, it appeared, had found a way to destroy Protestant England. They had closed down the main market abroad for broadcloths and kerseys at Antwerp. Forty English ships in the Thames had to be unloaded and cloth worth up to £700,000 had to be stored at the risk of damp, moth, and total loss.

Warwickshire would suffer with no cloth market. The Queen had used her wiles on the Spanish envoy—but early in 1564 the only Spanish envoy in England was a corpse, and creditors prevented the release of his body. With the cloth fleet blocked, merchants were desperate. The plague had begun to move north, killing children and the poor. On 14 March, before it struck Stratford, the vicar recorded the loss of his own sister Cicely, 'Sicilia Bretchgerdle soror Vicarij.'[12] With death and ruin on his doorstep, he even had to think of his unlucky chamberlain, whose wife had borne yet another child. As the father of two dead infants John Shakespeare, on this occasion, presented a boy. William, or *Gulielmus*, the vicar wrote on 26 April 1564, when infants were dying within two days' ride of Stratford parish,

Gulielmus filius Johannes Shakspere.

2

MOTHER OF THE CHILD

> At first the infant,
> Mewling and puking in the nurse's arms.
>
> (Jaques, *As You Like It*)

Mary Shakespeare at Henley Street

When her first son was born, Mary Shakespeare's town lay in the path of the worst plague since the Black Death. Yet the town's corporate council had been warned about the contagion, and for years the aldermen and chief burgesses had been trying to keep the streets clean. As early as April 1552 John Shakespeare had paid a small fine for keeping an unauthorized muck-heap (or *sterquinarium*) on Henley Street. At the town's northern end, this was an old, built-up street, traversed by horsemen riding through on the way up to Henley-in-Arden. Wagons drawn by oxen bumped over a cross-gutter in front of Gilbert Bradley's house, a few doors to the east of his fellow glover John Shakespeare. Once, in 1560, nearly every tenant had to pay for pavings broken by the damaging wagons. 'All the tenauntes in Henley stret from ye cros gutter befor bradleys doore', it was stated, were to blame, as many of 'the pavementes are broken befor ther doores & for not mendynge of them they stand amerced'.[1] A street also had to be kept clear, and Robert Rogers and others paid for leaving carts at their doors.

Wagons and pack-horses were less likely to use the parallel way known as the Gild Pits, or royal highway, since it was rutty. Crossing Clopton's bridge, a traveller would be led by a walled causeway into Bridge Street, and on past two inns showing the Bear and the Swan. This was a major market area, divided in the centre by a row of houses called Middle Row into Fore Bridge and Back Bridge streets. Riding up opposite the Crown inn and past the Angel inn, one turned into Henley Street, where orchards and gardens lay behind the façades. Here doors abutted pavings, and on the north side, leading east to west, stood a row of half-timbered tenements, some of which served as shops. A tradesman let down a wooden board or shelf before a ground-floor window to display his wares, and a glover would show an array of purses, belts, gloves of various quality, and other soft-leather goods.

In the street's north row, John Shakespeare's two houses were separate but adjoining. In later times the eastern one became known as the Woolshop, and the western as the Birthplace. He held these *libere* of the lord of Stratford manor on a burgage tenure (nearly the equivalent of a freehold) and paid a small annual chief-rent, or ground-rent, of 6*d*. for the Woolshop and 13*d*. for the Birthplace; with these rents, we find both houses linked to his name in 1590 in a list of manorial tenants of the late Ambrose, Earl of Warwick:

> Vicus Vocatus
> Henley Strete
> [The Street Called
> Henley Street]

Johannes Shakespere tenet libere unum tenementum cum pertinentiis per redditum per annum vj^d secta curie   vj^d

[John Shakespere freely holds one tenement with appurtenances for a rent per year of 6*d*. by suit of court   6*d*.]

Idem Johannes tenet libere unum tenementum cum pertinentiis per redditum per annum xiij^d secta curie   xiij^d

[The same John freely holds one tenement with appurtenances for a rent per year of 13*d*. by suit of court   13*d*.][2]

He had bought the Woolshop from Edward West, in October 1556, when its small chief-rent of 6*d*. is mentioned. We do not know when he began to inhabit the western house, or Birthplace, but the tradition that he lived in it early enough for his son William to be born there is respectable. After his son's time, workmen broke through a wall to join the two tenements, so that on Henley Street today there is a much-restored house of three gables as a shrine for Stratford's visitors.

John had a barn in the Gild Pits well behind the frontages, and he needed ample work-space. As a whittawer, he would have had to boil and scrape some of his animal skins—a job often given to a boy apprentice since it involved steam, human sweat, and stinking refuse. In 1556 he had bought an estate with garden and croft in Greenhill Street ('unum tenementum cum gardino et crofto'), and our improving knowledge of the town in his time suggests that he may either have transferred some of his work there, or leased that property to his helpers. Greenhill Street was then an area with open lots and storage buildings, and it was easily accessible to the Woolshop by way of Meer Lane.

In any case, he had more space. Soon after that purchase, or on a day between 25 November 1556 and mid-December of the year following, he married Mary Arden, whose father had leased a Snitterfield farm to John's father. Mary came from Wilmcote, a hamlet on a ridge of grassy land in Aston Cantlow parish where meadows rose to 400 feet at the Alne Hills and stone was quarried to repair Stratford's bridge. With its 'auncient name' Arden, as Leland found, the area north of the river was 'much enclosyd', lacking in corn if not in meadow-grass. Billesley, near Wilmcote, once had seventeen peasants and eight slaves; the Trussell family held its manor in declining circumstances which included the sentencing to death of one Trussell for highway robbery.[3] Poor families lost their homes as arable ground was fenced into sheep pasture, and fifteen families had been evicted over at Ardens Grafton. Enclosures of parkland tempted others; so many deer-poachers hunted at Shelfield Park that two commissions had had to look into the stealing.

Land seems to have changed hands rather quickly in this region. Thomas Finderne or Fynderne, a man of wealth, made two interesting purchases: he acquired—just when, we do not know—a holding that was called the manor of Great Wilmcote, as well as the farm that we know today as 'Mary Arden's House'. He sold both, five years after Mary's father died, to George Gibbes and to Adam Palmer; the latter had been a legal overseer of Robert Arden's will in 1556. These slim facts do not prove the Ardens' farm was 'Mary Arden's House', but the property that we see today on Featherbed Lane is of about the right size. The farmstead's sturdy, narrow main dwelling has low gables, close-timbered oak beams, a fair-sized kitchen. Outside is a dovecote, which supplied eggs and meat for winter. Either at this farm or at one close by, Mary Arden was born in about 1540, the youngest of eight daughters.

When Mary was young, her mother died. In 1548 her father married Agnes Hill, who brought two boys and two girls of her own to live near adze-roughened surfaces. Life on a Tudor farm could be bleak; the oddity of Robert Arden's household was that he lacked sons, and lost the help of his own daughters. Two years after Agnes Hill arrived, Margaret Arden was already married to Alexander Webbe of nearby Bearley, and Joan Arden to Edmund Lambert of Barton Henmarsh (or Barton on the Heath) fifteen miles south of Stratford. Other Arden daughters were wed later—Anne (or Agnes) first to John Hewyns of Bearley, and then to Thomas Stringer of Stockton in Shropshire; Katherine to Thomas Edkins of Wilmcote; and Elizabeth to a Skarlett. At all events, by 1556 Robert Arden found some merits in his youngest, unmarried girl and named Mary one of his will's two executors despite her youth; he also favoured her, leaving her not only the sum of 10 marks (£6. 13s. 4d.) but his most valuable property, Asbyes, at Wilmcote.[4]

The skills of Shakespeare's mother have been unknown, but it is not unlikely that she could read and write, and we have a sign of her hand. When selling her share in a land-holding to her nephew Robert Webbe, in 1579, she made her 'marke' on a deed and on a bond.[5] The deed (unlike the bond) is a large enough piece of parchment to have lain flat and offered her ample space to sign. Did she intend to write her initials on the deed? If she did, why does she appear to have written them in reverse, as S M and not M S, in between the scrivener's words 'the marke' and 'of Marye Shacksper'? Instead of drawing a stolid cross on the Webbe deed, Mary Shakespeare drew a small, neat, rather complex design suggesting the letters S M in a Tudor secretary style of script which her son William appears to have used; the 'S', in this design, is exampled in the handwriting of literate persons; the 'M' (if such was intended) lacks a final stroke or minim. She may have intended only a pretty design, and alphabetic letters in a 'marke' would not be proof of her ability to write. But what has become quite clear, partly because time has worn away some of her clotted ink, is that she drew her mark in one continuous movement. She appears to have been familiar with a quill pen.

If she was indeed able to write phrases and sums and to read them, she would have been of considerable use to her father. However that may be, Robert Arden's belief in her dependability is evident. She can hardly have been much older than 17 or 18 when he made his will. Young women, at that time, were seldom named in wills as executors, and Robert Arden's will is that of an alert, shrewd Catholic, who does not wholly trust his own wife. Whether or not he came from a cadet branch of the Catholic Park Hall Ardens, in Castle Bromwich in the parish of Aston near Birmingham, he seems to have shared the Arden piety. His father Thomas in 1501 had been able to use as a trustee the first of the intently pious Throckmortons, of Coughton Court, who died on a pilgrimage to Jerusalem and whose son, Sir George, spoke out against Henry VIII's divorce. Robert Arden joined Stratford's pious foundation. He chose as his will's first witness (as he had no need to do) a curate so stubbornly Catholic as to be dismissed later from a Snitterfield vicarage for adhering to the old faith. Wedded to John Shakespeare, Mary may have found his religious views problematic or unlike her father's, but John seems to have been brought up as a Catholic, and their son William was raised in the shadow of the old faith.

By the late autumn in 1557 she was living at Stratford. Young enough to have a chance of bearing a healthy child, Mary Shakespeare failed at first. Her son William's life itself was at risk in plague-time, and his birth-date was important to her and would have been lovingly recalled until Mary died. The wishful notion that he was born on 23 April was first mooted, so far as we know, by William Oldys in a marginal note written in all probability between 1743 and 1750, and properly belongs to legends about Shakespeare. 'The actual day of William's birth is unknown', wrote E. K. Chambers in a statement that still holds good; 'a belief that it was April 23, on which day he died in 1616, seems to rest on an eighteenth-century blunder.'[6] Oldys, writing a century and a quarter after Shakespeare died, presumably had no evidence as to the birth-date other than the ambiguous words on the tablet in the poet's monument at Holy Trinity, 'obiit anno . . . Ætatis 53' (he died in his fifty-third year), and Chambers believed that Oldys probably made 'an incorrect use' of these.[7] Edmond Malone, the exacting eighteenth-century Shakespeare scholar, expressed doubt that Joseph Greene, a curate of Stratford and Oldys's contemporary, had any authority for declaring 23 April as the birth-date other than the monument. It has been said to be 'especially appropriate' that Shakespeare should have been born on St George's Day, the day of England's patron saint; but the wish certainly does not add up to a fact. Had his birth and death really occurred on two 23rds of April, such a coincidence would surely have been noted within a hundred years of his death. Yet we have no sign of this. Strong family loyalty may well have moved Shakespeare's granddaughter Elizabeth Hall to honour his memory, just ten years after he died, by marrying on 22 April. Elizabeth's honouring his birthday as the 22nd remains only a good possibility, suggested at first by De Quincey; but it is supported by what we know of the closeness of John and Mary Shakespeare's people. Despite a record that includes lawsuits and a family fray, Ardens and Shakespeares knew the force of family ties (as when many of them helped young Robert Webbe, Margaret Arden's son, to acquire their own individual shares in an estate).[8] In brief, it is possible that Shakespeare was born on either the 21st, 22nd, or 23rd, but the day is still unknown. It is no more likely that his birth-date was Sunday, 23, than Saturday, 22 April 1564.

As a young woman who had known the death of her infants Mary Shakespeare must have been apprehensive that month. She perhaps lay on a bed supported by the same simple, cross-cross system of ropes used in most Elizabethan homes, and heard advice from servants or housewives in their stiff, practical white bodices of 'durance'—that stout cloth that appears in Stratford's records typically as 'boddies of durance'.[9]

Christening was a festival with apostle-spoons and a white chrisom-cloth, basins, ewers, and towels at the parish church. And yet the chances of a boy baptized in time of plague were not good. If a baby died, the town's bell might be sounded, as when the clerk records a 'ringing of ye grete bell' for three small children.[10] A boy who survived would wear swaddling-clothes until he was ready for a little russet-coloured dress.

'Hic incepit pestis'

In June plague broke out at Leicester, and soon after at Coventry. On 11 July, when the vicar wrote 'Hic incepit pestis' in his burials register, the plague was at Stratford. It burst into the town's centre, two houses from Ely Street where Thomas Deege lost an apprentice and then his wife Joanna. (The transmitting flea settled on black rats living in wattle-and-daub houses, in thatch or walls.) Plague was then 300 yards from Henley Street. John Shakespeare, as an officer of the council, did not leave town, and as a leading burgess in the Stratford Corporation he was unlikely to allow his wife to leave.

At these times, fires were lit in streets. Windows were sealed; doors admitted no visitors. William in infancy probably knew a hot, airless house—and yet work carried on in the town. The fright of Henley Street neighbours would have been evident, and the fear of a young mother—with her first-born son to protect—must have been considerable. In any case, death came close to the Woolshop. The terror of an epidemic was greater because people knew it was infectious—but no one could say why it crept into one house and not another. What was clear, in August, was that the infection had spread out from Deege the weaver's into High Street and Ely Street and beyond; it had seemed to fly over the Avon, not bothering with the bridge. Shakespeare's echoing in *Timon of Athens* of the belief that plague is caused by poison 'in the sick air' (IV. iii. 110–11) corresponds to his town's known experience.

Nearly two-thirds of the dead in the summer and autumn were women. 'Comfort's in heaven', Shakespeare would write in *Richard II*, and 'nothing lives but crosses, cares, and grief' (II. ii. 78–9)—but the fact is that in a well-organized town, women gave comfort nursing the sick. Plague bacilli of the bubonic variety are not transmitted from one human being to another, but a related variety of plague, which could have been present, is highly contagious. If one inhaled a few droplets of sputum sneezed or coughed into the air by a victim of pneumonic plague one's death was nearly certain. Victims of plague in its more common variety, in which the bubonic bacilli reproduce quickly and spread throughout the whole biological system, knew much pain. Some did survive, after noting the buboes (or swellings) in armpit or neck, and seeing on the skin 'God's tokens' of orange, reddish, or darker spots.[11] At risk, the council met four times in crisis, and levied its own members for funds to help the stricken. On 30 August burgesses and aldermen met in the Gild garden—on wooden benches— to avoid contagion.

By September, one out of every fifteen people in the parish was infected. Entire households began to perish. Working as acting chamberlain, John seems to have called in clerical help from outside. Later in the autumn, fewer died, but Dixon of the Swan lost two stepdaughters in November and December. In the last six months of 1564, Mary's infant was the object of more than a mother's usual care and vigilance, if only because the conditions of a severe plague were unusual. The emotional pressure of Mary's concern for William, her need for him to live, her prayers, tenderness, and watchfulness may be inferred from what we know of Stratford's suffering and Mary's previous experience of burying one or two of her girls. We have evidence of a situation, and of course must not suppose that we have access to her thoughts. But we need no psychological theory to explain a mother's ardent, sensible care for her son, day after day, when small children are dying. A pattern of Mary's special care for her son is also likely to have been set in these months. Her interest in him cannot have faded suddenly when Stratford was free of plague, and it is pertinent for us to think of his life ahead for a moment. William's confidence cannot be dissociated from the emotional support he must have found at home. As a man he would lack a quirky egotism, as seems clear from his relatively peaceful career in the theatre, a hive of tension. He was not involved in Ben Jonson's kind of embroilments, or Marlowe's. He has a calm, fine control of emotive materials, and his Sonnets, in the artfulness of their structures, reveal a lordly, easy play over feelings.

In early life he must have been the focus of Mary's very urgently watchful, intense love.

People had been warned of deaths. For the first time, London's corporation had printed plague-bills as broadsheets to keep towns informed; Stratford's council did well to preserve order, and women, not yielding to panic, consoled the afflicted at the risk of their lives. Shakespeare's feeling for civic order is related to what he came to know of Stratford.

Air and music

After a plague much was burned. Windows were flung open, rooms aired and scrubbed. By the time William was 3 or 4, his street would have been as dusty and filled with stray dogs as ever. (Unmuzzled dogs kept on troubling the council.) Henley Street also teemed with children, and George Ainge had two sets of twins to add to his numerous lot; he and his wife had thirteen offspring. George sold fine fabrics. John Ainge, the baker, also of Henley Street, had seven children including twins. An older boy might come in from Shrovetide football with a bloody face, and younger boys and girls shouted or fought, ran, babbled, and played. The area behind the houses on the Gild Pits side might have been a badly managed green kindergarten, and adults cared little out of doors for silence.

But indoors a boy was in a polite, much more orderly, reserved world—though the houses look hard and bare today. At John Shakespeare's now combined dwelling, an oak-beam frame rises on a stone foundation-wall, and at ground level timbers are close-studded or nine inches apart (an early Tudor pattern to keep thieves from breaking into a house). Wattle and daub, or plaster, fills in between the timber frames. The upper storey has rectangular panels, so that rooms upstairs have less timber and seem to invite decoration. John's hall, or the main downstairs chamber, has a floor of broken, blue-grey stone from the Alne hills. There is a brick-and-stone fireplace. Opening out of the hall and not at right angles to the main façade, the kitchen has a large hearth. Here one sees iron cooking-tackle, a hanger, a pothook and chain, and a pair of cobbards to hold up spits.

'Be not afeard', says Caliban in *The Tempest*, 'The isle is full of noises, | Sounds, and sweet airs, that give delight and hurt not' (III. ii. 138–9). A timbered house was full of noises, and a boy heard stories and legends to explain them. Good and bad fairies came into rooms to move objects about. Queen Mab, big as an agate on an alderman's ring, did no harm—nor did invisible fairies on Midsummer Night's Eve. Nor did ghosts, gliding on dim church-paths to return to clammy homes by sunrise. But villains in the wilds beyond Stratford *might* do as much harm as Mr Fox, in an 'old tale' Shakespeare seems to recall from boyhood when Benedick reminds Claudio of it in *Much Ado*:

Lady Mary, one day, on a visit to Mr Fox saw him pull a lady upstairs. Mr Fox cut off her hand, which dropped with a glittering bracelet into Lady Mary's lap. Lady Mary ran to her brothers' house, and when Mr Fox came to dine she told the guests of a dream. She spoke of her visit to Mr Fox's, and said at each turn of the story, 'it is not so, nor was it so'. 'It is not so, nor was it so, and God forbid it should be so!' said Mr Fox. 'But it *is* so, and it *was* so,' said Lady Mary, 'and here's the hand I have to show!' So all the guests drew their swords and cut Mr Fox into a thousand pieces.[12]

A Tudor boy heard dozens of such stories. He might hear riddles in *Demands Joyous*, which had appeared in Wynkyn de Worde's version in 1511:

Demand: Why doth a cow lie down?
Response: Because it cannot sit.
Demand: Who killed the fourth part of all the people in the world?
Response: Cain when he killed Abel.[13]

He would hear that deep quarry of human and divine truth, the Old Testament, and would learn to pray. Mealtimes began with a long grace before one touched a knife, spoon and trencher, or wooden plate. A boy washed his hands before and after eating and would be watched by his father, who wore a cap or hat at table; and he would be told to wipe his hands after picking at his meat—and wipe out the pewter or leather cup after sipping ale or beer.

At table and elsewhere, he was taught 'all obeysance and courtesie', or decorum—which turned him into a little actor at 3 or 4.[14] Decorum meant knowing how to choose the appropriate word suitable to the speaker and subject, or how to play one's role in a deferential society. Through years of discipline, one might acquire a well-fashioned mind, with good habits to discern what was proper in relation to all things, places, times, persons. At last, one would take a role upon the public stage befitting one's status.

John Shakespeare—much concerned for status—was to apply repeatedly for a coat of arms and learn that the College of Heralds conceded his father-in-law Robert Arden had been a 'gent. of worship'.[15] Mary's father may or may not have been of the Ardens who were descended from 'Turchillus de Eardene', or Turchill of the Arden Forest, whose lands in the Domesday Book fill over four columns. John seems to have believed that Arden was of the gentry; and as a parvenu himself, he would have credited his wife Mary's ability to *impart* courtesy. In any case, Shakespeare's courtesy is remarkable; it could hardly have been picked up quickly at gentlemen's or noblemen's houses (or at court, where there was too little to go round) since it involved more than knowing when to bend the knee, or doff the hat: deep courtesy is a habit of mind. In his plays his tragic kings, usurpers, and lovers fail in part through indecorous conduct, and so use language inappropriate to their character and status. Richard II and Bolingbroke both sin against courtesy, and Hamlet's real and imagined worlds have lost form, courtesy, or the balance and sanity of decorum. 'The baby beats the nurse, and quite athwart | Goes all decorum', Shakespeare writes in *Measure for Measure* (I. iii. 30–1).

His habit of mind in courtesy, even so, is in some ways that of an Arden, old-fashioned or pre-Elizabethan. In his usual attitudes, he is not so much coolly mercenary or aggressively thrusting as he is humane, receptive, and alert to tenderness and the public good, as if he had affinities with Warwickshire's past and the Gild his grandfather Arden had joined. (His audacity does not thrive coldly.) To be sure, 400 years of community life, a well-run town, and a Gild that linked the generations and influenced a local council in Elizabeth's day helped to form the mind of Shakespeare. In his early years religious troubles faded, and Stratford was not wholly torn from its past. The council had seen the town through sorrow. In London the Crown wanted settlement, stability, a tactical delay with Spain (before a war Elizabeth could ill afford); merchants had got round the Antwerp embargo and would have Hamburg as an outlet—cloth was being sold abroad. Stratford after its plague was fairly happy, and John Shakespeare was close to achieving high honour.

For his documents and dignity, John had a ring-seal with the initials I S, to press in wax. Mary had a delicate seal, showing a running horse.[16] Mary's pretty seal was typical of her time when simple but finely shaped intaglios, rings, and necklaces were much liked, along with bright colours in dress and decoration. At Wilmcote she had known painted cloths, which kept out the draughts. Their tempera tints on wide strips of canvas, for walls, showed biblical or mythological scenes adorned with mottoes or 'sentences' (Shakespeare recalls in *The Rape of Lucrece*: 'Who fears a sentence or an old man's saw | Shall by a painted cloth be kept in awe'—lines 244–5). Arden's house had eleven of such wall-cloths, including one in an upstairs bedroom worth 26s. 6d. (a good sum in 1556, the value of nine of his swine).[17] Their mottoes were no more subtle than the Elizabethan posies (which Hamlet mocks) engraved on the flat inner surfaces of rings: 'MY HEART AND I, UNTIL I DYE' or 'NOT TWO, BUT ONE, TILL LIFE BE GONE'. But the brevity, age, and universality of mottoes appealed to a people who liked old, well-rubbed, pithy truth as much as wit and invention. In Stratford's mainly oral culture, wisdom was stored up in commonplaces, which are one early basis of the art of a poet who could give audiences, at last, a maxim such as 'The readiness is all.'

The life in flowers and trees, gardens, orchards, and fields at all seasons appealed to Mary's son, and no poet has responded with more pleasure to nature. Yet the town was flat, and a boy's eyes might take in nothing more amazing at first than cowslips, burnet, and clover, or a river in flood, caterpillar swarms, or a 'curious-knotted garden'. The devotion of the mature Shakespeare appears with odd intensity in his making so much of banal nature, 'thistles, kecksies, burrs', or the domestic garden, or nature's excess or waste. It is as if in his early youth the drama of diurnal nature had been intense enough. A small boy could not travel far, and orchards and gardens between Gild Pits and the Woolshop perhaps had to satisfy him on many a day; later the shire's variety drew him strongly. What this boy saw and felt in early years was affected by his experience of Mary—who for thirty months had had him as her only child to adore, though she soon had others. Gilbert Shakespeare was baptized at Holy Trinity on 13 October 1566—and may have been named after the glover Gilbert Bradley who became a capital burgess in 1565.

When Gilbert was very small, William was in his fifth year, and well cherished. One of his greatest gifts was his understanding of feeling, and that was surely nourished by Mary. Heroines in his comedies would be notable for their stability and their resourceful minds, and be as affecting and vulnerable even when, like Julia or Rosalind, they had wit and capability. He was to respond easily to an Ovidian love ethic, and give a subtle and persuasive sense of how women feel and think. He must have studied Mary well, and she, after pleasing her father, was not likely to be hard with a son; he was not blighted by too many rules.

Richard Mulcaster, who taught the poet Spenser, wrote of the need to make a Tudor boy 'most able'. Music is a 'glasse', says that teacher, 'wherein to behold both the beawtie of concord, and the blots of dissension even in a politic body'.[18] If music helped one to know society it also changed moods at home and lessened the divide between fathers and sons. Parents danced and taught their children to dance, and many families had a tabor, lute, or recorder. Shakespeare was not the only boy born into the middling ranks to get a very expert, if informal, training in music's fundamentals. Even in the Midlands one might know the sonorous drone of a bagpipe. One could watch and hear morris-dancers at Whitsun, all dressed in garish costumes with bells on ankles and a hobby horse (or a horse's head in cloth or another light material) drawn over one dancer's head. The disguises, with the strange rhythms of the morris, appealed to many. This loud, outlandish ritual with its thwacking sticks had in it an aspect of drama or emotive performance common to all music, and a people in love with verbal rhythms fell easily under music's spell. Elizabethans loved music, too, as an antidote to boredom or low spirits; gloomy talk was disliked, though pessimism was attractive when travelling players feigned it.

In russet dresses, most often not of cotton but of coarse woollen homespun, children were much loved, but without status—as if they were mere nits, gnats. A boy, however, before he was 6, could leave off a russet dress. Till he did, he looked like a girl. Now he would wear a jacket or jerkin over a doublet, and struggle into skinny, long, knitted hose, though the hose often required mending and might be saved if he wore common loose fustian slops, or shiny breeches pulled in at the knee. He was then a small, unformed, man, eyeing his father's world.

William was to know his father's ill luck and downfall. (Partly because he served on the council, we have evidence of John Shakespeare's life and of the family experience of his son in years ahead.) In the late 1560s, however, John scaled the heights, and became head of the borough's council. He was then at last Master Shakespeare, mayor or High Bailiff of Stratford, and he knew his advantages as a townsman well enough since he was able to send his little son to school.

3

JOHN SHAKESPEARE'S FORTUNES

Paid for the foote stoole *tha*ᵗ Mʳ bayliff standeth on   ijᵈ [2*d*.]
(Borough accounts of Stratford-upon-Avon)

In the bailiff's family

*I*n the late 1560s Stratford had only about a dozen streets, fewer than 240 households, and a populace (lately reduced by epidemic) of 1,200 people at most; yet relatively speaking the market town was not small. A day's ride to the north, Birmingham with its lorimers (makers of metal parts for bridles and saddles), nailers, and other metal craftsmen was about the same size, and the red-walled, cloth-manufacturing city of Coventry less than twenty miles from Stratford had only 7,000 or 8,000 people—though it was one of the largest English towns. The largest city outside London was Norwich, with fewer than 15,000 inhabitants. Liverpool had 900 or 1,000, Gloucester about 5,000, Worcester no more than 7,000. A majority of the Queen's subjects lived in tiny, scattered villages and hamlets of fifty or sixty people or less.

Certainly, a borough town of some size and diversity of crafts gave one a chance to observe the nation's practical life—the real life of politics, trade, petty crime, religion, passion, and fate. Among those who best understood society and human aspirations in this age were Marlowe and Shakespeare, both products of market towns and sons of craftsmen. Christopher Marlowe grew up in a shoemaker's house in Canterbury, a town of about 700 families. Shakespeare had advantages in belonging to a mercantile governing class—he was, after all, the eldest son in a respectable bourgeois family which was one of the handful of families that ran Stratford.

John Shakespeare had become fairly affluent before rising to prominence. Keeping the borough accounts for well over three years, he even lent the town moderate sums of money; the council still owed him 7s. 3d. when he made his last report (15 February 1566).[1] The chamberlains' office kept up functions of the Holy Cross Gild's proctors, and John's work carried prestige. He served longer than he had to. He commissioned and constructed, repaired and hired, dealt with good and bad workmen alike. As a director of accounts, he was bound to rise to civic leadership. After William Bott—who was then living at New Place—was expelled from council for failing to 'cum to hys answer' for opprobrious words spoken, John Shakespeare was chosen alderman in Bott's stead in July 1565.

And yet John's rise, no doubt, was partly a matter of necessity. The Elizabethan Corporation found it hard to fill up its numbers; some of the men who were most eligible to serve, as aldermen and bailiffs, lived just outside the borough boundaries, and so declined their services without penalty. A chamberlain of John's experience was a prime asset, and any failure in his aldermanic duties would have been taken at the council as no small matter.

It settled on him as a good choice in 1565. Two years later John was nominated, with Ralph Cawdrey and Robert Perrott, to stand for election as High Bailiff of the borough. The council's election had a clear result, with only three votes cast for the glovemaker of Henley Street as a tally shows:

> o o o o o o o o o o o o o o o o Robart perot
> o o o John shakspeyr
> Raf Cawdrey[2]

After Perrott refused to serve, John declined, and with a good excuse. The bailiwick was onerous and he may then have lacked time for the office. A master glove-cutter was likely to keep three or four stitchers busy, and he had a glover's shop to run. But when elected the next year, he consented, and so in fur-trimmed robes and standing it seems on the bailiff's footstool, he began to preside over Stratford on 1 October 1568.

We have a clerk's report of his first meeting in 'hall', and this includes words said or sanctioned by the new bailiff. He agreed to fine stiffly men such as Perrott (who twice refused the bailiwick), but he was politic about solidarity and apparently referred to his group as the 'Brotherhode' or the 'Balyf and Bretherne' (words deleted in the official order of 1 October). John's tact was traditional, and effective at council, which was later told by arbitrators to 'be Lovers and ffrendes' even with the likes of Perrott.[3]

Stratford ruled itself well, and until William's thirteenth year his father, as a trusted, moderate alderman, with disputes to settle and rules to enforce, was at the centre of civic life. For a year John was a justice of the peace, and thus an agent of the powerful Privy Council at Westminster. He heard petty cases at Stratford's Court of Record, framed laws at halls, served as coroner and clerk of the market, and welcomed the judges after Easter and Low Sunday, and at the two Leets, or Law Days. For another year (1571–2) he was to be a justice and deputy bailiff, and his known duties seldom kept him far from home.

An alderman's son heard something of the *collective* good of town, brethren, and of course family. To one's own father, one owed love and respect. William was to refer to 'domestic awe' as being as natural to children as night-rest[4] and, in time, he was to exploit the rending, moving Tudor theme of the love and fealty due a parent. In his plays we have very good evidence as to what he came deeply to understand, or signs of his intimate knowledge. Filial ardour was a much-desired feature of Tudor life, and in the London theatres it would be a common theme: what is remarkable is that John's son later treated it so often with a masterly flexibility and confidence, as if felt along the pulse. 'To you your father should be as a god', Theseus warns Hermia in *A Midsummer Night's Dream* (I. i. 47), and in this ethic, at least in the theatre, cool compliance with a father's wishes is not enough. Cordelia's mere dutifulness drives Lear to rage, and Desdemona's cold subservience numbs her father's heart, before we hear that grief 'shore his old thread in twain' (V. ii. 213) when she defies him to marry the Moor. Filial love motivates Prince Hal, but it compounds Hamlet's anguish, and Macbeth's crime is the worse for its implicit and terrible element of parricide.

Moreover, no son is immune to a father's particular, idiosyncratic influence, and John Shakespeare was an impressive and versatile man. By and large, he pulled himself up by his bootstraps. His father Richard Shakespeare was probably born a few miles to the north, either at Balsall, Baddesley Clinton, Wroxall, or Rowington, the last a hive of Catholics and the home of more sixteenth-century Shakespeares than any other Warwickshire parish. It is certain that by 1529 Richard was a husbandman at Snitterfield—his name is copied as 'Shakstaff' four years later—and that he rented a house of Robert Arden that 'doth abut on the High Street'.[5] After his death his goods in 1561 were valued at £38 17s. 0d. (a sum befitting a prudent farmer) and his estate's administration went to his son John, who was relying on his own acumen and skill. Our earliest report of John in connection with a craft (when he is called 'Johannem Shakyspere de Stretforde, in comitatu Warwicensi, glover', on 7 June 1556, at the Court of Record) suggests that he was by then independent of his father. A glover acquired a fine touch after seven years' apprenticeship; cutting soft leather 'tranks' is an art, and holed leather is not repairable. John had to be shrewd to be free for civic duties, and his town service suggests an almost feudal commitment. He broadened his money-making ventures, as many craftsmen did, while competing with master glovers at Stratford and indirectly at Worcester and Oxford; in fact, in records of 1573 and 1578 he is also described as a 'whyttawer'. A whittawer (or white-tawyer) would buy pelts from butchers or other sellers, boil some of his sheepskins to make size to fill pores, tan the skins of goats, deer and other animals with salt and alum (aluminium sulphate), hang them out in his drying-sheds, and then shave them with paring knives and 'stake' the skins to render them soft—all before cutting, sewing, and finishing a product.

Without helpers, John could not have turned a profit, and his son had a chance to learn that success in a craft depends on co-operation as well as painstaking care. Tudor boys were made to emulate, and almost to revere, skilled male and female artisans,* and a wealth of

---

* But a skilled female sewer of leather tranks, for example, often earned appreciably less than a male sewer; it has been estimated that about half of London's apprentices in the crafts and trades were female.

gloving images in the plays suggests that William knew his father's craft well. In *The Merry Wives*, Slender swears 'by these gloves', and Mistress Quickly enquires of him, 'Does he not wear a great round beard, like a glover's paring-knife?', Romeo exclaims to his lady aloft, 'O, that I were a glove upon that hand', and Romeo's rash, wittiest friend understands the pliable, soft quality of kid-skin—or cheveril— used for the best, costliest gloves: 'O, here's a wit of cheveril, that stretches from an inch narrow to an ell broad', says Mercutio. 'Hang nothing but a calf's skin', mocks the Bastard in *King John*, and allu- sions to sheep-skin, lamb-skin, fox-skin, dog-skin, and deer-skin in the plays might conjure up a whittawer's drying-shed.

Any craft demanded *all* of the self, very strong commitment or *le cœur au métier* for a part of the day, a principle not quite incon- sistent with John Shakespeare's occupying himself, too, with grain, timber, and wool. Tudor work was suffused with spiritual significance and William was to plunge whole-heartedly into the hard work of an acting troupe, though his attitudes to his *métier* would be complex.

As handmade objects were costly, they called for ceaseless mainten- ance. A boy learned that his own body thrived on vigilance, exertion, and not too much sleep; his elders, in a rural town, often rose at 3 or 4 a.m. in summer; 5 a.m. in winter. Tooth decay was attributable to 'humours' or to little worms in the teeth, but he cleaned his teeth with a soft cloth and a sweet paste. He washed, dressed, heard morning prayers, knelt for a blessing, and after a light breakfast (often of bread, butter, and cheese) helped his parents if the day was not a schoolday. Mary, as an alderman's wife, may have had servants to direct; her hus- band, for his part, would have required help for a weekly market. On Thursday, stalls or booths were erected along High and Fore Bridge Streets as they converged at the High Cross—a square structure, on pillars, topped by a cupola and a clock with a brass hand (gilded in 1579); a chain and staple attached a standard measure. Here at the mar- ket centre, John Shakespeare and the glovers had pride of place in sell- ing wares. Some of their best gloves were bought as gifts: a fringed pair of Midlands manufacture, given to the Queen at Oxford, in 1566, survives as a sign of the craft.[6]

A bell closed Stratford's market at 11 a.m.; otherwise, church festivals, fairs, harvests, and the seasons set the rhythms of town life. A Bridge Ale raised funds for the two bridge wardens, and harvests influenced purchases: John Shakespeare had bought his Woolshop and Greenhill Street house in the worst harvest year of the century, and he would buy again when conditions were depressed.[7] The town's private life unfolded itself: moral faults were aired, when the vicar's court ordered a fornicator to stand in church. The 'bawdy court' held closed sessions, but later records show that adulterers and those who violated the Sabbath were cited and often on public view; William and his family knew some of these souls:

Elizabeth Wheeler: in the court itself she brawled with these words: 'Goodes woondes, a plague a God on you all, a fart of ons ars for you'; excommunicated.

Thomas Haman: 'for openinge his shopp windowes on Sabothe and holye dayes in tyme of divine service and sermon tyme'.

Hamlet Sadler: for not receiving the Eucharist: he appeared and petitioned time to cleanse his conscience; ordered a day to receive; he promised faithfully to obey; dismissed.

Judith, wife of Hamlet: for the same; she appeared; she promised as above; dismissed.

Richard Wheeler: 'for calling the wife of Richard Brookes whore and sowlike whore, with divers other filthy speeches' was ordered 'to repayre unto the parish church of Stratford the next Sabaoth at Morning Prayer and there to stand during the tyme of Morning Prayer before the pulpitt in his usuall apparell until thend of the second lesson'.

Anne Ward, spinster: for incontinence with Daniel Baker . . . ordered to do public penance in a white sheet.[8]

A wide variety of trades became known to the son of John Shakespeare, who by the 1570s, as a wool dealer and after two years as bailiff and deputy bailiff, knew some of the town's drapers, haberdashers, dyers, weavers, and fullers in the wool and textile trades, and those in leather such as skinners, saddlers, and shoemakers. John had dealt as an officer with tipplers, victuallers, and brewers, and he would have known those connected with farming such as corn-dealers and malt-sters, chandlers, coopers, smiths, wheelwrights, ploughwrights, and tuggerers (makers of carts and gear). He also dealt with men of the learned class such as John Bretchgirdle, who died in 1565, or the vicar's former pupil, John Brownsword, schoolmaster, who for Latin verse was to be cited in Francis Meres's *Palladis Tamia*, a rather lax but revealing survey of English poetry in 1598. William had a good intro-duction to the town's endeavour, and a boy who was to study people had much to observe in his own relatives, though he hardly knew his grandparents. Old Richard Shakespeare had died (his wife's death is unrecorded), as had Mary Arden's parents, before William's birth, though Mary's stepmother Agnes lived on at Wilmcote until her bur-ial on 29 December 1580. William's pious, eccentric uncle Henry Shakespeare, who farmed at Ingon and Snitterfield, assaulted one of his other uncles, Edward Cornwell, and at another time failed to pay for oxen and cooled off in prison. Mary's swarm of nieces and nephews was nearby, and strange fowl alighted upon neighbouring ponds: next door to the Woolshop lived Wedgewood the bigamist tailor, who had left a wife in Warwick to marry another while the first was still alive, though his reputation for 'noughty matters & quarelling with his honest neighbours' caught up with him and he fled when William was about 11.[9]

In contrast, William's early schooldays were tedious. Even if we dis-miss all mockery of school in his writing, we are left with the fact that no Oxford-educated master attended to younger boys, who instead usually went to 'petty school' classes, for boys and girls, under the likes of William Gilbard, alias Higgs. Higgs, a keeper of clocks, served now and then as under-schoolmaster up to 1574 and had a bent for Latin. He took pupils through the English alphabet, the Lord's Prayer, and an exorcism as seen on the shiny hornbook—a slab of wood tacked over with transparent horn. Its first line was the Christcross-row or 'crossrow', since it began with a cross. 'Yes, yes, he teaches boys the horn-book', we hear of Holofernes in *Love's Labour's Lost* (v. i. 45), and Clarence cites the crossrow on the way to prison to explain King Edward's fear of the name 'George' in *Richard III*:

> He . . . from the cross-row plucks the letter 'G'
> And says a wizard told him that by 'G'
> His issue disinherited should be.
>
> (1. i. 54–7)

Poets cited the well-known hornbook to advantage—but it was dreary work for anyone quick to learn, and slow plodding in primers followed it. William had to sit through an hour's catechizing (required of everyone over 6 and under 20) at the vicar's clerk's afternoon service, and it is certain that a chance to fish, to be footloose near the Avon, or to find Thomas Badger's or anyone else's eyrie of swans, and watch hunters who used trained hawks to catch waterfowl, or even to await a turn at archery at the 'butts', would have pleased a bored boy more than all he ever heard from an under-master or vicar's clerk.

As the world changed, public events touched home. People were aware of local musters, and of an urgency reminiscent of earlier upheavals under Queen Mary, caused by the revolt of the northern Catholic earls. That, however, was crushed, and Pius V excommunicated Elizabeth. Then pedlars sold ballads about the bizarre retreat from Scotland of Mary Queen of Scots, taken as a prisoner to Ashby de la Zouch and on to Leicester and Coventry. The tale of Leir or Lear, a fabulous King of Leicester, was cited at about this time in a letter appealing for clemency with the Scottish Queen. Driven from Britain by two unkind, unnatural daughters, Leir was restored to his throne at last by his third child, a 'noble Cordela'.[10]

But the Queen at Westminster did not play 'Cordela', and alarm over the nation's Catholic enemies increased after the beginning of a revolt in the Spanish Netherlands, and again after the massacre in France of thousands of Protestants in a bloodbath starting on St Bartholomew's Day, in August 1572. That confirmed a widespread, popular belief in a Catholic League to exterminate Protestantism. England's coast was put in a state of readiness. At Stratford, the borough council was alerted by calls for men, horses, armour, weapons, or for a 'dressing of harness' or a 'dressing of two pikes and a bow' day after day, with billmen on field parade and pikemen in corselets and canvas jacks (sleeveless tunics lined with metal plates). William knew that sight of armour and stir of alarm, and pikemen in tramped-down muddy meadows would have entertained crowds of young people. The young had other entertainers, too, in jugglers, sword-fighters, dancing bears, or sometimes bear-wards who set dogs on a bear chained to a stake.

Of delight for many, young and old—in Stratford's changing fairground activity—were the performers of 'pastymes', or plays and interludes. To imitate a custom at court and please their own households, noblemen kept player-companies at low fees, so the players travelled for part of the year to boost their income. William's father was the bailiff when two companies played in the Gild hall, and John's officer paid the Queen's men and the Earl of Worcester's men out of the borough purse. At least five times after John was bailiff, Worcester's players came back to impress townspeople with a compound art—their drums (and perhaps tabors), their spectacle, and their rhetoric. The young could be transfixed by what they heard, and the rare experience of watching a drama might burn into rural memories, and be recalled for a lifetime. At Stratford one saw some of the nation's best acting, as groups under the patronage of Leicester, Warwick, Derby, Strange, Berkeley, and Essex (among other companies) arrived during William's boyhood or early manhood. As a matter of record, he grew up with plays, within a few hundred yards of where fine actors, from time to time, performed in the Gild hall or the Bridge Street innyards or the market areas. And we speak here of recorded, authorized arrivals, and not of the wandering, illegal groups of actors who reached every town.

No one tutored at home in 'courtesie' or in care for the social situation and word, and no one being trained at school in affective discourse, would have been indifferent, for long, to the quality of plays or players. An alertness to manners in daily life improved audiences, and the troupes appealed to people who could judge their quality. Stale, stiff old chronicles creaked (not that they were unknown in the 1570s). Morality plays with the funny, coarse Vice, laughing his evil as he pared his nails with a lath dagger, gave way to a more complex moral play—avoiding wild mockery of Rome and other topics of the early years of Elizabeth's reign. Yet the players' menu varied. One might see, arranged for eight actors or more, Thomas Preston's lively, bombastic comic and tragic scenes in *Cambyses* (which Falstaff alludes to), and, in Coventry, the 'hogh tuysday' or Hock Tuesday play—staged on the Tuesday after Easter when women held sway over the town's men—or even the last of the superb medieval religious works, the Corpus Christi mystery plays, which were performed as late as 1579. To many a town outside London, the actors brought new, competitive plays, well acted and in their deft combining of elements offering something for everyone. People in Warwickshire waited for months between arrivals of touring companies, and in that respect William and other schoolboys were starved for theatre and would have been eager to hear the player's drums. He was not to forget innovative plays of a sort common at this period, or the sheer energy of carnival in older dramas—or the multiple planes of reality in mixed, antic works which the men of Worcester or Essex or Strange could set before a town.

Nothing suggests that John Shakespeare disliked the players. After all, he had seen two companies paid in his bailiwick. But there is no evidence that he went afield for reasons other than business or the law, or that he took William or Gilbert to the royal entertainments at Kenilworth in 1575. People did hear that an aleconner, an inspector of ales (who probably held the post as a sinecure), caused Coventry's Hocktide play-actors to perform there. And they heard of the Queen's arrival with her courtiers, ban-dogs, and bears, and of a pageant of the Lady of the Lake (on Monday, 18 July) when Triton rode on a mermaid, and Arion on a dolphin's back spoke verse to Her Majesty. In *A Midsummer Night's Dream*, the facts are changed since a mermaid rides on a dolphin, but Oberon reminds Puck, as if to conjure up the Kenilworth pageant:

> once I sat upon a promontory
> And heard a mermaid on a dolphin's back
> Uttering such dulcet and harmonious breath
> That the rude sea grew civil at her song.

> (II. i. 149–52)

It was never unwise to flatter the Queen, and even in the 1570s she protected the players. She enjoyed theatre, and very nearly squashed proposals to ban plays, games, and fairs on Sunday; she knew and spoke Latin, but had sat through so many university plays in that language (Plautus's *Aulularia* at Cambridge; modern Latin works at Oxford) that she was the keener to enjoy works in English. Her fondness for spectacle was shared by many, but she was the one who did most to ensure that her reign would be known for encouraging the drama.

Yet for months on end lawful touring groups were absent from Stratford. Amateur mummers, or a Lord of Misrule who presided over antics from Christmas to Twelfth Night, were the town's main dramatic relief. With card-playing in fashion, paper kings and queens were in anyone's power. Boys took up football, prison-base, wrestling, or cudgel-playing with a sharp, smacking violence that shook off the tedium of school hours; they also escaped into the countryside.

The town's common fields began near the Woolshop behind the Gild Pits, and here, a few hundred yards from Henley Street, one entered an arable Stratford field. William's sense of the country—and its terms—has a relation to the borough fields, one of which lay within sight of his father's barn, and the Bishopton and Welcombe fields were not far off. Borough fields were laid out in furlongs, and the furlongs were divided into yard-lands, separated by balks, or grassy ridges. Each yard-land had ninety little strips, or 'lands', of a third of an acre, which were 'eared'. Later, as a hopeful poet, he could write with simple elegance to his patron that if *Venus and Adonis* proved deformed, he would 'neuer after *eare* so barren a *land*, for feare it yeeld me still so bad a haruest'.

Rural Warwickshire impressed him, and nature and his feelings for it supplied a rich thematic basis for his imagery—and its keynote. He gorged on farming terms and would refer to *meers*, or banks and hedges (as in Enobarbus's 'the *meered* question'), or to *leas*, or tilled lands (as in Timon's command to mother earth, 'Dry up thy marrows, vines, and plough-torn *leas*'). Ploughed fields led up-river to Charlecote, where 'at the bake-syde of Mr Lucies huse', as Leland wrote,[11] a brook met the Avon. Among several Thomas Lucys of the same title, the Sir Thomas Lucy who was born in 1532 was tutored by

John Foxe and wed at the age of 14 to Joyce Acton, aged 12. Tearing down an old demesne structure, he built the great red-brick Charlecote House, where the Earl of Leicester knighted him and the Queen visited. With forty servants or retainers, a fine library and a touring group of 'Sir Thomas Lucies players',[12] he was as well known at Stratford as the wealthy Sir Fulke Greville, of Beauchamp's Court, who served as town recorder after 1591; both men once arbitrated in a suit brought by William's friend Hamnet (or Hamlet) Sadler. With reminiscent humour, but not necessarily to settle a score as has been imagined, Lucy perhaps was recalled in Justice Shallow's armorial coat of 'luces' in *The Merry Wives*. Anyone could see, beyond his barbican at Charlecote, the fine glass in a hall's bay window which showed a fishy coat of arms—three white pikes or 'luces' on a crimson ground.

To the south lay other elegant, ornamental domains such as the Rainsfords' at Clifford Chambers, where from the turf one had a view of Holy Trinity. The Warwickshire poet Michael Drayton was to summer with the Rainsfords and at last write an elegy on Sir Henry Rainsford, who married Drayton's beloved Anne Goodere. In youth or early manhood, William knew the locale if not the owners of Clifford Chambers, and both south and north of his town a line between affluence and poverty met his eyes. Beggars were in the lanes and ditches, at fairs and in streets. Wages sank and prices rose, and if farmers had pewter, glass, and feather-beds as luxuries, a surplus of labourers added to the homeless. Indeed, even market towns came into difficulties.

In the mid-1570s inflation began to affect the leather crafts at Stratford. In poorer times glovers became victims of their own workers, and William's father—whether or not he suffered from thievery—had begun to speculate and break several laws himself. In fact, Tudor laws affecting trade might have been kept in force for the purpose of being broken, so that the state gained a revenue in fines.

Debts and a downfall

Far from keeping all his eggs in one basket, John Shakespeare had been dealing in wool and lending money. In 1570, when William was barely of school age, John was twice accused of breaking a usury law by charging interest—high interest, £20 in both cases—on loans of £80 and £100 to one Walter Musshem, or Mussum, of Walton D'Eiville near Stratford.[13] Musshem appears as a sheep farmer and one of John's business partners; he may be the Musshem whose inventory is in the Worcester County Record Office and who possessed 117 sheep in 1588: we know that he and John failed to appear when Henry Higford, formerly town steward, sued them for debts of £30 each in 1573.[14] John's usury cases came before the Royal Exchequer and in one instance he paid a fine; but the wool trade relied on credit, and the unworkable usury laws amounted to a random tax on trade. (The system relied on informers who could receive for their services half the fine levied against a violator.)

Such a fine would not have disgraced a leading townsman; but John Shakespeare's other troubles were more dangerous, as when he was twice accused at the Exchequer in 1572 for illegal wool-dealing. The wool statutes were unevenly enforced, but violations annoyed the Merchants of the Staple, the main legal dealers. Glovers in particular were tempted to transgress: with no use for fell wool removed from pelts, a glover sold it as a matter of course to wool-dealers; yet it was only a small step to take from selling cheap, superfluous fell wool to breaking the law seriously to deal in fleece wool, and some Midlands glovers made large profits in fleeces. A 'wool brogger' had to be discreet, and it is more likely that John Shakespeare rode to Walton D'Eiville and beyond with his eldest son, or others he trusted, than with casual helpers. William learned facts of the wool trade that apply to his father's time, such as that eleven Midlands rams yield a tod of 28 pounds, or that a tod's worth at Stratford was 21 shillings.[15] He acquired a knowledge of shepherds and sheep farmers, sympathy for them, and an accurate sense of sheep-shearing feasts and of the farmers' talk, tones, and drollery. His sense of these men and their womenfolk is unusually sure, and so in *The Winter's Tale* he could go beyond his romance source (Greene's *Pandosto*) to write of more than pastoral puppets and give Warwickshire life to Bohemia's shepherds. His knowledge of details a 'brogger' knew in the 1570s suggests that he was aware of his father's dealings and was trusted. The Shakespeares of

Henley Street were close, defensive, and mutually dependent (so much we may infer), but they were not isolated, and John in his graver troubles was to depend on the leniency of the 'Brotherhode'.

Any brogger, by the mid-1570s, would have found it harder to get contracts for June shearings without risk of heavy fines. John had farming as well as his shop to fall back on. With acreage at Asbyes, an interest in 100 acres at Snitterfield, and a lease on 14 acres, in 1568, at Ingon Meadow, he was involved in corn-growing. He had sued the tanner Henry Field for a debt owing on eighteen quarters of barley (nearly 5 hundredweight), and he had at least 22 acres of meadow and pasture suitable for grazing; not all of his land was arable. Also, he was still buying land. In 1575 he paid to Edmund and Emma Hall, of Hallow, the sum of £40 for two houses with gardens and orchards at Stratford—his last recorded property purchase. In that year or the next, his application to the Heralds' College for a coat of arms and hence for gentlehood came to nothing, though he got a 'pattern' or sketch of his arms, before the matter was broken off.[16] In October 1576, the Privy Council ordered wool-buyers from London, Northampton, and other locales in for questioning. Wool middlemen were then being blamed for a sharp rise in wool prices (following a resumption of normal trade with the Netherlands, after some four years' interruption), and legal dealers of the Staple raged for the heads of broggers. Intervention and questioning by the Privy Council, just then, could be dangerous for Catholic families. Though he had married one of the strongly Catholic Ardens, John, it is true, was reticent about his own belief. Catholics had been accommodated in Elizabeth's tolerant Church, but, increasingly, the nation's climate of opinion had turned against the old faith.

How defiant in religion John truly was, we do not know; but he added to his troubles by not attending Anglican services. Did a Jesuit missionary in the 1580s persuade him to declare his faith? A paper booklet of six leaves stitched together, found by a bricklayer in April 1757 between the rafters and tiling of what had been John's western house at Henley Street, has turned out to be an authentic formulary; a 'John Shakspear' here makes a Catholic profession of faith, and appears to sign, as the last paragraph indicates, in his own hand. The formulary found in the rafters follows Borromeo's Last Will of the Soul, which Jesuit missionaries in England were making use of by 1581. But the booklet itself has vanished; and if John did mark or sign it, he kept his religious feelings as well hidden as the testament in his rafters. When cited in 1592 for recusancy, or failure to attend church, he evidently declared he had stayed away from Anglican service to avoid his creditors. 'It is sayd that', the wardens' not very rigorously enquiring 'Seconde Certificat' states, 'Mr John Shackespere' among eight others 'coom not to Churche for feare of processe for Debtte.'[17] But by then almost any creditor could have caught him at the Court of Record juries on which he served; he was not in fact in hiding, but available to make probate inventories and press claims at law.

It is true that his practical, financial position was poor by 1576. In a new effort to stamp out brogging, the Privy Council temporarily suspended all licensed wool-dealing that November; thus six months before the whole network of justices of the peace became involved in collecting £100 bonds from the broggers as security against their dealing in wool,[18] John Shakespeare—if he had any large debts—would have found his hands tied. By then a marked man and known offender at the Exchequer, he could not with impunity have made good to any of his creditors by buying or selling wool after about December 1576.

This was a turning-point for the Shakespeare family. We have good evidence that John failed to meet claims on his funds, and that his downfall was known in the Gild hall. He avoided borough council meetings. His affairs were so poor that when a levy to equip soldiers was passed, John was 'excepted' and had to pay only 3s. 4d. (just half the amount levied on other aldermen). He was excused from paying a fine for being absent on election day, in 1578, and excused again that November from paying 4d. weekly towards poor relief: 'm^r John shaxpeare', it was ordered, 'shall not be taxed to paye any thinge'.[19] It would be wrong for us to suppose that he avoided council meetings *only* because he feared trouble as a Catholic, at any rate. Incurring debts and lacking cash, he was able to raise £40 in 1579 by mortgaging a house and 56 acres at Wilmcote to his wife's brother-in-law Edmund Lambert, to whom he owed money. When the borrowed £40 fell due, John could not pay it—and so Lambert held the property until he died, after which John tried in vain to recover it from Lambert's heir, whom he sued at the court of the Queen's Bench. Later he renewed his effort in the court of Chancery, but John and Mary Shakespeare never did get back their land, which was a part of the Arden inheritance.

John had dealt illegally in a wool trade that relied much on credit. It is clear from borough records that he lacked ready cash to pay creditors after the assault on broggers, and that his colleagues freed him from fines, cut normal levies, and dropped him as an alderman after his nine years' absence (during which he appeared once to vote for his friend John Sadler as bailiff): 'm^r Shaxpere dothe not Come to halles when they be warned nor hathe not done of Longe tyme', as a clerk wrote in 1586.[20] John was concerned with self-preservation, and his long avoidance of halls may not be wholly attributable to a fear of debt. He kept his head down, it would seem, partly because he feared questions about his beliefs and background; and he was disgraced by absences before the town council expelled him. Yet he was not sent to ruin. He was in business or speculating after being dropped by the council, and in his last years was looking into toll-corn or pursuing Lambert's heir. As late as 1599 he tried to recover a thirty-year-old debt for 21 tods (588 lb.) of wool from John Walford, a clothier of Wiltshire and thrice mayor of Marlborough; and he was slow to give up a glover's shop.

Shakespeare 'was a glovers son', Thomas Plume, Archdeacon of Rochester, records around 1657 (and is thus more accurate than early biographers in identifying the poet's father's trade), ' — Sir John Mennis saw once his old Father in his shop — a merry Cheekd old man — that said — Will was a good Honest Fellow, but he durst have crakt a jeast [or jest] with him at any time'.[21] (Mennis was born in 1599 and could not have recalled a glover who died in 1601, but may have quoted someone else who heard and recalled John Shakespeare.)

That report of a merry-cheeked old man who jests with his son is credible, and John was not broken in 1576. In between William's twelfth and thirteenth birthdays, the father's behaviour simply changed. After being an honoured town servant, John became an absentee, plagued by threats of creditors and informers, and needing help rather than giving it. He was in shadow, and his household had less money but more mouths to feed. William's parents had named a second child Joan Shakespeare on 15 April 1569. She was the only one of their four daughters to survive childhood. Their last daughter, Anne, was baptized on 28 September 1571, and buried at the age of 7. Their son Richard was taken to the baptismal font at Holy Trinity on 11 March 1574, and their last child, Edmund, on 3 May 1580.

These births accentuated an eldest son's pride of place, and, far from being displaced in the family, William thrived. His well-being appears in his later dedicatory letters to his patron and also in light jokes and allusive, affectionate mockery—all of which seem to point back to happiness, self-love, and his family pride in the Stratford years. No deep distaste for Stratford would appear in any of his known actions, attitudes, or allusions. If he consciously made light of his sister Joan, in later times, by calling a hawk 'Old Joan' in *2 Henry IV*, or by playing on a name common for upstarts and servants (as in 'greasy Joan' or 'I can make any Joan a lady'), he kept his sister close to him in such references; and he was not likely to have forgotten the constables at Stratford, including his father, when conjuring up Dull, Elbow, or Dogberry and the watch in *Much Ado*. He had every reason to be amused and complacent in boyhood as his father's heir apparent. His ease or boredom in early schooling can only have left his mind free. In a town various in work, the comic human spectacle was instructive. But there would also be the profound enquiring force of his disillusionment—

> Othello's occupation's gone!
>
> (III. iii. 362)

What happens when our preconceived notions of life are abruptly changed, or when trust in a beloved person is shattered by experience? His father had risen to a bailiff's robes, and then after being exposed for usury and illegal dealing, neglected his role as an alderman until the council would have no more of him. What do the furred honours or rank, office, and reputation conceal?

> Through tattered rags small vices do appear;
> Robes and furred gowns hides all.
>
> (*Lear*, 1608 quarto, xx. 158–9)

In densely peopled Henley Street, an alderman's actions would in any case be judged by gossip, and his refusal to attend halls would be known. John Shakespeare had abandoned the 'Brotherhode'. The evidence would suggest that William was alert to his father's daily work, and well aware of his brogging. The neighbourhood cannot have been blind to an alderman's behaviour, and gossip and William's own eyes and ears would have told him about his father's setback. Yet many an idolized father has been found to have feet of clay, and for the sensitive young the act of growing up is perhaps inherently disillusioning. William is likely to have felt the strongest loyalty, sympathy, and love for his father, while being aware of depressed circumstances. At 13 he was being changed by one of the great experiences of Tudor life, inasmuch as he was going to a grammar school, and his education would have carried his mind away from his family's troubles with debts and credit. John Shakespeare's downfall is a matter of record nevertheless, and the household at Henley Street was affected by it.

4

TO GRAMMAR SCHOOL

Sweet smoke of rhetoric!

(Don Armado, *Love's Labour's Lost*)

A classroom

John Shakespeare knew his advantages well enough to take large risks in the early 1570s, and he won local notoriety as an entrepreneur. Once he was accused of illegally sharing in a joint purchase of 200 tods (5,600 lb.) of wool. Even before applying for a coat of arms, he must have looked with immense hope to his son and heir. As a deputy bailiff, he was unlikely to have sent William to any school but the borough one, the only grammar school for miles around. This was the King's New School on Church Street—scriveners refer to it as the 'free scole' or 'Kynges ffree Schoole'. Its registers are missing, but Nicholas Rowe writes in 1709 that 'Mr. John Shakespear' was a 'considerable Dealer in Wool' who bred William 'for some time at a Free-School'—and, though he was not always reliable, we have no reason to discredit Rowe's words in this instance.[1] Much more direct, certain evidence that William was in grammar school comes from his plays. The Latin authors he recalls are mainly those he would have studied in class—the 'grammar gods'—and since the school was open to sons of burgesses, he would have been enrolled in 1571, when he was 7.

Stratford classes before William's time, and down to the present day, have met in what borough records call 'the chapell'—that is within the chapel precincts, either inside or close to the Gild hall. That hall was the seat of the town government, and William was schooled within a few yards of the annexe in which his father met with other aldermen. Formerly pupils had convened in 'Scholehows' (or

Pedagogue's House), but after the Gild school was refounded in 1553 there was a slight move. We do not know just why. It may be that Scholehows was assigned rent-free to John Brownsword, a married teacher. A new room was set up, and a clerk notes in Brownsword's tenure (early in the 1560s) that this teacher gives 12*d*. 'towarde ye makynge of ye schole'[2]—a modest gift. (Bretchgirdle, the vicar, did at least as well by leaving to the new classroom his 'Elyottes lybrarie of Coopers Castigacion', which was a copy of Sir Thomas Elyot's Latin–English dictionary *Bibliotheca Eliotae*, revised in 1552 by Thomas Cooper, a valuable folio.[3]) By the 1570s, the boys were climbing stairs to the Gild hall's 'over hall', which is jettied, ample, and airy with heavy roof braces under a peaked ceiling of rafters, and two rows of windows, one row looking onto Church Street. The room was evidently subdivided with partitions; but in one part about forty-two boys—with a schoolmaster and his assistant, or usher—met six days a week for nearly the whole year.

The class was a quarter of a mile from the Woolshop, a weary way for Jaques' lad in *As You Like It* no doubt, though Jaques reduces each age of life to a cynical vignette:

> the whining schoolboy with his satchel
> And shining morning face, creeping like snail
> Unwillingly to school.
>
> (II. vii. 145–7)

Of course, somebody made the boy's satchel and one or two greasy Joans collected ashes and grease all winter to make soap for that shining face.

A grammar boy was part of an élite. Most children hardly finished 'petty' class. Setting out with his knife, quills, and ink, William would have been very special: an alderman's son was under pressure to behave well and do credit to his father. Later William was to mock rhetoric, Latin, and pedants—but not bitterly—and alluded often enough to school and its texts to suggest he had known classes from two viewpoints, the pupil's and the teacher's. He was impressionable enough to be at one disadvantage as a schoolboy, in that he might take in *too much* instruction and so be overly receptive, dutiful, and patient, if bored and a little flattened. He had to reach class at about 6 a.m., and, after a pause for breakfast, hear lessons till luncheon, and then from 1 p.m. to about 5.30 p.m.

Memory-work was endless. At Leicester's Free Grammar School—which cannot have been much unlike Stratford's—each morning's lesson was repeated by pupils next day 'without booke'. On Fridays, the week's lessons had to be known by heart, 'perfectlie'. From the age of 7 until about 15, William memorized Latin almost daily. Unlike the meandering, fuzzy, verbose English language—so unfixed and variable, so quickly changing that Chaucer was almost unintelligible after 200 years—Latin was lucid and precise. For a millennium and a half it had been the pre-eminent language of Europe, and since the 1540s it had become the vehicle for a fluent and elegant commentary in all fields of learning at Cambridge and at Oxford. In the 1570s the literary prestige of Latin was immense. The sound of a language—far more than its syntax or vocabulary—appealed to Elizabethans, and William's memorizing of Latin would, above all, train his ear. With a good memory, he would later be able to synthesize in his work a very great deal of verbal material that he had heard or read. Experience with the preciseness of Latin would help him to express himself with point, logic, and lucid continuity, and save him from larding his English writing with bombast, 'ink-horn' terms, or exotic and high-sounding words adopted simply for show.[4]

On the other hand, a narrow focus upon Latin could be stultifying. Grammar-school boys were taught nothing about modern history, society, politics, the life of their town or county or nation, almost nothing about the crafts, the trades, agriculture, the human body, or any other topic likely to be useful to them. Discipline was strict, and no doubt benches were hard—a clerk notes a new 'plank' for King's New School. A master arrived at about 7 a.m., when pupils bowed to him. In a leather jerkin, flat cap, and round cloak, or cassock of silk and woollen 'mockado', he was usually a lordly presence as he taught the older boys, who were in Upper School. In the same room the usher taught children of the Lower School the rudiments of vocabulary, accidence, and grammar. That training did not help William's spelling, to judge from 'Hand D' in the *Booke of Sir Thomas More* play manuscript, and he perhaps spelled no better than Stratford clerks if 'Hand D' is indeed his own (as we believe it is), since it shows spellings such as 'ffraunc' (France), 'Jarman' (German), 'graunt' (grant), 'scilens' (silence), and 'afoord' (afford). It is not true that teachers were indifferent to a boy's English, but English spelling was not regularized and they would have cared a great deal more for a child's Latin.

Learning by ear and memory, William would have read very little in the few, costly schoolbooks. But boys listened, and, since he heard his schoolmates' jokes, some origins of his puns, bawdry, and burlesque seem traceable to class. In reaction to endless obedience, town boys almost had to hear English bawdy humour in the Latin of 'horum, harum, horum' in William Lily's *A Shorte Introduction of Grammar* (a required text), if only to save their sanity.

In *The Merry Wives*, Mistress Quickly thinks she hears bawdy in those words, and in Act IV, scene i, the Welsh parson–pedagogue Sir Hugh Evans takes young William Page through a mock-usher's drill. In the scene's contemporary spelling we may catch tones of an Elizabethan first-year class, despite Mistress Quickly's commentary:

EUANS. What is (*Lapis*) *William?*

WILLIAM. A Stone.

EUANS. And what is a Stone (*William?*)

WILLIAM. A Peeble.

EUANS. No; it is *Lapis*: I pray you remember in your praine . . . What is the *Focatiue case* (*William?*)

WILLIAM. O, *Vocatiuo*, O.

EUANS. Remember *William*, *Focatiue*, is *caret*.

MISTRIS QUICKLY. And that's a good roote.

EUANS.   O'man, forbeare.

MISTRIS PAGE (to *Mistris Quickly*). Peace.

EUANS. What is your *Genitiue case plurall* (*William?*)

WILLIAM. *Genitiue case?*

EUANS. I.

WILLIAM. *Genitiuo horum, harum, horum.*

MISTRIS QUICKLY. 'Vengeance of Ginyes case; fie on her; neuer name her (childe) if she be a whore.

(IV. i. 28–57; *O-S* sc. xiii)

Mistress Page is so pleased that she says of William: 'He is a better scholler then I thought he was', and, in general, Tudor parents approved of grammar-school training. It made their sons polite and employable, and we must not assume that Mary Shakespeare—who had won Arden's trust for *her* early competence—would have lessened urgent pressure upon an alderman's son to succeed in school. And to succeed too well.

Certainly for many of the boys the slow pace and repetitions were soporific or numbing. They went from the *Grammar* to Lily's *Brevissima Institutio*, which is all in Latin except for an index and a Greek alphabet—and William tasted his 'lesse Greeke' (as Jonson termed it) by the age of 9. He did recall the *Grammar* with a clear, untroubled humour that contrasts with his paradoxical reactions to Upper School. 'An Interjection', he learned from Lily, 'betokeneth a sudayne passion' as of 'Laughing: as *Ha ha he*'.[5] So Benedick tells Claudio in *Much Ado*: 'interjections? Why then, some be of laughing, as "ah, ha, he!" ' (IV. i. 21–2).

Or the *Grammar* could remind boys (who rose before dawn) of the beautiful proverb 'Diluculo surgere . . .' (it is most healthful to get up early in the morning). 'Approach, Sir Andrew', Sir Toby Belch tells a woebegone Aguecheek in *Twelfth Night*, 'Not to be abed after midnight is to be up betimes, and *diluculo surgere*, thou knowest' (II. iii. 1–3).

Lower School dragged on for three or four years—and yet earlier scholars such as Erasmus, Colet, and Grocyn had put into the schools a potent originating force. Their Christian humanism had in it an ample, cheerful faith in the possibilities of each individual's capacity for wise action. They had transformed the old medieval *trivium* of grammar, rhetoric, and logic partly because their humanism was cosmopolitan, alert, and seeking. Some roots of their thought—and thus of Shakespeare's schooling—were in the writings of fifteenth-century Florentines such as Marsilio Ficino or his protégé, Pico della Mirandola, whose biography Sir Thomas More translated.

Pico held that we are not celestial or earthly, mortal or immortal, good or bad, but become the product of our choices. If so, young minds must be trained for ethical choice, and the aim of the British grammar school should not be to purify souls but to prepare the intellect for proper service in God's world. Since the ancients had refined the mind—or brought it to its highest attainments—Latin and Greek filled the Tudor curriculum, and indeed in 1571 the bishops asked every British schoolmaster to teach books 'whereby the fulnes and finenes of the Latine & Greeke toung may be learned'.[6]

The system—with its element of promise—at least ensured that Elizabethan playwrights would write for audiences reared in a literary culture. In practice, the system of course depended on many a Sir Hugh Evans—but William learned from his next classroom text. This was Leonard Cullmann's *Sententiae Pueriles*, with its lists of Latin adages for 'conversing', such as these:

Deferto neminem	Accuse no man
Multitudini place	Please the multitude
Pecuniae obediunt omnia	All things obey money
Felicitas incitat inimicitias	Felicity doth raise up enemies
Somnus mortis imago	Sleep is the image of death
Tempus edax rerum	Time is a devourer
Tempus dolorem lenit	Time doth assuage grief
Animus cujusque sermone revelatur	Each person's mind is discovered by his speech

If Polonius is here in bud, so is much more. Pupils used these and other adages—such as those in Erasmus's *Cato*—for 'amplifying' in themes. William learned to think in *sententiae*. As he looked for the best, he was to bring pithy commonplaces along with much of the subtle mind of the Renaissance into his work, and some 209 echoes of the *Pueriles* itself have been found in his poems and plays.[7]

Pupils had to think beyond the life of the classroom, now and then, for how else could they show that 'time doth assuage grief'? They imagined ancient Romans (they heard almost nothing about England since the time of Julius Caesar), and they met a few Romans in Terence's comedies, as in the delicate *Eunuchus* with its funny, greasy parasite Gnatho:

GNATHO.   plurima salute Parmenonem
   summum suom inpertit Gnatho. quid agitur?.

PARMENO.   statur.

GNATHO.   video.

num quidnam hic quod nolis vides?

PARMENO.   te.

[GNATHO. Gnatho wishes a very good morning to his great friend
  Parmeno. What are you on?
PARMENO. My legs.
GNATHO. So I see. You don't see anything here, do you, that you'd rather not?
PARMENO. You.][8]

If the usher ever went beyond a few scenes, the children became aware
of the five-act play structure, but Terence was admired chiefly for fine
Latin. William was to take much more from Plautus, whose comedies
were too coarse for most schools. When did he first read Plautus? That
is uncertain, but the classroom introduced him tantalizingly to
Roman comedy; and it is probable that from his father's friends, if not
from the schoolmaster, he could have borrowed, at last, as much of
Terence or Plautus as he wished to read.

He recalled the modern Latin moral poets well. Children memorized from Palingenius' *Zodiacus Vitae*, which has a brief defence of
comedy, and from a bucolic eclogue or two by the Carmelite poet,
Mantuanus (Baptista Spagnuoli), dear to the heart of the pedant
Holofernes in *Love's Labour's Lost*. In their third year, they began to
compose their own Latin with help of Withals's short dictionary, or
the Elyot–Cooper one left by the vicar. For more conversing, they
jotted lines from Corderius, Gallus, or Vives, or from the dialogues of
Castalio and Erasmus.[9]

In a sense, classes lasted seven days a week, since the children had to
account for themes they heard in Sunday sermons and briefer hom-
ilies. In school they translated back and forth, English to Latin and
Latin to English, from the Geneva Bible—and William's teacher most
probably favoured the Proverbs and Psalms as well as Genesis, Job,
and Ecclesiasticus.[10] His knowledge of the Bible was improved in
church by Henry Heicroft, a fellow of St John's at Cambridge, who
had an MA in 1570, and who earned extra pay for Lenten sermons and
who was among the best-prepared vicars the town had known. In
tenure from 1569 to 1584 (when he left for the richer benefice of

Rowington), Heicroft at least helped to impart that profound religious and moral sense that underlies Shakespeare's urbanity.

Schooldays began and ended in devotions, and the boys would have trudged into the Gild chapel to sing from the Psalter. A psalm was a dramatic, collective act, requiring pupils as they sang to assume in unison the 'I' of David, Christ, and the Church. They were saved, too, from literalness by Alexander Nowell's great *Catechisme*, which, after *ABC with the Catechism*, most grammar-school pupils knew by the mid-1570s. Nowell taught the mystery of God, 'which is a spirit, eternall, unmeasurable, infinite, incomprehensible', severed from every 'vaine shape', and he pointed to an evil so dark, foul, and dreadful (and full of emotion and drama) that it was nameless. Boys may have whispered 'regicide' as they memorized his warning: 'Yea surely', says the *Catechisme*. For if it is terrible to offend one's parents, 'and parricide to kill them . . . what shall we say of them that haue conspired and borne wicked armour, against the common weale, against their countrey, the most auncient, sacred, and common mother?'[11]

That was about as close as schoolchildren came to hearing of English 'bearers of wicked armour', although a new mood stirred outside schools in the 1570s with an implicit question. If teachers taught Latin, what of English? New books praised the nation's past as well as her tongue: William Lambarde's *Perambulation of Kent*—the first county history—argued in 1576 for the supreme value of the 'Hystorie of England'.[12] Raphael Holinshed's massive *Chronicles* a year later exalted the British Isles. One of its excellent woodcuts shows 'Makbeth', as he rides along with 'Banquho' under a crow-filled sky to meet three 'weird sisters or feiries', who scowl at him and his companion on horseback.[13] If the British past was important one might argue for the fineness of the native tongue—at least in the patriotic climate when William left Lower School. Up until then, his training was routine, but it would have prepared him for the arrival of Master Thomas Jenkins.

Rhetoric at dawn

On dark days in Church Street's over-hall, the living world faded and it was the ancients that mattered. Sallust or Caesar came to life in the accents of young boys—or miracles of animation were *supposed* to occur. Boys were told to recite 'pathetically', with feeling, and the bishops' canons asked them to stand up straight and speak 'openly, plainly, and distinctly'.[14] In Upper School, such recitals—of benefit to future actors perhaps—had to appeal to a university-trained master.

From 1571 Simon Hunt had taught the upper benches; he was fresh from Oxford with a BA. He may have been volatile, but his payment of 7s. 11d. 'towardes the repayringe of the schole wyndowes' (in his early tenure) probably means that he was a victim of 'barring out' when, on set days, pupils barred the door against the master and became rowdy. Windows were smashed and boys—such as William—might pay for 'a wyndowe broken at the shuttinge of [their] Master forthe'.[15] William knew a festive, topsy-turvy world of inverted authority in school and his comedies were to explore the more subtle and complex inversions—and deep releases—of antic mishap.

Hunt's troubles with the broken window-glass preceded his exit in 1575. He left Church Street either to become a Jesuit—if he is the Simon Hunt who matriculated at the University of Douai in the summer of 1575—or else to pursue a local career, if he is the Simon Hunt of Stratford who left an estate worth £100 in 1598.

The next two schoolmasters were Thomas Jenkins and John Cottom, both Oxford men. The master's pay of £20 per annum was reasonable, but not generous, and since the incumbent teacher had to pay the usher's salary, some masters left for more lucrative posts in the 1560s and 1570s. The departing teacher or the vicar usually recruited a replacement. So John Brownsword had been brought in by the vicar Bretchgirdle, his former teacher at Witton. Three years later in 1568 the new schoolmaster became John Acton, a fellow of Brasenose College, Oxford; he was replaced by Walter Roche, a fellow of Corpus Christi College, who after resigning from the King's New School practised law on Chapel Street and twice witnessed deeds with John Shakespeare.

Jenkins and Cottom had strong Catholic connections, but no doubt so did many other masters at a time when the English Reformation was still within living memory. A Londoner, Jenkins was the son of an 'old servant' of Sir Thomas White, founder of St John's College, Oxford. White was a pious Catholic who conformed, and in fact St John's welcomed men who preferred the Catholic faith but who wished to reconcile it with loyalty to the Queen. It was to this college that White's servant's son was sent. Jenkins took his BA in 1566 and MA in 1570; he was also a fellow of St John's from 1566 to 1572, when his college granted him the lease of 'Chawsers Howse' at Woodstock, probably for teaching.[16] Sir Thomas had favoured him with a letter of support, and so if Jenkins was not in fact a Catholic he had friends and well-wishers who were. Cottom—who succeeded him— had a younger Catholic brother who was martyred. It is sometimes confidently said that Jenkins was fetched over from Warwick in 1575, but the master from Warwick is not named in Stratford's records, and Jenkins does figure as renting rooms from the council in a rent-roll dated 10 March 1574, though these entries could have been added some time after that March:

m^r Jenkins for one Chamber o————x^s
of him for an other Chamber o————v^{s}[17]

(Schoolmasters had rent-free quarters. Ushers did not.) It is possible, then—but by no means certain—that Jenkins began as an usher, and that his teaching would account for William's recalling extremely well the moral poets who came near the end of the Lower School curriculum. However that may be, Jenkins impressed clerks, who called one of his rooms 'm^r ginkins Chamber' or 'm^r Jenkins Chamber' six and eight years after he left it;[18] and he was likely to have impressed boys. He seems, to mention one example, to have taught the class Book I of Quintilian, which no mere pedant would teach (a teacher interested only in rhetoric drill would skip it). As he became master in 1575, it was apparently he who introduced William to Ovid's *Metamorphoses* and perhaps to Arthur Golding's famous, 'equivalent' version, homely and useful at once, which schoolmasters often read from. One virtue of Golding's English is that it unfolds and expands the tight richness of Ovid's Latin. Shakespeare's fondness for Golding's version and reliance upon it, of course, cannot be taken to show that he lacked a good, independent sense of Ovid's text; still, he was to use Golding's details, which are compelling in descriptive pictures—as in that of a mortal Atalanta, beloved of gods:

The garment she did weare
A brayded button fastned at hir gorget. All hir heare
Untrimmed in one only knot was trussed. From hir left
Side hanging on hir shoulder was an Iuorie quiuer deft:
Which being full of arrowes, made a clattring as she went.
And in hir right hand she did beare a Bow already bent.
Hir furniture was such as this. Her countnance and hir grace
Was such as in a Boy might well be cald a Wenches face.[19]

Ovid's text was the Elizabethan classroom favourite. But William's fondness for Ovid was complex, lifelong, and, it would seem, always developing so that he found freshnesses in the *Metamorphoses* as if it were for him a many-levelled source of worldly and metaphysical insights. One of the best things he saw in that inexhaustible poem was a varying, rich image of spiritual and bodily transformation, which informs nature's processes and could inform the spirit of comedy.

A master's chief task was to teach rhetoric, or the devices that enabled a boy to create a voice on paper in his themes, epistles, and orations. Any boy who stayed the course would learn a little—and clever boys learned how to state an argument with the utmost emotional force in their *controversiae*, in which they argued now one view of a question, now another. That exercise gave William an early sense of the detached-yet-attached speech-writing needed for plays. They also learned from *imitatio*—or the process of assimilating many snippets of Latin to produce a text, like, yet unlike, the one to be imitated. If Ovid captured his fancy at 13 and 14, William was exactly trained in the techniques of assimilation from diverse sources.

To the extent that school influenced him, he was made to be a follower and assimilator—not a creative man. School probably reinforced his dislike of singularity. He was to take well-tried subjects for his plays and use his power for a fresh reworking of old texts, old themes, old truths, and so write works that seem uneccentric but are deeply original as well as universal. To a degree, any boy on the benches was battered into conformity and taught merely the habits and frames that helped him to be a pale shadow of Latin authors. William's chief guides for rhetoric were the *Ad Herennium* (then thought to be Cicero's) for general information, Quintilian for theory, Erasmus's *Copia* for variety and elegance, and Susenbrotus for tropes and figures of speech. It is not clear that he ever read a work by Cicero other than *Tusculan Disputations*; his texts at school were few. But the *Ad Herennium* did teach him that a speech must be written without much labour—boys tried for smart fluency—and it implicitly offered the theory that the physical world itself, as well as verbal phrasing and adornment, may be alike ornamental.[20] Possibly his teacher dissented from that classical notion—and William did not subscribe to it. He respected a distinction between reality and the airy fuss of words, and yet he valued the tropes and schemes. A good teacher would have stressed them. They unlocked language itself, and, in theory, helped the user to express feelings naturally. The trope was, in effect, a 'turn' in a word's meaning from a literal to an imaginative level, as when the word is used in metaphor, simile, or hyperbole, or again in devices such as synecdoche (where the part represents the whole) or metonymy (where the name of an attribute is used for the thing itself). The schemes involved repetitions of words, symmetry or balance in style, visual and aural patterns, as in isocolon and parison (equal length and equal structure in successive clauses) or paromoion (corresponding sounds with matching structures), and a variety of other devices affecting emphasis, tempo, or rhythm in phrases and sentences.

The trouble is that Tudor schoolboys knew too little of life to use such a language system well. They were trained in imitative synthesis, but the rhetorical system was complex enough to encourage artificiality, or mere technical facility. Even when writing in London, William would take a decade to learn to use the full resources of rhetoric. To judge from the stiffness of style in his early plays, he was slow to match his use of language to his sense of experience. He learned (as many did) to attend to manner in composing arguments for orations, but we must wait at least until *The Merchant of Venice* or perhaps *Troilus and Cressida* and the tragic soliloquies to find him fully at ease in the argumentative speech. He never abandoned the classical system of rhetoric, and, in time, made more powerful, ranging, and innovative uses of it than anyone else who has written for the English stage; but it is another thing to suppose that he quickly assimilated that system.

With its arid emphasis on verbal artifice, school evidently came too early for him, in some ways narrowing his mind and delaying his success; there are signs, for example, in his mature writing, that he had been too attracted by ringing changes on words, by varying, amplifying, and patterning. Even when mocking rhetoric in his apprentice work, he seems enamoured of the verbal excesses he comically attacks, as in the word- and sound-play of Speed and Proteus in *The Two Gentlemen of Verona*:

SPEED. The Shepheard seekes the Sheepe, and not the Sheepe the Shepheard; but I seeke my Master, and my Master seekes not me: therefore I am no Sheepe.

PROTEUS. The Sheepe for fodder follow the Shepheard, the Shepheard for foode followes not the Sheepe: thou for wages followest thy Master, thy Master for wages followes not thee: therefore thou art a Sheepe.

(I. i. 84–90; *O-S* sc. i)

He was dazzled by models of verbal patterning he was slow to outgrow, and one of his handicaps was that he was likely to imitate styles long out of date, or not to adapt to a later age that might possibly ask for more matter and less rhetoric. A grandson of Lily the grammarian was soon to charm him: the family name had changed from Lily to Lyly, and the patterned smartness of Lyly's *Euphues*, of 1578, became a fad. But fads do not last. Long after *Euphues* began to tire people, an ornate euphuistic style lingered in Shakespeare's writing. He never made his mind up about its excesses; he sends up euphuistic symmetry in Osric's speeches in *Hamlet* or Falstaff's in *1 Henry IV*—but he uses it in the serious verse, too, of *1 Henry IV*, *Richard III*, or *Othello*.

This fault is attributable to schools that were hotbeds of literary talent, but not always of self-sustaining life. William—and a few of his classmates—must have been agile at Latin, but as the agility spilled into English it outran the pupil's sense of himself and his observations. A deeper problem was William's enforced commitment to what he learned; the narrow channels of school were approved by his father, or John Shakespeare would not have seen the boy in class. But how could agility lead to inward development? An implicit protest against school is voiced in all of his light satire of pedants, but in the 1570s he prepared himself for no career more likely than the pedant's; if he evaded that, he still had no obvious way to reconcile his fondness for words and sounds with the sense of reality. As a schoolboy—even under an evidently humane, sensible Jenkins—he was in danger of being forced into a bright, shallow artificiality by verbal training, the narrow classicism of the course, and his imitativeness and receptivity. He did keep his fondness for rhetorical display in check—later—partly by laughing at its excesses, and indeed his comedians jest at academic absurdities with almost too much energy. His clowns are victims of rhetoric, and his most impressive themes exploit it; he was to portray in Hamlet a kind of ideal grammar-school prince, who can play, duel, and dream in words while staying in character, bookish and vital.

In the last stages of Upper School, the children took up Virgil and Horace, as well as Caesar and Sallust, for glimpses of Rome's history. If William began his Greek New Testament, it is probable that his career at Church Street ended before he learned much more to add to the modest amount of Greek he would already have had.

The Lord of Misrule

In recent years, his father's fortunes had changed. A boy who began in Lower School as a leading townsman's son found himself in a family short of cash and being treated leniently by indulgent aldermen—who did not see John Shakespeare at 'halls'.

Yet the times abetted a sense of release. There was a new audacity, a 'certaine deformitie and insolencie of minde' (as William Camden put it) that appeared in a rage for fashionable dress. This phenomenon was not confined to London but was a symptom of change 'all over England'[21]—and the flouting of old, sane sumptuary rules would have been evident at Stratford's Bridge Street inns and beyond.

Social barriers were eroding. Clothes no longer exactly reflected rank or degree. On a holiday from Upper School, William would have seen more than a little of the new anarchy—which was colourful. Men of mean rank wore cheap rosettes on their shoes. Embroidered waistcoats appeared in tuffeted taffeta or branched satin stitched in gold or silver, as if tradesmen's sons were noblemen, and grander young men had enormous padded doublets, effeminate shirts of cambric or lawn, even steeple-crowned hats of sarsenet 'with hat-bands of black, white, russet, red, green, or yellow, never the same for two days', hose after the French or Venetian patterns and slashed and embroidered shoes with high cork heels.[22]

That social revolution accented the audacity of seasonal rights of inversion, such as those of the Lord of Misrule in the Christmas feasts up to Twelfth Night and at harvest-time and Shrovetide. The wild-heads of a parish (says Phillip Stubbes in revulsion in the *Anatomie of Abuses*) with jangling bells and in 'liueries of green, yellow, or some other light wanton colour' either bemuse or deafen the godly, mock the Sabbath and invade churches, plead for money, dance and riot without hindrance—and may lay a cross over their necks, 'borrowed for the most parte of their pretie Mopsies & loouing Besses, for bussing them in *the* dark'.[23]

With the superiority of a grammar-school scholar, William may have avoided the ruffians of 'Mis-rule' and never figured among 'twentie, fortie, threescore or a hundred lustie Guttes' who followed their parish king; but he knew a spirit of inversion and defiance that abets self-discovery. The bottled-up life of the scholar did not appeal to him—and, partly in reaction to the artificiality of school, he seems (on the evidence of his attentions very soon in or near Shottery) to have had hunger enough for early experience. Even at 15 or 16 he was most certainly acquainted with Anne Hathaway, since the Hathaways of Shottery had had a friendly connection with his family since his infancy. Already his walks across the fields to the Hathaway cottage may have added to his parents' worries.

The restrictions of school and his hunger for experience affected his behaviour, and we cannot accuse him of incuriosity. As much as he absorbed in class, we have the evidence of his own writing to show that he was a close, almost famished, observer of the country—and the local Stratford lore of his deer-killing draws one's attention to his behaviour as he roamed with friends. In an early play he would cele-brate deer-killing and grammar-school pedantry in the same scene (*Love's Labour's Lost*, IV. ii).

In any case, deer-poaching was a sport for the adventurous. The

Tudor game laws in application were not severe. In theory (under the law of 5 Eliz., c. 21) an archer caught with a deer faced three months in prison and triple the cost of damages, and would have to provide sureties for abstaining from illegal killing for five years. But punishments seldom matched the statute.[24] Just because it involved outwitting the park-keeper, and a good deal of self-control and silent skill, deer-poaching appealed to the intelligent young. None of the poacher traditions attached to his name proves that William killed deer in these years or later, but so much smoke may suggest a little fire.

Poaching flourished at Oxford, and had had a lively history in Warwickshire. William learned about stalking, brakes, cover, the deer-herd, the herd's sensitivity to the slight 'noise of thy cross-bow',[25] and the ways of quiet, strategic poaching; he shows less knowledge of the legitimate chase with the hounds or the sounds of the horn. Even if he had studied the deer's anatomy in a Henley Street whittawer's shed, nevertheless he could not—one would think—have gained his fine sense of the herd's ambiance and habits in just that way.

Almost no escapade of his own would have caused his withdrawal from school, but straitened circumstances 'and the want of his assistance at Home, forc'd his Father to withdraw him from thence', says Rowe.[26] We have no evidence that he quit at an unusually early point. It was normal to leave at the age of 15 or 16, and it is probable that he left Church Street within a few months of his fifteenth birthday.

In April 1579 John Shakespeare would have needed 'assistance at home' if he lacked cash to pay helpers; as we have seen, by then the brethren were excusing him from levies he seems to have been unable to pay. The Shakespeares buried their daughter Anne that month. Joan was then 10, Gilbert and Richard 12½ and 5 respectively. Gilbert may have been to petty school, since he later affixed, in an Italian hand, his well-written 'Gilbart Shakesper' to a Stratford lease (of 5 March 1610).[27] As spring turned into summer in the parish there was a normal changeover at the King's New School when Master Jenkins was replaced by John Cottom. The two teachers agreed to—and signed—an arrangement as regards part-payment of salary, and Jenkins before leaving had one task laid upon him by the full weight of canon law: he had to recommend boys among those whom he had taught. He was supposed to send names of his abler pupils to the bishop of Worcester, for the 'Scholemasters' each year, as the canons read, 'shall signifie to the Byshop, what chosen scholers they haue of all their number, which are of that aptnes, and so forward in learning, that there may be a good hope they will become fitte, either for the common wealth, or for the holy ministerie'.[28]

William can hardly have spent months in class without revealing some 'aptnes', or a sign that he might 'become fitte'; his later writing does not suggest he had slept through school—and in the exercise of assimilating for *imitatio* he can only have shown promise. Yet we do not know that a borough teacher ever sent his name to the Anglican bishop of the diocese, ripe for advancement as he was. The evidence is still uncertain, but, with their known connections, Master Jenkins or Master Cottom may well have proposed for him an alternative way ahead, and a journey that led him to wear at a surprisingly early age 'playe clothes'.

5

OPPORTUNITY AND NEED

Proud of employment, willingly I go.

(Boyet, *Love's Labour's Lost*)

'In the Countrey'

*I*t is reasonable to think that at about the age of 15 or 16 Shakespeare helped his father, and that for an interlude he even found alternative employment. In the seventeenth century, John Aubrey was by no means certain that Ben Jonson's report of the Stratford poet's 'small' Latin could be valid. 'He understood Latine pretty well', Aubrey wrote of Shakespeare, 'for he had been in his younger yeares a Schoolmaster in the Countrey.'[1] This is a fairly well authenticated report. Using living sources of information, Aubrey was told of the schoolmastering by William Beeston, whose father Christopher Beeston the player had been a member of Shakespeare's company and had acted with him in Ben Jonson's *Every Man in his Humour*. Memories were long in the profession of the stage, in which recruitment was largely a matter of hereditary castes, and the elder Beeston had been an early member of the Lord Chamberlain's men. The 'Schoolmaster' report is not particularly surprising, unlikely, or merely gossipy.

At 15 or 16 William knew 'Latine pretty well', though with no other qualification he can hardly have begun as a grammar-school master. Unless he taught as an unlicensed teacher for a private employer, he would have needed a licence to be a schoolmaster, and no licence (or record of one) has come to light in his case. Most boys on leaving school either helped their fathers or contracted out, usually after paying a fee to be seven-year apprentices, and there was an exodus from

Stratford. A few boys, such as Roger Lock in 1577, or Richard Field in 1579, went to serve members of the London Stationers' Company, which controlled aspects of the book trade. As a son of Henry Field the tanner (whose inventory was later appraised by John Shakespeare), Richard Field was apprenticed from 29 September 1579 to the stationer George Bishop, and then agreed to learn printing for the first six years under Thomas Vautrollier, an immigrant from Paris, who brought out Calvin's *Institutes*, a Latin Book of Common Prayer, and Ovid, Cicero, and other schoolbooks.

If William had an explicit contract to teach in the Midlands, we lack it. We do, however, know of a family 'in the Countrey'—the northern family of Hoghton at Lea and Hoghton Tower in Lancashire—who have had a long-standing tradition that Shakespeare, as a young man, served two years with them.[2] Lancashire was then a poor county, backward and feudal, and known to be rough and dangerous for travellers. To the extent that they were religious, many of its people were Catholic. If Alexander de Hoghton wanted a 'Schoolmaster' for his retainers' children, he was wealthy enough to hire more than one. Yet among the retinue listed in his will, none is closer in name to Shakespeare than a 'servant', who is listed with a certain Fulke Gillom and is called William Shakeshafte. In the county there were a few families of Shakeshafte, but the name was not common; the name Shakespeare was very rare in Tudor Lancashire. An 'item' in Hoghton's will of 3 August 1581 interestingly associates Gillom and Shakeshafte with players, musical instruments, and 'all maner of playe clothes' or with a stock of players' clothes. In the will, Hoghton leaves his instruments and costumes to his half-brother Thomas, but, if Thomas refuses to keep an acting troupe, it is Hoghton's wish that his friend, Sir Thomas Hesketh of Rufford,

shall haue the same Instrumentes & playe clothes. And I most hertelye requyre the said Sir Thomas to be ffrendlye vnto ffoke Gyllome and will*ia*m Shakeshafte nowe dwellynge with me & eyther to take theym vnto his Servyce or els to helpe theym to some good m*aster* as my tryste is he wyll[.][3]

The phrase 'dwelling with me' is an odd one to use of servants, unless they 'dwell' in a special capacity. Also we cannot say that Shakespeare's name was not assimilated to the more familiar northern name of 'Shakeshafte' by Hoghton, or by his attorney or clerk. Surnames were not thought to be unalterable or fixed.[4]

This much of course does not prove the case, but it does leave open the possibility that Shakespeare spent some months in the north of England. In Lancashire the Hoghtons were second in influence only to the earls of Derby, their friends; and the young Stratford poet was to be associated with a Lancashire patron—none other than the fourth earl of Derby's son, Ferdinando Stanley, Lord Strange. A troupe or troupes under the Strange or Derby name performed two— perhaps four or more—of Shakespeare's early plays.

Moreover it is rather unlikely that he entered the theatre without influential help; we have no record of a Tudor playing company recruiting on the road, though a notion of his suddenly joining a travelling troupe of players is prized by romantic biographers. Some of his early work was to be linked with the men of Ferdinando, and we cannot deny that men under that patron formed the nucleus of the Lord Chamberlain's company. If Shakespeare never knew Hoghton or Derby, it is odd that he was known by their friends.

Certainly too in his youth, he knew a topography unlike Stratford's—and knew it well. In childhood he was sheltered by a well-run market town with its good borough council, mainly placid trades, seasonal festivals, and 'free scole'—and the climate was propitious: north of the Avon the low ridges are drained by the Salwarpe, the Arrow, the Alne, and other mild streams. This clement region produced excellent fleece (and a 'considerable' wool-dealer such as his father for a time had thrived). But western Lancashire has no such protection as the Welsh Hills. Climatic differences between the Midlands plain and the north enabled Warwickshire wool-dealers to market some of their best fleece in sheep-raising regions of Lancashire. In his early plays there are fine, closely observed images of mountains, the sea, and, it seems, of an estuary landscape such as appears in a soliloquy of Richard of Gloucester in *3 Henry VI*:

> Why, then, I do but dream on sovereignty
> Like one that stands upon a promontory
> And spies a far-off shore where he would tread,
> Wishing his foot were equal with his eye,

And chides the sea that sunders him from thence,
Saying he'll lade it dry to have his way—

(III. ii. 134–9)[5]

These topographical images correspond with nothing in Warwick-shire's landscape. They may suggest that William has followed the fleece, that he knows vistas around Lea, and that one of his teachers has sent him north, with John Shakespeare's compliance.

Grammar-school boys were often under scrutiny because the law enjoined masters to recommend promising pupils. Among five King's New School masters in William's youth, no fewer than three were Lancashire men—Walter Roche (whom John Shakespeare knew), John Cottom, and Cottom's successor Alexander Aspinall.

Thomas Jenkins—the retiring master at Church Street—was duly replaced by John Cottom. We know that on 9 July 1579 Jenkins received £6 from Cottom, a sum advanced to the latter by the bor-ough council, and so it is fairly evident that by around 9 July Cottom was assuming the duties of master at Stratford's school. (The cham-berlains accepted his receipt, from 'John Cottom, Scholemaster of the foresaid towne of Stretford', when they paid him wages 'for one half yere ended' on 21 December that year.[6]) Cottom (who preferred that spelling) was a son of Lawrence Cottam, whose ancestral estate was at Dilworth in Lancashire; adjacent to Cottam's estate was Alston, a country seat of Alexander de Hoghton.

It has become clear late in the twentieth century that Cottams and Hoghtons had had close family connections, and both families were Catholic. John Cottom was a graduate of Brasenose College, Oxford; he had taken his BA on 19 June 1566 (in the same year as Jenkins). Three months before Cottom began to teach at Stratford, his brother Thomas Cottam, also a graduate of Brasenose, entered the Jesuit novitiate of St Andrew in Rome—on 8 April 1579. A year later, in June 1580, Thomas Cottam left Rheims carrying on his person tokens of identification—including a medal, several coins, a gilt crucifix, and two pairs of beads—intended for delivery at Shottery. Whether or not Cottam considered Shottery a stronghold ripe for missionary work, the tokens were for members of the family of his fellow priest

Robert Debdale. One token was for Debdale's brother-in-law John Pace, who in the next year is mentioned as a chief creditor and as 'my neighboure' in the will of Richard Hathaway, the father of Anne Hathaway.[7]

Father Cottam's journey to Shottery was cut short. He was captured, arraigned and tried, and then executed at Tyburn on 30 May 1582. Leaving Stratford at about the time of his brother's death, John Cottom went back to Lancashire with his religious convictions evidently stiffened, since his name (along with his wife's) later appeared on northern returns for recusants, or those who failed to attend church.

However, there is no sign that obdurate Catholics succeeded one another as masters at King's New School in Shakespeare's time. Jenkins had Roman Catholic connections, and a London and Oxford background as Cottom did, and so may have helped to secure his successor. But even Cottom had to accept Anglican practices as a Stratford teacher, and indeed he could not have continued teaching after Michaelmas in 1579 without a certificate of conformity from the Bishop of Worcester. It would seem that Jenkins and Cottom alike—while at Stratford—met the approval of the borough council, whose clerk routinely cites them in the Minutes and Accounts. Yet the new master's Lancashire background is also clear. If Alexander de Hoghton did ask Cottom to recommend to him a clever, sympathetic young person to teach in the north, Cottom had Jenkins's former pupils to turn to.

Among them was William Shakespeare. We still lack a note in the hand of Hoghton, Cottom, or anyone else to show that he went north, though the risks of working for a distant, influential landowner may have seemed to his parents smaller than the benefits. Other bright, educated sons were leaving town; the times were uncertain. It is relevant, too, that the employer's religion was not necessarily a drawback; John and Mary Shakespeare appear to have been Catholics who conformed, as thousands of similar conviction did, and they raised a son who conformed: Shakespeare would show a close familiarity with Catholic practices, and at least as much intimacy and sympathy with the 'old faith', as any Protestant writer of his time. After his school years, he put his Latin to use, presumably 'in the Countrey', and so we may ask what a country experience would have held for him. We can only be tentative; an 'alternative narrative' can give us no more than pictures from beyond the edges of Shakespeare's known experience. But since there is a good possibility that he went to Hoghton, we may suppose that he had experiences not wholly unlike those a grammar-school boy would have had at Hoghton Tower and Lea, and that in 1579 or 1580, after what may have been rough journey, a 'William Shakeshafte' found himself in the employ of a great family in the north.

Upon a promontory

May we see this person in Lancashire?

If he was like Shakespeare just then, 'Shakeshafte' was no more than a country lad of 16, about as shiny and neat in doublet and hose, or as angular and graceful, as other boys would be. After school recitals he would have been articulate, yet he had been trained in civility, restraint, and the decorum of manners, so would have known enough to be mainly silent and deferential. He would have to merit the approbation of an employer in an odd milieu. If he had a prime Shakespeare family trait, it was his ability to please, or rather to ingratiate himself so as to win loyalty and trust, as William's father held the loyalty of burgesses who kept him on the council (long after his absenteeism began), or as Mary Arden had pleased her father enough to be a legal executor as a young woman. To inspire affection and trust—that, after all, counted for more than brains, talent, or other assets in a strict, hierarchical milieu, in which the young pleased in order to survive. If 'Shakeshafte' was like our William, he also had enthusiasm and energy, with enough imagination to offset the effect of any over-taught, Latin-ridden cleverness of his own, and an impressionable nature eager to absorb what it could.

Alexander de Hoghton was near the end of his life. A portrait, said to be of him, shows a lean-cheeked man with thin eyebrows and an intent, sidelong glance. Married to Dorothy Ashton and then to Elizabeth Hesketh, he was close to 60 when in 1580 he came into full possession of the Hoghton inheritance. A few years later this included over 20,000 acres of land, some two dozen mills and 400 cottages, and the manors of Alston, Hoghton, and Lea. Much of Lancashire was then a thinly peopled feudal domain with wide areas given over to moss and marshland. Justices of the peace were few; several of the gentry kept armed bands of retainers, and there was occasional violence, as when the house of Alexander's half-brother, his heir Thomas, was attacked at midnight by about eighty of Thomas Langton's armed men, using the rallying-cry 'The crow is white!' 'Black, black!' shouted servants within, but their master died in the mêlée.[8]

Giving the country a semblance of peace and order were the Stanleys, the family of Alexander's close friend Henry, the fourth Earl of Derby. With nearly regal powers and the county lieutenancy, the fourth earl lived in as ostentatious a manner as his father had—and, at least since 1536, the Crown had acknowledged the family's importance. In Lancashire, the queen in effect ruled through the Stanleys.

This meant that 'Shakeshafte'—and any other Hoghton servant—lived in a milieu that was partly anachronistic. On visits to Alexander de Hoghton, the Earl of Derby personified a regal political authority and grandeur as if he were in fact the domain's monarch. An earl whose household was the largest in Elizabethan England after the royal one, and whose family spent £1,500 a year on food and had 140 people in his entourage, expected ceremony and displays of loyalty.[9] Shakespeare himself may well have observed such an earl—when 'in the Countrey' or later—inasmuch as he shows an easy familiarity with the habits and psychology of men of enormous, medieval political power. In Alexander's time, a certain tension was developing between the earl and his son and heir Ferdinando, whose troupe were to have some of Shakespeare's early work. In a friendly letter in 1571, the Queen had asked the earl to send his heir, as a young boy, to her at Windsor.[10] Influenced by his training at court, Ferdinando became obsessed with something besides the theatre, namely religion in his county. He began to denounce his own father in discreet letters to William Chadderton, Bishop of Chester, whose diocese linked Cheshire and Lancashire. 'I ame throughe with my father', wrote Ferdinando on 15 March 1582. Separating himself from the ignominy of papistry in Lancashire the next year, he hoped that 'your lordship

66

will proceide to frame some better reformation in this so unbridled & bade an handfull of England', and signed himself, 'Youre lordships assured, yow know even verie assured, Fer. Strange.' To add to that, he told the Lord Bishop a little afterwards about the earl's backwardness in reducing Catholic recusancy, and referring to two actions that might avail, he added of his father:

I find him rather an enemye in substance to both actions, than anie frende to ether. . . . To be constant is noe common vertew, althoughe it be most commendable, most fitt, & least founde in noblemen. . . . But we must be patient *per* force, & make a vertew of necessitie, & folowe his humor. . . . This secreat letter I sent your lordship. The other his lordship [Earl of Derby] is privie to.[11]

By 1582 Ferdinando may well have over-dramatized his feelings about his father—but it is clear that the Hoghtons knew a troubled county: spies were common and families were divided. Yet, to an extent, recusancy thrived; even late in the century Hoghton's friend Lady Hesketh, of Rufford in Lancashire, was reported as a 'reliever of papists'.[12] A connection, faint enough, but interesting, has been traced between Shakespeare and this same Lady Hesketh: 'Shakeshafte' was recommended to the Heskeths of Rufford, in Hoghton's will of 1581, and eighteen years later Shakespeare with four colleagues chose as a Globe trustee (when its ground-lease was arranged) the Rufford-born London goldsmith, Thomas Savage, who left a bequest of 20s. to a close friend of Lady Hesketh.

How much would a visitor have heard of the county's past? Among the Hoghtons one was likely to hear at least of the Pilgrimage of Grace (the rebellion of 1536 against which the Crown had enlisted the third Earl of Derby's help, at a price), when two Cistercian abbots of Lancashire were hanged on the same day and when banners painted with emblems of Christ crucified, or showing the chalice and host, were hacked down. Many died. The quarters of one abbot's body were displayed, and the body of one of his monks was secretly cut from the gibbet and taken to Cottam Hall.[13] People prayed on All Hallow's Eve for such faithful; the northern Catholic sentiment was elegiac, intense, and yearningly nostalgic over the spiritual past and a thousand years of the Roman faith in England.

Shakespeare, it is true, may have acquired his own intense feelings for the past in another family, or at home. Eight or ten years after he left school, he knew more than most contemporary playwrights. He would devote nine of his first eighteen or nineteen plays to the history of his country; he knew a good library before he wrote his *Henry VI* plays, and he could hardly have made deft use of historical sources without developing his reading habits after grammar school. Any time as a 'Schoolmaster in the Countrey' perhaps helped him to seek in books for what might appeal to his hearers. One warm, favourable catalyst for an emergence of his talent, at any rate, was a milieu not indifferent to learning and to history.

Alexander de Hoghton, as we know, was anxious to attach 'Shakeshafte' and 'Gillom' either to his half-brother, or else to send them on with his stock of play clothes to Sir Thomas Hesketh. New measures, receiving the royal assent on 18 March 1581, were partly directed against the keeping of unlicensed schoolmasters. If hired as teachers, 'Shakeshafte' and 'Gillom' would have been in less danger as players, and after Alexander died in August 1581 they may indeed have gone, in accordance with his will, either to his half-brother, or to Sir Thomas Hesketh's players at Rufford Hall south of Lea.

Returning

We have only incomplete, uncertain evidence as to what may have happened to both servants. It seems that Fulke Gillom did cross the Ribble to serve at Hesketh's Rufford, ten miles to the south. His name is unusual, and 'ffoulke gillame' and 'ffoulke Gillam' occur in two papers in the Hesketh archives.[14] Since their names are linked three times in the will of 3 August, it would seem that 'William Shakeshafte' went with Gillom, some time late in 1581, to join Hesketh's players.

Our William was then past his seventeenth birthday. If he had something like the experience of a Hesketh servant by then, he already had taught children to sing and play the virginals. And both Hoghton and Hesketh had players skilled in 'mewsicks'. A later inventory of Robert Hesketh names a small orchestra of instruments—some or all could be those bequeathed by Hoghton—which includes 'vyolls, vyolentes, virginalls, sagbutts, howboies and cornetts, cithon, flute and taber pypes'.[15] A lad in Hoghton's ménage may have had a good chance to perform. At Hoghton Tower east of Lea, there was a grand banqueting hall with a minstrels' gallery; the hall could have accommodated an audience of 150 people and the gallery, if needed for a theatrical, could have served as an upper stage. Hoghton had lived chiefly at Lea, near the north shore of the Ribble estuary. Here, too, was an oak-framed hall where players could entertain. The locale—with its long vistas changing with swift regularity—was unusual. Nearby the tide brought in a sudden rush of ocean to part the shore, with a visual effect not unlike that of a striking image in Shakespeare's Sonnet 56:

> Let this sad int'rim like the ocean be
> Which parts the shore where two contracted new
> Come daily to the banks, that when they see
> Return of love, more blessed may be the view.

Shakespeare as a young playwright is almost too attentive to England's west; he has the west in mind when he means the Kentish coast and so has the 'day' sink in an easterly direction (*2 Henry VI*, IV. i. 1–2). In three scenes in *3 Henry VI*, the effort of crossing tidal waters against wind and tide is evoked, as if the playwright had known the crossing from Lea to Rufford, and, indeed, apparent images of an estuary have been noted in the same early play.[16] The young playwright is familiar with a sight that is common on a flat northern seashore when rough waves, in a strong offshore gust, after breaking appear to hesitate and retreat before the wind. Perhaps he would have needed to see this, as well as a play of light on low mountains such as those at the end of the Pennine chain, to depict such details as freshly as he does. Other images in *2 Henry VI* and *Titus Andronicus* suggest a sight of northern hills and seascapes.

So far as his identity with 'Shakeshafte' is concerned, Shakespeare's images of course prove nothing, but some are consistent with a Hoghton servant's likely experience. Did he join Hesketh's players at Rufford Hall? Apart from a folk tradition at Rufford that 'Shakespeare had been at the Hall as a young man',[17] we know, of course, that a contemporary from Lady Hesketh's small village of Rufford served as a Globe trustee. We know only a little more that might connect Shakespeare with Rufford. As an influential Catholic, Sir Thomas Hesketh in 1563 had been made High Sheriff of the county under Queen Elizabeth; he not only kept players, but remained friendly with ambitious player–patrons. His son and heir, Robert Hesketh, was to entertain 'Lord and Lady Strange' in the 1580s at Rufford.[18] Derbys and Heskeths had for years been on intimate terms. Thus if Shakespeare reached Rufford—as a local tradition suggests he did—Sir Thomas Hesketh was in a position to recommend him to Lord Strange, in a decade when Strange's men were on the way to becoming the premier playing troupe in London. Again, it may be a coincidence that Shakespeare's early plays, and knowledge of his unpublished sonnets, can be linked with people in the circle of Hoghton, Hesketh, and Strange; but the associations are factual enough. Certainly, too, Hoghton's sojourner was thought of as an actor in need of a patron. Sir Thomas was obliged by an item in Hoghton's will either to keep a 'Shakeshafte' or to send him to a good master who might 'manteyne players'.

At Rufford Hall, Hesketh's entertainers would have used an enormous, intricately carved screen for their rapid entrances and exits. The spectators watched in one of the loveliest halls that survive, nearly unchanged, from Tudor times. Carved angels peer out from heavy, hammerbeam trusses above rows of mullioned windows and a five-sided, tall bay window. However, the players could have disbanded temporarily in 1581, even before new servants reached them. Since Sir Thomas failed to suppress Catholic worship in his household, he was in prison late in the year.[19] Evidently he was released in 1582, then in custody briefly again in 1584, before he pledged reforms that kept him safe.

William returned to Stratford, presumably from some employment 'in the Countrey', either in 1581 when Sir Thomas was in custody, or soon after. He was at home within a few months of his eighteenth birthday, and not later than August 1582. In a changed political climate, not only unlicensed masters but other temporary servants in prominent Catholic families were then at risk. He may have been recommended to a patron such as Lord Strange, and, in any case, he could hope for interesting employment. Any experience of 'playe clothes' would have given him a measure of detachment, so that he would begin to see his town through a player's eyes.

To some extent, the ordinary, workaday life of any town is consoling. But in *A Midsummer Night's Dream*, the dignity and normalcy of the 'mechanicals', with their suppositions, seem to threaten the dream-world of the imaginative poet. Here there is a terror of the real, an absence of any complacency on the part of the playwright in the face of the normal and familiar. If William worked 'in the Countrey', it is likely that he came back with a troubled awakening to what as yet he had unsurely known. His instincts were theatrical, and with any opportunity to put on play clothes he cannot have been content to accept his position at home exactly as he had left it. He was ambitious, and an eager young poet in the making. He was no less charmed by books than Roger Lock or Richard Field—who, by then, were stationer-apprentices. But back at Henley Street, with any travel dust on his shoes, he was almost unpredictably complex, if we accept Beeston's remark about his schoolmastering, which is one of the best-authenticated reports we have of him. He was a smart, enthusiastic lad who had fled from pedantry, but prized what he had learned; and indeed with a remarkable, assimilating mind he found the world hardly too various for him; he might nourish any dissonances in his outlook, any number of mixed feelings or conflicting impressions while even hungering for books and learning, after being 'in his younger yeares a Schoolmaster in the Countrey'. But that experience would have whetted his taste for the full, sensuous enjoyment of the little world he found again. He was not likely to be guided by mere prudence and circumspection, and his life was to change very quickly at Stratford.

6

LOVE AND EARLY
MARRIAGE

I hope upon familiarity will grow more
contempt. But if you say 'marry her', I
will marry her. That I am freely
dissolved, and dissolutely.

(Slender, *The Merry Wives of Windsor*)

Anne Hathaway and the Shottery fields

*I*n a Tudor parish one's life was under review by parents, friends,
and neighbours so that almost no change in one's fate went unno-
ticed. One's private behaviour tended to be observable, too. A young
man in the 'May of youth and bloom of lustihood' might, of course,
sow his wild oats, but he was likely to hear from the vicar's apparitor
and have to explain his fornication and apologize for it. Anyone's sexual affairs, outside marriage, concerned the community, and William's
involvement with the Hathaways affected his career even as it touched
on a web of social relationships.

The summer of 1582 had favoured lovers and crops. Great spreading
green fields cultivated in strips, at Stratford and Shottery, lay in the
sun, and the nation's harvest was the best since 1570, or about 20 per
cent better than average.[1] Near the end of their new civic year Stratford's council in fact acted with largesse and, for the first time on
record, sponsored local mummers. The aldermen were to pay the
troupe's leader Davy Jones, whose wife Frances Hathaway was related
to Richard Hathaway's people at Shottery. Davy's troupe were to perform at Whitsun a week before Shakespeare's first child was baptized—and his familiar name would echo in Justice Shallow's

insatiable liking for a servant in *2 Henry IV*: 'What, Davy, I say! . . .
Why, Davy! . . . Davy, Davy, Davy; let me see, Davy, let me see . . .
With red wheat, Davy' (v. i. 2–13).[2] A good yield of crops often
induced a general, rational euphoria in the 1570s and 1580s, since
'good' and 'bad' years arrived in cycles. Stratford's aldermen met at a
happy seasonal time on election day, 5 September, with John Shakespeare, who had not been to 'halls' in months. The new bailiff to be
elected was Adrian Quiney, who once had been asked with William's
father to plead for the borough's corporate rights against the claims of
its obstinate manorial lord, Ambrose, Earl of Warwick.

By November, the Shakespeares certainly knew of their son
William's relations with Agnes or Anne Hathaway, the eldest daughter
in a family of the earl's copyhold tenants. Born in 1555 or 1556, if the
legend on her grave-slab is accurate, Anne at 26 or 27 was pregnant
with William's child. It is a modern myth that she was 'on the shelf', or
older than many women of the Tudor yeomanry at marriage, but
William was legally a minor. He probably felt obliged to seek his father's
consent to marry, and he may not have tried to do so before November.

It is unlikely that before this month he had any exact, careful wedding plans, and there are signs of his lack of reckoning, if not of last-
minute haste and turmoil, in events that caught him up. One may have
good reasons for loving, or none, but William, it seems, was partly
moved by an urge to purchase experience. The strictness of schooling
and almost any exigencies of work 'in the Countrey' would have
limited his free behaviour. *Every* grammar-school boy had known a
harsh discipline, and his eloquence had not been acquired cheaply,
but as he became more self-confident so he enriched his sense of life.
There can be no denying what he had done in August—but, then, he
could afford to be incautious: his father, despite financial irregularities,
had kept up a trade and the Henley Street houses. William would have
property to inherit, even a lucrative future if he found ways to use his
eloquence.

He may have tested that eloquence during courtship, as has been
supposed. The evidence is uncertain. But he was young for marriage,
and had been a suitor among practical farmers. Anne, with the
pride of her years, may have kept him in a 'woeful state', if the poem

later printed in *Shake-speares Sonnets* as no. 145 has autobiographical references and he plays on her name 'Hathaway' as 'hate away'. The pun, of course, is not very exact. In the sonnet, a lady's acquiescence is merciful. Her poet, it seems, has been so suave that she has hardly had a chance to be cutting, petulant, or severe with him:

> Those lips that Loves owne hand did make,
> Breath'd forth the sound that said I hate,
> To me that languisht for her sake:
> But when she saw my wofull state,
> Straight in her heart did mercie come,
> Chiding that tongue that ever sweet,
> Was used in giving gentle dome:
> And taught it thus a new to greete:
> I hate she alterd with an end,
> That follow'd it as gentle day,
> Doth follow night who like a fiend
> From heaven to hell is flowne away.
> I hate, from hate away she threw,
> And sav'd my life saying not you.

The poem's naïve diction and simple feeling suggest early work, and it may well date from about 1582.

However that may be, she would have a legacy. Her father Richard Hathaway, alias Gardner or Gardiner, a few days before he died in September 1581, had anticipated the wedding of his daughter 'Agnes' (pronounced 'Annes' and interchangeable with the name Anne). She was to have 10 marks, or £6. 13*s*. 4*d*., 'at the daye of her maryage'.[3] His will was proved on 9 July 1582, and the lovers, in the summer, could have plighted their troth with the hope of a legacy to come. A troth-plight was binding, and if spoken before witnesses it legitimized a child born out of wedlock—but it was not recommended by clergy-men of any persuasion. It would not necessarily save two young people from a summons by the vicar's court, and William may have been reluctant to force his people to accept his union with Anne as a *fait accompli* in this way before November.

At no time, in his school years or later, had he been a stranger at Anne's door. His father had twice helped her own father as a surety in

1566, and had paid Hathaway's debts of £8 to John Page, the iron-monger, and £11 to Joan Biddle.[4] The sums suggest that Shakespeares had not been unwelcome at the Hathaways' farm. A mile to the west of town, but within the parish, Shottery was then a scattered hamlet with about 1,600 acres of common fields under tillage, an area as large as Stratford's three other main fields put together. Richard Hath-away's house, with extensions added after his time, survives as Anne Hathaway's Cottage. The Forest of Arden was then nearby, and vis-itors now are reminded of Oliver's 'sheepcote' and of the pretty woodland setting Celia describes in *As You Like It*:

> West of this place, down in the neighbour bottom.
> The rank of osiers by the murmuring stream
> Left on your right hand brings you to the place.
>
> (IV. iii. 79–81)

Roses, herbs, and posy-peas still grow in the garden, though an orchard with fragrant apple trees and wild flowers must now be im-agined. A brook flows below the house, which is built on a slope and has stone foundations with timber-frame walls filled in by wattle and daub, under a steep roof of thatch. The dwelling was ample for a fam-ily of eight or ten, with its 'hall' or downstairs sitting-room, a kitchen with a heavy bake-oven, and several upper rooms. Crucks, or curved oak timbers, rose from the ground to roof-ridge in the oldest part (dating from the fifteenth century), and lately builders had added two fireplaces with chamfered oak bressumers or sustaining beams, eight and eleven feet wide, and an upper floor for rooms over the hall. In his will Hathaway mentions two bedsteads, which would have been valu-able if elaborately carved, and 'the Seelinges in my haule house' or his wainscots, which must have kept out winter drafts. Chairs, stools, cushions, brass pots, eight pieces of pewter—all later owned by his son Bartholomew—may originally have been in his own hall, where a high-backed bench or 'settle' is fixed near the hearth today.

For two generations, at least, Hathaways had been locally prom-inent, and their word had carried weight in Shottery and other parts of Stratford parish. Richard's father, John, had been one of the Twelve Men of Old Stratford's court, and had served as a beadle, a constable, and an affeeror while turning a profit in farming; his goods, in the subsidy of 1549–50, are valued at £10 (not, then, a low assessment). In turn Richard had carried on the farming, and, it seems, had married twice. Seven of his children were alive in 1579, when Shakespeare was near the end of his schooldays.

At that time, Shottery was fairly tranquil. Families here with recusants or with a Jesuit priest as a son, such as the Burmans or the Debdales, lived on good terms with church-goers. Though he apparently went to Anglican service, Richard Hathaway named in his will John Pace, a Catholic neighbour, and asked that his will's two supervisors be Fulke Sandells, a young farmer, and another of his 'Trustie ffryndes and neighboures' Stephen Burman, whose wife Margaret was a defiant Catholic twice cited by commissioners for avoiding church.[5] But by 1580 or 1581, Shottery had become the focus of an angry dispute over land at its western edge, Baldon Hill, claimed alike by the Protestant Earl of Warwick and the Catholic Mr Francis Smyth of Wootton Wawen. The dispute threatened to incite religious partisans.

Francis Smyth, with four peacocks in his coat of arms, was a son of the heiress of Wootton Wawen north of the parish; he openly professed to be a Catholic, but just avoided the usual penalties for his belief, and in his property claims if not in his religion he infuriated the earl. When the earl in court challenged his claim to Baldon Hill, the two main contenders at least were influenced by religious-party allegiance. Shakespeares and Hathaways were well apprised of the affair since one juror was Anne's father, another was Fulke Sandells (who also acted as a surety at Shakespeare's marriage), and a third was Anne's near neighbour Richard Burman.

Not long before he died, Anne's father had supported the earl's claim, but Smyth defied the jurors' findings around October 1582, when Anne was carrying William's child. By the time a new commission looked into the case, Baldon Hill was provoking sharp civic tension, and when the future playwright was 19 the Warwickshire equivalent of Capulets and Montagues, stirring for a fight, gathered one day at a vintner's at the corner of Bull Lane and Old Town where Sir Thomas Lucy was trying—upstairs—to examine witnesses. A real scene that Shakespeare and the parish would have heard about is apparent in court records. Stepping into the vintner's parlour, the Catholic Smyth was rudely met by the earl's man, John Goodman, then wearing a dagger:

GOODMAN. Mr Smyth, you do not like a gentleman.

SMYTH. Why?

GOODMAN. For you do my lord great injury.

SMYTH. Why, wherein?

GOODMAN. Marry, you go about to allure my lord's witnesses, and talk with them in corners.

SMYTH. I do not.

GOODMAN. You do.

SMYTH. I tell you truly I do not.

GOODMAN. But thou dost (*advancing upon him*). Thou shalt not.

SMYTH. I tell thee thou dost say untruly (*thrusting him away with his hand*).

GOODMAN. What, dost thou lay thy hands upon me? If thou dost lay thy hands on me I will lay my dagger on thy pate (*putting his hand to his dagger and offering to draw it*).

Smyth extricated himself, but his servant, Richard Dale, was set upon by two of the earl's men together—Goodman and Mr Fenton:

FENTON (*grasping Dale by the doublet*). Ah sirrah! What dost thou here? Thou art a knave of all knaves! Away, knave! Out of this place!

GOODMAN. What, villain, wilt thou not go? Go, or I will lay my dagger on thy pate. (*putting a hand to his dagger*)

(*Fenton gives Dale a blow on the side of the head, thrusts him partly through the door, and claps the door upon one of his legs.*)

DALE. I pray you, let me take my other leg with me! (*struggles with Fenton to open the door, and goes upstairs in fear and trembling*)[6]

Sir Thomas Lucy's commission made small headway with regard to that turmoil on 12 January 1584, and the case slowly dragged on until a final settlement for the Catholic landowner Smyth. Shakespeare—with the rest of the gossipy town—must have heard what had passed between Smyth, Goodman, Dale, and Fenton and possibly remembered 'Fenton' when he wrote *The Merry Wives*, though the young gentleman who steals away Anne Page (as the host describes him) is less like the earl's rough man than like a nonchalant, sprightly lover of

18—'he capers, he dances, he has eyes of youth, he writes verses, he speaks holiday, he smells April and May' (III. ii. 61–2).

Most Shottery jurors in the Baldon Hill affair, it appears, had *not* spoken or decided upon religious party lines; people were wary of a case with a strong doctrinal factor. Events dictated caution. In the year of William's marriage Cottam, the brother of Stratford's school-master, was hanged, and Robert Debdale of Shottery was to suffer the same fate as a missionary priest. William may already have learned to be discreet, but the mood of his parish would have affected him at least to the extent of making him a more seeking, fascinated observer. Even Baldon Hill exposed old religious fractures in a society, and local wits must have have enlivened the issues involved. William's own wit and imagination developed with enormous, buoyant force and humour as his head cleared itself of cobwebs left by the 'grammar gods', and civic contention appealed to him as he looked beyond the outward spec-tacle to the inward, private lives of individuals. If he was a neutral observer, he came closer to being a dramatic poet who would not 'take sides'. Perhaps the paradox of his courtship was that his imagin-ation out ran it, as he took in tangled, intriguing, or comic events such as those involving the pride and pretensions of Smyth or the earl.

No such tumult as that at the vintner's normally upset Shottery, and there was an air of placid well-being at Hewlands with its pasturage, meadow, and livestock. Richard Hathaway had left substantial leg-acies to seven children. It is likely that four of them—Thomas, Mar-garet, John, and William—were born to his wife Joan. Anne, Bartholomew, and Catherine, as his eldest children, must have been offspring of an earlier marriage; he left to his widow the option of refusing Bartholomew a bequest of land if she paid him £40, a normal provision if he was not her own son.[7]

Already an adult when three of Richard's children were born, Anne was about twenty-three years older than her father's smallest boy. Inevitably child-care had devolved upon her, as it did upon most women at a Tudor farm. Female work did not stop in daylight hours, and Anne's role would have included helping to wash, feed, and instruct the younger ones while seeing to other siblings. Her brother Bartholomew is asked in his father's will to be 'a Comforte unto his

Bretherne and Systers to his power', and there is sign of Anne's being kind or responsible if she was not so ideally tender-hearted as the person in William's 'hate-away' sonnet. Her father's shepherd Thomas Whittington, unless he was slow to collect his wages, later trusted her to hold in safekeeping for him his funds for the parish poor. 'I geve and bequeth', Whittington stated in 1601, 'unto the poore people of Stratford 40ˢ. that is in the hand of Anne Shaxspere, wyf unto Mʳ Wyllyam Shaxspere, and is due debt unto me, beyng payd to myne Executor by the sayd Wyllyam Shaxspere or his assigns, accordyng to the true meanyng of this my wyll'.[8]

The shepherd in old age sojourned with John Pace, the brother-in-law of Shottery's Jesuit martyr,[9] and one recalls that Anne's father named as an executor the brother of a defiant recusant. Still among several Shottery families of Hathaways in the 1580s or 1590s, no one appears to have been cited for avoiding church (though John Hathaway of Old Stratford was to be cited in a list of Catholic recusants for 1640–1). Anne's brother Bartholomew embraced the Anglican faith with evident readiness and ardour. He became a churchwarden (as did his three sons) and left a fervent statement of faith in his will. It would seem that a number of members of the Shakespeare–Hathaway circle were typical of those in old Catholic families who conformed, even if some, now and then, abstained from Anglican communion. Anne and William's own child, Susanna, as a young woman, was to hear from the vicar's apparitor for missing an Easter communion and would then ignore the summons. Their friends Hamnet and Judith Sadler, along with a servant of Hamnet's, were also to be called before the church court for not receiving the Eucharist; Hamnet, or Hamlet, as we have seen from the 'bawdy court's' proceedings, pleaded for time to clear his conscience—though it is hard to imagine this working man fretting over niceties of doctrine. As the heir of Roger Sadler the baker, he lived with Judith at the corner of High Street and Sheep Street next to the Corn Market, and normally, at least, brought himself to attend Anglican Easter service. On the other hand, Thomas and Margaret Reynolds were obstinate recusants, who appear once to have given refuge to a fugitive Jesuit priest; their son and heir William Reynolds was to be left 26s. 8d. in Shakespeare's will to buy a memorial ring.

One concludes that most of the poet's schoolmates and some of his friends were unexceptionally Protestant, but a nucleus of Catholics lay near the centre of his early acquaintanceship; he was surely not surprised by those of the old allegiance among Hathaway's friends—or perhaps by Anne's regular church-going. Like others, she had, at some point, accepted an Anglican faith which had kept an old order of priests and bishops with a doctrine that admitted of belief in the Real Presence in consecrated bread and wine; her conformity may or may not have been painful for her, but it was to be matched by William's practice.

Whether by calculation or instinct, he had been careful in one way. He had not courted above his social degree, or, in effect, matched the later presumption of his friend Richard Tyler, who was named in the first draft of the playwright's will. As a butcher's son, born in 1566, Tyler in the 1580s married Susanna Woodward of Shottery, after which Susanna was disinherited by an angry grandfather, who seems to have felt that a butcher's son was a poor choice for the eldest daughter of Mʳ Richard Woodward of Shottery Manor, who entertained the likes of Sir Fulke Greville.

On the other hand, William can hardly have acquired a maturity of outlook that years would have given Anne. She had not acquiesced at a casual moment, but when her circumstances were changed radically by loss. Less than three months after their father's death Bartholomew had wed Isabel Hancocks of Tredington and gone to live at Tysoe—twenty miles south of Hereford. He was the brother closest to her in age, and it is likely that Anne became a godmother to his child. (Bartholomew's daughter 'Annys'—or 'Anne' in her marriage register—was baptized on 14 January 1584 after he had decided to return to Stratford.[10]) It may not follow that, after her brother had left Hewlands, her loneliness, age, or a quarrel with her father's widow had led Anne to take a lover. But William was rewarded partly because of displacements in her life; she would have been of use to her father and brother, and after losing them she had found this rather elegant young man of Henley Street, a son of her father's friend, ardent in his need for her. Now, however, she had to face the consequences of becoming pregnant—her social humiliation and the ruin of her life. Just how much William valued her maturity, or the kindness Whittington appears to credit her with, we do not know. But he was evidently in love, and his problem in November was to arrange for his future as quickly as he could.

A licence for lovers

The urgency of his situation must have touched his parents sharply. Under the elms of Henley Street with its dogs, carts, dust, and clamour a few craftsmen knew a consoling normalcy, but in the troubled Midlands the glovers' trade had its endemic difficulties, as it fell into deeper decline. The Shakespeares' family included five living children—William, Gilbert, Joan, Richard, and the 2-year-old Edmund—and John Shakespeare with his large responsibilities had more cause for anxiety. In the last Trinity term (15 June–4 July 1582) he had been compelled, at any rate, to seek legal sureties of the peace against Ralph Cawdrey, William Russell, Thomas Logginge, and Robert Young 'for fear of death and mutilation of his limbs'.[11] The formulaic phrase might seem to apply literally to Ralph Cawdrey the butcher, who once assaulted John Shakespeare's brother-in-law, Alexander Webbe. But Cawdrey had become a respected figure at 'halls'. William's father had sat with him at council in September, and had sought sureties not because (in the legal formula) he feared 'death or mutilation', but because he needed a respite from suits by creditors.

A family scandal could further damage his trade. If the vicar's court noticed a sexual offence, the lovers might be asked to apologize publicly on a Sunday. That could bring a mild ignominy down upon a family. In fact, rash lovers did not always avoid semi-public disgrace even if they married: Fulke Sandells's son later heard from a vicar's apparitor simply because his wife gave birth too soon after their wedding.

Gossip and rumour, in themselves, could cause an alert court to summon a pregnant woman and her lover, and as Anne's condition became obvious it could have attracted attention, so she may have left Hewlands by November. But the evidence is unclear, in any case: her November locale is given as 'Temple grafton', in a Worcester entry that errs with her surname ('Whateley'). Temple Grafton was a settlement outside the parish but only three and a half miles west of Shottery and south of the Alcester road. (The hamlet was about five miles from Henley Street.) If she huddled there William perhaps felt obliged to ask for his father's consent to marry, and his mother's willingness to share a home with his bride.

Yet he was not quite so dependent on them as is often implied. Ecclesiastical laws had loopholes, and Richard Cosin (the bishop's chancellor at Worcester) had power to override a refusal of consent and issue a licence.[12] Nevertheless whatever their surprise, the young man's parents had reason to favour a wedding once they knew of Anne's condition, quite apart from a craftsman's fear of scandal and the real disgrace of bastardy. Anne, of course, was no stranger to them, but the child of an honourable yeoman William's father had aided; they were likely to find her age and practicality of benefit to their son, a young man lively, eloquent, with a 'mint of phrases in his brain' perhaps, but of small practical experience. In one light, William was both more and less than a mere individual; he was a guarantor of his family's futurity, his father's investment and hope, since he would inherit; and those with property to bequeath seldom objected to an heir's early marriage.[13] A son who wed early might count on having a grown heir in his lifetime, so that heritable land would not devolve (with wardship complications) on a mere child.

His mother, no doubt, wished him to acquit himself well, and as arrangements were made near the month's end, some wind may have gone out of William's sails. His real troubles, so far as one intuits them, began with marriage, as in a sense his possibilities did. He had no choice *but* to take on abrupt responsibility—to be a husband, a father. So his initiative was undercut; his situation in November was hardly that of August. In yielding to exigencies late in the year his summer romance must have begun to seem humdrum, undramatic, dull, without risk, boring to an active mind. Also there were besetting aspects of such a dilemma, for a complex young man sensitive to local opinion; he was likely to regard any excitement, dread, regret, or embarrassment he felt in November in many different lights, as his mind circled round all sides of a topic. He probably began, though, soon enough to see his predicament in ironic perspective, and so assumed a path that would help him to take a robust, amused, varyingly ironic view of marital affairs later. At the moment he had to think of banns, fees, sureties, a visit to the consistory court, a licence, and the inexorable approach of a hasty wedding.

He appears to have journeyed to the bishop's court at Worcester, late in November, with the farmers Fulke Sandells and John Richardson. Since the first was a supervisor and the second a witness of Hathaway's will, the two yeomen, in effect, represented Anne's father. Sandells, at 31, seems to have been as taciturn as his dry, laconic Baldon Hill deposition suggests; he had no reason to be convivial with a youth who had compromised Hathaway's daughter. But both Shottery farmers agreed to post as surety for the marriage licence the large sum of £40, to be forfeited if the validity of the union were impeached.

In the consistory court's licence entry, he was now matched with a ghost; the wording of the entry (dated 27 November) applies absurdly to a union 'inter *willelmu*m Shaxpere et Annam whateley de Temple grafton'. But clerks were lax with names of brides; one Stratford marriage bond later seems to permit a wedding of a bridegroom with his own curate, and another, in 1625, allows that 'John Francis and Edmund Canninge' may wed (but 'Joan' could be spelled 'John').[14] Some confusion about Anne's locale, perhaps, was bound to occur if she was living outside the parish. The chance that she was staying with Whateleys is remote, though Whateleys were in the diocese and the name had been prominent at Stratford since the town's incorporation. The best explanation of 'Annam whateley' may be that the court's clerk was beset by a tithe dispute, involving William Whateley, the vicar of Crowle, on the same day Shakespeare appeared. That suggestion with relevant evidence was offered by Joseph Gray in *Shakespeare's Marriage*, a main source for moderate commentators ever since (though Gray does not quite explain 'Temple grafton'). Anyway, a clerk's error has made 'Anne Whateley' into an enduring spook.

Substantially, on 28 November, the bond of sureties shows that William did not merit a 'special' licence of a kind issued to clerical bridegrooms and those of more exalted rank than his own. He

qualified for a 'common' licence, reserved for husbandmen, craftsmen, and the like. This document was addressed, as a rule, to the minister of the named church where the wedding was supposed to occur,
but we do not know where his own licence was sent.

Four conditions imposed on the young man all take the form of
unlikely negatives: he must not marry if a legal impediment exists, or
if a suit alleging an impediment is in process, or if he cannot guarantee
the bishop and the bishop's officers immunity from harm arising from
the issuing of a licence, or—more interestingly—if the bride's friends
do not approve the match. Two muddy-booted farmers, it seems, represented Anne's friends, and the word 'impediment' (which is in the
marriage service too) would be recalled by a poet who wrote, 'Let me
not to the marriage of true minds | Admit impediments'. By the end
of the day, he was free to marry. The bond itself allows

that will*i*am Shagspere on th*e* one pa*r*tie, and Anne hathwey of Stratford in
the Dioces of worcester maiden may lawfully solennize m*at*ri*m*ony together
and in the same afterward*es* remaine and continew like man and wiffe.[15]

With the flick of a quill pen Anne has returned, in this document, back
to Stratford parish—if she ever left it.

Richard Cosin or his registrar, Robert Warmstry, did remove one
'impediment'. The wedding, by licence, would need to be preceded
by only one reading of banns in church, not three as was more usual,
and that saved an unhelpful delay. The reading of banns was prohibited in the diocese between Advent Sunday (2 December 1582) and
the octave of Epiphany (13 January), during which time weddings,
too, were not customary and in principle not allowed.

Shakespeare's banns were probably read in church on St Andrew's
Day, 30 November, and the couple could have wed the next day,
before the prohibited season of Advent (otherwise they would have
had to wait until mid-January). Haste was welcome in light of Anne's
situation, and the ceremony took place in one of several possible
locales. John Haines, the curate, could have married them at St Peter's
Bishopton—north of Shottery—or, possibly, Thomas Hunt did at
All Saints' Luddington to the south. These were Stratford's two
chapelries. But likelihood, after all, favours Temple Grafton, though

its mention in the entry is not proof the wedding occurred there; it would have been an unobtrusive place. Four years later, a Puritan survey of Warwickshire described the vicar of Grafton, John Frith, as 'an old priest & Unsound in religion'. As a papist Frith was not up to much and was not very dangerous: 'he can neither prech nor read well, his chiefest trade is to cure hawkes yᵗ are hurt or diseased, for which purpose manie doe usuallie repaire to him'.[16] It is pleasant to think Frith's hawks watched the young couple. Yet whether they were married at Grafton or not, William and Anne began wedded life before winter came to Stratford parish.

After Davy Jones's show

By December the poet had almost certainly brought Anne to Henley Street, if she was not there before the wedding. It was normal for a groom's father to offer the bride room and board for a few years, and couples gratefully accepted shared lodgings. Anne had her bequest of 10 marks, and William may have had an annuity of £2, plus an extra year's pay, if he worked for Hoghton, or savings if he had worked elsewhere. Yet he would have found it hard to set up a new home with his wherewithal.

Even before any interlude 'in the Countrey', it seems, he had worked for his father. He kept on for 'some time' in that employment after thinking it 'fit to marry', says Nicholas Rowe, who explains the nature of the work only as 'that way of Living which his Father propos'd to him'.[17] At any rate, William could have found a pen in his hand rather than a glover's knife; he became very familiar with legal and business terms, though he could have picked these up later (he would write plays partly to suit Inns of Court men); he learned no more of the law than someone outside the field could have acquired, and he absorbed what he needed from other professions too. (Juliet's use of 'deed', 'counsel', or 'commission'—*Romeo and Juliet*, IV. i. 57–64—for example, need not suggest that he had trained as an attorney.) Probably he served as a clerk, scrivener, and part-time helper of his father.

Did a back wing at the Birthplace afford the newlyweds some privacy? The wing has been said to have been 'an independent little dwelling, with separate kitchen, staircase, and "solar", extending into the garden', but it is hard to imagine much independence for anyone in a glover's domestic arrangements.[18] The couple probably dined with William's parents, and Anne would have been obliged to co-operate in the common family work.

We cannot peer into the ménage, but it would have had drawbacks as well as a few advantages. That Anne seems to have stayed with William's parents until the purchase of New Place in 1597—some fourteen or fifteen years after she began to live with them—argues that she was welcome to Mary Shakespeare. Both countrywomen were pious daughters of affluent, conservative farmers. John Shakespeare had more in common with the two women than did William—a grammar-school scholar and poet too old for an apprenticeship and surely aching for better challenges than Stratford could offer. In this ménage he was in the position of a child twice over, first to his mother and then to his wife. He was in effect doubly fixed in his former home; he was his mother's flesh and blood, and of one flesh and blood with his wife: 'Farewell, dear mother', Hamlet mocks King Claudius, 'Father and mother is man and wife, man and wife is one flesh' (IV. iii. 51, 53–4). To an extent he was locked into a little, ever-present situation of half-understandings, or of much less than full communication, in which his elders could not have responded to much in his being. So it is often, with one generation and the next, but the gap between young and old in provincial towns in the 1580s was particularly great. William's Latin training had abetted his concern with books when more were being published than ever before and the nation's culture was becoming more complex, refined, challenging to the mind; the pace of sophistication was swifter than at any time in the past. There are signs of Mary's unusual capability, but we do not know that she read for pleasure; his father and wife were, at best, semi-literate.

As a person of intellectual acuity, he adapted outwardly to those who could not share his interests, as his later relations with the town suggest. In a sense, the security and routines of the day must have been welcome enough, and his imagination and intellect were free to conceive remote, ancient, or courtly pictures of an ampler existence. To judge from his plays and poems, he needed to lose himself in the distanced imaginary situation to explore his insights, and perhaps to make use of his experience. What is really new in his view of love is his understanding of its connection with loneliness, and one force that drives many of his stage lovers is misery in the isolatedness of being; some of his young men are convinced that love is a means chiefly of overcoming errors of pride, self-delusion, and presumption that victimize the estranged, misled psyche. In *The Comedy of Errors*, his Antipholus of Syracuse speaks to Luciana as if she had alighted as a force of sanity from a distant planet:

> Teach me, dear creature, how to think and speak.
>   Lay open to my earthy gross conceit,
> Smothered in errors, feeble, shallow, weak,
>   The folded meaning of your words' deceit.
> Against my soul's pure truth why labour you
>   To make it wander in an unknown field?
> Are you a god? Would you create me new?
>   Transform me, then, and to your power I'll yield.
>
>   (III. ii. 33–40)

Romeo easily and naturally regards Juliet as an exception to the human species, as one who lifts him as in a dream to a new state of being. Such love may accuse domesticity of its failure to satisfy, to enlighten, to make whole. Yet a belief in the gorgeous, ample, transforming possibilities of love does not suggest utter despair over the commonplaces of marriage, and William must have drawn upon sources of strength at home. Ambitious, dissatisfied, and restless as he undoubtedly was with no outlet for the energy of his talents at Henley Street, he was not to behave as a man ensnared by an unsuitable woman; his apparently regular visits to Stratford, his investments and care to establish himself there, do not suggest he found Anne immaterial to his welfare. And it is not irrelevant that his early biographers imply he chose marriage, not that he was trapped: 'in order to settle in the World after a Family manner, he thought fit to marry while he was yet very Young', wrote Rowe in 1709, and Theobald alludes to the poet's 'Force of Inclination' towards matrimony.[19] Certainly his wife and mother were from old county families traditional in their ways; Ardens and Hathaways would have connected him more closely with the civic past of Stratford, the Holy Cross Gild, the impassioned intelligence and relative simplicity of the community in its medieval, well-regulated order. The piety of Anne and Mary would have been unlocking and important, but it is useless to suppose that he was deeply contented at Henley Street or that he welcomed Anne's family as intimate friends; he was not to mention any Hathaway in his will, and it is not easy to find more than a handful of local people who can be called his lifelong friends. He was to be wary of certain aldermen; but just after his marriage it is unlikely that he shunned all of his former mates. A week before Anne gave birth the husband of another Hathaway in fact put on the Whitsun show, and later the chamberlains noted,

Payd to Davi Jones and his companye for his pastyme at whitsuntyde
xiij^s iiij^d [13*s.* 4*d.*]^{20}

Frances Hathaway—whose father Thomas figures in Anne's father's will—was evidently a first cousin of Anne's. Richard Hathaway had left to her two youngest sisters the bequest of a sheep apiece, and the two families must have been on fairly intimate terms. In 1579 Frances had wed the young widower David Jones, formerly married to a daughter of Adrian Quiney, and, among entertainers, Davy or 'Davi' Jones rose to local leadership. Shakespeare would have known something of Davy's performers, whose costumes and paraphernalia, on 19 May 1583, surely were as fine as the sum of 13*s.* could buy. Municipal eloquence and pageantry, strong ale and sports, dancing and rowdiness had taken over Whitsun holidays—but Whitsun was a time of flowers and gentler celebrations, too, and not every performer was 'o'erparted' as he spoke his lines. 'Come,' says Perdita in *The Winter's Tale*,

> take your flowers.
> Methinks I play as I have seen them do
> In Whitsun pastorals.
>
> (IV. iv. 132–4)

It is just possible that Shakespeare acted with or otherwise aided the 'companye', and he would have been well acquainted with craftsmen's or tradesmen's sons in the performance. He may have found Davy's troupe more laughable than they meant to be. Probably he felt himself drawn in other directions, or towards the possibility of writing acceptably elegant poetry. His literary taste at this time—in common with England's—was certainly becoming alert to refinements in the vernacular; he was well attuned, for example, to the music of the Earl of Surrey in the *Songes and Sonetts,* 'For my swete thoughtes some-tyme doe pleasure bring . . .', and, no doubt, even more sensitively responsive to Spenser's delicate effects in *The Shepheardes Calendar* of 1579, which a generation of new writers accepted as a landmark:

> How I could reare the Muse on stately stage,
> And teach her tread aloft in bus-kin fine,
> With queint *Bellona* in her equipage.

> But ah my corage cooles ere it be warme,
> For thy, content vs in thys humble shade:
> Where no such troublous tydes han vs assayde,
> Here we our slender pipes may safely charme.[21]

A week after Davy's troupe performed, William and Anne's child was baptized Susanna Shakespeare on 26 May 1583. Her name had come acceptably into local fashion, and her parents may have named her after a family friend: Sir Thomas Lucy had a sister named Susanna, and Richard Tyler would soon marry his Susanna Woodward—but the name is interestingly significant for its story. In the Apocrypha, Susanna as the virtuous wife of Joachim lives in accordance with Moses' law. Two lustful judges trap her; her screams of despair bring servants to her rescue, but, at an assembly the next day, the judges cause her to be condemned as an adulteress. God, however, sends to her aid the young Daniel, who makes the judges contradict each other so that they are put to death, and Susanna and her family praise the Deity for her deliverance.

There may be a defiant, proud virtue in the name 'Susanna' when parents choose it for a child conceived out of wedlock, and gossip over a sudden wedding might linger. The name asserts its purity and spiritual strength; it had been used by the Catholic Bishop of Ross in a defence of Mary Queen of Scots (he summoned up the biblical Judith, too, in describing Mary's virtues); Puritans favoured 'Susanna', and playwrights had not neglected her story. When the Shakespeares' daughter was born the name was a prime one for biblical drama, and more than a dozen Susanna-plays had appeared in Europe before Thomas Garter's grave 'comedy' *Susanna* was printed in Fleet Street by Hugh Garter, at the sign of St John the Evangelist, in 1578.

Much of the training of a daughter was left to her mother, but, in an age of new literacy, a substantial number of girls benefited from petty school. Brightly alert, mentioned later for her wit and apparently favoured as an eldest child, Susanna was taught household chores. It is likely that she learned to read and write, but it does not necessarily follow that she was prompted to make much use of these skills, or to read for her delight. Had Shakespeare been a conventional father he would not have desired that she should read many books, or wished her to be unlike most other women of the Stratford gentry. He hardly wrote *Venus and Adonis* or the so-called Dark Lady sonnets for Susanna's pleasure, and it is difficult to believe he would have offered a printed quarto of a comedy to her. Uppermost in Anne Shakespeare's mind would have been her daughter's piety, dutifulness, simple and cheerful amenity, and usefulness.

We shall look further into such evidence about Susanna's life as we have. She was brought up in a busy, and eventually prosperous, household where she saw her grandparents regularly and her father seldom. Soon enough, she had siblings. On the Festival of the Purification, Tuesday, 2 February 1585, the Shakespeares had their newborn twins christened Hamnet and Judith, no doubt in deference to their friends Hamnet and Judith Sadler. The boy's name was interchangeable with 'Hamlet'—in Shakespeare's will in a legal hand his friend would appear as 'Hamlet Sadler'—and among abundant local variants of the same name were (for example) Amblet, Hamolet, and even Hamletti.

The family home became more crowded, ample as it was. New evidence in the inventory of Lewis Hiccox, who after the playwright's death had a 'lease of the houses in henlye street' once owned by 'William Shakespeare gent', shows that at least six of the rooms where Shakespeare once lived were thought suitable as bed-chambers.[22] In the 'starehead chamber' with its 'green rugg', or even in the best room with its feather-bed, red rug, curtains, benches, and solitary table in Hiccox's time in the 1620s, the furnishings seem sparse, and they could hardly have been much more ample in the glover's household. John's business affairs were poor and deteriorating, and as his prospects became worse so the outlook for his son and for Anne's children must have seemed bleaker.

The birth of twins virtually assured that Shakespeare's future would be more problematic, that he would be concerned to make up for lost time in a calling, and would undertake nearly anything required of him to get money. He would also know, surely, the pain of separation for long periods from a substantial and consoling family. At 20 he had known more domestic complexities and responsibilities and probably a more intense emotional life than some people have known at 40, although he had done little to justify his fine grammar-school training and cannot have felt he had much of a chance to earn a fortune. If he lingered in the town as a resigned, respectable Prince Hal, he waited for a crown he did not want—it is impossible that he would have yearned to take over a glover's shop and debts. Exactly who drew him from Stratford, or when at last he left, we do not know. Since London-based troupes did not recruit on the road, it is unlikely that one of them picked him up in Warwickshire, even if he had served in a provincial troupe. What is quite certain is that an expansion of playing companies in the 1580s would have worked in his favour. New hands were needed for all varieties of work in connection with the popular public entertainments; and, again, the capricious Ferdinando, Lord Strange was patron of a troupe of acrobats and players in a position to expand.[23]

In responding to any encouragement or offer, Shakespeare hoped to better himself; he could serve his family best by removing himself from Stratford, though theatre work was hard, always uncertain. The profession had little status. He would be far from normal consolations. After his school years, he had married quickly and sired children as if to absorb such emotional nourishment and experience as he could. He must have overcome the results of the scholarly aridity of his grammar-school training to a large extent; regular employment and marriage would have been antidotes to his vanity, and he was eager to imitate, to observe, to adapt himself to new demands. His alert impressionable nature, with his energy and agility, would have made him hope to prove his talent as a player.

Influence was then working on his behalf, if at any time 'in the Countrey' he had made a connection that helped him in the mid-1580s. A summons to the theatre may have promised little, but he would take advantage of his chances. We cannot be sure that the young Ferdinando, Lord Strange provided those chances, but 'Shake-shafte' had been well recommended to Sir Thomas Hesketh, and the Heskeths were intimate with Ferdinando and the Earl of Derby. At some point in the bewilderingly rapid evolution of the playing companies, Shakespeare contributed to the success of Strange's actors.

His departure was likely to be trying for his family, to judge from his mockery of sentimental farewells in *The Two Gentlemen of Verona*. His life would be arduous, but he had surely been prepared for workaday London by many reports of it. His father had visited the city, and Stratford and Warwickshire apprentices had hoped to succeed there; a few, no doubt, had set themselves up in urban comfort. He would have known the value of social connections, and perhaps would not be slow to take advantage of countrymen who could help him. In any case, on a day of doubtful promise to himself, he would have bid farewell to his parents, three small children, and Anne, and set out on a road leading to the teeming, colourful, and oddly dangerous south.

II

ACTOR AND POET OF THE LONDON STAGE

7

TO LONDON – AND THE
AMPHITHEATRE
PLAYERS

Lyfte up thy heart and corage eke,
   be bolde and of good chere;
For fortune most doth favoure those,
   that all thynges least do feare. . . .
Great shame it is that vertue shoulde,
   for monsters hyde her face:
Go to therefore leave of thy lettes,
   and walk the depth apace.

   (Barnabe Googe's translation of
   Palingenius's 'Taurus'—an
   Elizabethan grammar-school text
   in the Latin version, 1560)

It appears, by their bare liveries, that they live by your bare
words.

   (Valentine, *The Two Gentlemen of Verona*)

Streets and conduits

*E*lizabethan London deeply impressed or astonished its visitors—
even if they knew beforehand of its long rows of shops and four-storey
houses, thronged suburbs and magnificently built-up London
Bridge, or of its fine, painted theatres and rich waterfront palaces. Foreigners praised the city, and some apprentices knew it as bewildering
or lethal. More people died in London than were born there—but
nothing stopped an influx of workers. Taking the city, its suburbs, and

Westminster together, one found here the nation's largest market and port, the nation's parliaments, great royal palaces and the hub of the Queen's administration, a centre of education in the Inns of Court and of Chancery, a royal mint, and even an ecclesiastical centre at Lambeth Palace and the Court of Arches at St Mary-le-Bow. The capital's many functions assured its growth—to about 200,000 people by 1600—and its educational establishments, booksellers, theatres, and high level of literacy tempted citizens to think of the rest of the nation as a cultural desert.[1]

Shakespeare, in his early twenties, was not unprepared to succeed there. Whether or not he had joined an acting troupe, he was ready for work; he had been trained in elocution by a London-born schoolmaster and would be likely to be *heard*. We cannot doubt his energy. In 'the Countrey' or at home, he must have become practised as a singer or musician—and he knew that a good player must have versatility. Better groups than the 'companye' of Frances Hathaway's husband had been entertaining his town: Worcester's men had come back to the Gild hall in the 1580s with a swelling reputation, after including in their main troupe Edward Alleyn, a promising tragedian—and two troupes in Stanley livery had played at Stratford. Under the auspices of the Earl of Derby or of his son Lord Strange, these had been separately paid by bailiff's order, as the chamberlains' accounts show:

Paid to my lord Straunge men the xj[th] day of february at the commaundment of M[r] Baliffe   v[s] [5*s.*]](2)

Paid to the Earle of Darbyes players at the commaundement of M[r] Baliffe
viij[s] iiij[d] [8*s.* 4*d.*]](3)

And there is no need to assume that Shakespeare, on leaving home, imagined that his *only* chance of success lay in the theatre. He soon had an eye on help outside that of player–patrons, to judge from the courtly tenor of his early writings. He might use a lucky recommendation to a nobleman of wealth, and it is unlikely that he hoped for no eventual future other than a player's.

Slow, jolting carriers' wagons took people south. Whether he walked or rode, there were two main routes from Stratford to London —and on horseback later he seems to have known both.

One way led through Oxford and High Wycombe, the other by Banbury and Aylesbury. The shorter route took the traveller from Clopton's bridge over sweeping low hills to Shipston on Stour, then to Long Compton, Chipping Norton, Woodstock—where schoolmaster Jenkins of the King's New School once lived—and on through Oxford, High Wycombe, Beaconsfield. For the other route one went from Pillerton Hersey over Edgehill to Banbury; on a side-road just eight miles south of Buckingham lay the village of Grendon Underwood where Shakespeare stayed over on a midsummer night and met a constable who became the model for Dogberry—but this is to believe a report of John Aubrey that may include wishful gossip.[4] From Buckingham, the way led over a small stone bridge and causeway into Aylesbury, then past the two Chalfonts to Uxbridge.

And here the two routes met, so that one highway took travellers past Shepherd's Bush, the stark Tyburn gallows, the Lord Mayor's banqueting house in Oxford road, and the pleasant rural setting of St Giles-in-the-Fields into the suburb of Holborn. From there, one went to Oldborne Bridge—and the sight of William Lamb's new, lead-lined water conduit over 2,000 yards in length—and then past the churches of St Andrew and St Sepulchre to the edge of the historic city at Newgate.

A high, battlemented prison with a portcullis and an opening for traffic, Newgate was one of seven gates on the Roman and medieval walls—thick, crumbling, running for more than two miles—that hemmed in London on three sides. Outside the walls were 'liberties', or districts within county boundaries but in some instances free of their jurisdiction and subject to the municipal one. Wagons and carts of all descriptions, drawn by oxen, horses, or mules, or pushed or pulled by men, went through the great gates. On the river side the gate had vanished, but Bishopsgate, Moorgate, Cripplegate, and Aldersgate separated citizens from a crowded jumble of liberties and suburbs to the north; Newgate and Ludgate looked west to Charing Cross and royal Westminster, and Aldgate faced east. The inner city and the suburbs alike were unsanitary: as animal corpses rotted in the open, so offal, urine, and faeces were dumped in London's streets. In mean alleys, the rickety hovels beat back fresh air and light, and conditions were worse in poor areas beyond the walls. The stench of the metropolis was appalling, its overcrowding severe—and yet some city wards were beautiful, with ornate façades, spacious gardens, and numerous wild flowers.

The city's pride, wealth, and self-confidence were evident on the Thames, with its hundreds of high masts, wherries, and barges, and on London Bridge with its three-storey structures, twelve-foot-wide passage—dangerous when sheep or cattle were driven over—and a garish, barbarous warning of sometimes as many as two or three dozen traitors' heads stuck up on poles. There was an unbroken sweep of public and private buildings on the curving river from the royal city in the west to the Tower of London in the east. The Tudor chronicler John Stow shows that the Tower under its turnip-like turrets had a number of functions. It was a citadel of defence and a royal venue for assemblies and 'treaties', a prison for the most dangerous, an armoury, a place of coinage, a treasury, even an archive; Stratford's council, anxious for the town, sent citizens to the Tower to ferret into its legal records. A recent writer adds helpfully that couples could be married at the Tower and that it had a menagerie. (Paul Hentzner noted in 1598 that this included lions, a tiger and a lynx, an old wolf, an eagle and porcupine.)[5] But just why Shakespeare alludes more often to the Tower than to any other building is another matter.

A visitor—at first sight—might view the Tower romantically. Though William the Conqueror built it, Shakespeare refers in *Richard II* to 'Julius Caesar's ill-erected Tower'; the myth of Caesar as its builder linked it with grammar-school days (every boy in Lower School met Caesar in Lily's first grammar). Royal Westminster pointed to the classical past, too, in the popular myth that British monarchs were all descended from a Prince Brutus, who fought at Troy. Yet Shakespeare hardly let myths keep him from studying an authentic city. His mind was romantic enough to surfeit of its excesses, so that he looked for the reason of things; he brought analytical intelligence to London's past in his early history plays. Penetrating the Tower's romance, he would see it as a gateway to England's real history—and as one enticing, blood-ridden and tragic locale of events.

Passing through Newgate, he would have entered a world of tall, leaning houses and shops, filled streets, mercantile energy. Though quiet by modern standards, the city with its sellers' cries and a myriad bells would have seemed a riot of noise. It was filled with young people—apprentices made up a tenth of its populace—and vagabonds, prostitutes, unwed mothers, 'masterless men' and part-time workers swelled the number.[6] There were over a hundred bordellos in and outside the walls: streets were erotic, with a grotesque bawdiness or a sleazy prettiness in the air. The Bankside 'Stewes' were closed (and prostitutes were licensed), but girls solicited even inside St Paul's Cathedral. The city, in many ways, would feed his talent as a playwright of love, bawdry, and tragic sensuality while appealing to his image-making interests.

Much of its working life was disciplined by guilds or livery companies which controlled trades, as well as by masters of shops—who had to support their apprentices' illegitimate children—and by preachers, local officials, and watchful neighbours. One in ten householders, directly or indirectly, was involved in the government in some way; this figure rose to about one in three in a wealthy inner-city ward such as Cornhill. Despite brawls, cut-purse gangs, and major civic unrest, by far the worst threat in London was the recurrence of bubonic plague and other epidemics.

Shakespeare was later to live among French Huguenots. Aliens, or 'strangers', mostly from France and the Netherlands, were resented, though the Elizabethan apprentices—who broke skulls—never did riot against them. Poets and actors came to know 'Petty France' in Bishopsgate ward, 'Petty Almaine' and 'Petty Flanders' in Thames Street; they learned of Italy in the city, and met Jews. So-called Marranos, or Portuguese and Spanish Jews in the east and north-west wards, added to overseas trading contacts, worked in retailing, the crafts, or medicine, and supplied intelligence to the Crown before and after the war with Spain began in 1585. A second small community of London's Jews, of sixty or a hundred, had originated in musicians recruited in Venice by Henry VIII; some descendants included royal musicians, a few of whom were likely to be known later to the author of *The Merchant of Venice*.[7] Cosmopolitan London broadened Shakespeare's outlook, and foreign stories and the talk of Europe were to give him dramatic material.

London's Jews—some of them observant—relied on the Privy Council's tacit approval. But though no more likely to tolerate Jews than theatres, London's preachers saw the players as the chief, glaring, abomination: 'The cause of plagues is sinne, if you look to it well', as Thomas White had preached at Paul's Cross in the shadow of St Paul's Cathedral in November 1577, 'and the cause of sinne are playes: therefore the cause of plagues are playes'.[8] Even before that syllogism, theatres had been built out beyond the city within the more lax jurisdiction of county authorities.

Yet the players' situation was complex. Sometimes the Queen's Council, in fear of riot or disease, saw eye to eye with the irate city fathers and forbade playing in the suburbs. At other times the city fathers—or the Lord Mayor and his aldermen and common councilmen, who could raise money by regulating vigorous and profitable theatres—issued such a weak, *pro forma* complaint as to encourage playing within the walls.

When Shakespeare arrived a demand for theatre was growing. As play-goers for a penny, apprentices might escape for three hours from their fixed drudgery, rules, and roles. The privileged needed release, too. The city was becoming a social centre for the gentry, who thronged there partly to wage their law-cases: London's need for grain was about 11.5 per cent higher during the law terms.[9] Merchants and their wives, courtiers and litigants, sojourners and students in the Inns of Court and Chancery—taking afternoons off from dancing, fencing-school, or even their law-books—made up elements of a sophisticated, trainable audience, and the 'termers' or law students were, in effect, to help train the playwrights. Art responds to the wit of its receivers, and London audiences helped a new, paradoxical, immensely powerful drama into being. Even the Puritan opposition helped. Puritans saved the age from a brittle rationalism by insisting on the necessity of divine revelation, and spoke for intense, inward operations of conscience—upon which high tragedy depends—as well as for literacy and the value of the word.

Since the beginning of the reign, plays had been put on in London's streets, inns, private houses, schools, and colleges. Biographers have said that the first purpose-built theatre, in use when Shakespeare was a schoolboy, dates from 1576. But we know of a free-standing theatre of earlier date: it was built in 1567 by John Brayne, a Bucklersbury grocer, with helpers at Whitechapel outside Aldgate. The site was near the garden of the Red Lion, which was not, so far as we know, an inn, but a 'messuage or farme house called and knowen by the Sygne of the Redd Lyon'.[10] A five-foot-high stage, a thirty-foot turret, and tiers of galleries were 'framed' (or prefabricated) by 1 July 1567, when a dispute between Brayne and his chief builder, William Sylvester, stopped work. An appeal to the Company of Carpenters dragged on, and though plays were put on here, the venture never prospered. Yet the Red Lion's structure was influential, whether or not it resembled Henry VIII's hall at Calais, or that of the banqueting house, partly of canvas, where *Othello* was to be performed in 1604.[11]

Brayne, a plucky investor, must have recalled the design when he collaborated in 1576 with his brother-in-law James Burbage. Failing to thrive as a joiner, or craftsman-carpenter, Burbage became a player with the Earl of Leicester's troupe and possibly its head (or at least its payee). He sought in the theatre a 'great profitt',[12] and his financial anxiety matched his ardour for the playing profession; he was to be a close associate of Shakespeare's. Lacking funds, he borrowed from Brayne, so that a new amphitheatre rose north of the city—the Theater.

Located in the liberty of Halliwell (or Holywell) where a Benedictine priory had stood in the Middlesex parish of St Leonard's, Shoreditch, the Theater, too, was safe from city fathers. Its name, from the Latin *theatrum*, taunted people alert to pagan vices; a few spelled it as the 'Theatre', which was closer to the root-word *theatrum*, in order to link the enterprise with the supposed riots and depravity of the ancient Roman theatre; but the two different spellings, in an era of unsettled spelling, were also used interchangeably by the literate (and, in retrospect, both are correct enough). Puritans hoped for the playnouse's ruin, and there is evidence that Brayne had built it in such a way that it could be dismantled in a crisis.

As a business enterprise it was wildly risky, with costs estimated at 1,000 marks (£666). Burbage hungered after profit, and the costs agonized him. 'The Theater he built with many hundred pounds taken up at interest', his son Cuthbert later claimed in a very filial tribute to Burbage's merits. But while Brayne and his wife Margaret had worked on the building site without pay, Burbage took a cut from assets during construction; when the structure yielded profits of about £190–£235 per annum he was caught, it seems, with a hand in the till. Using a secret key for two years, Burbage, it was alleged, filched from a 'commen box where the money gathered at the said playes was putt in', and thrust coins 'in his bosome or other where about his bodye'. In due course, there was violence. Feeling out-swindled by his partner, Burbage hit Brayne with his fist 'so they went together by the eares', and later reviled Margaret Brayne, calling her 'whore', while his son Richard (who was to play Shakespeare's tragic roles) beat one of Brayne's men with a broom-staff. Depending on his dutiful sons, Burbage shouted that if he saw Brayne's allies again, his boys would take pistols and shoot them in the legs with powder and hempseed.

Burbage, a 'stubborne fellow', apparently never denied that he had filched from Brayne and the players. Witnesses supported allegations against him.[13] At this distance, his conduct is hard to judge—but his warfare with Brayne and Margaret illustrates not only rivalries, suspicions, a knockabout atmosphere, but also a nerve-racking pressure in the 'business' which Shakespeare, as a player, was trying to enter.

The Theater or Theatre cost its entrepreneurs more than they had planned, and while expenses soared, rival venues multiplied. Two hundred yards to the south, the Curtain opened at Moorfields in 1577. Its builder Henry Lanman, or Laneman, a Londoner who rented land at Curtain Close, had financial worries himself, until the Curtain became an 'easer' to the Theater with profits at the two houses pooled. Late in the 1590s, it would serve as a venue for Shakespeare's company, the Chamberlain's men, who were then winning what Marston calls 'Curtain plaudities' for *Romeo and Juliet*.[14]

Within two years of Burbage's opening, plays were regularly performed at eight or more London venues. Troupes were using converted inns, such as the Bell and Cross Keys in Gracechurch Street, the Bull in Bishopsgate Street, the Boar's Head near the Red Lion in Whitechapel, and the Bel Savage on Ludgate Hill. With stands for spectators and changing-rooms for actors, innyard theatres were not then a novelty—nor were they obsolete. The boy companies, made up of children from élite schools, had also found a good year-round market for stage spectacles. By going to school for a few hours a day, the boys kept up the fiction they were performing not for money, but to show off their educational skills. Intermittently for a decade and a half after 1575 (and later from 1600 to 1606) the choristers of Paul's School drew people to a small, indoor hall-theatre near their Chapter House. Their little rivals of the Royal Chapel held indoor shows at their own hall—in Blackfriars—until 1583–4.

But somewhat nearer the time when Shakespeare was starting in London, much fiercer competition for Burbage (and for all northern theatres) began south of the river on Bankside. Watermen, for decades, had ferried people over to watch bull- and bear-baiting; the animal arenas were in Paris Garden and the Clink, south-west of London Bridge, and so beyond the city's jurisdiction at St Saviour's parish, Southwark. That parish was oddly split into three administrative areas: its eastern district of the Boroughside was in Bridge Ward Without (one of London's twenty-six wards) but its two liberties of the Clink and Paris Garden were subject to Surrey authorities.[15] Famous for its prison, the Clink was on low, marshy land within the river's flood plain, and protected by earthwork embankments. Fifty-eight acres were taken up by Winchester Park with its chestnut trees, and there were ponds for pike and carp, some orchards and bowling greens, a bear garden, and bordellos (despite attempts to close them).

Here Philip Henslowe, a former dyer's apprentice who had married his master's rich widow, took a lease on the Little Rose estate, near Rose Alley and Maiden Lane. Once the site of a rose garden, the lot had been charitably bequeathed to the parish of St Mildred, Bread Street, and Henslowe saw money in it. With John Cholmley, a grocer, he planned a theatre, and his deed, of 10 January 1587, refers to 'a playe howse now in framinge and shortly to be ereckted'.[16] (This seems to mean that the Rose playhouse, like the Red Lion, was prefabricated before it was set up.) Possibly Cholmley died or opted out of the project. But the Rose flourished. So did Henslowe, who became the age's greatest theatrical landlord, not above lending money to impecunious players and poets who did not always thank him. He jotted wryly in a famous account book, or *Diary*:

> when I lent I wasse A frend & when I asked I wasse unkind.[17]

Henslowe, too, had miseries. A theatre may have seemed to him (as to Burbage) a costly sink, with the Rose empty for months while playing companies favoured other sites, disbanded, or fled by road because of civic riots or plague. We lack lists of performances at the Rose until 1592, when Shakespeare's *1 Henry VI* (if it is 'harey the vj') reached its boards, by which time Shakespeare had possibly acted there. Arguably it was one birthplace of Elizabethan tragedy, since Kyd's *The Spanish Tragedy* and all of Marlowe's plays must have been staged there. It was a training ground for Shakespeare as a poet (its landlord notes a showing of 'titus & ondronicus'[18]). And the Rose is important in another way. The discovery and unearthing of its foundations near Southwark Bridge, in 1989, has given us more exact, reliable data about the design of Shakespearean playhouses than we had had from all other sources in three centuries.

Henslowe's builder, John Griggs, used a beautiful design. Under its thatched roof, the Rose had a polygonal shape. Its stage was a small, neat trapezoid, only fifteen feet six inches deep, with a curving back wall or *frons scenae*. That was unlike the big, rectangular, jutting stages which are sometimes said to be the only kind Shakespeare knew. Critics, before 1989, often based ideas about his theatres on a vague, unreliable copy of a sketch of the Swan playhouse. The Rose's sheltered stage, with its actors' changing-room or tiring-house, was wide at the back, but it tapered to a width of less than twenty-five feet at the front. Actors overlooked the 'groundlings', or standing spectators, who cracked hazel nuts and drank bottled ale in a firmly mortared yard, sloped or raked to the front. There was room for 600 people in the yard, another 1,404 in the galleries (three tiers or storeys of them with benches), so the Rose could accommodate audiences of 2,000.[19]

Yet Shakespeare was to find that this theatre afforded intimacy. It was so designed that, in roofed galleries, which began thirty to thirty-six feet from the stage, people were close enough to catch the actors' nuances of tone and facial expression. The Rose's properties included screens, painted objects, and backcloths such as 'Hell Mouth' or 'the City of Rome', and audiences were close enough to savour the gorgeous costumes of performers in their velvet, satin, or taffeta. The theatre was lavishly, stunningly painted—as was every London amphitheatre—but here, close to the stage, audiences were all the more likely to react to the assault of colour and to dazzling and cunning visual effects. Indeed, Shakespeare's extraordinary use of visual stagecraft was to be influenced by the Rose, where audiences were trained to see and to remember what they saw.

Acting was not always skilful or restrained, but at its best it had become highly sophisticated, and it was the more brilliant at the Rose because of the sensible proportions of the theatre. Lifelike realism combined with the utmost stylization; players could make use of stock reactions or stock attitudes, as Alan C. Dessen has shown, inasmuch as stage directions can ask the actor to enter 'as robbed', 'as from bed', 'as from dinner', or 'as newly come from play', and the psychology of impersonation was not yet well developed. In his own early plays Shakespeare could rely on audiences' reactions to very standard types of characters. But even so, at the Rose at least, effects on stage did not need to be exaggerated or crude. An actor hardly needed to roar, declaim, or 'tear a passion to tatters'; Hamlet's advice to the Players is proof enough that Shakespeare had known a theatre where naturalness was possible.[20]

The Rose's yard and galleries were extended in 1592, and later this theatre served other uses and then decayed—but it may have been standing when Edward Alleyn (Henslowe's son-in-law, who inherited his interest in the Rose) paid a tithe due 'for ye rose' in 1622.[21]

One reached a slightly older theatre at Newington Butts, a mile to the south of London Bridge, along the road continuing from Southwark High Street. Playing at Newington is first mentioned on 13 May 1580. Twelve years later the Privy Council admitted Newington was remote, but Londoners knew its playhouse well enough to call a bad pun a 'Newington conceit'.[22]

❧

These, in brief, were the main theatrical venues Shakespeare would soon have heard about. By around 1588, Burbage's and Henslowe's major playhouses were enhancing London's life—though a Londoner such as Stow, the chronicler, was aware of civic loss, and little compensated for what had been lost in the lasting changes of the English Reformation. Many older, religious, festivals which had once deepened the people's lives had ceased, and church attendance in urban parishes was low. The Catholic menace within the country seemed to fade after Mary Queen of Scots' trial and execution in 1587, and war with Spain aroused fervid patriotism; but Londoners were not relieved by a heady, nationalistic sentiment. Though not on the verge of rebellion, London was riotous and less stable than it had been.

No one, at any rate, better knew its mood than the Queen, who usually began her royal year in mid-November when she returned to London by way of Chelsea. She rode in by night, for a torchlight welcome. Ambassadors, the Lord Mayor, and citizens in chains and robes of office assembled for her. As she passed on dark streets, the people greeted their Virgin Queen with a depth of feeling that also responded to the tenuous beginnings of the greatest drama the world has known.

Hirelings, repertory, and poets

But in the late 1580s the quick rise and fall of playing companies, with financial troubles and changing members, made theatrical life chaotic. The troupes split, reorganized, and to save themselves often left the costly city to perform in the provinces. Trudging in mud, rain, or sleet behind a players' wagon and hoping for a few more pennies at a distant town, actors yearned for London. Shakespeare may hardly have reached the capital before he was out on the road; if he did travel, he returned when he could. But for a few years he is not traceable in our records, and the likeliest reason for this is that he began as a 'hireling' of other actors. Until he became a 'sharer', he would not be listed among a troupe's principal men.

He could not have begun at any time without soon learning about a company's organization, about patrons, repertoires, and 'poets' (not yet called playwrights) and their valuable but lifeless scripts or playbooks. He may have known the ache of a traveller's bones overseas, and peered 'in maps for ports and piers and roads', in Denmark, the Lowlands, or Italy—but we lack evidence of this.[23] Under foggy, raw British skies, he took his training.

He knew that an acting company was a hard-working unit with eight to twelve chief actors, or sharers, who had invested in it; they paid relevant debts, and took on hired men who received between 5*s*. and 10*s*. in weekly wages. Financially the troupes often existed precariously, at the edge of ruin, and even late in the 1590s the Chamberlain's men had low receipts and were in dire trouble. The income of an actor varied greatly, as appears for example from G. E. Bentley's exact figures for a later period. In the year 1634–5, William Bankes, a sharer in what was then Prince Charles's troupe, earned £40, and each of three actors in the King's Servants earned £180. In earlier years, profits were lower, and in the mid-1590s when plague or riot had not shut the theatres, an actor, in a sharers' group such as the Admiral's, might earn on average about 18*s*. or £1 a week.

The playing company's relations with the community were always problematic, and the troupes had many more enemies than just London's city fathers. Pamphlets and sermons attacked the actor for being ungodly in idleness—a dishonest usurer, improvident, diseased, obscene, or sexually 'variable'. Religious authorities feared that the actor would capture Sunday audiences, and some merchants resented his competition for Londoners' cash. Dazzling and charismatic on stage, the actor offstage fascinated people, but also repelled them; he might attract women from any of the social ranks, yet he was also seen as a filthy pederast who kept boys as his 'ingles' or catamites. His ability to arouse strong feelings and fantasies was instinctively feared by many. It was felt that the actor could fatally induce divine wrath, or that his alleged self-love or self-satisfaction could infect honest people who went to work at regular hours. Moreover, from 1579 until the closing of the theatres before the Civil War, the actor was invoked as a person of no more status or real worth than a common beggar.[24]

Yet despite its paradoxical reputation—and even because of it—the acting profession drew into its ranks hopeful, intelligent, versatile boys and men, most of whom would have felt lucky to have anything to do with a troupe. A young man entering the theatre found that his fellows had their own special customs and hierarchy. They dined together and went to the same, fairly inexpensive, taverns—a young actor was not likely to have much spare cash. As a hireling, Shakespeare would have earned little more than a skilled mason or carpenter. About a quarter of the hirelings worked as minor actors; the others were stagehands, craftsmen, the 'book-keeper' or prompter—and his assistant 'stage-keepers'—as well as tiremen in charge of costumes (one might pay three or four times more for a rich costume than for a new play), and gatherers to collect admission fees at theatre doors. Boy actors, for female roles, usually began as apprentices and received little but their keep.

A player–patron had no direct legal responsibility for men who wore his badge and colours, but he gained prestige from his actors—especially if they played at court—and might influence them. Ferdinando, Lord Strange had become a stellar patron. Related on both sides to the royal family, he soon exposed a madcap Jesuit plot to get him to lay claim to the throne himself; he lured and betrayed one implicated Lancashire Catholic, Richard Hesketh, who was hanged. Ferdinando had hardly forgotten his family's alleged leniency with papists. And yet proud, sensitive, and alert to talent as he was, he borrowed funds to support the arts and earned the thanks and praise of a long list of poets, including Peele, Greene, Spenser, and Chapman. It is possible that he sent a few of his protégés to his troupe; but this is speculation. He did watch his troupe evolve. Once mainly acrobats, Strange's men appear as players in the 1580s at Bristol, Plymouth, Canterbury, Gloucester, and London;[25] in contempt of a prohibition by the Lord Mayor they played at the Cross Keys inn on 5 November 1589, for which some went to prison. A restructured troupe emerged to act six times at court in a single season, before some of them formed, along with Shakespeare, the successful Chamberlain's company.

Still, we have only a few hints (at best) that Ferdinando, Lord Strange tried to help a young Stratford man. Shakespeare later departed from his sources to portray Strange's ancestor Lord Stanley (the Earl of Derby) in a better light in *Richard III*; and he may recall Ferdinando in the amusing grandeur of the King of Navarre (who has the unusual name Ferdinand) in *Love's Labour's Lost*—but the portrait is not flattering. *Titus Andronicus*'s title-page suggests this play was first performed by Strange's men, who also acted 'harey the vj'.

All of which, of course, does not prove Shakespeare began as a hireling of Strange's troupe. Speculation thrives; there were other patrons, of whom none was more important than the Queen. Her Master of the Revels (officially a dramatic censor and an impresario for shows at court) had been ordered to 'choose out a companie of players' on 10 March 1583.[26] The Master banded leading actors from existing troupes into the Queen's men, who wore red jackets and excelled in this decade. One of their two prime comedians was Richard Tarlton. Drumming on a tabor, fingering a pipe, then singing, curveting, skipping, and shuffling round and round in a jig, Tarlton acted out his 'court', 'city', or 'country' *Jests.* He moulded audiences by acting not so much *for* them as *with* them; by bantering, calling for replies, and using impromptu wit, Tarlton became a part of the community of spectators. And no doubt his fame is important. He exploited something basic—an audience's 'double awareness' of the player's dramatic role and of the player who is only pretending. The Elizabethan actor, as in soliloquies and asides, expresses his sense of being in fact a performer; the boy in female clothes remains for the audience a boy actor *and* an impersonated female.[27] Tarlton, among others, prepared the way for a great non-illusionist drama, in which Faustus or Hamlet speaks with a more affecting intimacy because audiences do not forget he is also a stage actor, frail as themselves.

The troupes divided and reformed; personnel moved about. If Shakespeare attached himself to the Queen's men, he could have gone with the actor John Heminges from there straight into Strange's troupe. For twenty years, Shakespeare was to be Heminges' close friend and colleague. At any rate, after Tarlton's death in 1588, the Queen's men split into two groups—one of them acting jointly with Sussex's men, the other probably helping to form Pembroke's company. Unlike the Queen's, Strange's men favoured dramas that were politically bold, or controversial in topic and fresh in dramaturgy to draw the crowds.

Still almost all London troupes were alike in one way. They were subject to a tight repertory system. Shakespeare knew its demands well, and they seem hard to imagine. A company in good, or ideal, times acted on every afternoon except Sundays and during Lent; they put on a different play each working day of the week, though some plays would be repeated in the weeks ahead. For example, the Admiral's men typically put on fifteen different titles in the course of twenty-seven playing days. An actor usually had to keep at least thirty parts in his memory, many more if he doubled in minor roles. It would have been normal for Shakespeare (if he worked as a typical hireling) to take a hundred small parts in a season. A leading actor such as Edward Alleyn or Richard Burbage, in any case, memorized about 800 lines for a part, and kept in mind up to 4,800 lines in a week.[28]

Each morning, a hireling actor had to rehearse a new play while getting up his lines for the afternoon's play, or rehearsing that one as well, and seeing that his costumes were ready. The 'book-holder' or 'book-keeper' along with several assistants or 'stage-keepers' saw that the actors were ready on cue, and that properties were at hand. But a hireling got along without a director's help, and probably without ever reading the whole playscript. His own written-out 'parts', for memorizing, included only single phrase-cues or line-cues from other actors' speeches. On stage he was guided—chiefly—by his previous experience of acting with the same fellows.

Shakespeare did not learn about 'character' simply by watching men and women; he had to *become* many an idiosyncratic person himself, if he had anything like the experiences of a typical Elizabethan actor. As a rule, players became skilled in a broad range of personation. Young Burbage had to play the old, hoary Gorboduc and the lustful Tereus in the same play, Part Two of *Seven Deadly Sins*, performed by Strange's men around 1590. In that drama, one of the female roles was played by an actor named 'Will'—presumably not Shakespeare, who would have been too old for the part, although women were sometimes acted by boys in their late teens.[29] And to make life easier there was type-casting. Now and then, an actor was lucky enough to take on character-types he was familiar with. When Shakespeare accepted roles in his own works, he seems to have played old Adam in *As You Like It*, or the Ghost in *Hamlet*—elegiac, affecting voices; small parts—and, says Aubrey in the seventeenth century, he 'did act exceedingly well'.[30] Aubrey could have heard that from the son of Christopher Beeston of the Chamberlain's Servants; but it may mean little more than that Shakespeare on stage did not usually upset his colleagues.

At 23 or 24 he submerged himself in a troupe. His survival depended on quick, instinctive co-operation; as a young player he must have seemed adaptable, enduring, useful. Our slim evidence suggests he avoided quarrels, then and later, and took pride in ordinary competence. Whatever wish he had to be exceptional in a group, he did not fulfil, and as a repertory man he became a professional.

But it is by no means clear that he enjoyed this hard work at first, and there are signs he was nearly broken by it. His success as a playwright and poet was delayed; he admired poetry, but found the theatre a quick-paced, disenchanting funfair, with jigs, dancing, dumb-shows and clowns' acts interlaced with drama. As an actor, he learned facile tricks to get by, or hurried effects to win applause; and so as a playwright he would repeat stratagems, or rely at times on the makeshift. He might disguise yet one more heroine as a boy, or trust in actors to bring static roles to life, or assume an audience would not notice minor contradictions or improbabilities in a piece.

The playbooks were mostly written by those who were gentlemen by virtue of their Oxford or Cambridge degrees. Their work was in demand and Shakespeare studied it, possibly without realizing that a common player such as himself could offend university men by writing at all. Clearly, the companies hungered for scripts. To make their plays, writers were ransacking a wide range of sources, as Stephen Gosson, a playwright turned pamphleteer, noticed in 1582: 'the Palace of Pleasure, the Golden Asse, the Œthiopian historie, Amadis of Fraunce, the Rounde Table, bawdie Comedies in Latine, French, Italian, and Spanish'.[31] A company needed fifteen or twenty new plays a year. This imposed an enormous demand on the writers, and on the whole fund of available stories and plots in history and literature. Fresh, exciting plays helped to fill galleries—to the despair of the stage's opponents. A letter-writer observes in 1587 how 'two hundred proude players jett in their silkes, wheare five hundred pore people sterve in the streets'.[32]

III

Much in demand were competent writers, such as the 'University Wits', who included men such as Nashe, Greene, Peele, Lodge, and Thomas Watson. A cut above them all, socially and artistically, was young John Lyly, who since writing *Euphues* had supplied the boys of Paul's School with the finest English comedies Londoners had so far seen. A holder, like Greene, of two MA degrees, fashionably married and, in 1589, about to become an MP, Lyly, it seems, hoped in vain to be Master of the Revels. As an enterprising, short-statured man living in the parish of St Martin's, Ludgate, he was the major dramatist of the decade.

Shakespeare—who knew *Euphues*—could have read Lyly's comedies *Campaspe* and *Sapho and Phao* in their 1584 quartos, or seen Lyly's *Endimion* or *Midas* acted a few years later. He may well have learned from Lyly's *Mother Bombie*, *The Woman in the Moon*, or *Love's Metamorphosis* after starting to write himself. In the most routine of Lyly's work—and nobody has argued that *Midas* is one of his stronger plays—there is elegant wit, specificity, and exuberance, as when in *Midas* the servants Licio and Petulus discuss Licio's mistress (and thereby explain to London's gentry why their wives are costing them so much in London's fashionable shops):

LICIO. Well, she hath the tongue of a parrot.

PETULUS. That's a leaden dagger in a velvet sheath, to have a black tongue in a fair mouth. . . . But now you can say no more of the head, begin with the purtenances, for that was your promise.

LICIO. The purtenances! It is impossible to reckon them up, much less tell the nature of them. Hoods, frontlets, wires, cauls, curling-irons, periwigs, bodkins, fillets, hairlaces, ribbons, rolls, knot-strings, glasses, combs, caps, hats, coifs, kerchers, cloths, earrings, borders, crepines, shadows, spots, and so many other trifles as both I want the words of art to name them, time to utter them, and wit to remember them. These be but a few notes.

PETULUS. Notes, quoth you! I note one thing.

LICIO. What is that?

PETULUS. That if every part require so much as the head, it will make the richest husband in the world ache at the heart.[33]

Lyly's juvenile pages can be obscene. His women are refined, winning, and natural skirmishers, in a tradition followed by many of Shakespeare's heroines. His dramatic style has been called dainty or delicate—so it is—but he brought to comedy a sense of form and a clarity new in England. He had his characters discuss the state of being in love for the first time on a London stage; and by combining various genres and modes—such as farce, bawdry, mythology, romance, political allegory—he gave drama a presiding, supple intelligence, a sense of its unlimited possibilities. Drawing on Ovid and Plutarch and emphasizing a beauty of style, his works suggested more dramatic possibilities to Shakespeare than those of any other comic playwright.

Still others improved on Lyly by combining new elements, and by writing parts for characters rather than classical types. Robert Greene, down from Cambridge, red-haired, self-indulgent, with a mistress, had discipline as a writer. His prose romances are often excellent; his style tends to be supple, copious, and incisive. His comedy *The Honourable History of Friar Bacon and Friar Bungay* (printed in 1594 and perhaps acted in 1587) duplicates a romantic triangle in Lyly's *Campaspe* and foreshadows one in Shakespeare's *Two Gentlemen*: wonderfully yielding to love's force, a lover relinquishes his lady to one who loves her more. Greene interlaces magic, kingship, pastoral effects, and love-rivalry with pathos, humour, and a quick pace. His women, here and elsewhere, are Patient Griseldas, though they seem lifelike in their narrow roles. George Peele, meanwhile, with a background in writing festive pageantry, was carrying out structural experiments. No Elizabethan play of comparable length has a more complex plot, for example, than his *Old Wives Tale* with its folklore elements and 'framing' devices[34]—in which some of its characters watch and comment on the unfolding stage-action.

The University Wits were excelling themselves, borrowing from each other with jealous eyes, lifting the drama to new heights, and pleasing the companies, when a grammar-school trained man—a mere actor—began to rival them. Shakespeare, it seems, had decided to write for his fellow players.

Crab the dog

He may not have done so without encouragement. Certainly he appears to have been a busy, obliging hireling; Greene would accuse him later of being a 'Johannes fac totum', a jack of all trades in the theatre, or a would-be universal genius. To be sure, Greene does not use 'factotum' in its modern sense to signify a man who simply does odd jobs, 'a man of all work', but, rather, to suggest the high conceit of a man who both acts in and writes plays. Shakespeare's repertory acting itself called for dexterity and boldness; he can hardly have concealed from the players his wit or sense of rhetoric, and he seems to have impressed one actor—Beeston—as a person well trained enough to have taught at school. If his fellows did ask Shakespeare to write a play, they must have felt they had little to lose.

A knack for dashing off a script was highly valued, but not well rewarded in practice: companies paid about £6 for a play, which had a normal run of eight to twelve performances over about five months. (By the eighth performance, as Roslyn Knutson calculates, the company might expect to recover its production costs and make a profit.[35]) Popular works were often revived, as Kyd's and Marlowe's plays were over the years—but there were costly failures. To speed up their writing, most playwrights preferred to collaborate. For example among eighty-nine scripts that Henslowe of the Rose tells us about in detail, fifty-five are jointly written, and only thirty-four are single-author plays.[36] In a small collaborative team, a writer might specialize in working up a few kinds of action, scene, or situation.

An actor who could write a good play by himself was a rarity, but in Elizabeth's time he would not have seemed 'literary' or set apart. It is clear enough that Shakespeare coveted the normalcy of being a group member, just as his father for years, and at cost to himself, had served with his aldermanic brethren at Stratford. The group offered consoling protections. A measure of anonymity, a guise of ordinariness, in time suited Shakespeare well—and he and his fellows would have thought of a play as a collective event. A script existed, above all, for performance, when it became a play-in-being. Indeed, their acceptance of the notion of a play as a group activity—not as words on a page—was one of the actors' most valuable legacies from the medieval theatre.

A play's performance was its virtual publication, although the dramatist Beaumont later praised what he called a 'second publication'[37] when a work appeared in print. Shakespeare may have authorized the publication of several of his plays after they had come out in inaccurate quartos. A play issued in 'quarto' was a thin, unbound object advertised by its title-page, whereas a 'folio' was a large, expensive volume—not used for collections of plays until Jonson's *Works* in 1616. Dramas were only an insignificant part of the book trade, and bookshops such as those in St Paul's churchyard, which were not mere 'stalls', but structures two and four storeys high, hardly bothered with them. Peter Blayney reckons that on average only five or six new plays a year were printed in Shakespeare's time. The notion that a printed drama was often stolen by a rival company is quite mistaken. The troupes, as a rule, did not poach from each other's repertories, and more co-operation existed between acting companies than is usually recognized. But the book trade could be flooded with even a few playbooks. Shakespeare's three most popular plays in quarto, *1 Henry IV*, *Richard III*, and *Richard II*, possibly advertised his company, but sales in the shops would have brought him no direct return.[38] About half of his plays were printed in quarto before the large Folio with thirty-six of his works was published in 1623, seven years after he died. Throughout his life, he had little to gain from seeing his name in a London bookshop.

Yet this is not to say that he cared little for play-texts. Far from being a spontaneous genius, pouring out work with no heed for it, he evidently took pains with scripts; he was a reviser, with a poet's concern for verbal style. He usually read omnivorously to make a play; he relied on his memory of sources, if not also on working notes in a 'table book', selected materials to transform, and produced an acting text about which he often had second thoughts. He undertook some very substantial revisions. Initially, a text might require only minor changes for production. In giving a script to his fellows, he might, however, leave a few major decisions unresolved to benefit from advice during staging.[39] Although he left minor discrepancies in his works, he must have improved his early plays as his experience increased, and, no doubt, repertory playing aided him more than it harmed him. As an actor–playwright, he gained an insider's awareness of stage effects, a feeling for tactics that would make a character's psychology at once distinctive and plausible, and, above all, a splendid sense of overall design and economy of effect.

We may lack his earliest piece. But if Lyly began with a drama as fine as *Campaspe*, Shakespeare may have begun with *The Two Gentlemen of Verona*, which has the simplest design of his seventeen comedies. The composition dates of his early plays still provide a misty battleground for scholars, and the text of this play may have been changed over four or five years. One version of *Two Gentlemen* could have been written around 1588–91, when its elegant Lylyan theme of 'love versus friendship' was being mocked in romances and plays alike. For example, after two genteel friends in Peele's *Old Wives Tale* agree to share gains, Jack thinks nothing of asking Eumenides for half of a lady. Happily, Delia is ready to be cut in two, since she honours the cult of male friendship:

EUMENIDES. Before I will falsify my faith unto my friend, I will divide her. Jack, thou shalt have half. . . . Therefore prepare thyself, Delia, for thou must die.
DELIA. Then farewell, world! Adieu, Eumenides![40]

But Peele's joke destroys a pretended reality. His scene is funny but it becomes slapstick; an audience will not believe Delia *might* be sliced. In contrast, Shakespeare mocks and believes in his story at once; in *Two Gentlemen*, he distances an action while arousing our concern for his characters, and shows that he can write farce and comedy simultaneously. He fails the more egregiously, now and then perhaps, when his effects, which are new, go awry. His story, in outline, is so simple I will risk telling it briefly. Proteus and Valentine, the two young gentlemen, lose their gentility, but recover it at last to wed Julia and Silvia. Leaving Julia, Proteus runs after his friend Valentine to Milan, falls in love with the friend's amour Silvia, and then treacherously gets Silvia's father the Duke to banish Valentine. Missing her Proteus, Julia disguises herself as a page to journey to Milan, where she enters Proteus's service. With new falseness, Proteus pretends to win Silvia for Sir Thurio, while trying to make love to her. Valentine— chosen by outlaws as their king, because he is handsome and a linguist—eventually confronts Proteus, who is about to rape Silvia. Moved by his friend's total repentance, Valentine renounces his own loving claim to Silvia—or, as he tells Proteus, in lines that can still mortify the play's critics:

By penitence th'Eternal's wrath's appeased.
And that my love may appear plain and free,
All that was mine in Silvia I give thee.

(v. iv. 81–3)

That ludicrous gesture, at least, signals to us that the friends are at last resuming the habits of gentility they left behind in Act I. After the 'page' swoons and reveals herself to be Julia, Proteus recalls his love for her. Valentine, with the Duke's consent, prepares to marry Silvia, and two happy couples will return to Milan for a double wedding and bliss ever after.

Technically—as Stanley Wells has ably shown—the young playwright's handling of this story has drawbacks. Unwilling or unable to orchestrate group scenes, Shakespeare relies on soliloquies, duologues, and asides throughout; in one bad mishmash, two soliloquies come together.[41] Some of the poetry (as in the lovely song 'Who is Silvia?') has an April-like freshness, but some of it is shallow, humdrum padding, and a few speeches might be spoken by disembodied voices. The outlaws, even as parodies, are feeble; they might be children trying to imagine what adults would say. Thurio and the Duke are pasteboard; Valentine is almost brainless, though affecting. Speed the page seems like a pert, saucy Lylyan page, and the play echoes sententious remarks on women and love in Lyly's *Sapho and Phao*.

But if it is close in temper to Lyly's world, *Two Gentlemen* is not quite Lylyan, and grammar-school training in *imitatio* has served the young playwright well. Borrowing and assimilating widely, as if he could hardly trust what he knows of life, Shakespeare is an accomplished parasite. He lifts part of the story from a Queen's players' drama known as 'felix & philiomena', of 1585, or from Nicolas Collin's French translation of Jorge de Montemayor's Portuguese story *Diana Enamorada*, upon which 'felix' is probably based. He apparently looks into Puttenham's *English Poesie* treatise, works up an incident from Ovid, and takes numerous details from Arthur Brooke's romantic poem *Romeus and Juliet* (1562).

But, extensive as it is, his deft borrowing is already more nearly a habit of mind—or habit of being—than an artistic necessity.

Shakespeare did not always depend on literary models or existing sources, and much of *Two Gentlemen* springs from invention. Images, devices, or plots he takes up he usually changes. He had learned to 'vary' from literary sources at school when he was hearing simple sentimental exhortations to bold action: 'Lyfte up thy heart', says Palingenius in the English translation of a school text, 'and walke the depth apace.' To make good use of a source was to 'walke the depth', or boldly to further one's new, appropriate enterprise. Borrowing from literary models helped one to escape from the vices of singularity and useless invention. Furthermore, despite the ambiguous evidence of the Sonnets, Shakespeare seems to have flourished with a certain annihilation of the sense of himself and a profoundly sympathetic absorption in other, imagined viewpoints. His conception of his fellow actors' preferences and abilities on stage—and his awareness of viewpoints implicit in his sources—must often have helped him to write more freely.

If he wrote *Two Gentlemen* before 1592, the play was modish. Its clown Lance—and Lance's dog Crab—would have been theatrically advanced at any time in the 1590s; for though there had been clowns before, the actor playing Lance—and the real dog on stage, who 'acts' what he is—keep up a fictive illusion but also break it, with new, uneasy, yet intense comic effects. Into an elegant, artificial world, Lance brings his earthy peasant realism, as when he takes the blame for what Crab did under the Duke's table in a 'pissing-while' (IV. iv. 19). He barely advances the plot, but by berating his dog as unfeeling he highlights Proteus's stony behaviour with Julia—and offsets the all-too-genteel silliness of Valentine.

Julia is so affecting that she nearly destroys an artful, fragile balance. The author invests her with religious imagery before causing her to suffer. He gives to both Julia and Silvia an inner strength denied his men, as if he were recalling the two pious women in his father's home at Henley Street. It is most unlikely that Julia is, in any sense, a portrait of Anne Shakespeare; but the playwright has learned from his women. He so expertly evokes Julia's feelings that she becomes more moving than is necessary for his play. Most of all, he reveals himself as an unemphatic and astute writer producing a script stronger than the sum of its gaucheries; he has a natural bent for romantic comedy—already he is out-distancing Greene—and a genial tolerance of absurdity, which may be one reason why actors liked him.

We know nothing of the *Two Gentlemen*'s Tudor performances. But in 1598 Francis Meres cites it first in a list of Shakespeare's comedies, so it had had a vogue. The play was mainly conventional, but witty enough to flatter refined London tastes. Its movement is brisk and light, its courtly symmetry pleasing. Its greatest character may be Crab, who speaks no line at all. Julia's role suggests the author's talent for tragedy, and at about the time when the *Two Gentlemen* was new, two writers of tragedy had begun to transform the London stage.

8

ATTITUDES

Up Fish Street! Down Saint Magnus' Corner! Kill and
knock down! Throw them into Thames!

(Jack Cade, *2 Henry VI*)

Marlowe, Kyd, and Shoreditch

*S*hakespeare's likely evolving duties in a troupe, as well as his attitudes to Marlowe and Kyd, his own plays, and even what is known of
his London milieu, give us a chance to examine him rather closely.
What is unique in his inward development? After some experience as
an actor and theatre-poet, how did he make the most use of his
talents?

Even in comparison with John Lyly, he bursts into flower as a poet
with astonishing suddenness. Lyly had had the two elegant prose
romances of *Euphues* and *Euphues and his England* behind him when
he wrote his first play. Soon after school, Shakespeare must have
penned something other than epistles and orations; his amateurish
'hate away' sonnet, no. 145, is not beyond the skill of a bright grammar-
school boy, and it is likely that he wrote more ambitious works
during his courtship; a few years later in London he may have revised
or added to works by other writers.[1] Yet in a work such as *Two Gentlemen* he proved his real value to a troupe. His exotic, rather Petrarchan and Italianate manner suited a fashion, as though he had
been able to capitalize on a vogue and please Inns of Court men, city
gentry and their wives, and foreign visitors. As Thomas Nashe put it in
1592, the afternoon was 'the idlest time of the day', and London had
many idlers waiting to be charmed, such as 'Gentlemen of the Court,
the Innes of Courte, and the number of Captaines and Souldiers
about'.[2]

Meanwhile as a receptive, impressionable actor Shakespeare was picking up hints on stage to guide his pen. His early work is saved from gross dramaturgical faults because it is a reciprocal affair; as a player himself for five or six days a week, he appears to suit players whom he meets. Tudor actors were quick to suggest and to adapt in order to survive. Work in a group abetted his stage sense, as if he had so many extra pairs of ears and eyes, and this was one of his advantages over Greene, Peele, Watson, and other 'Wits'.

Yet he was in danger of letting his facility outrun his experience of life, and of being too rushed to develop his talents well. As an actor he had to charm nut-cracking groundlings, and put up with clownish acts and lewd jigs, to which he seems to allude acidly in the Cade episodes of 2 *Henry VI* (for example, in III. i. 356–65 and IV. vii. 118–22). As a poet he had to please a tightly knit group, find time in a busy schedule to concentrate, and avoid the luxury of writing to suit himself. His first extant plays (in revised texts) are clear in structure, alive in imagery, and often felicitous in blank verse—but they can show stiff, wooden, academic writing, poor exposition, and some of the worst vices of school rhetoric. A few of his devices are extremely feeble, as when a barbarian 'army of Goths' comes on stage in Act V of *Titus Andronicus* to restore civil manners to Rome. He is more book-ish than observant, despite what actors tell him. His grasp of psychology is latent but undeveloped in *Richard III*, and several voices in *Henry VI* speak in the same well-oiled, undifferentiated manner; this was a fairly general fault in plays of the 1580s and early 1590s, and can be illustrated even from some of the plays of Marlowe and Lyly. At the outset he brings less deft felicity to exposition, or even to scenic structure, than may appear until we compare him with others; and, so far as we know, he did not supply scripts regularly until he was past 25. Few good contemporary playwrights found their stride so late.

At first, he would have had to live near other actors, and the facts are interesting. The Exchequer's Subsidy Rolls show that by October 1596 he was lodging at St Helen's parish in Bishopsgate ward, about a mile from the northern theatres. This was a well-to-do neighbour-hood near rows of small, narrow shops at St Ethelburga's and All Hallows on the Wall; it was divided by a teeming, bustling Bishopsgate

Street, which led down into Fish Street (of *2 Henry VI*) and the area of Falstaff's Eastcheap taverns and on to London Bridge. To the north the concourse led outside the walls to the liberty of Norton Folgate, muddy Hog Lane, and the theatre suburb of Shoreditch.

He came to know Shoreditch (which Stow also calls 'Soresditch' and 'Sewersditch') very well, and so did his fellow actor Christopher Beeston, whose sons Augustine, Christopher, and Robert were baptized at St Leonard's, Shoreditch, and buried there between 1604 and 1615. Beeston's younger son William—John Aubrey's acquaintance—lived near the theatre suburb as late as the early 1680s. Shakespeare must have seen its high street on many a dark morning, for when at St Helen's he had to follow a northern route to reach Burbage's Theater or the Curtain, and this took him among rickety, propped-up tenements and smelly alleys.[3]

Known for 'wenches and soldiers' Shoreditch also harboured unlicensed barber–surgeons, procurers, beggars, and others of no legal trade. The Privy Council noted in such an area 'dissolute, loose, and insolent' persons among dicing-houses, bowling-alleys, brothels, taverns, and alehouses,[4] but Burbage's men found the suburb convenient. Its cheap entertainments made it popular with young actors. Later the inquisitive Aubrey—it seems after hearing what William Beeston told him of the playwright's habits—jotted this undated note over Shakespeare's name:

> the more to be admired q [*quia*: because] he was not a company keeper
> lived in Shoreditch, wouldnt be debauched, & if invited to
> writ [that] he was in paine.[5]

Shakespeare is tactful by habit, if this is a valid memory in a family of theatre people. When actors invite him to carouse, he writes that he is 'in paine' (with toothache or worse) to avoid being debauched in a famous red-light area. How often did he use the same excuse? But Aubrey crossed out this report (for what reason we do not know) and of course failed to say when Shakespeare may have 'lived in Shoreditch'. Plague deaths were numerous there in 1592–4, and he perhaps moved a mile south when he could afford a more salubrious room.

In any case, he saw the suburb when he came up from St Helen's.

Passing the so-called Artillery Fields and Bethlehem or 'Bedlam' hospital for the insane, he would have come to Norton Folgate—where the poets Watson and Marlowe lived in 1589. To the north was Hog Lane; beyond were the bordellos that so troubled the Queen's Council, a four-aisled church, and a yard where actors were buried. To the west in trampled fields stood Burbage's Theater and the Curtain. By night the suburb must have been as lurid as Eastcheap—where Doll Tearsheet, Poins, and Pistol of *Henry IV* would disport themselves. But in the early 1590s as a poet bringing his aspirations and rhetorical training to his work, Shakespeare was slow to draw on the capital's common life; he had much more to do with players, book-sources, and scripts. Playwrights were concerned with company loyalty, parody, and imitation, and above all with fashion and 'box-office receipts'. They studied the successes of rivals, and so he came under the influence of a poet who was his senior by two months—Christopher Marlowe.

❦

Marlowe's provocative artistry affected Shakespeare more deeply than did works by other modern writers, and this poet's background was not entirely unlike his own.

Marlowe, too, was raised in a craftsman's house and schooled in the 1570s when the humanist curriculum was settled. Like Shakespeare, he received some of the best training ever available for English boys who would become poets. Most accounts of both his and the Stratford poet's schooling overlook the change that had come over intellectual life from the 1530s and 1540s, when new Latin texts poured from presses and the life of the mind was keen at Cambridge (spurred on by Cheke, Ascham, Haddon, Carr, and Christopherson among others) and, a little later, at Oxford. Masters carried over that stir into grammar classrooms, and Marlowe benefited from an excessive emphasis on poetics and rhetoric.

At Canterbury's fine King's School, he heard ritual in chapel, discovered Ovid, listened to an able master. Then as the son of a debt-ridden shoemaker who was to prove untrustworthy as warden treasurer of a local guild, he matriculated at Corpus Christi College,

Cambridge, and took on clandestine work for the Crown's secret service at some point before taking his MA degree.

His showy, blasphemous wit concealed a sensitive nature. Some of his reported statements might be no more than parodies of his gambits, and his wit, at least, is more evident in his verse than in what he is supposed to have said, such as that 'all protestantes are Hypocritical asses', or the homoerotic 'all they that love not Tobacco and Boies were fooles'. The wittiest of his supposed remarks as reported by the dubious, fairly stupid, Richard Baines compares Moses with a juggler: 'He [Marlowe] affirmeth that Moyses was but a Jugler & that one Heriots being Sir W Raleighs man Can do more than he.'[6] At any rate, down in London Marlowe was known among cronies for atheism, papist leanings, and buggery, the charge often depending on the literalness of those who listened to him. His escapades, even before his final one, could be lethal. In September 1589 he was set upon in Hog Lane by the innkeeper's son William Bradley. Intervening, his fellow poet Thomas Watson fatally drove a blade into Bradley's chest. Both poets went to prison, but Shakespeare (whether or not he 'wouldnt be debauched') may well have frequented theatre alehouses and seen Marlowe between 1590 and 1592, after the latter's release. In a comic image in *Venus and Adonis* (1593) for example, he seems to remember

> shrill-tongued tapsters answering every call,
> Soothing the humour of fantastic wits.

(lines 849–50)

The lines may be a Norton Folgate joke, with Marlowe among 'wits' in need of soothing, but we leave it to romantic biographers to take us inside smoky, suffocating alehouses. His Cambridge degree made Marlowe a gentleman, dividing him socially from a mainly unknown player, but the player seems to have acted in the Cambridge poet's *The Jew of Malta*—a work Shakespeare recalled closely in his own plays and which was not in print.

However, Marlowe helped him in other ways in a climate of feeling marked by the reign's most renowned event: the defeat of Spain's Armada of 1588. War with Spain continued through the decade of

Shakespeare's history plays, and the enemy was nearly supreme on the Continent in armed might and cultural vigour. (Sailing with the Armada had been a young unknown Lope de Vega, who with Tirso de Molina and Calderón became one of Madrid's prime playwrights.) The events of 1588 were memorable enough. At Tilbury before the sea-battle, the Queen had appeared at camp dressed in her armour 'like an Amazonian Queene', and other reports of her are possibly echoed in Shakespeare's portrait of Joan la Pucelle in *1 Henry VI*. Channel winds and four-wheeled gun-carriages had broken a giant, crescent-shaped flotilla, whose captured ensigns were later flown in London over Traitors' Gate or displayed at Paul's Cross.

In reaction, playwrights cannily wrote of earlier victories at Agincourt, Crécy, and Flodden Field. Not that the sea-victory quite preceded the making of history plays in London: we know that the actors Knell and Tarlton took parts in the popular *The Famous Victories of Henry V* at some point before the Armada's date. (Both actors died in or before 1588, and Knell's widow married John Heminges in March of that year.) But the Spanish war did set a mood for history scripts with strong political implications, and around 1587 and 1588 Marlowe appealed to that mood with his two-part *Tamburlaine*.

His hero—starting as a Scythian shepherd—rises as 'the amazement of the world' to defeat witless, effete, or blustering monarchs, and so suggests that most regimes are corrupt at the top. Mocking royalty, Tamburlaine famously shouts at his captive kings who trudge with bits in the mouth—

> Holla, ye pamper'd jades of Asia!
> What, can ye draw but twenty miles a day . . . ?
>
> (Pt. 2, IV. iii. 1–2)

Other daring plays followed from Marlowe, with intellectual features that affected Shakespeare's attitude to form and meaning. *Doctor Faustus* and *The Jew of Malta* mix tragedy with farce, and in dramatizing belief they suggest a defiance of the tyranny and prejudices of all ideologies. *The Massacre at Paris*, despite its Francophobia, probes into roots of state violence in Machiavellian speeches of its Duke of Guise that seem to have affected Shakespeare's own style—

> Give me a look, that, when I bend the brows,
> Pale death may walk in furrows of my face.
> A hand, that with a grasp may gripe the world;
> An ear to hear what my detractors say;
> A royal seat, a sceptre, and a crown.
>
> (I. ii. 100–4)

After Marlowe was murdered in 1593, Shakespeare was to pay a certain elegiac tribute, not to the craftsman or maker of plays, but to the poet of *Hero and Leander*. Marlowe had achieved a level of writing in *Hero* that Shakespeare probably felt he himself could not reach, and in fact his quoting a line of Marlowe's poem in *As You Like It* ('Whoever loved that loved not at first sight?') was an unusual gesture, though some professional esteem had been mutually signalled between the two poets. As *Tamburlaine* affected the form of *Richard III*, so the Stratford writer's early chronicle plays evidently helped Marlowe to write his spare, almost apolitical *Edward II*. And Shakespeare learned from a poet who had located drama in new psychological techniques. By isolating a Guise, Faustus, or Barabas, and letting him 'speak past' interlocutors, Marlowe showed other poets how to dramatize a fascinating, aberrant psyche, display its suffering, and get a mind to lend its tone to a drama. Shakespeare seems to borrow from these methods for his Titus, Henry VI, and Richard of Gloucester, and to develop them later with egocentrics such as Hamlet, Coriolanus, and Timon.

'Kind Kit Marlowe'—as he was recalled—forgave 'Wits' for attacking him in print. Shakespeare, too, could be amenable and forgiving; at least, after being attacked in a work published by Henry Chettle, he was 'civil' with Chettle. But he was never likely to imitate Marlowe's personal braggadocio, sensation-hunting, or relish of confrontation. As a man obliged to work in a troupe, Shakespeare practised a certain husbandry with such experience as he had. If he played many parts in a season, he was not eccentric, picturesque, or attention-seeking after rehearsals; he was taken by most of his fellows for the clever and reliable colleague he seemed to be. He was an agreeable, cautious person, whose offstage experience, so far, had been intense rather than very wide, as his early plays and sonnets suggest.

Yet, if slower than Marlowe to do so, he was now showing a remarkable power of development, and this marked him out in the 1590s. That power depended, in part, on an excellent memory which must have served him in boyhood among 'grammar gods', as later it surely did on stage.

As we have seen, other Tudor actors, of course, retained many lines, and what is quite unusual is not the tenacity of Shakespeare's memory but its evocative power. In recalling the countryside he invokes the tones, feelings, and ambience of a Midlands past, and his recollecting complicates and renews his life of the sensations and intellect. He draws on a deep, fresh well of impressions of provincial life; he connects easily in *Titus Andronicus* with the Roman culture of his school-days, and elsewhere with known, curricular lessons pointing back to history's grandeur. In effect he repossesses his grammar-school learning to elaborate on it, and Shakespeare's plays exhibit school techniques, as in *controversiae* and *imitatio*, which become ever more refined and sophisticated. He appears to benefit from early complications at Shottery, and what he knows of courtship culture is recalled with exactitude in London. It is not in writing tragedy or chronicle plays that he is at ease at first (or lucky enough to avoid expository blunders), but in writing romantic comedy. His past continually instructs him, and with a conservative impulse he carried a good deal of Stratford to London.

Moreover, one source of tension helping him to develop is illuminated by recent, close investigations of his Midlands town and of aspects of sixteenth-century London. He knew contrasting social orders: from the almost medieval, well-regulated parish of his youth he had come into the anarchic, splintered world of the suburbs, where success in the theatre depended on chance, luck, agility, and quick rational effort. Stratford had its mercantile competitiveness, too, but it was also a place of older, communal and religious values, with traditions in behaviour and feeling opposed to those of the pragmatic, opportunistic stage. Formed largely by the pieties and temper of his home he was likely to exert himself without feeling quite satisfied with anything he did, and he had some reason in the tatty suburbs to regret the theatre.

In his Sonnets, he smartens feelings that he knows well. One problem he alludes to more than once is the vulgarity of acting, or the stain imparted to the actor and the actor's reputation, and so he implies in Sonnet III that a 'guilty goddess'—such as Fate or Ill Luck—has placed him in an unseemly, raw, exposed calling which offers no better way of getting a living, 'Than public means which public manners breeds.'

He appears to apologize stylishly for a calling of low to middling repute, no doubt with a wish to please friends or patrons who read his sonnets. But his behaviour suggests that he could not forget the related matter of his own family's need for respectability in a Midlands town. Some facts of the matter are clear in official borough Minutes and Accounts. As we know, his father had absconded from the brethren's council, and the brethren, of course, had lost patience: in 1586 they had deprived John Shakespeare of an alderman's gown. A series of harvest failures lay ahead, but early in the 1590s Stratford's economic plight was already acute; the crafts and trades could not employ all the talented, able young. Gossip was sharp in a market town, and unlikely to diminish in bitter times. William Shakespeare had three brothers who needed work, two daughters who might require husbands, and a boy in Hamnet who might finish school at Church Street. His own choices had not enhanced his social status; he needed money to help his family, but the public mercenary actor had never emerged from a certain shade. It is not unpaid actors, but those who go on the stage for reward ('propter praemium in scenam prodeunt') who are blameworthy, as the Roman jurist Ulpian had declared. Modern Oxford took up that theme. Who vulgarizes our theatre? as William Gager asked in a scene he added to Seneca's *Hippolytus* at Oxford in February 1592. And he answers in his own Latin:

> Qui sui spectaculum
> Mercedis ergo praebet, infamis siet.
> Non ergo quenquam Scena, sed quaestus, notat.[7]

[Whoever puts on a show for gain, let him be infamous. Not acting on a stage, but doing so for reward, disgraces a man.]

And yet, though he cannot have been insensitive to notions of respectability, Shakespeare was sanguine enough to hope to improve his lot, and to move into some position of safety and profitability. He could hardly return with equanimity to the circumstances at Stratford. And the theatre offered him anonymity, at least; only a few actors' names had resonance with the public. The city's *cognoscenti* might know who wrote the best scripts, but attention fixed on stars, lively dramas, or scandal, not on the scriptwriters. Marlowe's name meant so little that the two *Tamburlaine* dramas were printed without it in 1590—and only a chance remark, by Heywood, tells us that Kyd wrote the most influential English play of the sixteenth century, *The Spanish Tragedy*.

❧

Shakespeare was quick enough to admire profitable works. Thomas Kyd had not been to university—a defect unlikely to be forgiven by some 'Wits'—but his father, a city scrivener, had sent him to Merchant Taylors' School under the gifted Richard Mulcaster. With a rare gift for play structure, Kyd around 1587 may have written *Hamlet*, the missing revenge tragedy now famous as 'ur-Hamlet' since it must have been a source for Shakespeare's later tragedy. Revived at Newington Butts on 9 June 1594, when even a Marlowe play did poorly, *Hamlet* earned a paltry 8s. for Henslowe.[8] But if (as we think) it played at the Theater and Paris Garden it held the stage fitfully for perhaps thirteen years before Shakespeare turned to the subject.

In *The Spanish Tragedy*, his masterpiece, of uncertain date but perhaps of the late 1580s, Kyd uses a patterned manner to evoke extremes of impassioned feeling. The effect upon Shakespeare might have been as if Mulcaster's rhetoric lessons at Merchant Taylors' had been superimposed abruptly on those of Jenkins' at Stratford. Kyd's hero—Hieronimo—is a decent Spanish magistrate driven to wild grief and then to a crazed, clever, bloody revenge in a play-within-the-play after his son is murdered. Alleyn or young Ben Jonson, as old Hieronimo, may have shattered the groundlings' hearts—

O eyes, no eyes, but fountains fraught with tears;
O life, no life, but lively form of death;
O world, no world, but mass of public wrongs,
Confused and filled with murder and misdeeds!

(III. ii. 1–4)

That was easily parodied—as were Marlowe's lines on the harnessed kings. But Londoners responded to Kyd's aural symmetries, and Shakespeare was to appeal to the same gusto of delight in orchestrated language. Also, Kyd's play has rich seams of interest. He uses a revenge theme cleverly to bring in a variety of other appeals and concerns, such as justice, sexual passion, politics, duplicity, even play-acting, as in Shakespeare's *Hamlet*. His Spanish court is believable, and he shows how the concerns of a well-meaning king thwart or impel those caught up in a diabolic tangle of court policy.

South of the river at the Rose, Kyd and Marlowe in fact made high tragedy profitable. They emboldened Shakespeare, who needed to enhance his usefulness as times became harder. Miseries of war and inflation threatened all the players—even before death came massively to the city, as we shall see. And Whitehall was capricious. Lately the Puritans had made a bold case for church reform in a series of illegal, vituperative 'Martin Marprelate' tracts. At first the government employed theatre-poets to reply to the outrageous 'Martin', and then turned viciously against their own helpers.

In fact, the Privy Council warned sharply of 'matters of Divinytie and of state' unfit to be suffered on a stage.[9] But actors feared penury as much as prison, and around 1590 Shakespeare had begun to take his chances.

'I am the sea': *Titus Andronicus* and the *Shrew*

After some of them had been in prison, an exceptional group of men and boys had met west of Shoreditch's taverns in 1590. Comprising former members of Strange's and the Lord Admiral's troupes, this was an amalgamated company which lasted for four years under Lord Strange's (or the Earl of Derby's) patronage as the most successful body of actors in England. To their book-keeper, Shakespeare appears to have given his first tragedy, *Titus Andronicus.*

Just when he wrote this play is uncertain, and it could have had a debut at Henslowe's Rose rather than at Shoreditch. But he planned the work on a grand scale: its first act requires at least twenty-six players if we allow for 'doubling' in roles. Stagehands and 'gatherers' might take parts at a pinch, but *Titus* was meant for a large company such as Lord Strange's, which is the first troupe listed on the title-page of John Danter's quarto edition of the play in 1594.

Shakespeare counted on skilled tragedians, too, and much talent had come to Shoreditch. Famous in the new amalgamation was Edward Alleyn himself, a golden voiced 'fustian king' of about 26, and a glittering figure as he turned on a platform in a long, brocaded coat or the crimson velvet breeches he had worn in Marlowe's *Tamburlaine*. Such a man wore large, false mirroring jewellery with metal lace to catch the afternoon light. Burbage's son Richard was on hand—not yet rivalling Alleyn—and so was a thin, spindly John Sincler, soon to act in *The Taming of the Shrew*. Other actors had been abroad: George Bryan, Thomas Pope, and Will Kempe had entertained the Danes at Elsinore, and Pope and Bryan had gone on to the Elector at Dresden before coming to Shoreditch. Kempe, the clown, was back in London by 1590, and if he did not join Strange's group at once, he soon played in their comic *A Knack to Know a Knave*.

Shakespeare faced a troupe hungry for success, aware of their excellence. He was, in effect, their servant. His personality and even his play are related to his lack of status in these years: even as a sharer he was not to be so important to a troupe as its most famous actors, and amenity, modesty, agreeableness, and a certain jocular, detached attitude to his script would have served him well. At this point, he wrote parts that might be instantly familiar to those who would act them. *Titus*, in some respects, is cautiously imitative; its black, Moorish villain Aaron, laughing at atrocities, is like a Marlowe villain, just as its aggrieved, half-crazed hero Titus resembles Kyd's Hieronomo.

Notoriously Shakespeare fills his action with bizarre, numbing atrocities: dripping pig's blood is called for. The worst happens offstage, but three hands in this tragedy are chopped off, and a tongue is torn out. Titus kills one of his offspring in fury, another in shame. Most of the characters are emblematic puppets, but the play ably exploits visual properties in a well-painted, sensuously pleasing theatre and posits a malignant, nightmarish 'wilderness of tigers', a Rome featuring sizzling entrails, rape, dismemberment, slit throats, vivid torture, cooked heads in a pie, a cannibal feast. Titus's and Aaron's roles have life, and it may be valid that the playwright's first wholly successful portrait is that of a black man. (Though not the first Elizabethan to praise black skin-colour, Shakespeare is without much competition the most eloquent: Aaron's 'black-is-beautiful' speeches in Act IV are compelling.) But Aaron is only a speechless supernumerary in Act I. Titus's own faults are hardly emphasized as he enters Rome with his dead and living sons, a captive Queen Tamora of the Goths, and her paramour Aaron, and in cold piety orders a son of Tamora to be butchered. His political mistakes expose him and the Andronici to exquisite torture, and at first there is no consolation whatever. When Lavinia totters on stage in Act II, raped, tongueless, without hands, she is greeted by her uncle Marcus with a picturesque speech imitated from Ovid.

The play, however, can be much better to see than to read, and stylistic defects which we imagine in the text can magically disappear in a good stage production. More than a young poet's insecurity is evident. Meeting the demands for a Kyd-like revenge script, he manages to absorb what others were discovering about tragedy. He is in some ways less tactful than Ovid in *Metamorphoses* or Seneca in *Thyestes* in handling myth, but he brings a well-considered attitude to events. He represents carefully a Tudor view of ancient Rome, a city which in its republican phase seemed to have benefited from austere family virtues, before sinking into impiety and hedonism under the later empire. His materials help him to think of cities old and new, of Rome and London. He finds an emblem in Philomela's change into a nightingale after her particularly cruel rape by Tereus, and in woods where Lavinia is raped, a change for all Rome is signalled in Marcus's allusions to Ovid's myth.

The classical myth of transformation in the play is somewhat febrile and overstrained, though it is anxiously pointed up, as when a copy of

Ovid's *Metamorphoses* is literally brought on stage in Act IV. Still it is by means of his intellect, even his academic excess, that Shakespeare in this case preserves his integrity; his use of Ovid helps him to organize a story, impose a meaning on events, and also consolidate his outlook, so that the play relates even to the comic *Two Gentlemen*, the *Shrew*, and his other early works in which metamorphoses in being, attitude, or awareness occur.

And *Titus* is a work of immense promise for his constructive abilities. His lovely, varying, and ominous uses of nature help him to highlight the bestiality he depicts. To some extent he brings into the work just such a view of London as a sensitive countryman might bring from the fields and forests of the Midlands. He had seen a workable, civilized order (by and large) within London's walls, beyond which were the vulnerable and chaotic suburbs. What preserves an urban society? What threatens it? His Tamora is an emblem of corruption, a woman no longer nurturing but bestialized, rather like the women who were reduced to selling their bodies for male pleasure at Bankside or Shoreditch brothels. Much that he had known at Stratford was replicated in the capital, but not the lawless sordidness, the dens, procurers, and syphilitic women whom the actors talked about. From a mean, often debased, life of the theatre areas he at first drew little, but implicit in *Titus* is the corrupt, desperate face of a London that would have impressed him most as new in his experience.

He has relied in the play not only on the precedents of Kyd, Marlowe, and Peele, but on Ovid, Seneca, and the Roman historians. No other urban playwright had drawn on so many diverse sources to produce such a coherent, well-planned work, though a few of the élite saw little beyond its dazzling show.

At some point most likely between 1604 and 1615, Henry Peacham was to draw a 'composite' scene from *Titus* in which the chief actors are seen in Roman dress, the others in Elizabethan. Whether or not he had seen the play, he gives a visual idea of it: his pen-sketch displays Aaron the Moor wielding a sword, while a tall Tamora on her knees pleads for her two rapist sons. Earlier, on 1 January 1596, Jacques Petit, a Gascon servant of Anthony Bacon, had been struck chiefly by the work's visual effects. This play had more value in the show ('la monstre') than in the subject, as he wrote of a country-house production by London players that he had seen at Burley-on-the-Hill in Rutland.[10] (That was about a hundred miles from London, and Shakespeare may have been among the actors if the Chamberlain's Servants came that far north.) Also, a cartoon which circulated with a broadside ballad, perhaps in the 1590s, shows Lavinia, blonde hair down to her knees, prettily holding a pan with her stumps to catch blood squirting from the neck of a Goth who has raped her.[11]

The play's spectacular nature and its Kyd-like qualities dated it, and in later years Ben Jonson mocked the mode of '*Andronicus*'. Yet Shakespeare was altering the traditions of the English tragic hero, especially in his depiction of Titus's pain and suffering. From this portrait there were lessons he would use later in representing Othello, Timon, or King Lear. Titus's verse is revealing in and through the stunning force of its beauty, as when in bitter isolation and despair he declares,

> If there were reason for these miseries,
> Then into limits could I bind my woes.
> When heaven doth weep, doth not the earth o'erflow?
> If the winds rage, doth not the sea wax mad,
> Threat'ning the welkin with his big-swoll'n face?
> And wilt thou have a reason for this coil?
> I am the sea. Hark how her sighs doth blow.
>
> (III. i. 218–24)

Writing to suit a troupe's strength, Shakespeare experimented with more complex plots and romantic stories. It seems *The Taming of the Shrew* was also staged at an early point, in all probability before June 1592, by Strange's men.

Based on old, brutal folk-myths of the young wife 'tamed' by a husband who beats and terrifies her, this play ostensibly focuses on an economic issue. A self-reliant suitor, on his travels, only need marry a wealthy gentleman's daughter to prosper. But the daughter is a 'shrew', and her wealth means less in the suitor's eyes than the game of shrew-taming. Granted that one Katherine Minola, of Padua, will not be dictated to by a man, how is a well-born Petruccio of Verona to make her yield her independence? Intensely erotic, the story takes on issues of subservience and power, a male dread of dominant females, and a Renaissance fear of women in domestic rebellion.

All of which tasks Shakespeare's structural talent. He weaves in three plot-strands—Kate in relation to Petruccio, her sister Bianca with suitors, and an Induction (or framing device) involving the drunken Midlands tinker Christopher Sly—and does so with a skill that may seem to leave *Titus* and *The Two Gentlemen* behind. He also opens a Pandora's box, and his view of his materials is ambiguous and unresolved. He has not quite made up his mind about shrew-taming—let alone about a society which can isolate a woman and quickly rob her of everything but her courage. Petruccio's and Kate's talk is colloquial, earthy, often bawdy, sharp as a slap in the face, enriched by snippets from country folk-tales and legends. The playwright looks into the mirror and over its edge into remembrances of his past, so that the *Shrew* in effect greatly expands his supply for play-making.

He considerably opens up Warwickshire at any rate and his allusions in the Induction are fascinating. Christopher Sly's name relates to that of Stratford's own Stephen Sly, who later resisted enclosure at Welcombe. Duped by a bored, prankish nobleman into thinking himself a wedded aristocrat, Sly has a 'wife' in the young page Bartholomew, whose name is that of the poet's brother-in-law, lately returned to Shottery and the sibling closest to Anne Shakespeare in age. Sly is from 'Burton-heath', which suggests the hamlet of Barton-on-the-Heath of the poet's uncle and aunt Edmund and Joan Lambert, whose son and heir was sued by John and Mary Shakespeare—with one 'Willielmo Shackespere filio suo'—in vain in 1588.[12] (Since Shakespeare is named in that legal action he must have heard of it, and his Barton relatives remained a thorn in his father's flesh.) A servant mentions 'Cicely Hacket', and Sly refers to 'Marian Hacket, the fat alewife of Wincot'. Here we are about four miles from Stratford—a Hacket family lived at Wincot's very small hamlet at the time of the play. On 21 November 1591, Robert Hacket's daughter Sara was baptized in Wincot's parish church at Quinton. The Induction also evokes a local playing troupe such as that of Frances Hathaway's husband, Davy Jones.

For the playwright such allusions are memory-devices, echoes of use, comic connections with a recent past. But the Induction also has an odd, hallucinatory sheen of memory, and Sly lives in a waking dream between falsehood and reality as he sits down to watch a play, 'a kind of history', as his 'wife' Bartholomew calls it, and *The Taming of the Shrew* unfolds before their amazed eyes. Or has Sly dreamed up all the action that follows?

Sly, in fact, is important enough to be in both scenes of the Induction, and he may well have been brought back to comment on the action *after* Act V (thus with Warwickshire scenes surrounding those of Padua). However, he reappears only at the end of a very similar play called *The Taming of a Shrew*. Did actors on the road reconstruct the weaker *A Shrew*, from memories of performing in Shakespeare's *The Shrew*? Scholars debate this point; we do not know. Clearly though, there was a disruption in Strange's company: for example *Titus Andronicus* went out of their hands to be acted by Pembroke's men, and later, it seems, successfully at the Rose, by Sussex's players.

The most serious convulsion we know about in the amalgamated Strange–Admiral troupe split it apart. In May 1591, Alleyn had cornered the crusty impresario James Burbage in the Theater's tiring-house, at the back of the stage, to ask what had become of money due the players. As usual, his friend knew nothing of money. Alleyn heated up. On behalf of others, he told Burbage sarcastically that 'belike he meant to deale with them, as he did with the poor wydowe', the survivor of Burbage's partner in the Theater—Margaret Brayne. If things came to that, he, Alleyn, would complain to the Lord Admiral! With an oath, Burbage shouted that he cared nothing for the three 'best lordes of them all'.

The result was that Alleyn withdrew from Shoreditch. He took leading actors, such as Bryan, Pope, Augustine Phillips, and possibly John Heminges, down with him to Henslowe's Rose on Bankside, married Henslowe's stepdaughter within a year for good measure, and led the Strange–Admiral troupe in evil times of touring during plague. Shakespeare may possibly have stayed behind at the Theater with men such as Richard Burbage, Sincler, Condell, Tooley, and Beeston.[13] Some of these actors, at any rate, soon turned up in Pembroke's company, which had several Shakespeare plays in its repertory and came to such grief on the road its members had to pawn their own playing apparel.

Annihilation of some of the troupes and the closing of all theatrical venues in and near London was at hand. Like others, Shakespeare had very little security as a theatre man, but before the plague he had attempted something new; in taking English history as his subject he had begun to make one of the most sustained efforts of his life.

The white rose of York

In a sense, he had begun to do so just in time. His dramatization of Henry VI's reign drew comments in a plague year—1592—during the latter half of which no London theatre was open. But all three parts of *Henry VI* must have been penned before the plague, and he may already have begun to write *Richard III* or completed that fourth work in a historical sequence or tetralogy about the Wars of the Roses.

His subject—the fifteenth-century Lancastrian wars—sent him to the English chronicles, and here he found many problems. To justify his own claim to the throne Henry VII, the first Tudor king, had hired an Italian humanist named Polydore Vergil to write a proper history of England. Whitewashing the Tudors, Vergil had portrayed Richard III as a blood-mad fiend whose death at Bosworth in 1485 had brought Henry's own glorious line to power. In an ironic biography Sir Thomas More had further established an image of Richard III as a lip-gnawing, crook-backed killer whom people loved to hate.

But chroniclers wrote more and more about reigns before the Tudors, and early in the 1590s antiquarian works of many kinds came from London's presses and beyond. By 1576 Cambridge had its own press after appointing John Kingston as their printer, and eight years later Oxford's Convocation had loaned £100 to the bookseller Joseph Barnes to set up a press of its own. New data about the British past increased national pride and self-consciousness, but also whetted interest in royal power and abetted a certain popular cynicism. People were sceptical about authority, disenchanted by economic hardship. Royal pageantry and civic ritual abounded in London as if to show the smooth, superficial face of authority, whereas the chroniclers, now and then, offered intimate glimpses of power.

Strange's men had featured Henry VI as a vague morality-play hero in *Seven Deadly Sins*. But to look for a king in history or to attempt to see him realistically was to plunge into a welter of annalistic detail—for instance in Robert Fabyan's *New Chronicles* (1516), Edward Hall's *The Union of the Two Noble and Illustre Families of Lancaster and York* (1548), which lifts *in extenso* from Polydore Vergil, or Richard Grafton's *Chronicles* (1562–72), John Stow's *Chronicles* and *Annales* (dating from 1565), or the immense composite *Chronicles of England, Scotland, and Ireland* (1577 and 1587) which we call Raphael Holinshed's, though they incorporate work done by other Tudor historians for over seventy years.

In the expanded edition of 1587, Holinshed's *Chronicles*—three folio volumes with seven title-pages, and 3½ million words—was to be an oceanic source for at least thirteen of Shakespeare's plays. This work is not limited to any single ideology or historical thesis, and although it divides its chronicle, starting with William the Conqueror, into reigns, it opens up history on the basis of a giant random inclusiveness. It does not overrule the viewpoints of its many component sources. For Shakespeare this great text was a spacious library and supplier of detail; its jumbled vastness, multiple viewpoints, and fertile inconsistencies allowed space for his imagination to play. He reacted to Holinshed—somewhat as he did to Golding's version of Ovid—as to a very literal, unfanciful version of what was in the true 'thing' itself, in this case the documents of British historical experience, with judgement about the 'thing' left open. Beset by problems of form, he seems to have found that Hall's *Two Noble and Illustre Families* at least gave a shape to the fifteenth century in depicting a curve of events over eight reigns from Richard II (1377–99)—from the time of the Mowbray–Bolingbroke quarrel—to Richard III's death in 1485 and the union of the red and white roses of Lancaster and York under the first Tudor king. Hall moralizes, without really showing the hand of God shaping events. Before *Richard III*, Shakespeare eschews any emphasis on a 'providential plan' in history, but gains coherence in his use of abrasive conflict, ritual, and sharp ironies in all three parts of *Henry VI*.

He had set himself the most challenging of tasks, in that he now had to respond imaginatively to history's chaos. Nothing in Hall or Holinshed has anything like the appealing dramatic order of an Italian or French *novella*; yet he had to bring the liveliest order to *Henry VI*. The stage asked for clarity, intensity, and expert design as he re-embodied the English dead. The chronicles allowed him to expand upon details, but he was working within terribly restricting boundaries, and thus forcing his imagination and analytical intelligence to act to produce a cogent structure while always being aware of facts he had to exclude. The notion that his talent was 'miraculous' undercuts the many small, conscious efforts he had to make in his choices and deft borrowings. In *Henry VI*, he was relying on more than the chronicles, fusing with them elements of popular culture: he took something from the sportive, festive and impudent antics of Lords of Misrule, something from political cabaret, from Robert Wilson's popular patriotic dramas, and from Peele's and Greene's sentimental history scenes. He was helped by Sidney's *Arcadia* (1590), which, under the guise of pastoral convention, explores the idiosyncratic faults of aristocratic regimes, and he learned from Spenser's delicate finesse and insights into human power and temptation in the first three books of *The Faerie Queene* (1590).

Arguably, for his history series he wrote *1 Henry VI* first. A work of some expository stiffness, though it rises to masterly stagecraft in its 'Temple Garden' scene for example, it involved him in a ruthless selection from sources. The politically weak and morally good Henry VI had acceded in infancy and reigned for forty years. Later the first Tudor king tried to have Henry canonized, after his alleged miracles interested Pope Alexander VI. Wisely keeping the good king offstage at first, Shakespeare brings to the fore Lord Talbot, who has among his titles 'Lord Strange of Blackmere' (IV. vii. 65). Talbot's chivalry is considerably heightened in the play—as in his relations with the Countess of Auvergne, the most charming of would-be assassins— and the contrasting cowardice of one Sir John Fastolf, or Falstaff, who fled at the battle of Rouen, is also emphasized. One doubts that topical satire is aimed at Falstaff's living descendants, but in his heroic view of Talbot, Shakespeare, rather like Nashe in *Pierce Penilesse*, may go out of his way to flatter Lord Strange.

Most of the characters in *1 Henry VI* are quite unheroic. The play shows quarrels at home and calamity abroad, from Henry V's funeral in 1422 to Lord Talbot's death and England's final loss of France in 1453. Brutal, acerbic confrontations occur, but mere sensation is avoided. Here the stage does not symbolize a fictive violence as in *Titus*, but rather, shocking events of a bitterly terrible past reality. France is no worse than England. Talbot's mortal enemy Joan la Pucelle at first seems recognizably Jeanne d'Arc. She is imaged as Deborah, as 'Astraea's daughter', even as 'France's saint' (I. viii. 29). Later she is as duplicitous as Spenser's Duessa in *The Faerie Queene*, but Shakespeare includes a fictive siege of Rouen, and he may have been obliged to show Joan in a patriotic light—British troops under the Earl of Essex were in fact besieging Rouen from November 1591 to April 1592. Even so, Joan turns to devils and venery when the powers of light fail her, claims to be pregnant to avoid martyrdom, and is no worse at last than an amusing, pragmatic witch.

Shakespeare's French hardly seem Catholic, except for an allusion to Joan's Mariolatry, and he does not refer to Catholic repression. His satire is that of a moderate Anglican, and at its root is a resigned, calm gravity as if death were history's chief fact. He ridicules a vain, meddling Bishop of Winchester for getting money from bordellos, yet not for doctrine. Implicitly he has pity for the fatally mistaken, and admiration for wasted splendours of feeling in his doomed barons. His battle scenes are little more than brief calamitous testimonies to man's ignorance and absurdity.

In *2 Henry VI* he gains an advantage in placing his weak, unworldly Henry, now subject to a vicious Queen Margaret, at the centre of the action, so that the paralysis of a state can be depicted ironically.[14] His Jack Cade episodes in their fresh, mordant humour comment indirectly on his own Tudor audiences. Aiming to overthrow the Crown by stirring up unrest, the Duke of York has enlisted a headstrong Kentishman, 'John Cade of Ashford', for the purpose. Cade's rabble soon conquer London on the rampage. Parodying inversions of Misrule, and of 'barring out' when pupils smashed school windows, Cade inverts civilized codes with cheerful blasphemy. He legalizes his lust: 'There shall not a maid be married, but she shall pay to me her maidenhead' (IV. vii. 118–20). Heads of nobles are made to kiss on poles. A clerk is hanged with 'pen and inkhorn about his neck' (IV. ii. 108–9). Literacy is a crime—all lawyers are to be killed in Cade's London, while the city's 'pissing-conduit' (IV. vi. 3) flows conveniently with claret wine. Cade's rabble in mindless enthusiasm are like sensation-hunting play-goers, and as he is likened to a capering 'Morisco' himself, he is a type of the lewd jig-performer who dances at the end of dramas at Burbage's Theater. Still, Cade can be a spokesman of thematic truth as when he impugns the vain peers who 'consult about the giving up of some more towns in France' (IV. vii. 150–1).

Cade's quick fall foreshadows that of the Duke of York. Early in *3 Henry VI*, the author brings his nightmare story of feuding nobles to a pitch when the Duke of York, without his sons Edward, George, or Richard to save him, falls into the hands of a bloodthirsty Queen Margaret. That 'She-wolf of France', as York names her, with her 'tiger's heart wrapped in a woman's hide' provokes him with galling mockery:

> And where's that valiant crookback prodigy,
> Dickie, your boy, that with his grumbling voice
> Was wont to cheer his dad in mutinies?
> Or with the rest where is your darling Rutland?
> Look, York, I stained this napkin with the blood
> That valiant Clifford with his rapier's point
> Made issue from the bosom of thy boy.
> And if thine eyes can water for his death,
> I give thee this to dry thy cheeks withal.
>
> (I. iv. 76–84)

Hatred is evoked with an intensity new to the stage—and Shakespeare's rival Greene was jealously to recall this scene. Margaret's hatred arises in a fine pattern in *Henry VI*, though there have been no villains; the author refuses to promote one political doctrine over another, and his events seem ritualized in history's fixed past. To some extent he makes the theatre a ritual for the public, and indeed his early history plays have a strong liturgical aspect—which may be too overtly developed in *Richard III*.

But here in *Richard III*, brilliantly, he carries into a single individual's consciousness the allegorical method of many medieval morality plays. No doubt he could hardly have avoided the Tudor myth of Richard of Gloucester as a 'divine scourge', sent by heaven to punish and purge the realm. Rather more than a symbolic scourge, however, Richard is as idiosyncratic as Aaron of *Titus Andronicus*, whom he resembles. He has won his father's praise: 'Richard hath best deserved of all my sons', as the Duke of York says in *3 Henry VI* (I. i. 17). Unlike Hamlet to come, this son is not bent chiefly on avenging his father's death. Since peace has robbed Richard of his identity he will entirely refashion himself:

> I in this weak piping time of peace
> Have no delight to pass away the time,
> Unless to spy my shadow in the sun
> And descant on mine own deformity.
> And therefore since I cannot prove a lover
> To entertain these fair well-spoken days,
> I am determinèd to prove a villain.
>
> (I. i. 24–30)

To achieve that end, he is endowed with several of the author's own attributes, such as a talent for artful language, a delight in dry wit, and a belief in the inexhaustible powers of acting and make-believe. He becomes a Machiavel with a lustrous veneer of grace, and at first a merry Vice, an actor on delightful terms with the audience. No more charming and fascinating killer had been seen on the Elizabethan stage.

Opposed to carping politicians, stupid power-seekers and depleted moralists, he is even endearing up to Act IV. Like Jack Cade, Richard has the advantage of enduring for a while without the baggage of human conscience, which with its aspect of nemesis is transferred to Clarence, Lady Anne, or the railing spectre of Queen Margaret. With the intelligent gaiety of a *poseur* he is never more effective than when courting Lady Anne, whose husband and father-in-law he has murdered.

Here the playwright squeezes historical events together so that

Henry VI's actual funeral rites in 1471, Richard's courtship of Anne in 1472, Clarence's murder in the Tower in 1478, and Edward IV's death in 1483 occur at the same time. With glee, Richard scurries from one challenge to the next. Meeting Henry's funeral cortège in the street, he confronts Lady Anne, who is played by a boy, and boy actors were trained in speed of repartee. He flatters his indignant lady by pleading for a 'slower pace', matches Anne's own word-rhythms, exchanges 'angel' for her 'devil', drops or increases beats in his blank verse, and in effect wins Anne through consummate verbal agility. His conquest is the more amusing because boy actors were more highly drilled than adult actors[15]—and Anne's own articulateness itself is a part of her undoing.

In *Henry VI*, the device of having actors speak aloft from galleries seems artificially over-used, but here, for once, a stage gallery is exposed for the stage device it is. Prayer-book in hand between two bishops, Richard appears aloft in Act III to enchant London's aldermen with his virtue in order to appear reluctant to take a crown. (The playwright's father having been dismissed by his brother aldermen, the gallery drama obliges an audience to scorn aldermen as fools, just as Richard does.) By implication, Shakespeare interestingly suggests that the skilled actor, though possessed of great flexibility, may be nothing more than a hollow drum. Richard's excellence as a *poseur* rests on his miserable isolation and inadequacy—and he succeeds, as a showman, partly because his inward life is feeble and uninhibiting. His creative destructiveness is brilliant, but it has a short run. His 'character' does not change—but our intimacy with him lessens after he loses theatrical and political initiative. A chorus of wailing Queens precedes an innovative group of choric ghosts, and Richard is so distanced at last that his thoughts, not his feelings, are in focus. His opponent faces him at Bosworth, and after the tyrant is killed, a symbolic Earl of Richmond predicts the Tudor glory.

With its clever design, *Richard III* creates the illusion that history writes itself on stage. That play gave young Burbage his first rich, complex Shakespearean role and remained popular throughout the author's lifetime and the reigns of James and Charles I. Audiences and censors had a chance to judge the *Henry VI* series first. Henslowe's receipts for 'harey the vj', if we assume that this work was *1 Henry VI*, suggest an unusual financial success. Performed at the Rose by Strange's men on 3 March 1592, 'harey', at any rate, made Henslowe richer by £3. 16*s*. 8*d*.—the highest 'take' noted in his diary—and the play ran fourteen times more until 19 June.[16]

Censorship of *Henry VI* was surprisingly moderate, so far as we know. The Master of the Revels was irritated by reckless, feuding nobles in their contempt for a monarch. Dialogue had to be cut. Jack Cade's brags at Blackheath, such as 'bid the King come to me . . . ile have his Crowne tell him, ere it be long' and 'for tomorrow I meane to sit in the Kings seate at Westminster' must have been excised, as they are missing in the play's Folio text.[17]

But in June 1592, as rioting suddenly put the theatres in jeopardy, the authorities had more in mind than a few insults in a company's playbooks. And the success of *Henry VI* hardly bettered its author's life. His professional calling was new, turbulent, and unprotected by any guild; and since no one had been a city playhouse writer before 1576, he had no way of really envisioning how his career might turn out. As it was, summer brought him bad news, as we shall see, even before he found himself under personal attack. On the road Pembroke's men constructed brief texts of his *2* and *3 Henry VI*. These scripts, in due course, they were forced to sell as *The First Part of the Contention betwixt the two famous Houses of Yorke and Lancaster* and *The true Tragedie of Richard Duke of Yorke*. Shakespeare's own scripts with their large casts would have been difficult for any company to take on the road. But then he had not designed *Henry VI* for travel, and he could not have foreseen the coming of the plague.

9

THE CITY IN SEPTEMBER

Envie is seldome idle.

(*Greenes Groats-worth of Witte*, 1592)

[Your wife] prayeth unto the lord to seace his hand frome
punyshenge us with his crosse that she mowght have you
at home with her hopinge hopinge then that you should
be eased of this heavey labowre & toylle

(Philip Henslowe in London, to the actor Edward
Alleyn on tour with 'my lorde Stranges Players',
14 August 1593)

Plague and prospects

Viewed from the bankside south of the river, London would have
seemed tranquil and beautiful in the late summer of 1592. Then as
now, some days brought haze over the Thames. In low-lying southern liberties near the amphitheatres, the air could be hot and humid.
Here, though the tenements were sealed off from the Thames by rising embankments, the working lives of people within the river's flood-
plain were influenced by the river's commerce and the city to the
north. Above a line of public and private houses on the north bank,
steeples and towers rose into the September air. Wherries and barges
would have moved on the river deliberately as ever—but watermen
did not bring play-goers over to Paris Garden and the Clink.

What were Shakespeare's relations with a city which was about to be
struck by the worst plague since his birth? About 14 per cent of London's populace were to die. That calamity—with the fear, disruption,
suffering, and bitter loss it entailed—is so overwhelming that his attitude to the theatre, or the effects of pamphleteering by University

Wits on his career, must have seemed comparatively minor matters. Yet the attack upon him in Chettle and Greene's *Groats-worth of Witte* belongs as much to our picture as do the effects of the plague. Before we turn to the epidemic and to the 'Wits', however, it will be well to consider a little further his relations with the London theatres.

In the worst of the plague to come, deaths in theatre suburbs—in Shoreditch and Southwark—were to be proportionately much higher in number than those in London's heart. The central parishes were surrounded by a less than well-to-do riverside belt and by poor, tawdry districts north and east, and yet recent studies have shown that in each urban parish there was a wide range of wealth. It is true that those in the same trades might congregate in the same districts: there were for example shipwrights and sailors in St Dunstan's parish, weavers and cobblers in St Giles Cripplegate, and silk-weavers in All-hallows Honey Lane. But even the West End was not purely gentri-fied, since one might find goldsmiths in Holborn, the Strand, and Fleet Street, or cutlers and engravers, locksmiths and silversmiths else-where in the west. Each part of London was socially varied, and the various ranks were not segregated in daily life.

Generally, the public theatre reflected the 'mix' of parishes. By 1592, this theatre was nearly a universal one—it could be plebeian and courtly, ribald and refined in the same afternoon or play. All sorts, cer-tainly, had come to see *Titus*, the *Shrew*, or *Henry VI*, and Shakespeare had deliberately appealed to varied audiences since he needed to bring in receipts. So far, one might add, he has not suggested London's real variety in any production. In *Henry VI* he writes as if he could hardly see below the heads of nobles; his social contexts are surprisingly weak, vague, or thin. He looks at the urban populace with reserve, an aloofness, and now and then, as in the Cade episodes, with mild dis-dain, as if he had an eye upon a fastidious patron. How fairly has he pictured a society in *any* epoch? His vulgar clown in *Two Gentlemen* seems an afterthought; and nostalgia and memory help to prompt Warwickshire earthiness in the *Shrew*. In behaviour or in rank his pro-tagonists are aristocrats, and it may not be enough to say that he shared with many Londoners the notion that life in its 'fullness' could be realized only by the gentry and nobility.

In his concern for elegance—despite schoolish excesses—he had written as a poet who might find his fulfilment offstage, or without any very deep commitment to the theatre. His early plays are better than those of his contemporaries, with the exception of Marlowe at his best, but not astonishingly 'original'. They have more in common with other dramas of the 1590s than they show in differences. In *Henry VI* he strips drama of bombast or turgidity and makes it more intelligent, but this achievement suggests not so much his faith in the public as his dislike of mere sensation and crude sentiment.

On the other hand, we cannot suppose that he was not extremely attentive to 'sharers'. He hardly let the *actors* down. 'Your Poets', says Gamaliel Ratsey to players in *Ratsey's Ghost*, a fictive Jacobean account of a real highwayman, 'take great paines to make your parts fit for your mouthes'.[1] And he had taken pains to make parts fit for mouths and memories—his rhymes, striking images, and rhythmical styles made his early works fairly easy to memorize. (He would not be so kind to actors later on.) He cares little about historical causation in *Henry VI*—one never quite knows why York quarrels with Somerset, or Gloucester with Winchester—but tapsters and silversmiths at the Rose may not have cared much either, and it is more important that he tried to suit London's amphitheatres. At these venues an actor confronted a high, abrupt cliff of spectators ahead, to the right, the left, and people in the yard below. Those watching the stage also watched and reacted to each other, and as a wave of excitement swept round, the emotive intensity of speeches in *Henry VI* would have had a strong effect, with the audience's reaction forming part of the drama.

Shakespeare learned from that reciprocity and he and the public, in the months before the bubonic plague, were beginning to develop together. Lyly's, Peele's, Marlowe's, and his own works prepared the public for more subtle dramas, and chapels and churches, while denouncing the theatre, also aided it. Puritan vestries as in St Botolph Aldgate had 'concionators'—special lecturers[2]—who gave up to three talks a week: these frequent disquisitions trained the popular ear, and listeners might develop an appetite for livelier fare at the Rose, Curtain, or Theater. Bishops and grudging universities helped too, at least by sending more Doctors of Divinity to town, and by the 1590s few non-graduates were being instituted to an urban cure of souls.

Yet opponents of the theatre were stronger than ever—and some of its fiercest detractors, in effect, were among its enthusiasts. No one on record complained of snow, rain, hail, or frozen feet at an amphi-theatre. Londoners accepted the stage as a sport, an open-air, all-weather game. With jostling, shouting, hurled missiles, and a noisy stage, a playhouse could be a wild, alarming chaos. Stephen Gosson complains of actors in a 'heate' with 'their foaming, their fretting, their stampinge', and though he was no friend to actors he could expect to be believed.[3]

City authorities eyed the theatre as a sink of disease, lethal in epi-demics and unhealthy at other times—though some playhouse cus-toms, oddly, may have warded off death. We know that the rat-flea carrying the bacillus of bubonic plague is repelled by some odours—including the smell of nuts. If the loud cracking of hazel nuts in the middle of Romeo's love-scenes at the Curtain upset actors, the practice seems nonetheless to have been a healthy one. The flea that carried *Yersina pestis*—that tiny destroyer of Renaissance London—was hardy. Infected in October, it could awake to transmit plague in March after nestling in white fabrics, bedclothes, or neutral-coloured garments; since the rat-flea favoured these colours, the bright clothes of the public and the actors were fortuitous. Alert to a disease that was mysterious, savage, and evasive, aldermen and their advisers forbade acting when the weekly plague-toll rose sharply. When it stayed below a certain number—such as twenty or thirty deaths—play-acting might be allowed, though officials took varying views as to what constituted a crisis, and the city or Privy Council could impose a 'precautionary restraint' for nearly as long as they wished.[4]

Crowds disturbed the authorities for other reasons, too. Political unrest, destruction of property, disorder and rowdiness, or the disaf-fection of apprentices and the falling off of work might, among other ills, be blamed on the theatres. One drama such as Jonson and Nashe's *Isle of Dogs* (in the restraint of 28 July to 11 October 1597) might cause a suspension of all play-acting in the capital. Official views of the stage were constant mainly in their arbitrariness.

In common with other actors, Shakespeare viewed the plague as a fact of life—and stoicism befitted his calling. As for other kinds of interference with the stage he exercised his wit on a large variety of grievances. 'Tired with all these, for restful death I cry', as he writes in Sonnet 66 with its allusions to

> strength by limping sway disablèd,
> And art made tongue-tied by authority,
> And folly, doctor-like, controlling skill,
> And simple truth miscalled simplicity,
> And captive good attending captain ill.

No doubt he feels the weight of these things—or of some of them— though the complaints are commonplace and his delight in his poem's wit and smart concinnity is apparent. On the other hand, his stoicism in the Sonnets is convincing partly because its contexts are relatively fresh. For example, he is nearly immune to the external environment in Sonnet 124—inasmuch as his supposed sturdy passion, his 'love'

> suffers not in smiling pomp, nor falls
> Under the blow of thrallèd discontent
> Whereto th'inviting time our fashion calls.
> It fears not policy, that heretic
> Which works on leases of short-numbered hours,
> But all alone stands hugely politic.

Such an elegant declaration seems written by an imaginative man pleased with himself and well removed from Henley Street's flock bolsters, truckle bedsteads, 'the Roome over ye celler', or simple wooden stools, coffers, and chests in his father's house.[5] Yet the elegant lines take us closer to the theatre man, and the attitude of being 'hugely politic' or boldly and supremely prudent was a concomitant of Shakespeare's stoicism.

At 28, he had become prudent and enduring enough. His most basic professional strength was his constructive power or his ability to supply practicable scripts, and this was the power that would bring him rewards. To exercise it and survive as an actor–playwright, he had to be rough and ready, thick-skinned despite his sensitivity, humorous or lightly ironic. Good actors needed to find setbacks amusing in order to keep their equanimity in a profession known for its violence, and he could not have worked six months in the theatre without normal pluck and simple, shoulder-shrugging endurance. It is certain that, for as long as he felt he could be in the theatre, he meant to keep on 'making things' to get money. His acting, so far as we can tell, aided his constructive facility by acquainting him with a troupe's needs, and so far his talents may have seemed to him adequate to the purpose.

But his situation would have become more doubtful than this after *Henry VI*. As he gained notoriety and became an object of envy, his relations with other actors could change: and such a man benefited from harmony in a troupe. His modesty, agreeableness, and unpretentious 'open' manner were natural and yet self-protective—and he might have seemed, in 1592, as free and easy as Ben Jonson would find him. Amusingly, in both the so-called Chandos Portrait (in the National Portrait Gallery, London) and in his effigy in Stratford's church he is unbraced and relaxed. In the portrait, which may date from the Jacobean era though its authenticity has been debated, the sitter has unbuttoned the collar of his shirt and untied the dangling strings of a neck-band. In the effigy Shakespeare's fine gown, laced with silk, hangs easily open in front. The conventional poses prove nothing, but they might have seemed appropriate to Jonson, who implies that Shakespeare was normally frank, unaffectedly candid, not at all secretive.

And if he lost himself in his imaginative constructions or identified with his Titus, his Katherine, or even his Richard, and found fulfilment in humiliating himself, he was also hard-headed: concerned with the whole structural order of a script, at least as practical and down-to-earth as other suppliers of dramas, and evidently did not seem to be a protean wonder in daily life. He found it wise to be 'open' and simple: so much depended on his normal relations with his fellows that his amenity had a value. He brought rewards to players, and he was responding to much in the theatre such as its richness of colour and costume, its endless possibilities in the challenge of staging. But he was not likely to forget the low status of his calling or that his livelihood depended on chance, luck, and official whim.

❦

Late in June 1592, Shakespeare found London's playhouses forbidden to him. Authorities shut the theatres after a public riot near the Rose, and their restraint was supposed to last until Michaelmas, or 29 September. Then in midsummer, official notice was taken of plague in the city, and, except for two short winter sessions, the theatres were shut (in principle) for twenty months.

Apart from Lent, Shakespeare normally knew no let-up in repertory-playing which might have allowed him to visit Stratford, though he may have contrived to see his family each year (as Aubrey believed). Actors needed to work the year round. When London was closed, most companies were forced to break up or to go on tour, and though touring was a normal duty (not an act of desperation), Lord Strange's large group went on the road with difficulty: 'oure Companie is greate, and thearbie o*ur* chardge intollerable in travellinge the Countrie', these actors petitioned Whitehall, 'and the Contynuaunce thereof wil*l* be a meane to bring us to division and separacion, whearbie we shall not onelie be undone, but alsoe unreadie to serve her ma*je*stie when it shall please her highenes to commaund us'.[6] It was 'hugely politic' to refer to the Queen since her Privy Council acceded to the notion that she needed plays for her 'solace'. And the Queen lost little by throwing crumbs to actors. Strange's men were paid in arrears at a standard £10 for a court performance—a sum of 10 marks (£6. 13*s.* 4*d.*) as the official fee plus another 5 marks (£3. 6*s.* 8*d.*) as her gratuity—and the Queen paid for no plays at all during eight or nine months of a year (her fee barely equalled the total weekly profit of a troupe's chief actors). Her Council did agree, perhaps this season, that the Rose might stay open if free of 'the infection of sicknes', but in September there was no abatement of plague.

Lord Strange's company had been touring since 13 July; now they were forced to remain out of London for many more weeks. Whether or not Shakespeare travelled with them, he would have been aware of new setbacks. The sickness worsened slowly. Then, after a brief abatement in winter, plague returned to the city with a virulence which might have made the hardships of actors on the road seem trivial by contrast. Civic disruption in a major epidemic was enormous. Masters often discharged servants and apprentices; trade dwindled, marts shut down, grain might become scarce. What Shakespeare observed of wishful males and sensible females is submitted to a high-courtly comic order in *Love's Labour's Lost*, and ideas for that play were confirmed by what he heard or saw in plague-time.

Lord Strange's men, for example, were at Bristol, devoted to make-believe and applause. In London were some of their womenfolk, contending with hunger, terror, or death. An actor such as Alleyn felt that devoutness and a few nostrums would protect his wife Joan back in plague-ridden Bankside. 'My good sweet mouse', he writes, 'kepe your house fayr and clean which I knowe you will and every evening throwe water before your dore and in your backside and have in your windowes good store of rwe [rue] and herbe of grace.'[7] Alleyn was then anxious to have Joan darken the colours of his fine woollen, orange-tawny stockings before he came home. Philip Henslowe, Joan's stepfather, wrote that Joan as a good wife was imploring the Deity to cease punishing with a Cross. Over 700 men, women, and children were dying in the plague at Shoreditch, it appeared; over a thousand people had died in London in one week. On the Bankside over against the Clink, the plague had been in one house after another, as Henslowe writes to Alleyn in a hasty passage that deserves a translation:

Rownd a bowte vs yt hathe bene all moste in every howsse abowt vs & wholle howsholdes deyed & yt my frend the baylle doth scape but he smealles monstrusly for feare & dares staye no wheare for ther hathe deyed this laste weacke in generall 1603 . . . & as for other newes of this & that I cane tealle youe none but that Robart brownes wife in shordech & all her chelldren & howshowld be dead & heare dores sheat vpe[8]

[Round about us it [the epidemic] has been almost in every house about us and whole households have died, and [I can tell you] that my friend the bailiff does escape but he smells monstrously for fear and dares stay nowhere, for there have died this last week, in general, 1,603 . . . and as for other news of this and that I can tell you none but that Robert Browne's wife in Shoreditch and all her children and household be dead and her doors shut up.]

Robert Browne, an actor who was then in Germany with Worcester's men, evidently lost his wife, all of his children, and every household servant. In the country, troupes were often thought to be carrying the plague and so could be barred from towns and villages. Actors and their boys had begun to die of hunger or exhaustion, and at least one troupe was never heard from again. As for Strange's players, they had been afoot with baggage for almost the entire second half of 1592. However, when the worst suffering in the lanes, alleys, and subdivided tenements of London's suburbs lay ahead—and players had been on the road for less than three months—both Shakespeare and Alleyn, as the chief actor of Strange's troupe, received some encouragement. Early that September, Thomas Nashe in the city published his racy, nervy social satire *Pierce Penilesse his Supplication to the Divell.*

Taking the form of a witty address to the devil, this pamphlet was popular in plague-time. It was twice reissued in 1592. Before citing Alleyn's talents, Nashe praises a 'Tragedian' who has been playing in *1 Henry VI* with enormous success. 'How would it have joyed brave Talbot (the Terror of the French)', writes the pamphleteer,

to think that after he had lyne two hundred yeare*s* in his Tombe, hee should triumphe againe on the Stage, and have his bones new embalmed with the teares of ten thousand spectators at least (at severall times), who, in the Tragedian that represents his person, imagine they behold him fresh bleeding.[9]

The indirect praise of Shakespeare is strong—this is the first printed allusion to his plays—but it came from an odd quarter. Nashe was partial to scholars who saw play-writing as their own preserve. At 24 he was the sharpest, most original satirist among the Wits, making the pamphlet a vehicle for scorching but brisk polemic, humanist critiques, and stylistic verve. He seemed a wonderful boy. Thin and slight with a haystack of hair and a merry gaggle-toothed look as his teeth poked out at angles, he had come down from St John's College at Cambridge with a BA in 1588. He sympathized with the plight of men who worked for the theatres, and his early writings are influenced by fellow graduates. Asked in 1589 to write a preface to Greene's story *Menaphon,* he surveyed the tight little world of the theatre-poets. Nashe now adopts Greene's views. Opposed to university-educated poets, he argues, are parasitic actors and fluent 'Art-masters', or 'Alcumists of eloquence' who 'thinke to out-brave better pennes with the swelling bumbast of bragging blanke verse'.

But just whose are the unlearned pens?

Fond of punning on proper names—as when in *Anatomy of Absurdity* he evokes the puritanical Phillip Stubbes as one who will 'stubbe up sin by the rootes'—Nashe paints a picture-frame into which an enemy might fit Shakespeare's face. He seems to have in mind a follower of Thomas Kyd. Such a man 'will affoord you whole Hamlets, I should say handfuls of Tragicall speeches' to exhaust bloody Seneca, writes Nashe, 'which makes his famished followers to imitate the Kid in *Æsop*'.[10]

Perhaps neither Kyd nor Shakespeare meant to hang himself after reading this. Nashe was then just down from Cambridge—a university as hostile to the players as Oxford. Officials at Cambridge were about to petition to renew an edict of 1575 banning 'any open show' there or for five miles round. At Oxford of course travelling players were banned by the university but oddly not by the town, which forbade them only the use of municipal buildings. In fact Oxford's town chamberlains record a payment of 6*s*. 8*d*. 'geven to the lord Stranges players', and if Shakespeare was with the troupe he may have acted near Oxford's High Street on 6 October 1592.[11] But the Vice Chancellor was reduced to the humiliating policy of giving good money now and then to the troupes of actors of various noblemen (*diversorum nobilium histriones*) simply to leave Oxford quietly. Nashe regrets that any graduate must compete with ignoramuses, but he hopes graduates will save English poetry and sounds a clarion call for the Wits. With a flourish he mentions as possible revivers of the Muse Matthew Roydon, Thomas Acheley, and George Peele. (Marlowe's name may be missing from the short list because he had of late offended Greene.)

At any rate, Nashe takes one close to the dilemma of the University Wits. As author of a fine 'Elegie', Matthew Roydon enjoyed prestige, and George Chapman dedicated two works to him. With an Oxford MA, Roydon had come down to study law at Thavies Inn in Holborn, where Acheley may have joined him. Both young men would have found the law more profitable in the city than poetry, of which there was a glut; few of their works survive.

Peele was of very different mettle, but after depleting his first wife's inheritance he found he could barely support himself. At Christ Church, Oxford where he took his MA in 1579 he had been the fellow student of such men as Richard Hakluyt, author of the *Voyages*, Sir Philip Sidney, and the dramatists Richard Edes, Leonard Hutton, and William Gager; the three last became clergymen, but Gager had praised his verse, and Peele wrote pageants as well as his pastoral *The Arraignment of Paris*, which a children's company played at court. However, his courtly chances were few, and he earned less from pageants than Shakespeare's fellow dramatist Anthony Munday would earn from producing Lord Mayor's shows. He did not forget to honour a player-patron when he could, as in his lines for the Accession Day tilts in 1590:

> The Earle of Darbies valiant sonne and heire,
> Brave Ferdinande Lord Straunge, straunglie embarkt,
> Under Joves kinglie byrd, the golden Eagle.[12]

Few hopeful poets failed to nod at Lord Strange. However, Peele's play-writing was neither flexible nor abundant, and he sank into poverty and stasis. He might have illustrated Nashe's point that graduates are ill-used by players, and rivalled by too many other pens. The trouble was that, after leaving supportive medieval halls at the colleges, young men who were set on being poets found only a splintered community of fellow graduates in London; the Wits were proud, abrasive, quarrelsome, more or less in competition with one another, and they lacked institutional power.

But among Nashe's friends, Robert Greene, at least, had learned to thrive, although he saw actors as his enemies. Boldly prolific and talented, he had plunged into the sleazy, liberating life of Bohemian neighbourhoods with delight and a certain proud, dignified reserve as a gentleman of academic mark. Baptized near Norwich on 11 July 1558, and of a family that may have had prosperous connections with Yorkshire gentry, Greene had taken his BA at St John's College, and MA at Clare Hall in Cambridge five years later. Married, but having left his wife and child, he seemed 'a good fellow' in the suburbs among women and cronies, an artist in greasy silk stockings and what Nashe calls a 'very faire Cloake' with sleeves of 'goose turd greene'. He was 'of face amiable, of body well proportioned', says Henry Chettle, 'his attire after the habite of a schollerlike Gentleman, onely his haire was somewhat long'. The hair was a concession to his poetic life, but there was something immaculate, precise, and showily trim in Greene's look, even apparent in a printed cartoon which shows him at work though attired in a winding-sheet. Over his green cloak was his pendant 'jolly red' beard, long and pointed 'like the spire of a steeple'.[13] Thriving on books, adapting the Greek romances, and keen on Ovid, he was much concerned to show off his brilliance.

Though his workmanship often lacked polish, Greene discovered so much as an artist that Shakespeare studied his work with profit. In opening up many sources in his prose tales and bringing a Greek zest to them he was to have an influence on *Pericles* and *Cymbeline* as well as *The Winter's Tale*. In 1592 he had in his rogue pamphlets about pick-pockets, cut-purses, and other con men of the city extended literary diction and subject-matter fascinatingly downwards. Greene did not interview pick-pockets and purse-cutters, 'foisters' and 'nippers', but the dens and brothels gave him authority to use written sources freshly. Troubled, and unable to impose a moral system on his facts, he avoided moralistic comment by depicting the trickster as hero. His career had run parallel to and a little ahead of Shakespeare's. Fascinated by Ovid, he had written about wonder, about love and the mind's 'inward metamorphosis', and far from merely imitating John Lyly he had expressly reformulated Lyly's *Euphues* in his own *Mamillia* to comment on lust. Again, he took up Castiglione's *Il Cortegiano*, not to comment on the perfect courtier, but to explore love and eloquence in his story *Morando*.

Yet he was capable of plagiaristic excess. At a troubled time not long before he died, he replied to the fussy, scholarly Gabriel Harvey of Cambridge in a fine pamphlet, *A Quip for an Upstart Courtier*, most of which, though in easy prose, is closely copied from Francis Thynne's verses in *The Debate Betweene Pride and Lowlines* which was in print by the 1570s. Rather more cynical was Greene's irresponsibility in exploiting national prejudices. In his play *James IV* he humbles Scotland and then depicts a reconciliation between that country and

England on the understanding that the Scots are an inferior, bemused people. In the play, the English teach a sharp lesson, killing 7,000 Scottish lairds in battle—far exceeding the facts of Flodden Field— after which the Scottish king is sentimentally forgiven for trifling with the English: 'Youth has misled—tut, but a little fault. 'Tis kingly to amend what is amiss' (lines 2509–10).

Yet Greene was obsessed by his own moral lapses, and in 'repent-ance' pamphlets he took up his sins. He has given himself to drink and women. ('In one year hee pist as much against the walls', Nashe told Gabriel Harvey, 'as thou and thy two brothers spent in three'.) Tak-ing a prostitute as his mistress, he left this anecdote about women in *The Royal Exchange* (1590) without comment, though he claimed he was translating from an Italian source: '*Tymon* of *Athens* who was called *Mysanthropos*, seeing a tree whereon divers women had hanged themselves, wished that everie tree might yeelde such fruite.'[14] Repeatedly he told the sad tale of his decline into writing plays, and used a favourite image from Aesop for the players, as when he has Cicero rebuke the Roman actor Roscius in *Francesco's Fortunes*: 'Why, Roscius, art thou proud with Esops Crow, being pranct with the glorie of others feathers?' The 'feathers' were words supplied by artful, hard-working playwrights, and so an actor had no reason to 'waxe proud'.[15]

But his complaints ran a little deeper than this. He found in play-writing, which he respected, no way to come round—or to discover a satisfactory picture of himself or the stability he needed. He looked into the same situation that underlay Shakespeare's career, and saw that the making of scripts for a mercenary theatre subject to vulgar taste reduced the maker, the poet, to gross servitude. Shakespeare pursued his artistic life in public as a kind of popular entertainment and so far had found that circumstances 'did not better for my life pro-vide' than 'the public means'. But whereas Greene saw himself as a puppet of the actors, Shakespeare had regarded them so far as pro-tectors, intimate associates, and allies.

And yet even in 1592 Greene's plays were popular on the London stage. *Friar Bacon* had been bringing in an average of 23*s.* a day for Henslowe, and seemed so attractive that it demanded a sequel, the play we call *John of Bordeaux*, which has a few lines in Henry Chettle's hand in an extant script. Greene's *Orlando Furioso*, his *A Looking-Glass for London and England* (written with Thomas Lodge), as well as *Friar Bacon*, ensured that he had something produced every month from February to June that year.

But he was accused in April of selling *Orlando Furioso* to both the Queen's and the Strange–Admiral's players. Then, when theatres were under a double interdiction in the summer, Greene became ill. Nashe did not deny that a 'banquet' of Rhenish wine and pickled herring with this friend was the cause. Abandoned it seems even by his mistress, Greene fended for himself, wrote a confessional pamphlet and some acerbic notes about the players and Shakespeare, and apparently collapsed in the street one day near Dowgate wharf. He was taken in by a shoemaker, one Isam, and near Dowgate's water-carriers he feebly lingered on. Lacking clothes, he borrowed a shirt when his own was being washed—a fact that led Harvey later to sneer over his poverty. Early in September 'he walked to his chaire and back againe', and wrote to his wife after nine o'clock that night, but the next day Robert Greene died. The shoemaker saw to his burial after wrapping a wreath about the scholar's waist.

The first to descend on Greene's papers, it seems, was Henry Chettle, formerly a partner of the printer John Danter (who brought out a quarto of *Titus Andronicus*). Chettle, at the time, would have lacked a first-hand knowledge of the theatre, but he was inclined towards the stage and would write for it, in penury, after his daughter Mary died (in 1595). At the moment he had in hand some fascinating material. On 20 September 1592 he licensed a work to be called *Greenes Groatsworth of witte, bought with a million of Repentance. Describing the follie of youth, the falshood of make-shifte flatterers, the miserie of the negligent, and mischiefes of deceiving Courtezans. Written before his death and published at his dyeing request.*

The 'waspish little worme' and 'upstart Crow'

Greenes Groats-worth, printed from a text in Chettle's handwriting, was virtually a rape of Shakespeare, or an insinuating attack on not only his plays but his person, and it had the force of seeming to be a candid statement by a dying man. Greene uses a popular formula in which a parable is told, embellished with damaging details to fit an individual. Complex and witty, *Groats-worth* begins with a 'prodigal son' story about a bookish Roberto—who is meant to resemble Robert Greene. Having accused his greedy father of usury, Roberto is left one coin to buy a 'groats-worth of witte', and after luring his rich brother to ensnarement by a prostitute 'in the suburbes', he is cast out to starve.

Cursing his fate, he now meets a stage player, who has been a 'countrey Author' and has an odd voice. 'Truly', Roberto remarks with distaste, it is strange 'you should so prosper in that vayne practise [of acting] for that it seemes to me your voice is nothing gratious.'

Who is the country poet and actor with vile tones? Is Greene thinking of another enemy, or does he imply that Shakespeare's pitch, timbre, or Midlands vowels were unpleasant? At any rate, Roberto becomes a playwright himself. His purse swells like the sea until, demoralized by servitude, he cheats actors, takes up with lewd friends, and ends with just one groat. At this point, Greene intervenes to admit that his life has been like Roberto's and to advise Peele, Nashe, and Marlowe apparently about the actors. 'Base minded men all three of you, if by my miserie you be not warned', he says, 'for unto none of you (like mee) sought those burres to cleave.' The 'burres' may be the Burbages, and the next lines are the bitterest and nearly the most famous lines ever written of Shakespeare. 'Yes trust them not', writes Greene,

for there is an upstart Crow, beautified with our feathers, that with his *Tygers hart wrapt in a Players hyde*, supposes he is as well able to bombast out a blanke verse as the best of you: and beeing an absolute *Johannes fac totum*, is in his owne conceit the onely Shake-scene in a countrey. O that I might intreat your rare wits to be imploied in more profitable courses: & let those Apes imitate your past excellence, and never more acquaint them with your admired inventions. I know the best husband of you will never prove an Usurer . . .[16]

Does the 'upstart Crow' resemble proud, vain crows in Macrobius, Martial, and Aesop, or is he like the thieving crow in Horace's third *Epistle*, and so a plagiarist? Only vaguely is Shakespeare linked with dishonesty, but he is vicious (with a '*Tygers hart*'), presumptuous, and

common, if not ungrateful ('upstart' and 'beautified' by the achieve-
ments of others), and smug and conceited ('the onely Shake-scene').
In coining '*Johannes fac totum*' from *dominus* or *magister factotum*
Greene makes him as reckless as Jack Cade, who was known as 'Jack
Mend-All', and links him also with the author's pettily cruel Queen
Margaret. The Duke of York's phrase in *3 Henry VI* ('O tiger's heart
wrapped in a woman's hide!', I. iv. 138) is aptly misquoted, and that
allusion echoes Margaret's earlier attack on Gloucester in *2 Henry VI*
('His feathers are but borrowed, | For he's disposèd as the hateful
raven', III. i. 75–6).

Greene had listened very well to his rival's works, since none of *Henry
VI* was in print, and he conveys a final hint that Shakespeare had viciously
refused to lend money. A poor, starving Grasshopper approaches a
busy Ant for aid. Like the cruel, maleficent Shake-scene with his tiger's
heart, the Ant has the inner being of a 'waspish little worme'. And so
when the Grasshopper calls for food, the Ant waspishly replies:

> now thou feelst the storme,
> And starvst for food while I am fed with cates.
> Use no intreats, I will relentlesse rest,
> For toyling labour hates an idle guest.[17]

The pamphlet was not written by a deranged observer. Its charges
against a Stratford man, whose voice cannot be mistaken for a Cambridge graduate's, are not very precise; but they add up to a glimpse of
an actor–poet—seen through a thick glass of hatred—who holds himself aloof from other poets, blends with a group such as Burbage's
players, serves a troupe diversely, and writes scripts to rival those of his
social betters. In brief, its assertions are not fantastic. Shakespeare perhaps avoided Wits and others at Shoreditch, but whether or not he
ever refused to aid Greene is unknown.

Printed in an edition of about 500 copies, *Groats-worth* did not sell
very briskly—it was not reissued until 1596—but its *recherché* theatre-
allusions would have had some effect. The proof of Greene's straits
was that he was dead, whereas *Henry VI*'s success might well imply a
'Shake-scene'. Warfare between Nashe and Harvey in the autumn
called attention to Greene's strange demise: 'what a coyle there is with

pamphleting on him after his death' wrote Nashe, adding that *he* had
had no hand in a 'scald trivial lying pamphlet' called *Greenes groats-
worth* which is 'given out to be of my doing'.[18] Others took Chettle as
the work's real author, a matter that still fuels speculation.

With his integrity under attack, Shakespeare must at first have felt
sharply cut, and his stoicism cannot have left him immune to embarrassment and pain. Some 'friends' who read his manuscripts presumably heard of a scandal touching him, and he may allude to it. In
Sonnets 110–12, the Poet refers to his dire troubles, the stage's ini-
quity, and defects in his own behaviour. He has gone 'here and there'
in miserable, compromising journeys,

> made myself a motley to the view,
> Gored mine own thoughts, sold cheap what is most dear,
> Made old offences of affections new.
> Most true it is that I have looked on truth
> Askance and strangely.

The public stage even now colours him like a dye: 'my name receives
a brand', he declares,

> And almost thence my nature is subdued
> To what it works in, like the dyer's hand.
> Pity me then.

One scandal burns, whether or not he refers to the name 'Greene' in
'o'er-green'—a word used only this once by Shakespeare and printed
in 1609 as 'ore-greene'. 'Your love and pity doth th'impression fill',
the Poet begins in Sonnet 112,

> Which vulgar scandal stamped upon my brow;
> For what care I who calls me good or ill,
> So you o'er-green my bad, my good allow?
> You are my all the world, and I must strive
> To know my shames and praises from your tongue.

Events in his life may not be pictured exactly in the lyrics, but if he
refers here to his mood after the attack, his 'brow' clears. Yet he did
not forget easily. His exposure to 'ill' and 'shames' would continue if
he stayed in the theatre, and the pamphlet made his choice of a stage

career riskier. However little Greene's words continued to nettle him, he appears to mock his own sensitivity to them, as when in *Hamlet* he refers to Greene's 'beautified' in Polonius's saying, of the Prince's letter to 'the most beautified Ophelia': 'that's an ill phrase, a vile phrase, "beautified" is a vile phrase' (II. ii. 110–12). Later on in the same scene, an actor in Polonius's role apparently ad-libbed with the surprising remark 'beautified lady', since Edward Pudsey jotted oddly in a commonplace book around 1601: 'The sunne breedes mag *Beautifyed Ladye* gotes in a dead dog beeing good kissing carrion etc.'[19] But by then it appears, Shakespeare was amused by the 'vile phrase'.

At some point he, or another hand, did remove from *2 Henry VI* a line about 'Abradas the great Masadonian Pyrate' which he had picked up from Greene's *Menaphon* or *Penelope's Web*; this line is used in the quarto of *2 Henry VI*, but not in the Folio version, where it is replaced by 'Bargulus the strong Illyrian pirate'.[20] And late in 1592 he was well in control of his feelings when, it seems, he saw Henry Chettle. In *Kind-Harts Dreame*, licensed on 8 December, Chettle apologizes for *Groats-worth* and states that he had had no previous knowledge of Marlowe (whom he has no wish to know) or of Shakespeare either. His phrase 'the qualitie' refers to acting, and of late he has discovered Shakespeare to be a splendid actor—a stunning feat since the public theatres were shut that autumn—and, furthermore, has found him to be a perfectly civil or polite man: 'my selfe have seene his demeanor no lesse civill than he excel*l*ent in the qualitie he professes. Besides, divers of worship have reported his uprightnes*s* of dealing, which argues his honesty, and his fac*e*tious grace in writting, that aprooves his Art.'[21] Chettle's arm has been twisted, it seems. Persons of higher than ordinary standing, or 'divers of worship', had spoken to him about the playwright. Just who they were is unclear, but Shakespeare had been attracting very smart young bloods and men of rank.

Shagbag, *The Comedy of Errors*, and *Love's Labour's Lost*

Groats-worth itself was a symptom of a lasting feud between the troupes and the poets who wrote for them, and in time the playwright Thomas Dekker was to carry it on. 'O you that are the *Poets* of these sinfull times, over whom the *Players* have now got the upper hand',[22] Dekker would lament, and, in the wake of Greene's comments, Shakespeare in his straddling work as an actor–poet had reason to be on guard. But he had begun to amuse some of the keenest theatre enthusiasts, or law students and others at London's great law Inns, the Inns of Court and Chancery. Less than thirty months after Greene's allusion to '*Johannes fac totum*', law students at Gray's Inn's Christmas revels were warned, facetiously, of a 'Johannes Shagbag'. This vile man is potent since he waylays literally 'all' in his part of London.

Whether or not 'Shagbag' was meant to be Shakespeare, the 'termers', who were *au courant* with theatre news, had seen *The Comedy of Errors* a few days earlier in Gray's hall where invited actors had staged it after some uproar. When too many invited guests turned up and in the crush some stalked out, 'it was thought good not to offer any thing of account, saving Dancing and Revelling with Gentlewomen', reports the *Gesta Grayorum*, 'and after such Sports, a Comedy of Errors (like to *Plautus* his *Menechmus*) was played by the Players. So that Night was begun, and continued to the end, in nothing but Confusion and Errors; whereupon, it was ever afterwards called, *The Night of Errors*'.[23] Shakespeare's comedy was well suited for Gray's Inn and for Innocents Night on 28 December 1594—though it may have had a Bankside debut, if it is Henslowe's 'the gelyous comodey' (or *Jealous Comedy*), staged at the Rose during a break in the plague in January 1593.[24]

Many students and gentlemanly sojourners near Holborn had time to frequent public theatres, to seek out actors, and hear gossip of the stage, and around 1594 Shakespeare would have been known particularly at Gray's Inn. As the largest and most fashionable law Inn, Gray's recruited members from wealthy families north and south, and here men from great northern Catholic families were in evidence. One Gray's Reader (later knighted) was Thomas Hesketh, an executor of the wills of Alexander de Hoghton, and of his own namesake Sir Thomas Hesketh of Rufford in Lancashire, who had known Lord Strange and kept players. Gray's, indeed, had more Lancashire members than any other Inn; and whether or not Shakespeare had known Hoghton and Hesketh, Stratford had its Lancashire-born schoolmasters.

Among Gray's members from the south, none was a keener patron of the arts than a delicately handsome Henry Wriothesley, third Earl of Southampton. Historically, the Inns had sponsored drama almost as a loyal duty to the monarch, and they had poets and future dramatists in residence; also they were hives of sonneteering in the 1590s. Michael Drayton of Warwickshire refers to the Inns, and to judge from his sonnets he knew unpublished lyrics by his Stratford countryman.

In brief, *The Comedy of Errors* was staged in a milieu not uncongenial to its author. As Shakespeare's funniest play it advertises his considerable technical powers. It outdoes its main source, or Plautus's funny, unsentimental *Menaechmi* about identical twins, by having two sets of twins for confusion, even as it deftly mixes poignant comedy and farce. Shakespeare's Antipholus of Syracuse is a foreigner—as Johannes Shagbag is said to be—who fails to cope with a dauntingly quick-paced, haunted society of Ephesus, which takes him for his twin. He is like a confused actor who has lost track of his own identity, as if he has had too many bizarre roles to play, and though he falls in love with an urbane, pretty Luciana, the sister of his brother's wife Adriana, he never quite imposes himself on a foreign society.

Mistaking him for her husband and shocked by his coldness, Adriana beseeches him as one terrified by loss of love. Her pathos in its tragic aspect is urgent and unanswered, as if she were replying to the Poet of the so-called Dark Lady sonnets. 'Ay, ay, Antipholus, look strange and frown', she cries imploringly,

> How comes it now, my husband, O how comes it
> That thou art then estrangèd from thyself?—
> Thy 'self' I call it, being strange to me
> That, undividable, incorporate,
> Am better than thy dear self's better part.
> Ah, do not tear away thyself from me;
> For know, my love, as easy mayst thou fall
> A drop of water in the breaking gulf,
> And take unmingled thence that drop again
> Without addition or diminishing,
> As take from me thyself, and not me too.
>
> (II. ii. 113, 122–32)

Does Adriana in effect address the author from a 'Stratford view-point'? Interestingly, Shakespeare most nearly indulges in autobiography in a play when depicting illusory states of mind. *Errors* is a many-layered comedy with hints of Stratford's life in it. The 'confusions' of the Antipholi, though farcical, result in sharp, realistic mercantile tensions before the denouement: old Egeus, saved from death, is reunited with his wife the 'Abbess', who is as practical about medicinal herbs as about faith. Like the dramatist's father, Egeus has lacked money at a crucial time, and also faced a law as arbitrary as the Tudor usury statutes which affected John Shakespeare. He yearns less for his wife than for his progeny, and his Syracusan son, Antipholus, has been as bereft of family as a travelling actor might be.

Such autobiographical aspects of the play—which I risk over-emphasizing here—at least help the author to detach himself from the tone of his literary sources. Whereas the Latin *Menaechmi* is hard-edged and cynical, *The Comedy of Errors* tells a healing story befitting a drama twice performed on Innocents Day. Shakespeare explores problems of lasting intellectual importance to himself, such as the fear of non-being, or the need for self-redemption, and this light comedy really looks ahead to matters of identity in *Hamlet* and to reconciliations in the late romances. If it was written after September 1592, as is probable, *Errors* also suggests that he was more deeply troubled by the attacks on his integrity in Greene's *Groats-worth* than is often supposed. *Errors* is not so much a vindication of himself as it is an enquiry into the matter of how he can judge himself at all. Unrecognized by other people, Antipholus of Syracuse has no 'self' to be certain of, or to defend. Adriana's selfhood, even the nature of her 'blood', depends not merely on her own behaviour, but on her husband's. Funny as it is, *Errors* is in some ways a troubling work by a proficient author seeking to know himself. Gray's students—if the play was audible—must have been amused by mentions of the 'Phoenix' (the sign of a shop in Lombard Street and of a London tavern) and 'Porpentine' (a Bankside inn), as well as by a tour of modern Europe and America focusing on fat Nell's geography and by bawdy jokes on baldness. Losing his hair perhaps at about 30, Shakespeare finds baldness a sign of wit, or syphilis, or both.

It has been suggested that he also wrote *Love's Labour's Lost* during or just after the plague and with an audience of students and lawyers in mind. The work has bawdy enough for Inns of Court 'termers'. It was to be staged at the royal court, and it must have served in a public amphitheatre. Though its verse is adroit, *Love's Labour's Lost* has signs of having been penned very quickly in a relatively unplanned way. It opens with the King of Navarre's quixotic, limp wish to defy 'cormorant' time and win fame with his lords in three years' study during which no woman is to sully their academe; but the scheme is quickly subverted, and the drama nearly runs out of plot. Its wooing-games and funny shows of the Muscovites and of the Nine Worthies are at least well improvised by Shakespeare, and before Mercadé arrives with news of the King of France's death in Act V, the play is an exquisite frolic—a Lylyan work in which wit, word-play, and drama about words aspire to music's condition.

Biron, the most astute of the lords, for example uses the word *light* gracefully and half a dozen times in three lines, quite as easily as he breathes—

> Light, seeking light, doth light of light beguile;
> So ere you find where light in darkness lies
> Your light grows dark by losing of your eyes.

(I. i. 77–9)

He also summarizes the whole truth of Navarre's 'academe' at the outset with little or no effort:

> Necessity will make us all forsworn
>> Three thousand times within this three years' space;
> For every man with his affects is born,
>> Not by might mastered, but by special grace.

(I. i. 147–50)

Yet—within a leisurely framework—Shakespeare appears to carry out in part an exercise in recollection, or in comic criticism of his own early attachment to prosody and rhetoric. The ambience, in some respects, might be Church Street's in the 1570s. The hothouse of the grammar school is resurrected with affectionate gusto. Armado,

Holofernes, and Nathaniel all together suggest Upper and Lower School pedantry—but Holofernes does not have the name of Pantagruel's tutor in Rabelais for nothing. He is no mere fool, since he thinks the best poet who ever woke up in Italy was Ovid, or Naso, the great nose ('for smelling out the odoriferous flowers of fancy'). Indeed, 'Ovidius Naso was the man' (IV. ii. 123-5). In his Ovid-veneration, he speaks for his creator. What might seem, in Act IV, to be a satire aimed at a modern writer's excessive dependency upon Ovid turns into astute praise for Naso, or the Nose. Shakespeare's affection for Ovid mutes or qualifies an exceedingly mild criticism here of grammar-school ideals, as if Ovid's charm at one time had suffused the air of Church Street and softened Master Jenkins's very benches. Primed by Ovid, Holofernes has learned from Book X of Quintilian that, for poetry, imitation alone is not sufficient ('imitatio per se ipsa non sufficit') and that grace, facility, and invention count most, as they did for Naso.[25] So he offers an expert critique of a Biron sonnet, and Act IV itself seems to point Shakespeare away from a dramatic career and towards a lyric poet's one.

If Holofernes is indulged by the dramatist, so is Biron. This lord's role appears to have been slightly expanded as a result of Shakespeare's second thoughts, *currente calamo*, during the actual writing of *Love's Labour's Lost*. And in the action, Biron is the most fully defined ghost from the Gild hall's overhall. Suitably chastised, he frames a vow to give up taffeta phrases in a speech which is itself a perfect sonnet (V. ii. 402-15), and his penance will be the hardest of the lovesick lords. If he visits the groaning sick and makes a 'painèd' impotent smile, as Rosaline asks, the power of his dancing wit is likely to be confirmed by invalids.

The question might be whether Shakespeare could give up Bironic lyric grace, or could find a way to adapt lyric gifts further to his uses. *Love's Labour's Lost* suggests his diminishing commitment to the theatre, and in some ways a failure in dramatic nerve. Its women after all are remote, untested, enigmatic, and seemingly not in need of love of any kind. The play looks out on its time very tentatively—though it is filled with newsworthy names. The Earl of Essex had banqueted with Navarre or Henry IV, with Biron the French general, and with

Longueville the Normandy governor in 1591. The play's topical parallels are vague, and its satirical targets are not clear (if it really had any). Armado's page-boy Mote at least is not an explicit caricature of Nashe, though a boy actor could have mimicked Nashe's swagger, or shown off his funny, angled teeth.

Nashe may well have heard Biron compared with the real Armand de Gontaut, duc de Biron, since he noted how 'busie wits' look for non-existent allusions. 'Let one but name bread', wrote Nashe, 'they will interpret it to be the town of Bredan in the low countreyes; if of beere he talks, then straight he mocks the Countie Beroune in France.'[26]

Shakespeare in the play mocks very little, so far as we know, apart from the euphuistic style and his light, parodying glances at Marlowe or Spenser. But if the attack in *Groats-worth* and the long, discouraging closure of the playhouses did nothing to reconcile him to the theatre, it is likely that hardships had made a new path ahead for him more attractive. In his refined dramas, he had aimed to please actors and large crowds—but not without implicit defiance of his calling. He had written with an elegance that belied the normal constraints and tawdriness of an actor's days. Financially insecure at the best of times, he and his fellows had to predict what the crowds might like, and what might not offend authority. In the bitter hiatus of the plague, the solvency of every troupe was at risk, no matter what dramas they had on hand or how cleverly they were performed.

Furthermore, there is evidence of Shakespeare's acute and undiminishing concern for his own (and his Stratford family's) respectability. He would have been tempted to adopt a new calling if he profitably could, and as a sanguine and energetic man he might hope to find the ingenuity to please a great poetry-patron of England. Having spent his working life in the theatre, he cannot have been certain of his way ahead. There can be a prospect of self-betrayal in new undertakings. His Sonnets, to the extent that they are autobiographical, approach his identity uneasily, as if he were taking the lid off a jar of worms. They are urgently preoccupied with illusions of selfhood, and a picturing of the self. In any case during the plague, so far as we know, he looked beyond the stage to a new circle, a new audience, and with some hope to a remarkable young man.

10

A PATRON, POEMS, AND COMPANY WORK

How can it, O, how can love's eye be true,
That is so vexed with watching and with tears?

(Sonnet 148)

To the 'Earle of Southampton'

*W*ell aware of a sophisticated readership among courtiers, lawyers, and others in the professional and mercantile ranks, Shakespeare published two erotic works in the plague years. These poems were meant for readers of either sex. Yet they were especially well suited to young men with leisure to admire tales of rape, seduction, and female grief told with Ovidian grace and wit. With *Venus and Adonis* and *Lucrece*, he made a strong bid to be recognized as a poet by refined society.

And the poems contrast with a bleak, plague-ridden London. Early in 1593 Shakespeare had done much. If he had suffered as an upstart 'Shake-scene', he had Chettle's apology in print. And now for a few weeks actors resumed work in London, until plague closed the theatres on 28 January. Strange's and Sussex's players lingered near a wintry city before returning to the road. In fact, Sussex's troupe did not get a Privy Council warrant to play beyond a seven-mile radius of London until 29 April. Strange's larger group had a warrant on 6 May, by which time they had left with Alleyn for Chelmsford. In the interval the acting companies prepared for hard tours, which took the likes of Kempe, Pope, Heminges, and other sharers with hired men and boys as far north as Newcastle and York.

London's streets—in this year of *Venus and Adonis*—were

thronged with beggars, some of them maimed soldiers back from abroad. Among greasy crowds at Paul's Churchyard, booksellers did a fair business, but in the suburbs there was misery enough. Philip Henslowe, of the Rose, turned to pawnbroking, gouging clients at a 50 per cent rate of interest and taking in meagre, cloth-wrapped bundles of children's clothing, mainly from women.

Shakespeare would have been of use to a troupe readying for the road, and there is reason to think he had a collaborative task at about this time. He must have seen his dramas altered by improvising actors or other hands, and perhaps already had written some of *Edward III*, a work still outside the accepted Shakespearean canon, though scholars usually agree that he contributed to its first two acts. A history play with a fresh view of kingship and a moderate view of France, *Edward III* concerns a king's efforts to govern his own nature. Shakespeare's style is evident, for example, in a scene in which a nobleman advises his daughter in a grave list of school-like *sententiae* on the corruption of power:

> . . . poison shows worst in a golden cup;
> Dark night seems darker by the lightning flash;
> Lilies that fester smell far worse than weeds.[1]

Shakespeare used the last line, word for word, in Sonnet 94. Other phrases from the play are in his Sonnets—which relate lightly to *Edward III*'s text.

This year it is likely that he collaborated on a more volatile play; and the theatrical manuscript of *The Booke of Sir Thomas More* may give us—briefly—a chance to see him at work at about the time of his *Venus*.[2] We know that Anthony Munday—a government informer fond of volatile topics—had a major hand in working up a script on Sir Thomas More, who had been martyred by the Queen's father. The play was timely. It involved London's 'Ill May Day' riots against foreigners in 1517; these were ominous, unforgotten risings which had been echoed in a Southwark riot of 11 June 1592—the very cause of an official closure of theatres two months before the plague alert of August. On the latter occasion, mobs were angered by the government's slowness in protecting apprentices from competing 'strangers' or workers streaming in from France and the Lowlands. Munday's play about More's role in the historic riot was meant to be sensational, but the writing ran into trouble. Revisers were called in, and Shakespeare's handwriting in *More*'s manuscript has been found in three folio pages known to us, today, as those of 'Hand D'.

'Hand D'—or Shakespeare, as we think—writes at speed in a clear, cursive 'secretary' hand with ease, lack of restraint, and economy of effort. He dithers confusedly over names, abbreviations, and other incidentals, and may imagine a scene in life rather than a play on a stage, not unlike Shakespeare who elsewhere has 'Enter before Angiers' or 'Citizens upon the walles' as untheatrical stage directions.[3] But 'Hand D' evokes a firm, compassionate Sir Thomas More, who speaks in a rapid series of images as if the poet were compulsively caught up in them. The emotive force of an image sets up a rhythm of feeling, so that the poet follows and fills out More's psyche, but does not seem to create it; a vivid delineation of 'character' may be too external a matter to be involved in his aim or process of composing. If the quill of a theatre-poet could move rapidly, we have little sign of that speed in our modern texts of Renaissance plays. We punctuate More's lines to the London rioters rather heavily today:

> What do you to your souls
> In doing this? O desperate as you are,
> Wash your foul minds with tears, and those same hands
> That you like rebels lift against the peace
> Lift up for peace, and your unreverent knees,
> Make them your feet.

What 'Hand D' actually wrote is very quick, with its spontaneity and harmony all the more evident because the punctuation does not mark out every breath-pause for the lungs of an Alleyn or Burbage:

> what do yo^u to yor sowles
> in doing this o desperat as you are
> wash your foule mynds w^t teares and those same handes
> that yo^u lyke rebells lyft against the peace
> lift vp for peace, and your vnreuerent knees
> make them your feet[4]

The writing by 'Hand D' reminds one of Heminges' and Condell's memory of Shakespeare in the Folio of 1623, as a sure writer of such 'easinesse' his 'mind and hand went together'. Even if it were shown that he did not write More's speeches, they display just such theatrical qualities—rapidity, flow, expressive tone among them—as we find in his narrative poems and Sonnets. *Thomas More* in any case alarmed the censor's eye of Edmund Tilney, Master of the Revels, who asked for material that dramatized the insurrection to be narrated instead, and added for the script's revisers, 'nott otherwise att your own perrilles [perils]'.[5]

Despite the work of six 'hands' as poets or scribes, *More* languished—and one doubts that it reached the boards of any stage.

Almost as if in response to weariness of the plague, Shakespeare prepared *Venus and Adonis*. The erotic poem was ready by spring. With verve and colour, it plays upon a wide view of time, and reminds one of how easily Elizabethans imagined vast stretches of time ahead, even in legal documents. (They hardly needed our science fiction.) In the month of Shakespeare's birth, one Simon Saunders typically sold a lease on a 'Crofte' for a term of 2,995 years. Again, Thomas Sharpham acquired Devon lands until AD 3607, and John Hodge signed for property to be his family's until AD 4609, as if our twenty-first century were a 'tomorrow'.[6] Shakespeare's expansive view of time is not unusual, but it appears to good advantage in his poems. He inscribed *Venus and Adonis* to the refined, well-schooled Henry Wriothesley, third Earl of Southampton, and found a Latin epigraph to suit that patron of poets. It reads, in one version, 'Let base-conceited wits admire vile things, | Fair Phoebus lead me to the Muses' springs'.[7]

After that, he appends a letter which suggests he barely knows the 19-year-old earl. As printed by his Stratford acquaintance Richard Field, then in London, to whom he sold *Venus*, the letter ends with the name 'William Shakeʃpeare'—and the spelling is interesting. Field probably inserted a neutral *e* between the two syllables of the last name—'Shak' and 'ʃpeare'—because, in a Tudor press, both **k** and the long letter ʃ kerned (that is, the *face* of each letter projected beyond the tiny *body* behind it, and when set together such letters bent or broke in printing). None of the poet's six known signatures shows an *e* in the middle of his last name; but surnames were not thought of as fixed. Out of habit, or to the extent that he cared, he was perhaps happy to be 'Shakspere', or 'Shakspeare'.[8]

'Right Honourable', he writes tactfully within a few weeks of his twenty-ninth birthday for the earl and other readers of *Venus and Adonis,*

> I know not how I shall offend in dedicating my vnpolisht lines to your Lord-ship, nor how the worlde will censure mee for choosing so stronge a proppe to support so weake a burthen, onelye if your Honour seeme but pleased, I account my selfe highly praised, and vowe to take aduantage of all idle houres, till I haue honoured you with some grauer labour. But if the first heire of my inuention proue deformed, I shall be sorie it had so noble a god-father: and neuer after eare so barren a land, for feare it yeeld me still so bad a haruest[.] I leaue it to your Honourable suruey, and your Honor to your hearts content, which I wish may alwaies answere your owne wish, and the worlds hopefull expectation.

> Your Honors in all dutie,
> William Shake∫peare.

He is newly reborn, as if with a 'first heire' of his brain he begins his career again, and there is a hint of the muddy Midlands whence he comes in the allusion to 'so bad a harvest'. Southampton's fashionable name advertises a work about which the poet has doubts. He follows Thomas Lodge's *Scillaes Metamorphosis,* lightly, in matters of style.

But his own erotic epyllion or short epic uses light borrowings well. His Adonis is a prim, amusing child hardly past puberty, with a nice-ness and gaucherie that might suit a new boy in an acting troupe. Adonis fears sex with a 'bashful shame' and maiden 'blush' that make him seem over-mothered.

Venus appears as a Shoreditch bordello-madam on the rampage, or at first as a fleshy, sweaty, pantingly grotesque woman as she lugs Adonis under an arm or lecherously hungers for his virginal body:

> Backward she pushed him, as she would be thrust,
> And governed him in strength, though not in lust.

(lines 41–2)

His red lips might save England from plague or drive infection from

the 'dangerous year' (perhaps the year 1592–3) as she tells him pas-
sionately, 'that the star-gazers'

> having writ on death,
> May say the plague is banished by thy breath!
>
> (lines 508–10)

Early readers did not find her comical, but sexually exciting. And
whereas treatments of Ovid's story had shown Venus and Adonis as
mutual lovers, here the goddess is more affecting because her frantic
appeals fall on deaf ears. In this poem she lusts rightfully, as if the
author drew on an early experience of his own with a woman in making her alarming, then motherly, luscious, sympathetic. There is a
deep, possibly autobiographical, aspect to Shakespeare's fascination
for the sexual initiatives of women—as in Titania's farcical but compelling wooing of Bottom in *A Midsummer Night's Dream*, or Rosalind's wooing of Orlando in *As You Like It*, or Helena's pursuit of
Bertram in *All's Well*. The poet hardly wrote to make an earl give up
bachelorhood, but in line with his procreative Sonnets 1–17, he has
Venus argue for a begetting of children. After Adonis's horse bolts off
to breed with a mare, Venus gets the boy into a coital position, hanging with plump arms round his neck till he falls on her belly, and she
on her back:

> Now is she in the very lists of love,
> Her champion mounted for the hot encounter.
>
> (lines 595–6)

But he is not 'pricked' just then for her delight, in a phrase of
Sonnet 20, and next day a boar's priapic tusks nuzzle in his groin.

Venus weeps angry tears at his death. In her vision of misery for all
lovers and her flight to the skies, the poet hints at what she bequeaths,
to us, on earth—a miasma of sexual guilt, betrayal, and nagging torment which, in effect, Shakespeare takes up in the Sonnets.

Licensed on 18 April 1593, *Venus and Adonis* had a delayed debut,
but Richard Field, who bought the work outright, printed it by mid-
September and sold its very marketable copyright to John Harrison
the next June. The poem's painterly appeal, sensual quality, and smart

pace ensured its success with courtiers and students; it had gone
through at least six editions by 1599, and within a year of its publication Thomas Edwards, Michael Drayton, and Thomas Heywood (all
in works licensed between October 1593 and May 1594) alluded to it in
verses of their own.[9]

One consequence was that Shakespeare's name became more familiar in literary London. Dramatists and other poets knew one another,
and *Venus* would have been noticed by those in Southampton's circle. Patronage networks were fluid and fragile, but distant informants
could affect a poet's career. Southampton, as we know, came to court
with the poet Fulke Greville—whose father had become honorary
recorder of Stratford-upon-Avon, after aiding bailiffs and aldermen
when John Shakespeare was going to 'halls'. We do not know this, but
it is possible that Southampton had heard a little of Shakespeare from
the younger Fulke Greville—no mean judge of the talented—and felt
the more disposed to be encouraging.

It is certain that with poets such as Drayton and Heywood astir over
Venus and Adonis its author was talked about, and that he received a
mark of the young lord's favour. The earl gave what Shakespeare simply calls a 'warrant' of his 'disposition', which, as vague as that is,
implies a sign of approval. With a chance to learn more of him, what
did Shakespeare—around the autumn of 1593, or, at any rate, before
the next spring—find in the young 'Henrie Wriothesley, Earle of
Southampton and Baron of Titchfield'?

For the earl's family, the very hour of his birth was affecting and
memorable, and yet—born at 3 a.m. on 6 October 1573—he was the
fine product of an unhappy match. Much that Shakespeare either
heard about or would have been quick to notice, such as the young
man's love of action, art, and drama, or his self-display and ambition,
his homoerotic friendships, and his highly strung, rather unreckon-
ing, temperament, must surely have had causes in his upbringing. His
father was a fervent Catholic, imprisoned more than once for treason,
and his mother a beautiful, sentimental, rather silly person who was
said to have taken a commoner as a lover.

As a boy, Henry Wriothesley had been a go-between for his parents.
Then, when forcibly parted from his mother, he developed a deep

suspicion of women—and he was to turn often to male friends for stimulus or affection. Nearly 8 when his father died, he became third Earl of Southampton, and a ward of the Queen's powerful Lord Treasurer—Lord Burghley—who trained him superbly at a school for young noblemen at Cecil House in London's Strand. Having met other royal wards, including perhaps his future hero the Earl of Essex, he went on at the early age of 12 to St John's College, Cambridge. His guardian also thought that the law might be useful, and enrolled him at Gray's Inn.

But the comely, refined earl, who took his MA degree at 16, hardly had time for law-books at Holborn—though his own Southampton House was near Gray's. He came to revels at Gray's Inn at about the time *The Comedy of Errors* was staged there; yet he mainly glittered at court. He was with the Queen at Oxford when, as a poet put it, 'his mouth yet blooms with tender down'. For a time, he was to see 'plaies every Day', and delight in Lord Strange's younger brother, who wrote playscripts.

But Shakespeare at the time of *Venus* would have found him in hot water. Ordered by Burghley to wed the latter's granddaughter Lady Elizabeth Vere whose father was the Earl of Oxford, the young man baulked. That alliance might happily have cleared him of a papist taint; his mother's own Catholic crimes, on manuscript evidence, were hardly worse than her appeal to free an 'olde poor woman' charged (it seems) with recusancy,[10] but his father's link with a regicidal plot had led to the Tower.

Still the boy refused to wed; and the law held that if an heir would not marry 'at the request of his lord', on coming of age he must pay him what 'any would have given for the marriage'.[11] The earl faced paying a stupendous fine (said to be £5,000) on turning 21 in October 1594. Hence it was to a rather plucky nobleman that Shakespeare pledged love 'without end' (in his letter with *Lucrece*) and wrote 'what I have to do is yours, being part in all I have, devoted yours'. Southampton was becoming an exhibit. He enhanced a slender, lightly built form with delicate fabrics; his clinging white silk doublet, dancing hat-feathers, and purple garters could be offset by a lovely tress of auburn hair falling to the breast. Was he homosexual? The unreliable William Reynolds, who was perhaps schizophrenic, wrote later that Southampton slept in a tent in Ireland with Piers Edmondes, a brother officer, and 'the earle Sowthamton would cole and huge [embrace and hug] him in his armes and play wantonly *with* him'.[12] Reynolds expected to be believed, but even if we dismiss that report, there are signs enough that the young earl preferred bisexual or homosexual friends.

Buggery was a crime, but close, very affectionate friendships between males were much respected in this period. Male friends might desire with honour to be together always, and so the Cambridge tomb of the dramatist Thomas Legge signals his love for a man: 'Junxit amor vivos sic jungat terra sepultos' ('Love joined them living and so may the same earth link them in death').[13] The Sonnets show Shakespeare's understanding of homoerotic feeling. He admired a patron who seemed, to many, to be Sir Philip Sidney's possible heir in valour and art. At least at the fringes of Southampton's set were Michael Drayton and his close friend Richard Barnfield, who wrote homoerotic lyrics. Barnfield had been at Brasenose College, Oxford— as had Barnabe Barnes, who wrote a sonnet alluding to Southampton's lovely eyes. Gervase Markham in a sonnet praised the young earl's 'well-tun'd' sweet voice. Barnes and the poet Daniel were close friends of the earl's great tutor John Florio (who was to translate Montaigne's *Essays*).

At little cost as a rule, Southampton sweetly encouraged such writers, and Nashe complimented him justly, if flippantly, in the dedication of *The Unfortunate Traveller* in 1594: 'A dere lover and cherisher you are, as well of the lovers of Poets, as of Poets themselves.' It is not clear that the cherishing earl really entertained poets at his Titchfield estate in Hampshire, but here Shakespeare is said to have found the name 'Gobbo' for Shylock's servant.[14] However that may be, he soon dedicated a new poem to his patron.

The erotic subject of Lucretia or Lucrece, her rape and suicide, obviously intrigued Shakespeare—and this may be the 'graver labour' he had promised Southampton in 1593. His new poem's seriousness itself compliments the earl. This lady's Roman name had been synonymous with marital virtue since the Middle Ages, although her death troubled Christian piety. In *Lucrece*, Shakespeare freshly reworks her story in the 'complaint' tradition, using the rhyme royal of Daniel's recent *The Complaint of Rosamond*, and wrings pathos from the helpless exposure to Tarquin's savagery of Lucrece's white bosom's 'blue veins' and 'round turrets'.

Tarquin's tense, interesting, rationalizing debate with himself fore-shadows the psychic terrain of *Macbeth*. The rapist disappears, as shat-tered as the lady's husband Collatine whose boasting of her virtues implicates him in the rape. But the benefit of the subject lay in chances it gave Shakespeare to plumb tragic feeling and effects. Minimizing outward action, he gives himself access to Lucrece's mind after the violation and so explores her agony, inanition, and self-accusing doubts. He might be a viewer in a plague-ridden city, musing on pain as he takes up tragic picturing:

> To see sad sights moves more than hear them told,
> For then the eye interprets to the ear
> The heavy motion that it doth behold,
> When every part a part of woe doth bear.

> (lines 1324–7)

Lucrece is a work of great technical innovation and of much aes-thetic appeal. It has the inward force of a spiritual 'retreat' in its spa-ciousness, slowness, and graphic depiction of mental suffering even in a dramatic context that is barely viable; the reader's mind fixes on an epitome of the fall of mankind and has time to contemplate it. Here, too, as Hallett Smith has said, is 'an examination of what constitutes tragedy and an explanation of how it operates'.[15] Or at least in the sun-light of an earl's eye, the author pursues his interests. A dozen or more passages echo imagery or phrasing in his *Titus*, and here he looks into the rationale for such a play.

Even so, his design is slightly compromised, and one might think that he had been anxious to show his fitness to talk with the learned. The heroine's set-pieces, such as her denunciations of Night, Time, and Opportunity, show rhetorical agility, but lose her own accent—a dozen other speakers in Tudor poems might have said them—and easily detachable stanzas were to appeal to Elizabethan anthologizers.

In *England's Parnassus* (1600) Robert Allott selected thirty-nine passages from *Lucrece* (he took fewer from all the author's plays then in print) and a mere twenty-six from *Venus*, and John Bodenham's *Belvedere* (1600) used ninety-one from *Lucrece*, only thirty-four from the more prurient *Venus*.

Printed in 1594 as *Lucrece*—later as *The Rape of Lucrece* from Field's early running-titles—the poem as a whole was marginally less popular than its predecessor, if more instructive for the author, and went into six known editions in his own lifetime.

Inscribing *Lucrece* to Southampton, Shakespeare is less reserved, more intimate in tone than before. 'Right Honourable', he begins around the spring of 1594,

The loue I dedicate to your Lordship is without end: whereof this Pamphlet without beginning is but a superfluous Moiety. The warrant I haue of your Honourable disposition, not the worth of my vntutored Lines makes it assured of acceptance.

All of his poems, written and unwritten, are to be for the earl's honour:

What I haue done is yours, what I haue to doe is yours, being part in all I haue, deuoted yours. Were my worth greater, my duety would shew greater, meane time, as it is, it is bound to your Lordship; To whom I wish long life still lengthned with all happinesse.

> Your Lordships in all duety.
> William Shake∫peare.

Yet certainly a large, unbridgeable social gap divided the young, keen earl from an actor who wrote verse. Class consciousness in the age was very acute; Southampton for instance saw plays with his friend, the Earl of Rutland, but Ben Jonson remarked that one day, when he was at Lady Rutland's table, 'her husband comming in, accused her that she keept table to poets'.[16] Shakespeare was not a narrowly calculating man, but a hopeful enthusiast eager to improve his social credentials; in effect his dedicatory letters acknowledge a gap between himself and the earl, but they also make use of the young man. So far he had been rather limited by actors' demands, haste in production, and shifting public taste as he served up playscripts to be changed as occasion required; he had to plunge boldly ahead of himself, touching on topics he might later develop. Actors and playwrights felt time pressing them, but, to the eye of many an observer, the nobility lived at another pace. Imaginatively, it was as a leisurely sonnet-writer that Stratford's poet most nearly entered his patron's privileged, less mercenary, world.

Sonnet-writing had come into vogue among courtly poets, even as it appealed for a while at the law Inns. Having tried his hand at them, Shakespeare wrote sonnets over the years for private perusal. In this mode, he had a certain freedom denied a dramatist, in that he could allow himself to fail. Keeping his sonnets out of print, he might revise them or abandon them as he wished. In fact his Sonnets 138 and 144 were published without his authority and in what appear to be early drafts in a curious volume, *The Passionate Pilgrim*. The work's first edition now exists only in eleven leaves in the Folger Library, but we know that its second edition was printed by Thomas Judson for William Jaggard in 1599.

In 1598 Francis Meres referred to Shakespeare's 'sugred Sonnets among his priuate friends'[17]—without saying who the lucky readers were. Recent evidence suggests that the 'friends' were rather few. At some point, he settled upon a plan of contrasts for a series, with one group of sonnets to be about an admirable love for a youth, and another group to be about uncontrollable lust for a married woman of dark complexion. The myth that Shakespeare's nameless Young Man and Dark Lady had exact counterparts in his life only began in the late eighteenth century. The Sonnets—which profoundly explore love— are replete with bawdy puns and sexual jokes; the lyrics about adultery, for example, include allusions of a discreet sort to the vagina, and much plainer ones to the rising and falling penis. For years he had little to gain by printing his lyrics, and it is, of course, possible that he felt that intimate Sonnets with bawdy wit, carnal imagery, and exposés of lust might have troubled Mary Shakespeare, if she, or a literate neighbour at Stratford, saw a volume of them. He had the feelings of others at home to consider, and yet when well into his forties, he perhaps found reasons to publish his lyrics (a matter best judged in view of his life in 1608–9). Time changes circumstances, and at last a series of 154 numbered sonnets with his narrative *A Lover's Complaint* appeared under the irreproachable city imprint of George Eld, for the publisher Thomas Thorpe, soon after the volume was registered in 1609.

The sonneteer

The order in which he penned the Sonnets is unknown; but those to the lovely youth increase in syntactical complexity and were hardly begun later than 1593 or 1594. He appears to have started with a few, well-tried themes, before turning to some of the guilt and anguish he knew.

It is likely that he took up for his youthful patron's eyes the theme of begetting children. In urging a young man to beget heirs in Sonnets 1–17, he echoes his *Venus*, which has a 'warrant' of Southampton's favour.

In the sonnet vogue of the 1590s, poets tried to hint of dark, personal secrets in their lyrics. With artful verve Shakespeare himself played the game, and no one has ever complained that his Sonnets leave us with too few riddles and problems. I shall solve no puzzle here and advance no major theory, but it is worth glancing at a difficult matter at first—did he write lyrics to please a nobleman other than Henry Wriothesley?

If he did, the most probable candidate is young William Herbert, who was born at Wilton on 8 April 1580, and became third Earl of Pembroke in January 1601. He and his brother Philip were to have the large Folio of 1623 dedicated to them. By coincidence, in 1597 this boy's nervous parents urged *him* to marry another child of the Earl of Oxford and granddaughter of Lord Burghley—Bridget Vere.

Pembroke, of course, may have influenced the sonneteer at some point, and that cannot be ruled out. But there is no sign that Shakespeare met the future earl in the 1590s, though Michael Brennan's historical research, for instance, takes one close to the milieu of the Pembrokes at Wilton in Wiltshire and to its concerns.[18] No visitor at Wilton, none of its residents, and no one connected with William Herbert or his father suggests that the playwright had anything to do with the family in the 1590s. Lord Herbert was only 13, and not yet living in London, when *Venus* was printed; there is no guarantee that the opening Sonnets were written first, but they relate in style to the Ovidian poems and early plays, not to the poet's manner late in the decade. Moreover, up to 1594 Shakespeare acknowledges only one poetry-patron. On telling Southampton 'what I have to do is yours' in 1594, he apparently aims to delight that patron in future with something besides *Lucrece.*

He is gravely elegant in Sonnets 1–17—which, even as they allude to time's ravages and beauty's fading, are truly an actor's lyrics. If something is missed when the Sonnets are recited, they are impressive even then as the most beautiful poems in our language, so truthful that the poet's nasty, ugly, and finally near-insane outlook is not muted or compromised. The Sonnets have been effectively recited, not with any halting emphasis on phrases or images but with whole lines as units of speech. 'The meaning of the line very often resides in the second half', remarks the actor Simon Callow.[19] And at the start, the Poet's misogyny is mild, aristocratic, tactical. Abasing himself, he implies that a lovely, well-born youth needs a wife for childbearing, but not of course for love, wit, wealth, talents, companionship, or anything else she may offer.

In Shakespeare's time, or soon afterwards, one of these decorous opening lyrics was well liked. More manuscript copies of his Sonnet 2 ('When forty winters') survive from the seventeenth century than do all similar copies of his other lyrics. Whether he or Drayton was the borrower, a line in Drayton's *Shepheards Garland* of 1593—'The time-plow'd furrows in thy fairest field'—resembles a line in a manuscript of Sonnet 2,

> And trench deep furrows in that lovely field.

Shakespeare apparently revised this to read,

> And dig deep trenches in thy beauty's field.[20]

His image becomes military, and has a military echo of course in Sonnet 16 ('Make war upon this bloody tyrant, time'). It was for military glory, one notes, that the young Southampton yearned; unfortunately Shakespeare (so far as we know) lacked any such military credentials as those of two brave sonneteers who praised the earl: Barnabe Barnes, two years before he wrote his sonnet to Southampton, had joined the army expedition to Dieppe; and Gervase Markham was to have a captaincy in Ireland when Southampton became Essex's General of the Horse.

In Sonnets 1–17, Shakespeare at any rate does not vaunt his originality. He neither flatters a patron's learning, nor links him with a vain, naïve young man. But in praising mutable human beauty, he tests the language of praise while avoiding panegyric staleness, and so pays tribute to a reader's good taste before pledging loyalty to one of implicitly high rank:

> Lord of my love, to whom in vassalage
> Thy merit hath my duty strongly knit,
> To thee I send this written embassage
> To witness duty, not to show my wit;
> Duty so great which wit so poor as mine
> May make seem bare in wanting words to show it. . . .

(Sonnet 26)

A 'Lord' of culture might wonder if the tired, well-worn sonnet *form* could any longer be fresh, a suitable vehicle for a poet's 'wit'. By the 1590s the form was becoming *passé*. Shakespeare writes with a sense that sonnets are indeed toys, little games in which a mystifying poet (aided, if possible, by a publisher's mystifications) pretends to unlock autobiographical secrets 'consecrated to silence' in an inner self.[21] He derides sonneteers in his plays, and lightly mocks 'wailful sonnets' as early as *Two Gentlemen*. In a sense he had grown up with sonnets: Wyatt's and Surrey's sonnets were popular in his boyhood. He knew Thomas Watson's versions of some of Petrarch's and Ronsard's sonnets, and Spenser's *Ruines of Rome*, with its pleasant, fairly close versions of Joachim Du Bellay's allusive sonnets on time and the past in *Les Antiquités de Rome*. Spenser's *Ruines* was of 1591. In that year, Sidney's brilliant sonnet sequence *Astrophil and Stella* appeared, five years after Sidney's death, along with twenty-seven of Daniel's smooth sonnets to Delia in a pirated edition with Nashe's exuberant preface.

In this 'Theater of pleasure', wrote Nashe of the *Astrophil* lyrics, 'the tragicommody of love is performed by starlight' and 'you shall find a paper stage strewed with pearle'.[22]

But in the deluge of English sonnets that followed, the paper-stage became soggy. A new, wittily acerbic poetry of argument by Inns of Court coterie poets with young John Donne at the forefront did not bode well for the sonnet vogue. Daniel in his lyrics to Delia, for example, had offered Shakespeare a good example of a smooth, tonally fine English Petrarchan manner:

> Seeke out some place, and see if any place
> Can give the least release unto thy griefe.
>
> Autentique shall my verse in time to come,
> When yet th'unborne shall say, 'Loe where she lyes,
> Whose beautie made him speake that else was dombe.'[23]

But Daniel soon despaired over that 'naked' style, and thought of himself as an old-fashioned Elizabethan. Drayton tried to 'harden' his own sonnets in repeated revisions. Even Meres's praise of 'sugred Sonnets'—*sugared* meaning smooth or graceful—would have seemed outmoded to some at Holborn, or in the west of London, by 1598. When Shakespeare's lyrics resurfaced in a second (pirated) edition in 1640, their editor touted them as being no more than 'Serene, cleere and eligantly plaine', and made a virtue of outmodedness.[24]

Well alert to literary fashion, Shakespeare nonetheless found an old lyric genre congenial. He does not invent a new form, but uses the English or Surreyan form which George Gascoigne had defined in 'Certayne notes of Instruction concerning the making of verse' in *The Posies* (1575), a revision of *A Hundreth sundrie Flowres* printed two years earlier: 'some thinke that all Poemes (being short) may be called Sonets', wrote Gascoigne,

as indeede it is a diminutive worde derived of *Sonare*, but yet I can beste allowe to call those Sonets whiche are of fouretene lynes, every line conteyning tenne syllables. The firste twelve do ryme in staves of foure lines by crosse meetre, and the last twoo ryming togither do conclude the whole.[25]

Katherine Duncan-Jones thinks that another passage in Gascoigne's 'notes' may have caught Shakespeare's eye. This is likely in view of

Sonnet 130 ('My mistress' eyes are nothing like the sun'), though such a lyric transforms any suggestion in a source. 'If I should undertake to wryte in prayse of a gentlewoman', declared Gascoigne, 'I would neither praise hir christal eye, nor hir cherrie lippe, &c. For these things are *trita & obvia* . . . I would undertake to aunswere for any imperfection that shee hath, and thereupon rayse the prayse of hir commendacion.'[26]

Shakespeare borrows from other sonneteers. He even imagines rival poets in Sonnets 78–86, but without evoking Barnes, Markham, Chapman, Marlowe, or any others known to us; his nameless rivals belong to a strategy of praise for a youth who grants access to a truer, purer language than other poets use. The Sonnets are too paradoxical and mixed to be labelled as either 'fictions' and 'literary exercises', or as straightforward 'biographical revelations'. Helen Vendler calls attention to 'the successive intellectual position-taking' which is a fea-· ture of them, and yet, as she suggests, what counts is a pressure of inwardness, or the poet's ability to transform idea into intense experi- ence.[27] Certainly these poems take us inside Shakespeare's mind, and the real importance of the Sonnets in his life is that they became a means of developing his artistic sensibility. In this theatre of the mind it is rehearsal time, as he tries out this and that, tests his style, moods, and perceptions, brings some lyrics to the highest level of his art, or leaves others as simpler experiments. His Sonnets partly account for a new lyricism in his plays, and also for the more individuated verse that he uses to give depth to his dramatis personae, and so, especially in the 1590s, for his stunning progress as a dramatist.

❦

Most of the first 126 sonnets focus on a lovely youth while painting their speaker's—or Poet's—portrait. The topic of childbearing dies away, as the Poet declares love's urgency. He lives for the youth, no one else, and shares a mistress with that gentle thief: 'Take all my loves, my love, yea, take them all' (Sonnet 40).

The lyrics are self-effacing almost to the point of masochism, oddly troubled in emotion under smooth surfaces, and as their syntax becomes more complex they suggest a rather over-responsive author, easily pained, weary of his faults, but unable to endure a friend's disloyalty. Though pleased or touched by simple banalities of nature, and by his mind's eye's image of the youth, he is oddly removed from real people; he feels while observing. Adoring from a distance he is nearly tranquil, or only at the mercy of his intellect's questioning pictures; to be involved closely in reciprocal feeling is to know his own worthlessness along with disquiet, turmoil, or despair. To be sure, despair belongs to the sonnet vogue. Shakespeare's sonnets are more flexible and varying, also more parodying, subtle, and intelligent than those of his rivals. He sees much, holds to rather little, and contradicts nearly everything he can say about time, love, the youth, or the self.

In no sonnet sequence of the 1590s is there much narrative continuity, and Shakespeare's triangular love-story of a Poet who loves a youth and a Dark Woman (who in their own affair betray him) is a slender one. Far more elaborate than that 'story' are stylistic and thematic links between groups of sonnets. To increase the psychological interest of yearning, the author gives it a homoerotic or, at times, bisexual aspect. Shakespeare delights in sexual ambiguity and his little parable in Sonnet 20 is odd enough (one imagines) to stun the lovely boy's brains. As the Poet's 'master-mistress', the youth is told he was 'first created' as a woman,

> Till nature as she wrought thee fell a-doting,
> And by addition me of thee defeated
> By adding one thing to my purpose nothing.

Nature in her doting at first shows homoerotic feeling, which perhaps seems natural enough to the author, but then, inclined to be heterosexual, she gives 'one thing', or a penis, to the boy, though even after this event the Poet's feelings remain sexual. And if never the boy's possessor, he is 'proud as an enjoyer', as he says with sexual innuendo:

> Now counting best to be with you alone,
> Then bettered that the world may see my pleasure;
> Sometime all full with feasting on your sight,
> And by and by clean starvèd for a look.

> (Sonnet 75)

The effect is to universalize his feeling without loss of context, and to picture a deep yearning in all human love, both male and female.

Instead of describing the youth Shakespeare has the novel aim of 'writing' an equivalent beauty into his lyrics. So he draws on a lucid simplicity learned from the stage, and on imagery of the seasons, often with irony as his Richard does. He catches the rhythm of nature famously at his best as in Sonnet 18 ('Shall I compare thee') or writes, with less irony and more passion:

> How like a winter hath my absence been
> From thee, the pleasure of the fleeting year!
> What freezings have I felt, what dark days seen,
> What old December's bareness everywhere!
>
> (Sonnet 97)

Or he reaches pathos in an opening line, 'From you have I been absent in the spring', and develops it in speaking cadences and severely simple, graphic details. Almost as often multiple meanings coalesce, check, or reinforce each other, as in the variant words, *substance*, *shadow*, and *shade* in Sonnet 53, which has the syntactical clarity of his limpid style. Elsewhere he can include meanings that contradict themselves and find no resolution.

He also begins to reveal the price he pays to write as he does, and the oddities of his imagination and memory. He exaggerates feeling; but Tudor drama rested on the ability of poets to plumb recesses of motivation that are obscure, and feeling, of every kind, was a guide. He can bring human loss, debilitating grief, and dead and lamented friends to bear on ardour. 'Thy bosom is endearèd with all hearts', the lovely boy is told,

> Which I by lacking have supposèd dead,
> And there reigns love, and all love's loving parts,
> And all the friends which I thought burièd.
> How many a holy and obsequious tear
> Hath dear religious love stol'n from mine eye
> As interest of the dead, which now appear
> But things removed that hidden in thee lie!
>
> (Sonnet 31)

Even if it is a poetic conceit that the lovely boy is a 'grave' of love, the lines offer an unforced view of memory. For Shakespeare, memory has concentrative and animating effects; those 'supposed' dead or 'thought' buried, as it were, return. They seem reborn, because what was once felt for them is recovered forcefully in memory, and this emotive force has creative uses as in picturing the boy or the fond Poet's ardour. If Shakespeare's memory works in this way, things 'removed' in time or space have startling freshness for him, and his creative resources are immense. Anne Shakespeare is in the Sonnets apparently, since the turmoil of his courtship (for example) is memorially recoverable as he writes of love and betrayal.

Is the self-effacing artist, in some way, a victim of the imagined being or emotion into which the past momentarily pours? The lovely boy is fickle, but the Poet is obsessed with his own faults, his self-conceit or worn face, 'Beated and chapped with tanned antiquity' (Sonnet 62). 'Being your slave' and 'your vassal', as the Poet repeats, 'O let me suffer' (Sonnets 57–8). Parted from any sight of the youth, he is subject to restless, petty moods, or feels 'outcast' and 'all alone', almost self-despising, and summons up regrets:

> I sigh the lack of many a thing I sought,
> And with old woes new wail my dear time's waste.
>
> (Sonnet 30)

This in the language of patronage may imply that a patron's love or aid is needed for one's well-being; indeed the melancholy in the Sonnets is often conventional—but their anxiety, restlessness, and sense of time lost are not.

Death is a promise of stasis and of deliverance from hope, desire, and shame alike. An elegiac note in the Sonnets was to surprise John Keats, but the author's tone is seldom more assured than when he takes up death's law,

> But be contented when that fell arrest
> Without all bail shall carry me away
>
> (Sonnet 74)

or church-bells ringing out death, as in plague-time,

> No longer mourn for me when I am dead
> Than you shall hear the surly sullen bell
> Give warning to the world
>
> (Sonnet 71)

or death's bleak, beautiful season with a possible allusion, after all, to 'our ruined monasteries':

> yellow leaves, or none, or few, do hang
> Upon those boughs which shake against the cold,
> Bare ruined choirs where late the sweet birds sang.
>
> (Sonnet 73)

Yet the Poet's odd exhilaration belies any death-wish; he tirelessly forecasts his demise to play on a boy's shallow heart. And images of death work as symbols of thematic integration which the Poet's splendid, varying reflections do not quite achieve: he imagines a time 'When all the breathers of this world are dead' (Sonnet 81) and the lovely boy—his follies of less account—will 'live' in lyrics that never deny his beauty. These sonnets rest in no other less ironic truth; and the author perhaps acknowledges the moral failure he sees in their tentativeness, and in his inability to hold fast to anything but a picture of removed, faulty beauty. 'My name be buried where my body is', writes Shakespeare, 'For I am shamed by that which I bring forth' (Sonnet 72).

That would not have hurt him in the eyes of a noble patron, and in Sonnets 127–52—mainly to the Dark Woman—he is implicitly harder on himself. His sexuality is perhaps more overt; he might be obsessed with sexual experience since he has included bawdy puns even in poems on ideal love. In a degrading affair and unable to break off his liaison, the Poet has ruminated nearly to 'madness'. His Dark Woman is a composite portrait, with details of her colouring or eyebrow 'mourners' echoing Sidney's seventh sonnet to Stella. We hear of her in incongruous reports. She can be 'thy sweet self'—or she cups her hand over the virginal's jacks prettily—but in a lightly or (more often) mordantly joking perspective she is also ugly, with her dun breasts, sallow face, and cosmetics, 'black as hell', dangerous, vile, and whorish, a 'bay where all men ride' with so foul a face as to prove Cupid a blind fool, and love a 'false plague' or self-deceiving disease.

As an index of the Poet's rage against himself she is intentionally out of focus, as we might say. 'Me from myself thy cruel eye hath taken', the Poet bitterly accuses her; he proposes various frail, temporary objectifications of himself to endure at all. In one of these he is a victim of love's 'fever', longing for more of the disease that agonizes him. In another, he is no more than a phallic drudge.

'Flesh', he assures his lady, .

> rising at thy name doth point out thee
> As his triumphant prize.
>
> (Sonnet 151)

Yet as he has violated social codes that properly bind men and women, his isolation remains. Shakespeare's lyrics are not moralistic but tragic, as they take up in these various views of the 'self' the manner in which alienation may influence perception and language. The author may well explore his own sexual nausea, the better to understand Hamlet's, Angelo's, Othello's, or Lear's horror of sexuality. His interests here are at once psychological and social. For Elizabethans adultery implied bastardy and so threatened family succession and the survival of names. Quibbles or puns on the name 'Will' are appropriate. The Poet's name is 'Will'; so is the name of the Dark Lady's husband. Shakespeare mocks the pretended self-revelation of the sonnet vogue by neatly dissociating his *own* name from 'Will' with allusions to non-existent persons of that name in proverb and popular riddle. Yet Sonnets 135 and 136, on Will, pick up slang meanings of *will* as both penis and vagina, and obsessively condemn the adulterer. 'Wilt thou', the Poet obscenely asks his lady,

> whose will is large and spacious,
> Not once vouchsafe to hide my will in thine?
>
> (Sonnet 135)

Still, the author avoids moralizing even in his fine sonnet on lust. Here he echoes a pun on *waist/waste* which Barnabe Barnes had developed in the same volume (of 1593) in which he praised the Earl of Southampton. For Shakespeare, a 'waste of shame' implies a 'shameful waist'. In modern editions of the Sonnets, grammatical punctuation may abet the clarity of this great discourse on lust, but Shake-speare's intimacy of tone is perhaps more apparent in the text of 1609:

> Th'expence of Spirit in a waste of shame
> Is lust in action, and till action, lust
> Is perjurd, murdrous, blouddy full of blame,
> Savage, extreame, rude, cruell, not to trust,
> Injoyd no sooner but dispised straight,
> Past reason hunted, and no sooner had
> Past reason hated as a swollowed bayt,
> On purpose layd to make the taker mad.
> Made In pursut and in possession so,
> Had, having, and in quest, to have extreame,
> A blisse in proofe and provd and very wo,
> Before a joy proposd behind a dreame,
> > All this the world well knowes yet none knowes well,
> > To shun the heaven that leads men to this hell.

(Sonnet 129)

If the Sonnets were set from his manuscript, he may have written 'In pursut and in possession so', and then inserted 'Made' (for 'Mad') in line 9 without changing the capital letter of the next word.[28] Quick and flowing as this poem is, its vision of lust is nightmarish. Developing his art typically by pressing situations to extremes, he etches the bleakest side of passion. He pictures a sexual reality that other sonneteers of the 1590s fail to show, and ends his series with two wry, ironic sonnets on venereal disease.

Politics and *King John*

By the time *Lucrece* was printed in 1594, the theatre offered some illusion of hope for a few actors as plague abated. Among playwrights active just before the epidemic, few survived it for long. John Lyly lived on unproductively and sat as MP for one 'pocket borough' after another. Greene was gone; Peele and Nashe had only a few years left. Lodge was about to renounce the theatre. Kyd dragged out his last months in squalor, and on 30 May 1593 at Deptford—along the river south-east of the capital—Marlowe had been killed in a knife-fight with three of the scum of the government's intelligence network (Ingram Friser, Robert Poley, and Nicholas Skeres).

Shakespeare's soft-voiced, glittering patron now faced paying a fine to Burghley, and another vast fee to get his estates out of wardship. In November 1594, the young earl was leasing out part of Southampton House, and a few years later selling off five of his manors, including Portsea and Bighton—the last to relatives of the poet George Wither. He did little else tangibly for poets, and in fact the young earl was not well placed to offer great sums of money, a semi-permanent house-hold office, a sinecure, or other large benefits of patronage. The myth that he once gave Shakespeare £1,000 for a 'Purchase' was invented by Sir William Davenant, and strained even the credulity of Rowe (who noted it in 1709).

But having used the earl's fashionable name, Shakespeare in *Venus* and *Lucrece* had offset the slurs of Greene and advertised his worth as a poet who pleased beyond the public stage. He might yet attract political patronage, and early in the spring of 1594 he could not have been certain of his way ahead.

Throwing in his own political lot with the brash, vigorous Earl of Essex, Southampton began to offer a lively spectacle. Railing at the Burghley–Cecil faction in government and quietly scheming for James VI's succession, the Earl of Essex was drawing Puritan and Catholic followers alike. In 1599 he set sail to crush the Earl of Tyrone's or 'the O'Neill's' rebellion in Ireland and took along as his cavalry general Southampton—who, just lately, had offended the Queen by seducing and marrying one of her doll-like Maids of Honour. In the most cautious patriotic way Shakespeare spoke out. In his only clear, specific allusion to a contemporary (and extra-dramatic) event, he has the Chorus in Act V of *Henry V* comment on the Earl of Essex's possible return from the Irish bogs.

Had not Londoners cheered King Harry after a rain of arrows at Agincourt? (Not that the famous use of arrows and stakes against the French cavalry is explicit in the play.) 'As, by a lower but high-loving likelihood', says the Chorus, with imperfect faith in the Earl of Essex's military luck,

Were now the General of our gracious Empress—
As in good time he may—from Ireland coming,
Bringing rebellion broachèd on his sword,
How many would the peaceful city quit
To welcome him! Much more, and much more cause,
Did they this Harry.

(V. O. 29–35)

This is no propaganda for Essex and Southampton—and Shakespeare's doubt about their expedition was prophetic. After the débâcle of the army overseas, Southampton, Rutland and his brother, and a few other rash romantics joined the Earl of Essex in a rebellion against the Queen in 1601. But Londoners failed to rise against her, and Essex was executed. Southampton luckily was merely imprisoned in the Tower—with his cat for company.

Finally, when nearly retired from the stage, Shakespeare gave a very slight sign of his feeling for the Essex conspirators—and indirectly for his former patron—by devising an *impresa* for Southampton's friend the sixth Earl of Rutland. Such *imprese* were insignia, with mottoes and allegorical designs, usually painted on banners or paper shields. Shakespeare was paid 44s. for devising the work, his friend Burbage the same amount for painting it, and Rutland carried the insignia at a tourney, on 24 March, to mark King James's Accession Day in 1613.

These late, almost nostalgic, gestures are indicative at least of Shakespeare's regard for the fate of the Essex faction. No doubt his caution was prudent, but it was also a sign of his wish to keep his poise, his freedom of enquiry into political motives. And that much is evident in his *King John*, a play which may date from around 1593–4 or a little later. *King John* has a relation to the Sonnets and to *Lucrece*'s style, but the date or dates of its composition are in dispute and it could be a revised play, originally written before its author had read the anonymous, crude, anti-Catholic drama *The Troublesome Raigne of John, King of England* which was printed in two parts in 1591.

Shakespeare, in his play, in effect looks at modern political motives by taking up a thirteenth-century subject. King John, in defying the

193

pope, seemed a hero to Elizabethan Protestants. In the play he is weak and wavering, living in a world of deceit and compromise in which religion itself is political. Significantly the play offended Catholics, and William Sankey SJ, on the authority of the Holy Office, was to censor much of it in the 1640s for students at an English college in Spain. Shakespeare's papal legate Cardinal Pandolf has a grand subtle intellect and is by no means corrupt, but he is worldly, cynical, and capable of political blackmail on behalf of the pope.

The play's boldly sardonic, developing hero—the Bastard Falcon-bridge—begins as a self-interested adventurer equipped in his rough and ready way for survival. He might be an ideal play-actor, ready to serve, detached from events, observant, and not inhibited. As the play's moral agent he is sensitive to politics as an arena of deceit, chance, treachery, self-delusion, and cowardice, and he interestingly rails against the refinement of court circles in a manner that might imply effeteness and ineptitude in Shakespeare's own patron.

The yearning at the root of *King John*—and conveyed by the Bas-tard—is for a blameless, wise ruler in a just commonwealth; this is set against the realities of viciousness, weakness, and guile in the political world. The play's portraits are at once subtle and given in highly rhetorical and somewhat overwrought verse. *King John* might have suited a weary, if well disciplined, troupe on the road, since it nearly 'acts' itself and demands unusual restraint. Its portrait of Constance, the mother of King John's victim, young Arthur, reminds one of the technical experiment of *Lucrece*. And its Bastard's patriotism is thoughtful and questioning, at least partly because the author has tested his own paradoxes of attitude as a sonneteer.

Though distanced from pieties of his upbringing, Shakespeare had not lost his Christian faith, or his belief in the worth of his nation under its Queen. He sympathized with Catholics, but he shows King John cowed by the pope's legate. Cardinal Pandolf tells the king with reference to the French threat to England:

> It was my breath that blew this tempest up,
> Upon your stubborn usage of the Pope,
> And since you are a gentle convertite,

My tongue shall hush again this storm of war
And make fair weather in your blust'ring land.

(v. i. 17–21)

The Bastard, however, has another counsel for a confused, enfeebled king. 'But wherefore do you droop? Why look you sad?' Falconbridge tells John,

> Away, and glisten like the god of war
> When he intendeth to become the field.
> Show boldness and aspiring confidence.

(v. i. 44, 54–6)[29]

Such an antidote to discouragement seems meant for a weary company, as well as a king. *King John*'s overall form is poorer than in its best scenes, and the play is not a strong one. But its Bastard speaks with hard-won authority, and suggests an author who knows the pain of plague-time and the struggle of actors to endure.

II

A SERVANT OF THE LORD CHAMBERLAIN

I am as vigilant as a cat to steal cream.

(Falstaff, *1 Henry IV*)

Sharing with the Burbages

*I*n the bleak, cold spring of 1594, plague abated in southern England and players returned under grey skies to London. Few people could remember such an odd, dismal spring. The past two years had punished the acting troupes; none had thrived on the road and plague had brought total chaos to the entertainment world. Pembroke's men had broken up and had sold their playbooks, which thus came into print like debris from a sinking ship. Keen to advertise themselves, it seems, and stay afloat, other troupes released plays for publication. Hertford's small troupe faltered, and after losing their own patron, Sussex's men disbanded. Then, on 16 April, Ferdinando Lord Strange (lately fifth Earl of Derby) died in such bizarre circumstances that it was rumoured he had been poisoned, as likely he was, and his death, a few months after that of the Earl of Sussex, meant the theatre had lost two of its keenest patrons. Ferdinando's troupe performed in the name of his widow, the Dowager Countess Alice—who will concern us—but his death was like a bad omen. Cold skies, moreover, foretold a poor grain harvest (the first of four utterly disastrous annual failures) with rising prices and new hardships.

So far, Shakespeare had kept his options open: in the letter accompanying *Lucrece* he looks ahead to writing poems, not more dramas, while implying he will accept patronage. In May the government interfered—as if a giant were regrouping the children in a vast urban sandlot—and set up a kind of theatrical monopoly in London. That would give him a new chance; but biographers have underestimated his real situation, just as they neglect the difficulties faced by his new troupe in the mid-1590s. In some ways, his troubles only deepened as his career became more settled. Once committed to the theatre, he was unlikely to write another *Venus* or *Lucrece*; and it was unlikely that any stage drama could have the status of such works. He cut himself off from the hope that is implicit in his two letters to Southampton, and a curious, cold sense of loss and disappointment runs in his Sonnets. Whatever he did, he might be less than respectable in a Midlands town; but the low status of actors was an old ache, a grievance felt by colleagues such as Phillips and Pope, and not the worst of his problems. Some dissatisfaction with himself saved him from complacency, while quickening his intellectual life; he adjusted with some cunning to a milieu he felt he had to accept to earn his livelihood. But the financial outlook of his new company was uncertain; he had nothing else to fall back upon, and might return home with nothing. If he had followed the path of his *Titus* playbook and gone with Burbage from Lord Strange's company, after May 1591, into Pembroke's, and then Sussex's, he had been obliged to do so to survive; in later years his fidelity to one troupe would be unique among poets. Yet that loyalty is no sign of his contentment, and there are underlying complications in his ambiguous writing to suggest that he opposed his vocation as much as he accepted it. He subverted many norms of the theatre and defied his medium as he made use of a compromised way of life in 1595 and 1596; he mocked popular assumptions even in his first great mythic plays *Romeo and Juliet* and *A Midsummer Night's Dream*, before creating a radical, ebullient mocker in Falstaff and virtually turning English history on its head. How did his new situation come about, and how did his new duties really affect him?

Certainly in the plague, old James Burbage, as proprietor of the empty Shoreditch Theater, had not been quite idle. In good times, as recent evidence shows, Burbage broke city trade-laws in his manner of selling fruit, nuts, and drink to playgoers. He was fined, indicted, and banned from catering. Yet even when the Theater was shut he sold food illegally at Holywell Street, despite summonses from the

Middlesex justices (each year from 1591 to 1594). He felt the freer to do so, it seems, because of a connection in high places. He claimed to be 'Hunsdons man', while wearing the livery of old Henry Carey, Lord Hunsdon of the Privy Council.

This lord had a rather downright manner, a 'custom of swearing and obscenity', and the outlook of a politic old hedonist.[1] When his mistress Aemilia Lanyer, who was the daughter of a court musician, bore him a son called Henry in 1593, Lord Hunsdon was not very badly inconvenienced; the child, after all, had a notional father in her husband, the spendthrift musician Alfonso Lanier.[2] Hunsdon hardly concealed his follies, and in the obdurate old James Burbage, defying the law with his nuts and drink, he had a loyal and rugged admirer. More than once, Hunsdon's intervention saved the Theater from hostile voices on the Privy Council, and Burbage played Falstaff to a rather wheezy, ageing Prince Hal. Hunsdon was the Queen's first cousin (he was the son of Anne Boleyn's sister) and in view of Henry VIII's appetites he was said to be Elizabeth's half-brother, too. If not always on perfect terms with the Queen, he was one of her more trusted advisers. Moreover not long after his son-in-law Charles Howard, Lord Howard of Effingham, became the Lord High Admiral, Hunsdon was appointed the Queen's Chamberlain with control of funds and play-censorship in the Revels Office.

In that office, economy was vital. Hunsdon knew for instance that it cost his office three times as much to stage a masque for the Queen as to pay for a play, and so, in league with Charles Howard, he usually protected actors from the worst demands of Guildhall, while quietly favouring the Queen's troupe, which was set up in 1583. But the Queen's group split in two twice, and in the spring of 1594 its remnants were in decline. Other acting companies were nearly bankrupted, melting away, and two of the best player-patrons—Sussex and Derby—were gone. Hunsdon and Howard had to move boldly to keep a stable, durable troupe in the capital.

If the lords took advice, two women would have heard of plans affecting the fate of Shakespeare and other actors. It is unlikely that Hunsdon took five major actors from the troupe of his own relative, Alice, Countess of Derby—Ferdinando's widow—without consulting her. Derby's men performed in her name in May. Litigious, abrasive, and later dissatisfied in a second marriage, the Dowager Countess Alice oddly took a generous interest in poets and actors. Hunsdon's daughter and Howard's wife, Catherine Carey, who was closer to the Queen than either of them, would probably also have given advice. What emerged, at any rate, was a sensitive theatrical plan of considerable help to Shakespeare. Though nominally sponsored by two Privy Council lords, it was not strictly a measure of the Queen's government, and that made the plan somewhat fragile. But it ensured the continuance of London playing, and, in the long run, the greatest cultural success a modern nation had ever known.

Hunsdon and Howard's plan had a double-insurance feature in that two troupes were set up with a 'family' at each centre for stability; the two groups would straddle London, one north of the walls, one just south of the river. Hunsdon would sponsor men and boys under the Chamberlain's name at Shoreditch and thus oblige the profit-hungry old Burbage and his two sons. (Cuthbert Burbage, lately a servant, had been baptized on 15 June 1565: he was now almost 29; young Richard, the actor, baptized on 7 July 1568, was 25, with his main success still ahead of him.) In turn, Howard would lend the Lord Admiral's name to a troupe on Bankside with Edward Alleyn, his wife Joan, and father-in-law Philip Henslowe at the centre.[3]

For the Admiral's men, Howard thus had the most famous actor in Alleyn, the wealthiest impresario in Henslowe, and perhaps the most up-to-date theatre in the Rose, along with all of Marlowe's dramas and the rest of Henslowe's rich stock of playbooks. The actors were not to be sworn in as Gentlemen of the Privy Chamber but would wear the badge and colours of Hunsdon or Howard. Among Howard's dependable, well-tried actors were Thomas Downton from Derby's troupe, John Singer of the Queen's, as well as Edward Dutton (prominent by 1597), Edward Juby, Martin Slater, and Thomas Towne. All of them wore a badge of the Lord Admiral's players—a noble white lion with a blue shoulder-crescent.

Yet Hunsdon was not quite outdone. His troupe began with seven or eight shareholders, though the number would rise. As Chamberlain's sharers—or leading actors who would jointly own and manage the company, pay expenses, and take profits—Richard Burbage and Shakespeare probably came in before the summer. Five more sharers were found in the Countess Alice's troupe in George Bryan, John Heminges, Will Kempe, Augustine Phillips, and Thomas Pope, along with some lesser recruits. These men and boys wore the insignia, on a round arm-badge or on a brooch pinned to the hat, of a flying silver swan.

Shakespeare had to pay about £50 for a Chamberlain's share, unless he was excused from that. In lieu of paying, he may have agreed to write for the company two new plays a year—one comedy and one serious work—for which he would be recompensed. The Burbages knew something of his value. All of his early plays came into their hands, either because he had kept his rights, or because old Burbage shrewdly had bought the *Henry VI* scripts and a few others.

Much else doubtless came into company hands, and it is likely that they acquired four other playscripts of some note: a *Hamlet* which was perhaps Kyd's, a recent *King Leir*, *The Troublesome Raigne of John, King of England*, and one of several texts of *The Famous Victories of Henry V*. The titles are interesting. *King Leir* definitely, if not versions of the other plays, had once belonged to the badly depleted Queen's troupe, which in the spring quit London to go 'into the contrey to play', as Henslowe recorded; for one reason or another they did not return. The regular poet of the Chamberlain's men, it seems, was to ensure that new versions of those same four playscripts would not be forgotten.

❦

Without much time for planning, the Admiral's and the Chamberlain's men shared a ten-day run at Newington Butts in June. This was miserable; the takings up to 13 June were thin. Two days later the Admiral's Servants were at the Rose near the river, and here they had a fairly brilliant run—putting on nearly three dozen plays in fifty weeks and breaking only at Lent and midsummer.

The Chamberlain's men had unknown problems—the Theater may not have been ready, or the venue gave difficulty—and in September they were out at Marlborough in Wiltshire. But, not meaning to starve in the winter, they made it plain to their great patron that they needed to be in the city's heart at the Cross Keys inn in Gracechurch Street. On 8 October 1594, Hunsdon sent an odd letter to the Lord Mayor, something in between a fiat and a request, to 'requier and praye' that Shakespeare's company be allowed in the city. He implies they are *already* there, and promises the actors will begin at two o'clock, instead of nearly four. They will be less noisy than in the suburbs, not using any drums or trumpets at all,

for the callinge of peopell together, and shall be contributories to the poore of the parishe where they plaie accordinge to their habilities. And soe not dowting of your willingnes to yeeld hereunto, upon theise resonable condicions, I comitt yow to the Almightie . . . this viijth of October 1594.

Your lordships lovinge freind,
H. Hounsdon[4]

For a few days at least, Shakespeare and his fellows were at the Cross Keys, near the arterial road leading up to the city's north-east gate.

Playwrights, we imagine, must have waited for elaborate civic occasions to see symbolic, colourful ceremonies from which they could learn. But after the plague, a wealthy inner parish of London would have shown its own rainbow. Colours, at the time, were not just anarchical; and streets were encoded with a thousand symbols of rank, trade, and profession, with heraldry on flags and even on shop signs. One saw the badged coats of liveries, ecclesiastical and civil robes, now and then the black gowns of students or magistrates, and many blues of apprentices. On a working day, London would have given Shakespeare vibrant examples of a symbolism of colour. London also offered books, and not far from the inn was the bookshop of William Barley—soon to be a music publisher.

How did Shakespeare get his books? By late 1594 he must have owned a copy of the second edition of Holinshed's *Chronicles*, and he would soon make use of 'The Life of Theseus' in North's version of Plutarch's *Lives*. After the Earl of Derby died his widow Alice in fact presented a copy of North's Plutarch to a man named 'Wilhelmi'—or

William—but the last name is lost. A Latin inscription (not in her own hand) has been cut to leave the words:

> Nunc Wilhelmi
> dono Nobilissima
> Alisiae Comitissae[5]

Perhaps Shakespeare, perhaps someone else. But Alice's book—whoever her William was—suggests that patrons gave volumes as desirable gifts and so a poet might acquire books in this way. Patrons, such as the third Earl of Pembroke, even gave money for book-buying. At Stratford today is a copy of Henri Estienne's *Katherine de Medicis* (1575), a work full of allusions to the King of Navarre;[6] it was once in Shakespeare's hands if we accept a legend, not very sound, that his daughter Susanna later gave it to a royal chamberlain. What seems true is that in an age when books were costly, he acquired from sellers or patrons a few that he most needed, and borrowed others on short-term loan. One evident resource was the printing office of his friend Richard Field, since it appears that soon after Field printed Richard Crompton's *Mansion of Magnanimitie* early in 1599, the poet was able to consult a copy for *Henry V*.

At the Cross Keys, he was near the Eastcheap taverns of Falstaff, and, at about this time, his interest in London quickened. His men had a repertoire to plan in 1594, and at taverns a new play might be recited for a troupe's approval: so the Admiral's men vetted a script 'at the Sun in New Fish Street', and wine flowed at such recitals.[7] The Chamberlain's men had time for the wine, but the Guildhall's general anxiety and mortal fear of civic riot, it appears, ensured that they were never again allowed at a city inn. After moving up near Holywell Street they acted twice at the royal court in December, and later, to collect the fee, Shakespeare went along to Whitehall with Richard Burbage and Will Kempe on 15 March 1595.

As joint payees, these men were key figures in the troupe. But the usual payee became John Heminges, who as a 'business manager' held bonds, deeds, and other legal papers and looked after financial interests of his fellows. Meanwhile, the actors had begun an almost frantic routine. At the Curtain or Theater in 1595, morning rehearsals preceded the afternoon's show, and Shakespeare was then partly responsible for a pyramid of half-sharers, supporting actors, boys, and hirelings.

The first condition of his own success was a troupe's smooth order, but actors were flamboyant, living on their feelings. Offstage fights were known. His actors were not especially dangerous, but extreme cases probably suggest an underlying tenor in behaviour. John Heminges had married a widow of 16, whose actor-husband had been killed by a player, and the actor whom Ben Jonson later killed had himself murdered a man. Robert Dawes was dispatched by a fellow player. John Singer, then working as a 'gatherer', killed a play-goer who argued over the price of admission. The creator of Tybalt and Mercutio had much to observe, not least the love-affairs, flare-ups, mix-ups (as with lovers in the *Dream*), petty arguments, jealousies, and minor tumult of his own actors. And in the sharers' group he became part of a conservative phalanx which at least tacitly reinforced order. Clowns were more independent, 'solo' players, and Will Kempe presumably was not among his coterie. To judge from wills and bequests, Shakespeare was not attached to clowns, though he may have felt better about the dwarfish, subtle, literary Robert Armin than about Pope and Kempe. He perhaps had friends whom wills and bequests tell us less about, such as the boys who were to be his Juliets and Rosalinds and who were usually apprenticed to individual actors.

His special, known friends included the popular, level-headed Heminges as well as Henry Condell, Augustine Phillips, and Richard Burbage. These four had in common a certain natural plausibility, and an influence on and off the stage. Starting in the group as no more than a half-sharer, Condell in 1596 married a city heiress with twelve valu-able houses in the Strand west of Somerset House, and after that, though he did not win fame as an actor, he was of value for business acumen and somewhat stolid efficiency. Augustine Phillips was a cau-tious, dependable musician and actor who was to testify for the troupe, as will appear, in a crisis over *Richard II.* After moving up from Bank-side, he made elaborate provisions to protect his modest wealth, bought himself a coat of arms to which he had no right, and must have seen his practical-minded friends Condell and Shakespeare fairly often offstage; he favoured them both with 30*s.* bequests and left lesser sums to other actors. Richard Burbage, whose tragic roles concern us especially, became the leading actor of his time and an adept, amateur painter who peers today, rather abjectly, from a supposed self-portrait at Dulwich Picture Gallery in South London. He had a reputation for temper, but, unspoiled by success, he was one of the troupe's more stable elements. Shakespeare, it is said, was obsessed with money—but this myth has been partly dispelled by recent evidence. Neither he nor any of his settled, married friends among the sharers, to judge from allusions to their finances, was very money-hungry, though all cared for social status and the troupe's profitability. Famous as he was, Burbage had land worth only £200 to £300 a year when he died— about the annual worth of Shakespeare's total property in 1616 (and a trifle compared with the riches of the Admiral's star, Alleyn, who could invest £10,000 in a manor at a stroke).[8]

Without obvious compromise, they attended to patrons and authorities, and may have buttered them up. Burbage befriended the wealthy William Herbert, Earl of Pembroke, even before that patron had the chamberlaincy, and Shakespeare and Heminges dealt with licensors of the Revels Office, whose trust Heminges very clearly won. 'Teste [so states] W. Shakespea*re*', one finds in a note in an early seventeenth-century hand about the author of *George a Greene*, a comedy revived at the Rose. In the play, George a Greene is 'Pinner of Wakefield', an officer in charge of impounding stray beasts. If one can trust the note, an official (such as Sir George Buc) had asked the poet about the play's authorship. *George a Greene* was written by 'a minister', Shakespeare is reported to have said amiably, 'who acted the pinner's part in it himself'.[9]

In an Elizabethan company, all the sharers performed in each play, though there must have been many exceptions. Recent evidence from computer studies, involving the lexicon or vocabulary of each of his dramatis personae, in quarto and folio texts, yields a rather eerie, problematic view of Shakespeare acting. Much of his play-writing, it appears from these studies, was done in his favoured 'season' for sitting at his writing table, November to February, but he acted the year round, often taking two or three minor parts instead of a major one.

His striking, more energetic, roles in his own works, or so we are told, included that of black Aaron in *Titus Andronicus*, Antonio in *Twelfth Night*, and Ulysses in *Troilus and Cressida*. He played several kings (as it was reported in the seventeenth century that he had done), but more typically old men, churchmen, or 'presenter figures'—such as *Henry V*'s fine Chorus—roles which called for eloquence rather than much acting skill. He spoke on average as few as 300 lines in a performance, chose parts that took him on stage in opening scenes (sometimes to a drum-roll or trumpet-flourish), and often had the first line in a drama. In his *Romeo and Juliet*, Shakespeare, as we hear, played Friar Laurence and later the Chorus. In *A Midsummer Night's Dream*, he was usually content to be Duke Theseus, who discourses on poetry. On separate occasions in the same drama, he played either Mortimer or Exeter in *1 Henry VI*, Ferdinand or Boyet in *Love's Labour's Lost*, and Leonato or the Friar and Messenger in *Much Ado*. He doubled as old Gaunt and the Gardener in *Richard II*, impersonated King Henry in both parts of *Henry IV*, as well as Rumour in Part 2, the Garter Inn's Host and then Master Ford in *Merry Wives*, the King in *All's Well*, and Duncan in *Macbeth*. Shakespeare perhaps liked to stun the groundlings with finely tonal, 'aria' speeches. He consistently took the sentimental Egeon's role in *The Comedy of Errors*, and he did play Adam in *As You Like It* and the Ghost as well as the First Player in *Hamlet*.

All of this, anyway, is what computer analysis says or implies: he would have had to memorize a role to act it, so with high frequency, in theory, his 'rare' or seldom-used words in that role will crop up in his subsequent work to tell the computer that he did take each of the parts just mentioned, or such minor parts as Flavius in *Julius Caesar*, or Desdemona's scandalized old parent Brabanzio in *Othello*. Anyway, so much for theory. Facts are another matter: the computer's results may be explained in some other way, and, so far, at best, we have frail hints as to his acting roles—not proof.[10]

But there is no hint that he took major parts; he was likely to be protected because his composition rate was high, and his friends knew it. Collaborators often had a hand in more titles overall, but few poets wrote more than an equivalent of two whole new plays a year. He was exceptional before he joined the Chamberlain's men, but even with his deep, abiding tensions and his regret—not about the money he was earning, but, it seems, about the way he earned it—he excelled in a fairly stable troupe in which membership did not quickly change. Stage demands suited his rapid intellect, and his writing suggests a needed release. His productive tensions may be related to an obscure, residual, and not quite unevidenced self-contempt, and to the problem of unbalanced excesses from time to time in his work; but it is a good deal less speculative to say that in the late 1590s he lived to an unusual degree in and through other viewpoints. Like most Tudor playwrights he was not especially proprietary about his scripts, and he gave the actors chances to mock their calling and also their poet, as in several of his solemnly absurd plays-within-plays. His troupe's solidarity—which he abetted—would have kept outsiders and the curious at bay while helping him to know the sweating, hard-worked actors well. He took pains to show how lightly he regarded himself, or at any rate there are more 'in-jokes', theatre references, and self-deprecating allusions in *A Midsummer Night's Dream* or *Hamlet* than in all the dramas by his rivals. In a small group of managers, with close colleagues among the steadiest, he worked in the midst of a troupe to achieve results—and as they acted his plays the troupe expressed his own inner being.

His company was under threat from a puritanical Guildhall, from competition, plague, and dwindling receipts, but the public theatres were more stable than before 1594. The audiences included many habitual play-goers. Not only leading actors, but Phillips, Shakespeare, and individual boys in their wigs and luxurious dresses would have been identified on stage, and if Burbage missed a line in *Richard III*, it was perhaps shouted down at him. Audiences knew Shakespeare and he knew them, so that despite disruptions, there might be a complex, subtle communicative exchange when a play was acted.

Thus he had some incentive to pursue his interests, and he might have felt he had little to lose. He did not write *Romeo* or the *Dream* much before 1596, but in their fresh, artful use of locale these plays at least begin to show what he found in the Chamberlain's group. They are in part correctives; they make up for a feeble sense of locale in *Lucrece*, or for a nervous, overwrought ingenuity in some of its stanzas, as well as for slack, almost timid, imitativeness in a few of the Sonnets. He has found naturalness, the right detachment, and he succeeded not only because of his talent. The more self-abnegating he became, the more his imagination really flourished. His daily self-effacing duties would have given him a sense of routine as he sat at his table, and he found he could supply his troupe best by complicating his work and giving it multiple layers of appeal. In the same play, he can affirm and repudiate popular attitudes, and in a sense, by writing plays with subversive, troubling aspects, he remained inside and outside his vocation, and abetted his own development.

Performing even in minor roles, he learned from acting; and the paradox is that he drew now from an audience's intelligence and energy, only to overturn the city's static, predictable attitudes. In fact he challenged Londoners and their views in his soaring, witty, lyric styles, as he told them about love in his two greatest works so far.

Dreams and the doors of breath

In the summer of 1595 Londoners were alarmed by severe rioting over food prices. At Southwark butter was snatched from vendors who were paid for it at 3*d.* a pound, instead of 5*d.* asked, and such high-handedness led to violence. At Tower Hill crowds of apprentices and other youths throwing a hail of stones and inspired by a trumpet-call drove local warders back into Tower Street.

Not only the Lord Mayor, but the Crown took alarm. A curfew was decreed, public assemblies were banned. All theatres were closed by order. By 26 June Shakespeare had lost his means of livelihood. By then the Rose had shut, and the Admiral's men toured to stay solvent. The Burbages' troupe suffered until late in August—when acting resumed—but as if to mock Hunsdon and Howard's plan, the new Lord Mayor recognized no truce and asked that the Theater and the Rose be pulled down.[11] How long would an ailing, elderly Lord Hunsdon protect his troupe? Shakespeare prepared *Romeo and Juliet* for a tense city, and his tragedy reflects the civic tension and obtuseness that make violence endemic in life.

A great love story which he knew in Arthur Brooke's poem *Romeus and Juliet* dictated an Italian setting. Italy suited Shakespeare's experiments, and with her pagan, triumphal Rome so often compared with the English capital, this was the cultural land of his schooldays. The beauty and elegance he associates with Italy have a curious effect upon him, freeing his pen from normal inhibitions even as he adheres to an outmoded Petrarchism in his Sonnets. His path to Elsinore is partly Italian. He set most of his early comedies and six of his ten tragedies in Italy or ancient Rome—and no other country gave him freer leave to test unbalanced extremes in his dramaturgy. In creating absurd, febrile lovers in *The Two Gentlemen* or the sharply articulate pain of his Roman Titus, or the piercing beauty of Juliet, or the pithy, unassimilated grandeur of his Italian Shylock, he supplied the stage while opposing its norms, boundaries, stereotypes, and predictability—and there is a note of defiance in *Romeo and Juliet*. The author, as *poet*, upsets his medium and redefines tragedy, but on the other hand his play's rhymes, sonnets, intense bawdy wit, and soaring images drenched with the classics almost topple his new work into bathos.

No doubt economic and social facts of the theatre were influencing him even as he took rivals into account. Keeping in step, his own company and the Admiral's both soon had plays on Henry V, Jack Straw, Owen Tudor, King John, Richard III, or Troilus and Cressida. The Admiral's took a conservative 'good citizen's' attitude to love and marriage, but Shakespeare's fellows, offering more radical and subtle love-dramas, were getting a following among Inns of Court students, courtiers, members of Commons, lawyers, merchants, and their ladies. Beyond these were ranks of tradespeople, carriers, labourers, and many apprentices, and the latter were of no small interest to the entertainment industry. Most of the city's apprentices—contrary to what is often said—were not boys but young people in their late teens or early twenties, who might wait years in the metropolis or return home before they could marry.[12] If the bordellos and bear-pits drew some of them, so did love plays and even popular history plays in the suburbs. With its numerous young of both sexes, London by the mid-1590s was the nation's training college. The trainees of course had reason to complain, but they indulged in no mass riot after 1595 and many would have come to see *Romeo and Juliet* at the Curtain—and to see its author.

In the play, Shakespeare's Friar propounds a theme in Act II, scene ii, reminiscent of thoughts that an English boy might have heard from a vicar's clerk. 'O mickle'—or much—as he says over a basket of greenery,

> is the powerful grace that lies
> In plants, herbs, stones, and their true qualities.
>
> (II. ii. 15–16)

Does botany offer instruction in life?

> Within the infant rind of this weak flower
> Poison hath residence, and medicine power
>
> .   .   .   .   .   .
>
> Two such opposèd kings encamp them still
> In man as well as herbs—grace and rude will.
>
> (II. ii. 23–4, 27–8)

Grace and rude will—or love and hate—inhabit all sensate things and so must occur in each heart, each town. That truth may relate to the author's childhood, but it is borne out here with a dazzling sophistication and particularity which exalt brief love ironically above all else.

Romeo and Juliet begins as a romantic comedy. After servants of the Capulets and Montagues appear there is a minor street fight, and Romeo—as a Montague besotted by a black-haired Rosaline—even sounds like the butt of a romantic farce: 'O me! What fray was here?' he asks his friend Benvolio,

> Here's much to do with hate, but more with love.
> Why then, O brawling love, O loving hate,
> O anything of nothing first create
>
> .   .   .   .   .   .
>
> This love feel I.
>
> (I. i. 170, 172–4, 179)

But if love-struck and unaware, he is not rash. His family's enemies are well disposed to him, and when he invades old Capulet's feast that enemy is not unkind or hostile. 'To say truth', as Capulet admits,

> Verona brags of him
> To be a virtuous and well-governed youth.
> I would not for the wealth of all this town
> Here in my house do him disparagement.
>
> (I. v. 66–9)

In a play about love in rival Italian families the true lovers, oddly, have no obvious obstacles to surmount. The town's lawgiver is Escalus, Prince of Verona, who angrily ensures that penalties for violence will be extreme. Romeo and Juliet fall in love in an instant, and might prosper except that they neglect moment-to-moment realities in a drama of competing awarenesses. The tragedy occurs in four days. Images emphasize clock time, morning and night, days of the week, sequences, the exact lapse of time since a fatal event.

The most chilling murder in Shakespeare's plays occurs on Verona's streets. No violence in *Othello* or *Macbeth*, even the blinding of Gloucester in *King Lear*, has the chancy, terrible immediacy of Tybalt's killing of Mercutio with a thrust under Romeo's arm. That is untheatrical murder, of a kind known in each London parish. In keeping with that realism, the balcony scene—the most famous scene in any drama—is dependent on fleetingness, enclosure, sharp disruption, and a defiance of locale. Town, balcony, stony courtyard, perilous walls are inimical to sexual love, but love battens on opposition as if wished for by the lovers, rises to the stars, drawing the terror out of death, and defying all that mocks love's constancy. Romeo and Juliet are right—the world is wrong—or they are right to defy the time and circumstance that begrime everyone else.

Elizabethans would have seen them as ideal in honouring love, silly in flouting parental wishes, and their tragedy as being the result of a conflict between rationality and impulse. Yet the lovers are not tainted. The Franciscan Friar upbraids Romeo for his ardour while loving him the more for it. Capulet loses charity to become a testy old cormorant who will wed his daughter Juliet to Paris willy-nilly, and he is one of the play's fine achievements, his wishfulness fore-shadowing Falstaff, then giving a ground-note to offset the lovers' lyric flights. Even the obtuse are in love with words, from Lady Capulet with her book-imagery, to the illiterate Nurse who is obsessed with the 'R' of the hero's name: 'Doth not Rosemary and Romeo begin both with a letter?' she asks. (For Elizabethans, R was the dog's letter since its sound was like a growl.) But the literary images and gorgeous lyric flights might be no more than commercial features of Chamberlain's and Admiral's rivalry. Dekker—a prolific dramatist—wrote of dramas good enough to tie an audience's ears with 'golden chains' to verbal 'Melody', and so make the ignorant

> clap their *Brawny hands*,
> T'*Applaud*, what their *charmd* soule scarce understands.[13]

If this refers to Shakespeare, it slanders him, since his scenes are usually clear for those of 'brawny hands' and for the refined alike. But 'Melody', or fine, well-worked verse helped such a play as *Romeo* to keep its appeal so that it might stay in the repertoire for two years, be taken off for three or four, and then put back again later. The 'high style' was profitable.

Still his lyricism here, as in *A Midsummer Night's Dream* or *Richard II*, has other causes. Shakespeare had a realistic view of himself and nobody of discernment around 1596 would have ranked him with Sidney, Spenser, or, perhaps, even Marlowe. In the commercial theatre he could not have hoped to match the first two, nor need we assume that he secretly thought of himself as Sidney's or Spenser's equal. He was in his own view in this decade a functionary, or a minor cause of a troupe's ability to endure; and his verbal grace, after all, was the essence of his usefulness. In emulating the best poets he knew, in opposing the stage's banalities and exercising lyric talents he had developed in the plague years, he hoped to profit with his troupe, but, then, he also kept open for himself an option to decipher and picture his own complex, inner sense of society and behaviour.

He takes risks in Juliet's 'high style'. She speaks in rather magnificent literary images with the cadences of a Roman goddess rallying the legions, as in her frank display of sexual ardour while awaiting Romeo in Act III, after he has killed Tybalt:

> Gallop apace, you fiery-footed steeds,
> Towards Phoebus' lodging! Such a waggoner
> As Phaëton would whip you to the west
> And bring in cloudy night . . .

(III. ii. 1–4)

Juliet's 'high style' divides her from the impercipient around her. The intensity of her love infects Romeo, who is like an adolescent glad to find the proper, inevitable role. (One forgets that he is indirectly responsible for six deaths.) Juliet's suicide in the Capulet tomb, at last, is saintly, and Romeo's has a touching, histrionic grandeur: 'O, here', he says, bemoaning his 'world-wearied flesh' as he leans with a poison vial over pale Juliet for one final kiss,

> Eyes, look your last.
> Arms, take your last embrace, and lips, O you
> The doors of breath, seal with a righteous kiss
> A dateless bargain to engrossing death.

(V. iii. 109, 112–15)

Finally, the dead lovers seem asleep. The Friar retells their tragic story for the benefit of Verona, as if to underline his lesson that grace and hatred are interrelated, always present. Pure love is brief. Hatred or violence, in a modern city, may be expected to endure.

For all its point and great power, the play has trivial weaknesses (as critics rightly notice). Its heaped-up coincidences, or the poor exposition which brings the Chorus on again in Act II, or the inexplicably sudden failure of the Nurse's sympathies, or the Friar's awkward exit from the Capulet tomb, suggest an author troubled by structure as he develops a new kind of romantic tragedy. However in *A Midsummer Night's Dream*—which is likely often to have been staged a few days after *Romeo*, which it sends up—he offers a funny, self-mocking summary of what he has achieved in comedy and tragedy so far. This play is so brightly unique it can seem to have no sources—though it fuses much from folklore and legend, as well as from works such as

Plutarch's *Lives*, Chaucer's *Knight's Tale* and *Merchant's Tale*, and Lyly's plays, while being unlike any model.

Was the *Dream* written for a private occasion? We hear sometimes that it amused Queen Elizabeth at the wedding of the sixth Earl of Derby and Elizabeth Vere (on 26 January 1595), or that it was designed for the wedding of Lord Hunsdon's granddaughter Elizabeth Carey and Thomas, the son of Lord Berkeley (on 19 February 1596). Both brides were god-daughters to the Queen, who had over a hundred god-daughters and seldom went to weddings, though she did attend the Derby–Vere one; but masques (not plays) were performed at Tudor aristocratic weddings and we do not know of a play's being acted at a court wedding until 1614. The *Dream*, moreover, opens with references to a bleak, cold virginity unflattering to a Virgin Queen. If Hermia will not wed the man her father chooses, she must live as a nun, a 'barren sister all your life', and Theseus warns her with ducal firmness:

> earthlier happy is the rose distilled
> Than that which, withering on the virgin thorn,
> Grows, lives, and dies in single blessedness.

(I. i. 72, 76–8)

It is hard to believe that these lines, vital to the plot, were deleted if and when the play went to court, but 'barren sister' or 'virgin thorn' may not have upset Gloriana. The play elsewhere seems to compliment her. The author was not hostile to his Queen, but he would have jeopardized his troupe's profitability by court-toadying, and nearly all of his plays would have been acted first on the London stage, before being taken to an Inn, to court, or anywhere else. Aware of Lyly's examples he uses a free, brisk method in balancing and combining the *Dream*'s personae—who include Theseus and Hippolyta, a quartet of lovers, the fairies, and the artisans who will perform with sublime bungling 'Pyramus and Thisbe' for Theseus's nuptial day. Most of the mortals quickly retreat to woods where Oberon, King of the Fairies, his Queen Titania and their fairy troupe and the spirit of Puck live.

Do fairies cause our misery? Puck puts Cupid's love-juice on Lysander's eyes as Oberon does on Demetrius's—so both men are attracted to an exasperated Helena. But Helena had noted love's absurdity before entering the magic wood, and Demetrius has been fickle beforehand. Theseus, whom critics have cited as the Tudor ideal, has seduced or raped Ariadne, Antiopa, Perigenia, and Aegles, names the author derives from Plutarch's 'Theseus'. In being only lightly individuated, Lysander and Hermia, Demetrius and Helena the better suggest in their yearning and pain that love's 'madness' is universal.

Marital peace and fidelity everywhere may be slight: the Fairy King and Queen, in coming to bless Theseus and Hippolyta, are torn by bickering and jealousy. Suave aristocrats, in Act V, deride working men who, with no very clear hope of profit, have come to entertain them, and the human mind is implicitly seen to be irrational, out of control, faithless, thankless, unkind, and viciously changeful.

At the heart of Shakespeare's comic view of life is his tragic sense, and the *Dream* is evidence that the tragic sense had fairly early roots. The play explores what must have been memories of 'midsummer madness', magic times and features of a country boyhood such as Midsummer Eve with its greenery decoration, divinations, and religious connections with nature. The artisans themselves relate to Stratford days. Snout the tinker is to animate Wall for the artisans' play of 'Pyramus and Thisbe'. 'Some man or other', says Nick Bottom, 'must present Wall; and let him have some plaster, or some loam, or some rough-cast about him, to signify "wall"; and let him hold his fingers thus, and through that cranny shall Pyramus and Thisbe whisper' (III. i. 62–6). Of similar materials 'the wall' outside Stratford's grammar school bordering the Gild chapel's garden was busily repaired and rebuilt in the 1570s. About 5 per cent of all official payments by council in a year focus on it, so the Wall has an amusing life today in the Minutes and Accounts:

Item for reparacions of the wall . . .
p^d to *Wever* for hernes ['earnest' or pre-payment for repairs] of the walle . . .
p^d for syx Rafters to ley vpon the Chappell garden wall . . .
p^d for the peare of Rafters for the wall . . .
p^d Thomas Tyler for his two men, iiij [4] dayes worke about the garden wall of the Chapell
p^d to wever to make an ende of the wall
p^d to Thomas tyler for his men working at the Chappell wall . . .[14]

Endless work on a wall at Church Street, in days when the author was going to school, puts one in mind of a Midland town's slow, puttering normalcy in contrast to the tenor of an actor's days in London. The funny artisans are sketched with compassion, if not with nostalgia. What enriches the *Dream* is the breadth of human experience always implied in it, and its workers in their authentic dignity do not seem to be caricatures. Ease of style masks the *Dream*'s profundity, but that ease is biographically interesting as a sign of the author's long familiarity with themes he can handle most lightly: a person of his quality of memory gathers in time past, and may 'compose' quickly what has been in gestation half a lifetime.

Darkness at the play's heart makes its humour the more affecting. Changed into an ass and loved by an exquisite Fairy Queen—another Fairy Queen, one notes, was even more humiliated at about this time[15]—Bottom sums up his experience in 'Bottom's Dream'. Echoing St Paul in 1 Corinthians 2: 9 and confusing the senses, he suggests that the mind's dominance over the eye is a means of gaining divine grace from woodland ritual. The 'bottom of Goddes secretes' cannot be known, as one reads, for example, in the Bishops' Bible (1568) or the Geneva Bible (1557). 'The eye of man hath not heard', says Bottom earnestly,

the ear of man hath not seen, man's hand is not able to taste, his tongue to conceive, nor his heart to report what my dream was. I will get Peter Quince to write a ballad of this dream. It shall be called 'Bottom's Dream', because it hath no bottom (IV. i. 208–13).[16]

In farce, Shakespeare can allude easily to matters that involve his own past or his present. These religious motifs have early naïve origins, and 'Bottom's Dream' appears to reflect schoolboy lessons of the 1570s about God's unknowability, if not a classroom's jokiness as well. The 'Dream' as a dream within the *Dream* gets some of its edge and comic depth from a poet's mature, pessimistic reflections on what he had once understood simply. Significantly Bottom stars in Peter Quince's 'Pyramus and Thisbe'. Here self-directed satire is apparent. Peter Quince is like Shakespeare in writing a drama and acting in it, in being versatile, assigning parts and dealing with actors, arranging rehearsals and making textual changes. Shakespeare burlesques himself as a *Johannes Factotum* whose efforts produce nonsense, and 'Pyramus' in fact explicitly parodies *Romeo and Juliet* and has mocking allusions as well to *Titus, Comedy of Errors*, and the *Two Gentlemen*.

Theseus, on the other hand, is gallant enough to defend even the stage's feeblest performances. 'The best in this kind are but shadows', he tells his warrior-bride, 'and the worst are no worse if imagination amend them' (v. i. 210–11). After his days of rape and conquest, the Duke is politically astute. Indeed, in his noble, good-natured authority and concern with illusion, as in his freshness of thought and charity towards the 'rude mechanicals', he might almost typify Shakespeare's interest in the ideal leader of a modern political state.

Falstaff, Hal, and a Henriad

The Chamberlain's men needed many plays. Inevitably they took in poor scripts to fill up a week, but, no matter what was done, the outlook deteriorated, and financial straits and worse trouble lay ahead in a time of ruined harvests, inflation, hostile city aldermen, rising numbers of the poor, and intermittent plague. Dull afternoons with feeble dramas, and half-empty galleries, could bring ruin quickly. Their resident poet noted failures: 'I was lately here in the end of a displeasing play', Shakespeare writes for one of his curtseying Epilogues.[17] He also had noted a hunger for political plays evoking shames of the state and cutting close to the bone, and, partly because of the success of *Henry VI*, he soon turned again to politics and history.

In fact he wrote *Richard II* as the opening work in a series of four dramas about the Lancastrian kings who had reigned before the period of his first tetralogy—or in the seventeen years between Bolingbroke's quarrel with Mowbray in 1398 and the aftermath of Agincourt in 1415.

This was the riskiest of his projects, and the first drama in the series nearly ruined his company. For one thing, with *Richard II*, he doubtless irked the Queen. 'I am Richard II, know ye not that?' Elizabeth later told the antiquary William Lambarde at Greenwich Palace on 4 August 1601. Her political enemies had compared her with

Richard II, who had lacked a direct heir as she did and had been deposed. The Essex-and-Southampton faction pressed that analogy fatally, and she felt that the theatre was partly to blame. 'This tragedy', she told poor Lambarde (who died fifteen days after the interview), 'was played 40^tie^ times in open streets and houses.' Lambarde tried to mollify her, but she returned to Richard II and 'demanded', as the old antiquary put it, ' "Whether I had seen any true picture, or lively representation of his countenance and person?" ' 'None but such as be in common hands', she was told.[18]

The scene in *Richard II* in which the king is forcibly deposed was censored or never printed while the Queen was alive, but, luckily, the rash acting of the play by the Chamberlain's men at the request of five or six of Essex's conspirators on 7 February 1601 (only a day before their abortive coup) did not bring down the company; they were cleared of conspiracy in the Essex revolt. On behalf of Shakespeare's men, Augustine Phillips at a trial on 18 February—perhaps in one of the star performances of his life—claimed that his actors had told Essex's men that the play was 'so old & so long out of use as that they should get no company at it'. Actors, like newborn babes or sheep in a meadow, knew nothing of politics; that was implicitly clear, but, as a respected sharer, Phillips stuck to the point. He recalled that his troupe had heartily wished to put on 'some other play' for the Essex conspirators, who, nevertheless, gave them 40s. above the ordinary fee to put on this one.[19]

One feels, anyway, that the actors had reason to be pleasant with the Queen's officials. The Revels Office had been tolerating a good deal of political comment. But in the mid-1590s, Shakespeare had taken risks with *Richard II*. An unusually ceremonial play, it balances the story of King Richard's fall with that of Harry Bolingbroke's ominous and deadly rise. Richard talks, but Bolingbroke takes steps. Law and tradition have ensured Richard's right to the crown, and yet having had his uncle Gloucester killed by means of the Duke of Norfolk, he falters, and while picturing his guilt and self-pity, he foolishly relies on the crown's mystique to save him.

Shakespeare had taken very special pains with the work, using details in Holinshed's *Chronicles* but looking into more alternative sources than for any other history play. Also he lavished care on verbal texture, to the extent that his text has an unusual verbal decorum. Few plays demand more of the 'ear', and its rhythms or quirky negative verbs ('unkiss', 'uncurse', 'undeaf', 'unhappied') are intendedly medieval in a very Elizabethan way. Just as Marlowe's *Edward II* affects the portrayal of Richard, so Spenser's deliberately archaic manner in *The Faerie Queene*, for example, influences Shakespeare's language.

The play's choric figures hardly seem medieval. As if he were one of Elizabeth's clergy, the Bishop of Carlisle implores a lax Richard to use strength to resist Bolingbroke—and Aumerle rubs in the lesson:

> He means, my lord, that we are too remiss,
> Whilst Bolingbroke through our security,
> Grows strong and great in substance and in power.
>
> (III. ii. 29–31)

Rather so did the Queen feel about British military laxity and Spain's threat in 1595—when a Spanish invasion was expected, her troops had withdrawn from the Continent, and Ireland stirred in revolt. In one respect, Shakespeare offers a sad object-lesson almost bound to please a militant anxious Queen and her Privy Council. He makes Richard even more passive than any historical source had shown him to be.

But, then, Richard is potent in his fall. There is a metaphysical aspect in his tragedy, even as his faith in the crown is mocked by a nasty, emergent pragmatism. How patriotic was Shakespeare? The dying Gaunt very poignantly evokes an England which the young king wastes and neglects:

> This earth of majesty, this seat of Mars,
> This other Eden, demi-paradise,
> This fortress built by nature for herself
> Against infection and the hand of war,
> This happy breed of men, this little world,
> This precious stone set in the silver sea,
> Which serves it in the office of a wall,
> Or as a moat defensive to a house
> Against the envy of less happier lands,
> This blessèd plot, this earth, this realm, this England . . .
>
> (II. i. 41–50)

But even Gaunt can be less impressive than the spectacle of the decline of medievalism in Richard's talk in Acts IV and V.

Shakespeare designed his plays to be open to multiple interpretation, and all have inexhaustible problems. But with more intellectual confidence here than in earlier history plays, he uses patriotism as a theme to be balanced against deeply upsetting ideas. *Richard II* shows how easy it is to be rid of an anointed king. Not God's power, but presumptions about divinity are radically at issue: the play demystifies monarchy by undercutting its godly sanction, and implies that a divinely ordained ruler is no concern of heaven. The idea that God no longer 'guards the right' has a dramatic shock, and counters tenets of belief which have supported armies from Tudor times to ours. As a key work in its author's development, *Richard II* also opens a path for his tragedies. If even the anointed servant is not protected by divine favour, history may be nothing more than a product of human volition; and emphasis falls upon choice, responsibility, and resourcefulness as factors that may determine the fate of a Macbeth or a Lear.

After this prelude, the author explores ambiguities of modern politics in *1* and *2 Henry IV* in which the terse, practical Harry Bolingbroke—now Henry IV—contends with a single armed political rebellion and has a truant-rebel in his eldest son, Prince Henry or Hal ('my unthrifty son' and 'a plague' in *Richard II*). In an early part of *The Civil Wars* (1595), Samuel Daniel had made Hal and Hotspur of about the same age, and so foils and rivals. More boldly, Shakespeare puts Hal at the centre of an evolving familial, military, and political picture which involves most of British society.

Looming in the foreground is the bulky, dissolute colossus of Falstaff, who might be the soul of the suburbs or an urban Lord of Misrule expert in Nashe's raillery, or Tarlton's repartee, except that he is more inclusive. He is more complex than any of his sources: 'it is hard to get one's mind all round him', William Empson once noted, though there is no reason why Falstaff should be consistent, as modern critics of stage performance (such as Samuel Crowl in his *Shakespeare Observed*) often imply. Falstaff was probably acted by Kempe, whose artificial girth on stage would have been telling. A Jacobean drawing shows a reduced and tidy Falstaff in doublet and breeches with lace-topped boots, but the architect Inigo Jones (born in 1573) could have seen Kempe's clown, and Jones later specifies 'like a Sʳ Jo*h*n fall staff' in describing a similar figure: 'a roabe of russet Girt low', he writes, 'wi*t*h a great belley' and 'buskines to shew a great swolen lege'—a figure with a 'great head and balde'.[20]

As in the *Merchant* or *Much Ado*, Shakespeare could hope to appeal to idlers and lawyers at the Inns of Court and of Chancery and well beyond. Falstaff, as the most intelligent of clowns, has been an Inn of Chancery law student of Clement's Inn, who began to crack skulls as a mere lad (*2 Henry IV*, III. ii). He appears with Hal in a very Tudor Eastcheap, which had in Gracechurch Street a street of haberdashers pronounced as 'Grass Street', as well as what Stow calls a 'flesh Market of Butchers' and the Boar's Head among other taverns.[21] Prince Hal's education includes bouts of heady enjoyment and combats of wit with a glutton. Both are canny actors, and yet, though Falstaff lies, he counters the worst shams of wartime patriotism. The Prince has an authentic self only when with him. Like Doll Tearsheet, the clown even becomes a standard of social truth, as when, as a captain, he reports on his men at Shrewsbury: 'I have led my ragamuffins where they are peppered; there's not three of my hundred and fifty left alive, and they are for the town's end, to beg during life' (*1 Henry IV*, V. iii. 35–8). That condemns the army system, not the fat clown. Similarly when Doll is scandalized by Pistol's captaincy, she really derides the Tudor practice of giving offices by court favour. 'You a captain?' she screams at Pistol,

You slave! For what? For tearing a poor whore's ruff in a bawdy-house! He a captain! Hang him, rogue, he lives upon mouldy stewed prunes and dried cakes. A captain? God's light, these villains will make the word 'captain' odious; therefore captains had need look to't.   (*2 Henry IV*, II. iv. 139–44)

Yet it is Falstaff who best exposes a gap between Renaissance language and action, and to the extent that he pictures the excesses of humanist faith in the word, he might be a rebel in the advanced grammar-school era of the 1570s. He is the only being through whom the Poet of the Sonnets might speak the truth. Cat-like and alert, despite his bulk, he is in his odd, aggrandizing passivity, easy sociability, and detachment so much like the author that a resemblance may have amused the actors. Both poet and clown are pretenders; both exploit royalty; both try to control reality through words; both appear to seek male affection and approval with the utmost urgency. Both are insouciant but not arrogant—and perhaps only a writer of unusual receptivity and great personal modesty could have brought such a clown into being. Falstaff symbolizes nothing exactly because he engrosses so many meanings.

Critics, more often than audiences, nonetheless find fault with *Henry IV*. If Falstaff's lying is not thought to be objectionable, the Prince's lying can seem slick and self-interested: it is impossible to know when, or if ever, he tells the truth, and commentators fault him in all three parts of the Henriad. 'Hal is an anti-Midas; everything he touches turns to dross', writes Stephen Greenblatt. 'Hal is the prince and principle of falsification—he is himself a counterfeit companion.'[22] Certainly Hal lies in order to manipulate appearances as he waits to amaze the world and to redeem himself by rejecting Falstaff, but he comes out of the chrysalis as a rather stiff butterfly.

His interior life—if it exists—is not on display even in *Henry V*. Shakespeare concerns himself here with the theatre of politics and writes his most effectively playable history drama. It is likely that he added the apologetic Chorus at a late point, and just how vital that is to the play's success can become clear when the Chorus is missing, as in the brief quarto of 1600. Shakespeare never wrote with a narrower, more coercive purpose than he did for a Chorus which steadily praises King Harry and amplifies his settings:

> Now entertain conjecture of a time
> When creeping murmur and the poring dark
> Fills the wide vessel of the universe.

> (IV. 0. 1–3)

Yet the Chorus might have wandered in from another play. It describes wrong settings, contradicts the stage-action, or sends Harry off to Harfleur from two different ports. It refers to honour 'in the breast of every man' just before we see the Eastcheap rogues. On the eve of Agincourt, it speaks of a 'little touch of Harry in the night', though Harry cheers up neither man nor devil in the night. What we read in a text of *Henry V* is not what we usually hear and see on stage, or in the heroic films of Laurence Olivier (1944) or Kenneth Branagh (1989), though Branagh's Henry at least watches as Bardolph is hanged. A modern editor notices that the King lies to his troops about brotherhood, that he cannot be honest with anyone, and that after a doubtfully just war he claims the French princess in a kind of diplomatic rape.[23]

Written when the Chamberlain's men were short of funds and in other difficulty, *Henry V* reveals patchwork composing or, at least, uncertain revision. Shakespeare's trouble with Hal, in any case, appears in no fewer than three plays. However, *Henry V* might testify to the value of external and conceptual difficulties in his career, for he depicts the politician and military hero at last in an exciting drama of action, in which the ambiguities perhaps are not fully realizable on a stage. Harry may be nobly perfect and likeable, or a kind of sullen, political chunk of ice who is false with everyone, but he is certainly heroic; and just as Richard II is hard for actors to get right, so Henry V seems nearly impossible for them to get wrong. The gusto, humour, and sureness in Falstaff's portrayal are the more effective because ironically he is a test of truth in *1* and *2 Henry IV*, but in *Henry V* there is no such standard, and the pragmatic Harry suggests the author's deep uneasiness with political heroism and with a nation's barbarity in war.

As it turned out, Falstaff caused some unexpected trouble. At first in *Henry IV* Shakespeare had called him 'Sir John Oldcastle' after the Protestant hero and Lollard martyr. Descendants of Oldcastle's widow including Henry Brooke, the eighth Lord Cobham, must have protested, and the clown's name was changed to Falstaff. In *2 Henry IV* the Epilogue eats humble pie to say that Falstaff might 'die of a sweat', but 'Oldcastle died a martyr, and this is not the man'. With the clown's new name in place, *1 Henry IV* was published in quarto in 1598 and reprinted more often, in the next twenty-five years, than any other Shakespeare play. Immensely popular, Falstaff thrived even in private theatricals. At Surrenden in Kent, Sir Edward Dering went so far as to abridge the two parts of *Henry IV*, link them with a few original verses, and arrange for the revamped work's staging by his relatives, friends, and 'Jacke of the buttery' a year before the first Folio.[24]

Long before that, Falstaff had featured in *The Merry Wives of Windsor*, in which the great clown purges a provincial town of folly at the price of losing his skill at evading blame. The comedy is a strong one with its roots in old, suggestive folk-myths of social purgation. The text was written in a mere two weeks at the Queen's command, according to a legend fostered in 1702 by John Dennis, who had a financial stake in *The Comical Gallant*, his revision of *The Merry Wives*. Seven years later Dennis's legend was embellished when Rowe added the detail that the Queen had asked Shakespeare to show Falstaff in love. Falstaff is not in love, just broke, and hopes with identical love-letters to seduce both Mistress Page and Mistress Ford and so live off both. Unfortunately, he lacks a photocopier. 'I warrant', says Mistress Page, 'he hath a thousand of these letters, writ with blank space for different names—sure, more, and these are of the second edition. He will print them out of doubt—for he cares not what he puts into the press when he would put us two' (II. i. 71–6). Not many Tudor country folk talked so readily of printing and the press. The comedy was written for an urban audience, and, no doubt, too, for a royal occasion. Posing as the Fairy Queen in Act V, Mistress Quickly alludes to 'Windsor Castle' and to the Order of the Garter. It has been argued that the play was staged at the royal Garter Feast at Whitehall Palace, Westminster, on St George's Day, 23 April 1597. For the first time in four years, knights were then elected to the Order of the Garter, and invested in St George's Chapel, Windsor, a few weeks later. Still, there is no proof that *The Merry Wives* was acted then, and it could have had a court debut as late as the winter of 1597–8.[25]

Does the author take revenge on Henry Brooke, Lord Cobham by letting jealous Ford assume the name 'Brooke' in negotiating with Falstaff? The name *Brooke* in the play was altered to *Broome*, in any case. Shakespeare glances at a real Frederick, Count Mömpelgard, later duke of Württemberg, whom the Queen had pledged to elect as a Garter Knight. From the German states Mömpelgard was sending letters about a missing Garter. Thus Bardolph, out beyond Eton, spies 'three German devils, three Doctor Faustuses', but it is left to the

French physician Dr Caius to demolish foreign pretensions. 'It is tell-a me', says Caius to the Garter Inn's host, 'dat you make grand preparation for a duke de Jamany. By my trot, der is no duke that the court is know to come' (*Merry Wives*, IV. v. 65, 80–2).[26]

Shakespeare did not always mock 'Jamany', and would send Hamlet to one of the German universities most favoured by the Danes. The heroine and her brother are called 'Anne' and 'William', as if the author had in mind two persons of the distant past. A sighing, wistful Slender, missing his book of Songs and Sonnets, describes the pretty heroine as well as he can. 'She has brown hair and speaks small like a woman', he says of Anne Page; we don't know whether that is a clue to the colour of Anne Shakespeare's hair. Slender manages to lose Anne for good in this very funny comedy, the only one the author ever set in an Elizabethan town.

12

NEW PLACE AND THE COUNTRY

She has a housewife's hand—but that's no matter.

(Rosalind, *As You Like It*)

Gains and losses

*I*n these years, the poet who supplied repertory with works as effective as *Romeo and Juliet*, the *Dream*, and *Henry IV* did not hang up his hat after morning rehearsals. He appeared on the stage himself, and with his writing, rehearsing, acting, planning with his fellows, and vetting of scripts he was very unlikely to leave London often. His income was substantial by 1596. As a matter of record 'William Shackspere' was one of the seventy-three rateable residents at St Helen's parish that October, but since he forgot or neglected by the next February to pay his tax—just 5s. on goods valued at £5—the Petty Collectors of Bishopsgate ward sent his name to the Exchequer. No doubt the low assessment of £5 was simply nominal. Sharers in the Admiral's Servants were earning about £1 a week (perhaps the equivalent of £500 or more in London at the end of the twentieth century). This was four times the fixed wage of a skilled city worker, and his income would have been between £100 and £160 a year from all sources by the end of the reign. Few of his schoolmates ever earned so much.

There is no evidence that he spent money on London property until near the end of his life, but there is every sign that he was concerned to establish himself respectably at Stratford. His wife, his two daughters, and his small son Hamnet awaited him there in 1596. John Aubrey twice records that Shakespeare went into Warwickshire 'once a yeare', and there is a good tradition that he favoured summer visits when the city's theatres might be shut. On 22 July, an outbreak of plague had closed all of the suburban theatres. This was a hard, miserable, testing time, since Lord Hunsdon died at Somerset House next day; and later the old lord's cortège was followed (as one manuscript account puts it) by large numbers of yeomen in 'black coates'.[1] So the Chamberlain's men lost their patron. His successor, in the chamberlaincy, the seventh Lord Cobham, was less partial to the public theatre, indeed he was descended from the Oldcastle who is mocked in *Henry IV*; but for other reasons there was a danger now, if not a likelihood, that he might collude with the Lord Mayor against the playhouses.[2]

Sponsored by their former patron's son, the Chamberlain's men became Lord Hunsdon's Servants. When they toured after 22 July in Kent, Shakespeare apparently had a chance to return home, and he was to be in Stratford well before he bought a house there. What would he have found as he crossed Clopton's bridge, and went up beside Middle Row at last into Henley Street?

❧

Stratford was feeling the effects of harvest failure—and of two serious local fires. One saw charred timbers and ruined barns. Though houses and shops in the main streets were usually tiled, on 22 September 1594 and again in the following September the flames had leapt to street frontages. Leather fire-buckets, ladders, and fire-hooks to pull down burning thatch had not saved many dwellings, and it was said that damage and loss of property and goods amounted to £12,000. The second fire had reached the Henley Street tenements of Cox and Cawdrey—though John Shakespeare's double house was spared. Funds had poured in from nearby shires, and the city of Oxford, for instance, had sent 'tenne shillings towards the relief of those that had their howses burnt'.[3]

William Shakespeare, in his will, left twenty times that amount to Stratford's poor—a generous bequest. In his expenditures he ran a tight ship, but he was not simply tight-fisted, obsessed with land, or harsh with debtors. A man of his means recovered debts through Stratford's Court of Record with its jurisdiction over sums up to £30, and we know that he took local debtors to court just twice—once to get Philip Rogers the apothecary to pay for twenty bushels of malt plus a borrowed sum in 1604, and again to recover a debt of £6, plus damages, from John Addenbrooke in 1608. This may be the Addenbrooke who speculated on land rights at Tanworth, near Henley, or the one who sold starch licences at Warwick, but he lived within the borough.

Apart from rebuilding in the High, Stratford was much as it was in the poet's youth. Time moved slowly here, and the townspeople were in touch with their communal past. The council still met regularly at the Gild hall's annexe, outside which the public sweeper 'Lame Margaret' had at last given way to old 'Mother Ashfield'. Margaret Smith had long since lost her full name, to be called Lame Margaret as if she were an animal, but the burgesses had admitted her to an almshouse. In succession she and Mother Ashfield swept the channel of a small, often noxious, stream as it crossed the road from Tinkers Lane to Chapel Lane at New Place, which the poet was to buy. It is likely that he knew their old, coarsened or reddened faces.[4] From his viewpoint many women in the town might have been younger versions of Lame Margaret, valued for childbearing or hard work.

At his parent's house on Henley Street, there was incessant work for women to do. In any home there was wool to card, after it had been treated with swine's grease, and spinning to do, with the spinner leaning forward over her work. There would be netting for coverlets and curtains, and sewing for most garments worn indoors or out, as well as weaving hats and baskets, and candle-making with kettles of boiling water and melted tallow for wicks.

Even a poet had to rely on quills from some source. A stocking was pulled over a goose's head and down would fly everywhere as quills were plucked. Shakespeare's wife Anne would have known comparable tasks, even if she had servants. This summer she was nearly 40. Hard work etches lines in a face and colours the hands. 'I saw her hand', says Rosalind in *As You Like It*, as she mocks a love-letter from Phoebe the shepherd-girl,

> She has a leathern hand,
> A free-stone coloured hand. I verily did think
> That her old gloves were on; but 'twas her hands.
> She has a housewife's hand.

(IV. iii. 25–8)

But there is sympathy for the plight of rural women in several of Rosalind's remarks: 'Maids are May when they are maids', Shakespeare writes for that heroine, 'but the sky changes when they are wives' (IV. i. 140–1). Along with his wife Anne, he of course found his ageing parents at Henley Street. In this same year, he apparently ensured that his father John had a grant of arms from the Heralds' College. Two surviving drafts of the grant suggest it was Shakespeare who sat with the heralds in London to supply data and pay fees. His father was optimistically declared to be worth £500, and there was comic trouble with the family motto (which the poet never used). A clerk jotted it as 'non, sanz droict' and then as 'Non, Sanz Droict' and finally in capitals without the comma as 'NON SANZ DROICT', meaning 'Not without right'. Supposedly this later incited Ben Jonson in *Every Man Out of his Humour* to have the clown Sogliardo (who pays £30 for arms) mocked and deflated by a motto suggested to him, 'Not without Mustard', a phrase which Jonson lifts from Nashe.[5]

At any rate, John Shakespeare and his offspring were granted for all time a shield or arms showing:

Gould. on A Bend Sables. a Speare of the first steeled argent. And for his Creast or Cognizance a falcon his winges displayed Argent. standing on a wrethe of his Collors. supp [MS torn] A Speare Gould steeled as aforesaid sett vppon a helmett with mantell & tassel

[Gold, on a bend sables, a spear of the first steeled argent, and for his crest or cognizance a falcon, his wings displayed argent, standing on a wreath of his colours, supporting a spear gold, steeled as aforesaid, set upon a helmet with mantles and tassels][6]

A sketch of this fairly simple trick of arms appears in the upper left-hand corner of both drafts of the grant made at the Heralds' College in 1596. Three years later, John gained the right to impale his arms with those of Arden, his wife's family, as C. W. Scott-Giles points out, so that the shield could be 'divided vertically into two halves, the Shakespeare coat being placed in the dexter and the Arden coat in the sinister half'.[7] John, evidently, chose not to impale with Arden.

Shakespeare seems to have been amused by these prodigious efforts. The heralds—it seems at the poet's own bidding—had lifted up the rank of his grandfather Robert Arden from 'gent'. or *generosus* to the higher rank of 'esquire', *armiger*. In *The Merry Wives*, the insipid Slender proudly hails his uncle—Justice Shallow—as one 'who writes himself "Armigero" in any bill, warrant, quittance, or obligation: "Armigero" ' (I. i. 8–9). For their part, Shakespeare's fellow actors were hardly amazed by his minor triumph of arms. Augustine Phillips, his colleague and friend, simply bought one day from a heraldic painter the arms of Lord Bardolph (William Phillips), and the actor Thomas Pope bought the arms of Sir Thomas Pope, the Chancellor of the Augmentations. Richard Cowley and Shakespeare had legitimate claims to arms, but, as actors, both were later cited in a complaint of Ralph Brooke, the York Herald, to the effect that Sir William Dethick as Garter King-of-Arms had made grants to 'base and ignoble persons'.[8]

Gentlehood had a serious bearing on the chances of younger Shakespeares. Possibly the least helped was the poet's sister Joan, soon to marry William Hart, a hatter down on his luck. Shakespeare's three living brothers were more likely to benefit. Gilbert Shakespeare, who never married, was in this year 29. His brother Richard was 22, and Edmund 16. Gilbert tried to succeed in the nation's capital, since he was a haberdasher at St Bride's in 1597 when he and a local shoemaker put up £19 bail, in the court of Queen's Bench, for the clockmaker William Sampson. Gilbert must have been back in the Midlands in 1602. Then or a little later he became associated, probably in business, with Peter Roswell (or Ruswell) and Richard Mytton, who are both mentioned in the only existing letter addressed to Shakespeare.

In the twentieth century, Mark Eccles discovered a court case involving Gilbert Shakespeare and his rather unsavoury acquaintances living in, and also to the south-west of, the parish. We know that Gilbert had to appear at the Court of Requests with Roswell, Mytton, Mary Burnell, and others in November 1609 to answer certain charges. The charges are still unknown, but we know that Roswell and Mytton had been in the employ of Stratford's Lord of the Manor, whose men, as will emerge, were involved in the killing of the Shakespeares' friend Richard Quiney when Quiney was bailiff. Roswell appears as a brutal bully, among other bullies, even at the outset of the case involving Shakespeare's brother Gilbert. Tempers flared when Elionor Varney, a serving-girl of 21, first handed Roswell the subpoena to appear in court: 'he did violently snatch from [Elionor] the said writ and refused to re-deliver it unto her, and delivered his staff he then had in his hand to a stander-by who therewith did assault and beat this deponent out of the house'.[9] It is of interest to find Gilbert Shakespeare among violent associates who in themselves worked for a vicious manorial lord, but a dark curtain falls over this obscure court case; we may yet learn more about it. The poet's brothers Gilbert and Richard, anyway, drew little opprobrium down upon their own heads, and left almost no mark in life. Gilbert was to die in his forty-sixth year; he was buried as a bachelor (*adolescens*) at Holy Trinity, Stratford, on 3 February 1612. Richard admitted a fault at the church court in July 1608, for which he was fined 12*d*., but he was blameless in the local court's eyes after that. Having nearly reached his fortieth year, he was buried at Stratford on 4 February 1613.

The case with Shakespeare's youngest brother was otherwise, for Edmund, unluckily, became a city actor. Among the dangers that threatened an actor were indiscipline and sexual disease, and the young man was rashly imprudent. In London he sired a son who was baptized at St Leonard's parish in July 1607 and buried a month later, at Cripplegate, as 'Edward sonne of Edward Shackspeere Player base borne'. The father barely survived the infant: Edmund died at 27 and was buried on 31 December 1607 at St Saviour's church, Southwark, where Shakespeare must have paid to have the great bell rung for him.

Would the 'Dark Lady' sonnets, in their fitful story of sensuality, have been lost on Edmund? In our time, fanciful writers of course suppose that Shakespeare himself fell into the clutches of a dark-haired vamp, such as Lucy Negro, bawdy-house keeper of Clerkenwell's stews, or Hunsdon's mistress Aemilia Lanyer, or else Pembroke's silly paramour Mary Fitton (despite a lack of factual proof that he ever met any of them). It is not difficult to imagine that actors were terrified of syphilis, and, in a 'homosocial' culture, very close male friendships could help a few actors to avoid fornication. Homosexual relationships must have been common, though boy apprentices were likely to be well protected. No one knows if Shakespeare was especially chaste, but when living with Huguenots later, he was respectable enough to be trusted in a delicate family matter. The Sonnets suggest he knew sexual liaisons, but that his horror of adultery is unusually strong.

Nevertheless if he was a penitent husband, it is odd that Anne Shakespeare bore him children in only three years of married life. His own mother had offspring over a span of twenty-two years, but Anne gave birth to no child after Susanna and the twins Hamnet and Judith were born. It is perhaps less likely that she was hopelessly estranged from her husband, than that damage to her reproductive system, caused by the carrying and birth of twins, had made it impossible for her to have more children. This of course is no more than a possibility. Robert Bearman of the Shakespeare Birthplace Trust notes that of 'thirty-two instances of twin births in Stratford between 1560 and 1600, both children survived at least the first three months of infancy in eighteen cases'. In eight cases of twin births, however, the mother bore no more children—at a time when children were much desired in all of the social ranks.[10] Twin births could be particularly horrendous as a barber-surgeon stood by, with his unsterilized instruments, to cut, crush, and extract the unborn to save the mother, who might suffer irreparable harm even if the births were successful. Shakespeare and his wife would presumably have had more children if they could, and it is by no means certain that they had a choice in the matter. A child was a fragile treasure, and, among the gentry, it was normally felt that a family's well-being and the likely survival of one's estate depended on one's having a living male heir.

At the time, belief in the sacredness of marriage reinforced unions, and Shakespeare had much to benefit from harmony at home. In his dramas from *Hamlet* to *Coriolanus*, he is, interestingly, less concerned with opposition between husband and wife than with problems a son faces in coming to terms with images of a parent. He was to take Anne from the double house at Henley Street, and live with her among pleasant amenities at Chapel Street; the poet's house was convenient and hospitable enough for Thomas Greene to stay there as a guest for at least a year. Anne's looks, dress, or manners can hardly have surprised Shakespeare, and, certainly, his family had known her own family since his infancy. But to judge from the available facts, her Hathaway relatives gave him cause for alarm. We recall that Anne was close in age to her eldest brother Bartholomew, who was back at Shottery. As an act of family piety Bartholomew had given the name of his father, Richard, to his first-born. There was persistence in that, since Bartholomew and Anne had earlier lost two brothers named after their father. At Shottery Anne's father had thrived, but the rewards for his energy, or good luck, were not bound to be equalled by fresh, young Hathaway men in need of advancement in depressed times. Anne's brothers were unlikely to offend her, and there is no sign that she renounced any of them. It has been said that one reason why Shakespeare's will appears to treat his wife shabbily, or negligently, is that she became mentally ill—but nothing supports that. If Anne held money in trust for her father's shepherd in 1601, she was not ineffectual then, nor do Whittington's phrases hint at any incompetence on her part. What does clearly emerge, though, is the fact of strong family loyalty among the Hathaways as Bartholomew's children began to settle not only in Shottery but within the town itself. Their warm interest in Anne Shakespeare was normal, but since Bartholomew's branch produced churchwardens, aldermen, and a bailiff there was a trace of social ambition in their friendly ways. Bartholomew had very good credentials for his attentions to Anne. His own father, a friend of John Shakespeare, in his will had urged Bartholomew to look closely after his sisters, or to be a 'Comforte' to them 'to his power'. Returning from Tysoe, he was not simply a farmer; he took an interest in the town and had a lease in Ely Street by 1583. Visiting Anne, he came to be on friendly terms with her children; and through the poet's daughter, Susanna, Bartholomew later developed a trusting relationship with her physician husband, John Hall. Shakespeare's will firmly excludes Bartholomew and literally every other Hathaway, while chiefly empowering Susanna and her spouse. Ironically, Susanna's spouse was to be appointed as an overseer of Bartholomew's own will.[11]

What, then, in all likelihood irritated Shakespeare? The friendliness of Bartholomew and his sons was hard to guard against, if Anne's loyalty to them was keen. As they were by no means disreputable, he could hardly have turned them from his door. Absent for long periods, he cannot have returned home to find matters exactly as they were when he left, and his brother-in-law's needs evidently confronted him. Just how Bartholomew came to have £200 in 1610 to buy back Hewlands and adjacent property at Shottery is unknown, but E. I. Fripp believes the money came from Shakespeare. It was a large sum; the buyer was not wealthy. Other Hathaways were very nearly the poet's neighbours. Bartholomew's son Richard set up as a baker in Fore Bridge Street, and became host of the Crown inn, before rising to the bailiwick.[12] Whether or not the poet welcomed early signs of such success, the weak point of his own estate was soon to become its terrible lack of a male heir. If he died before his wife, there was a possibility that her relatives might try to get, through her, some access to his heritable wealth, or to the entity of an estate intended for male Shakespeares. He was vulnerable to his in-laws through Anne, and even if she at last did nothing worse than to receive or encourage them, that could have aroused his anger.

The unusual arrangements he made for his Blackfriars property kept it safe from Anne even three years before he made his will. His will is an extraordinary document when compared with other actors' wills, and it reflects further troubles in 1616. One oddity is not its lack of endearing phrases for Anne (such as 'my loving' or 'my beloved' wife), since other testators could omit those, but his failure to leave Anne any jewel, keepsake, or other artefact that might show tenderness. One might be reminded of the Sonnets' speaker who resents those to whom he is emotionally close. The poet had a sudden, dark temper, it has been implied, since two men he knew used the word 'offence' to describe him. He was forgiving with Henry Chettle, but Chettle added that *Groats-worth* was 'offensively taken' by the poet, and Thomas Heywood reported that Shakespeare was 'much offended' by Jaggard the printer who presumed 'to make so bold with his name' on the title-page of *The Passionate Pilgrim*. Ben Jonson wrote with conventional hyperbole that his 'beloved' was capable of rage: 'Shine forth, thou star of poets', he urges in his elegy on Shakespeare, 'and with rage | Or influence, chide or cheer the drooping stage'.[13]

The trouble is that the poet had good cause to complain to Chettle of *Groats-worth*, and about a printer's unauthorized use of his name. It does not follow that he was easily upset. He believed in loyalty and stability, and his wife kept his house and raised his children. There are signs of his satisfaction at New Place, an estate large enough perhaps to emphasize his distinction in social rank from relatives who appeared cap in hand. He mentioned a wish to invest in Anne's 'Shottery'—and civility prevailed in Shakespeare's household or he would not have tolerated the prolonged stay of any visitor. How did Anne respond to him? Stoical or dutiful compliance, at the time, is noticeable in wives of the privileged. Even as a person from an old, respected Shottery family, Anne may not have been so amenable as two other wives recently widowed, but there is no outward sign, so far, that her attitudes greatly differed from theirs: 'I carried always that reverent respect towards him in regard of my good conceit which I had of the good partes I knew to be in him', wrote Lady Mildmay in 1617; 'I could not fynde it in my heart to challenge him for the worst word or deede which ever he offered me'. Or again, Ann Clifford's attitude was not altogether uncommon among the gentry: 'Sometimes I had fair words from him and sometimes foul', she recalled of her husband, 'but I took all patiently and did strive to give him as much content and assurance of my love as I could possibly.'[14] Did Shakespeare believe in a marriage of equals? His dramas show a wide range of marital attitudes, and his outlook on marriage may not even begin to appear in Macbeth and Lady Macbeth, or Cornwall and Regan, who might represent unions of equals in villainy. In the *Merry Wives*, there are companionate marriages, despite Ford's air of authority. The *Shrew* and *Comedy of Errors* debate the rights of a wife; Capulet in *Romeo* is shown to be a foolish autocrat in a disastrous marriage. In his plays, Shakespeare at least entertained an idea, not attributable to Puritan notions but to traditions as old as his town's Gild, that marriage is a partnership based on mutual acquiescence. He feared at times that Anne could not protect herself from her brothers; for the likelihood of this, even if we put aside what is known of the Hathaways, we have signs in two kinds of evidence in the Blackfriars transaction and in the poet's legal will. From what is known of Shakespeare's behaviour, he was easy and companionable but also rapid and fluid in his respon-siveness and adaptability, and likely to hold to not more than a few central moral principles as he observed and reflected the viewpoints of others; his plays develop their ideas in a complex dialectic. He valued the stability he could have found in normal relations with his wife, and there is enough evidence to suggest that he worried over his heritable estate and thought it vulnerable. Certainly, in 1596, the prospects of that estate depended on a crucial emotional bond he had with Anne in their children.

And yet that bond, in effect, involved their boy's life. Their son Hamnet Shakespeare, at 11, may have completed Lower School. This would have been normal, and one need not suppose the boy was as precocious as children can be in his father's plays. For the parents of any child, death seemed an ever-present threat. A third of all children born in England never reached the age of 10. Frighteningly, infectious diseases killed quickly, and one was seldom under the illusion that a child might not be lost. As it happened, nothing saved the Shake-speares' only son, who died early in August of some unknown cause. On the 11th, the little boy was buried at Holy Trinity, and a clerk noted in the burials register:

Hamnet filius William Shakspere[15]

Such a loss could affect a wife even more sharply than it did her hus-band. If Anne was moved to cry out, that was not quite forbidden, but excess grief showed 'weakness and lack of control'—and any display of pain was less befitting than joy over an innocent soul saved.[16] Death was very public in Stratford, and one calmly discussed one's dead child. The poet, in his verse, chose not to do so, though it is some-times said that Sonnet 37 bears on his loss: 'As a decrepit father takes delight', Shakespeare begins,

> To see his active child do deeds of youth,
> So I, made lame by fortune's dearest spight,
> Take all my comfort of thy worth and truth.

But that, at best, vaguely alludes to his young boy. Heavily moved by a son's death, Ben Jonson, for instance, was eloquent in writing of his own boy's loss. In contrast, Shakespeare in these years devoted himself to comedy, to finishing up his history series and turning to Caesar's Rome. Had he died in this decade, he would be well remembered as the best in a group of Tudor playwrights, but he lived on to write plays that hardly allow one to compare him with anyone else, and his son's death changed him. He seems never to have recovered from the loss. What evolved was an intelligent complication of his view of suffering, so that he came to identify with those in extreme, irremediable pain; his grief increased his inwardness while perhaps making him mock any worldly success he might achieve. It is useless to argue that he could not have written his most intellectually assured tragedies had his son *not* died; he was not yet writing such plays in 1596. But Hamnet's death, this bitter and terrible loss, deepened the artist and thinker: that loss would have helped him to avoid the last, lingering drawbacks of his technical facility, that legacy of his youth, and to gather up his strength for the most emotionally complex and powerful dramas the English stage has known.

Two murders, New Place, and Mʳ Quiney's little faults

About a year after Hamnet died, the playwright was able to settle his wife and two daughters in an ample house just across from the old Gild chapel. The grammar school, of course, was close to the chapel, and in a sense Shakespeare was back where he began. Anne with her children Susanna and Judith, then aged 14 and 12, moved into New Place late in 1597, or in any case not after February 1598. The house was almost excessively roomy and very pleasant, with five gables, three storeys, and wide grassy borders setting it back from the corner of Chapel Street and Chapel Lane (also known as Dead Lane and Walkers Street). Ten rooms were warmed by fireplaces—at a time when fireplaces were taxed as a luxury. There were two gardens and an orchard, as well as two barns and other outbuildings. Built by Sir Hugh Clopton late in the previous century, New Place was said to be the second-largest house at Stratford with a frontage of over sixty feet, a depth along the lane of about seventy feet, and a height of twenty-eight feet at its northern gable. But by odd coincidence, for a poet who made a living in the melodramatic theatre, the house was linked with dire crime, or with two murders, one of which occurred as his wife was about to move in.

Shakespeare's knowledge of savage, calculated family murder is interesting. It was a murderous time—but New Place might have been a magnet for victims and killers. First called 'the Newe Place' when Adrian Quiney the elder lived in it, this pretty edifice of brick and timber had been leased by one of the Catholic Cloptons to Thomas Bentley, a physician to Henry VIII. After Bentley, the house fell into bad repair, and while its Clopton owner was away in Italy, William Bott managed to take possession in 1563. In that year, Bott murdered his daughter Isabella, according to the shoemaker Roland Wheler who claimed to be an eyewitness. Others who knew of these events seem to have credited Wheler's deposition. First, it was alleged, Bott cleverly had forged legal deeds to acquire the property of Isabella's husband, if she died childless; then he mixed poison in Isabella's drink. The shoemaker said he was in the house when this happened; he saw the 'spoon', the ratsbane, the drink, and noted that Isabella 'did dye sodenly and was poysoned with rattes bane and therewith swelled to death'.[17] Bott never faced a murder charge, for if he were hanged, the shoemaker said, Isabella's widower as well as the house's true owner would 'lose all their lands which the said Bott had beguyled them of'.[18]

A second major crime, nearly on the heels of Bott's occupancy, jeopardized Shakespeare's right to the house. Bott sold the estate to William Underhill, whose son and namesake eventually sold it to the poet. Shakespeare paid about £120 for New Place; the exact amount is unknown, but it was likely to be double the £60 cited in the 'fine' or Final Concord pertaining to the sale (the 'fine' usually cited a fictitious price). An existing copy of the Latin 'fine' does not call Shakespeare *generosus* or mention an orchard (both defects were remedied later), but this document of 4 May 1597 assigns to him a messuage with two barns and two gardens ('uno mesuagio duobus horreis et duobus gardinis').[19]

The vendor William Underhill, who lived part of the year at Idli-
cote, was a Catholic recusant who appeared to Stephen Burman to be
'subtle, covetous, and crafty'. However bad he was, his elder boy was
somewhat worse. Two months after the sale to Shakespeare, Underhill was killed by his son Fulke, then a legal minor, to whom he had
orally bequeathed his lands. Once again, apparently, a murderer connected with the house used poison, as Claudius does in *Hamlet*, and
Underhill died at Fillongley near Coventry on 7 July 1597. As a result,
New Place was forfeited to the state for felony, and Fulke was hanged
for murder in 1599.[20] Even when working on *Hamlet*, Shakespeare
virtually had Fulke's parricide at his elbow, since the crime kept his
right to the house insecure until the victim's second son Hercules
Underhill came of age in 1602. In that year Hercules (who was born
on 6 June 1581) secured a clear grant of the estate and confirmed its sale
to the playwright. In buying the property, Shakespeare thus got in the
strange bargain a father's alleged murder of a daughter, and the murder of a father by his son. He made good use of what he knew, and the
Bott and Underhill stories familiarized him with the raw, primitive
theme of family murder, which he was taking up with psychological
realism. And indeed, what is important about *Hamlet*'s origins is that
the play was created not merely out of literary sources, or by a 'supposing' of events, but by a poet who took in ingredients from real life
to assimilate them thoroughly with experiences of his own family,
schooling, and town, and with his private aspirations, hopes, disap-
pointments, and intellectual life. He knew Underhill, just as his father
knew Bott; and the murders in *Hamlet* are not like pictures out of
Ovid, not *Titus*-like, but intimately known happenings based in part
on real, acutely judged events.

The house was a lucky purchase, whether or not tales of murder dis-
tracted his wife from her loss. On three sides, the place was surrounded by greenery. In front was 'a little court yard', according to
George Vertue, who in 1737 made a pen-and-ink sketch of the house,
and a second drawing showing servants' quarters on either side of the
court. New Place was partly torn down and rebuilt on neo-classical
lines by Sir John Clopton in 1702 (though the house was not finally
demolished until 1759, by vicar Francis Gastrell of Frodsham), so

Vertue had to rely, partly, on what others told him. But he is consistent with the memories of Richard Grimmitt (born in 1683) who
recalled that in his childhood, he and a Clopton boy, when playing,
would cross 'a small kind of Green Court' before entering the house
which was 'fronted with brick, with plain windows, consisting of
common panes of Glass set in lead, as at this time'.[21]

In the orchard and gardens which ran down parallel with a water-
channel on the other side of the lane, Shakespeare planted roses and
apple trees. Writers gravely add up the number of horticultural allusions in the dramatist's works, and sure enough the poet refers to
apples about thirty times, and cites a number of varieties—the crab,
pippin, bitter-sweeting, pome-water, applejohn and leathercoat. He
also refers to roses on at least a hundred occasions, and gives us no
fewer than eight sorts, the white, the red, the variegated, musk,
damask, rose of Provence, canker or dog-rose, and sweet-brier.[22] Gardens at the time were often planned with ingeniously laid out beds,
paths, arbours, and trellises, all surrounded by a brick wall or a high
hedge cut into odd, eccentric shapes.

Did his keenness as a gardener lead him to a book such as Gerard's
Herbal (1597)? Gerard anyway shows that the pretty, blue-petalled
speedwell relates to the leek, and is, in Welsh, called *fluellen*. The most
sympathetic captain in *Henry V* becomes Fluellen of Wales, but there
were Fluellens in the local parish. Tudor gentlemen compared what
they found in books with lessons from the soil. And Falstaff, perhaps,
would not have gone thirsty here. New Place's vines, evidently grape
vines, thrived so well that Sir Thomas Temple later asked a servant to
get some of its 'vine settes'. Shakespeare's 'cousin', the attorney
Thomas Greene of the Middle Temple, enjoyed 'a pynte of
muskadell' of a morning, and his tastes were well served at New Place
to judge from his long stay there.[23] There are two allusions to malt on
the premises, and monthly brewing would have been normal. Anne
Shakespeare no doubt looked after the brewing, and she had plenty of
malt in the winter of 1598.

Yet in connection with using malt for ale-making, tempers were
running high at Stratford. Malt derives from barley—a staple food
so costly it was nearly out of reach of the poor. Just then, people

were enraged by malt-hoarders, and the town was close to open rebellion.

In buying a fine house Shakespeare had caught the eye of some of the gentry. Old friends of his father such as Adrian Quiney and his son Richard, a man of genial advice, took a keen interest in him. In fact he was of special use to Richard Quiney and Abraham Sturley. Both were amiable, well-educated aldermen, who happened to be in trouble. Bad harvests had affected the price of grain cruelly, and Quiney and Sturley had been hoarding malt to release their stocks at inflated prices.

Faced with a starvation crisis in the Midlands, the Queen's Council cracked down on hoarders and ordered a Stratford survey. The results appear in a 'Noate of Corn and Malt', dated 4 February 1598, and, oddly, in Quiney's handwriting. Out of seventy-five local households with grain or malt only thirteen barns have more than Shakespeare's own, with its ten quarters (or eighty bushels):

> 10   Wm Shackespere x q*uar*^{trs}[24]

That was a large supply. To be sure, the schoolmaster Mr Aspinall had eleven quarters, and the vicar Mr Byfield six of his own, four of his sister's, but it is hard to believe that Anne needed eighty bushels.

Her husband was then in London, and lately he had talked of investing. Apparently he had spoken to his father about putting some money into land. On 24 January, Sturley, at any rate, had written to Richard Quiney, who was himself then in the capital, to say that 'our countryman Mr Shakespeare is willing to disburse some money upon some odd yardland [about 30 acres] or other at Shottery or near about us'. This hint comes from Quiney's old father Adrian, a close friend of John Shakespeare for three decades. The Quineys were mercers, or sellers of fine cloth, silk, and oddments, but their trade declined, and malting had become the town's chief industry. Often in London on town-council business, young Quiney typically interviewed the Exchequer, obtained fire-relief funds, pressed for a new town charter, or secured Stratford's exemption from taxes. Much like his friend Sturley, who had been at Queens' College, Cambridge and who sent him news, Quiney was a civic-minded man who, now and then, con-

Shakespeare's Birthplace at Stratford. Richard Greene's watercolour, made around 1762, is one of the first pictures of John Shakespeare's double house on Henley Street. The so-called 'Woolshop' was to the right, and the 'Birthplace' to the left.

(*Below*) The earliest known drawing of Mary Arden's house at Wilmcote, in John Jordan's sketch of about 1795.

Top to bottom: (1) From an engraving of a copy of Richard Greene's *South-east Prospect of Stratford-upon-Avon*, 1746. (2) A sketch of the High or Market Cross, next to which the glovers sold their wares. (3) Stratford's Middle Row, shortly before it was pulled down. From the south, one rode up beside Middle Row's houses, before turning into Henley Street.

The skills of Shakespeare's parents

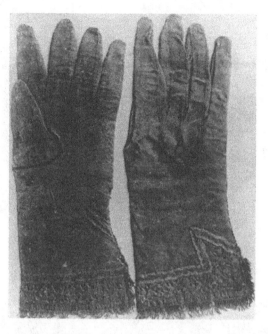

Elizabethan gloves, of a kind familiar to the glover John Shakespeare.

(*Below*) Between the words 'the marke' and 'of Marye Shacksper', Mary Shakespeare wrote her marke on a deede that conveys interest in a Snitterfield estate to Robert Webbe in 1579. Her neat design, made in one continuous movement, shows some familiarity with a quill pen.

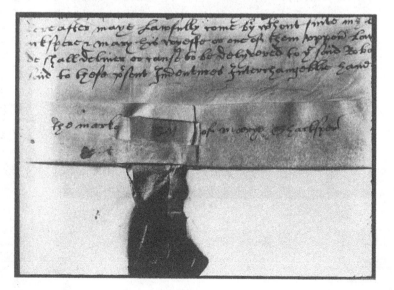

Macbeth and Banquo meet three 'weird sisters or feiries', in Raphael Holinshed's *Chronicles*, published in 1577 when Shakespeare was at school. (*Opposite*) Sir Humphrey Gilbert's *A Discourse of a Discovery* appeared in 1576, with a surprisingly accurate world-map despite its view of a northwest passage between the Atlantic and the Pacific.

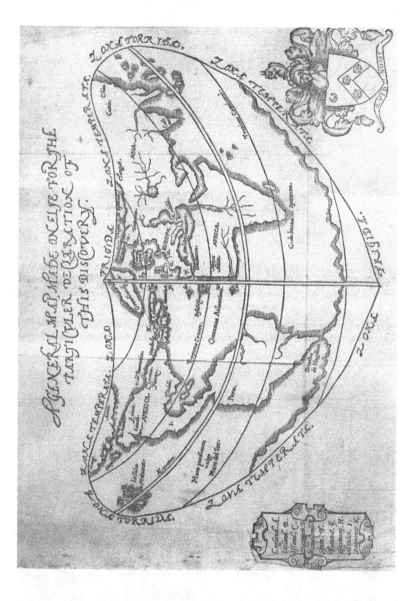

A GENERAL MAP MADE ONELYE FOR THE
PARTICVLER DECLARATION OF
THIS DISCOVERY.

Shakespeare's Consort. This drawing by Sir Nathaniel Curzon is dated 1708. It is less likely to be an authentic portrait than a playful sketch of Anne Shakespeare in her Elizabethan cap and ruff. With verses signed 'NC 1708', it is inserted in a copy of the Third Folio (second issue, 1664), now at Colgate University Library.

(*Below*) Anne Hathaway's cottage, as viewed by Samuel Ireland in *Picturesque Views on the Upper, or Warwickshire Avon, from its Source at Naseby to its Junction with the Severn at Tewkesbury* (1795).

The Grafton Portrait. An oil painting, on oak, reputedly owned by the dukes of Grafton and now in the John Rylands University Library of Manchester. If the inscription at the top (Æ SUÆ · 24 1 · 5 · 8 · 8 · ') is genuine, the young man was born in the same year as Stratford's poet. No evidence links the work with Shakespeare, but the facial proportions are similar to those in Droeshout's engraving.

London Bridge and the city. A copy of a detail in a panoramic view of London from the south, made by the Amsterdam engraver Claes Janszoon de Visscher in 1616. In the foreground is St Saviour's church in Southwark, also called St Mary Overy, the parish church for the Globe.

(*Below*) The Bear Garden and the Globe, from a copy of another detail in Visscher's view.

The Chandos Portrait, painted in oil on English canvas, is typical of British portraiture of about 1600–10. Though its origins are obscure, there is a good possibility that it shows Shakespeare; he has greyish eyes, brown moustache and beard, and a gold ring in his left ear. The drawstrings of the shirt hang down over a black doublet. Once owned by the Duke of Chandos, later by the Earl of Ellesmere, in 1856 the work was the first picture to be presented to the National Portrait Gallery.

(*Above*) Shakespeare's two greatest clowns. Will Kempe dances on the road to Norwich in 1600, and the dwarfish Robert Armin strikes a pose in a long coat, in Armin's *Two Maids of Moreclacke*, printed in 1609.

(*Below*) Two enemies. Six years after attacking Shakespeare, Robert Greene rises from the grave to write again, in a cartoon of 1598.

(*Below, right*) The York Herald's disgusted note that Shakespeare, 'y^e Player', qualified for a coat of arms in 1596.

Shakespear y^e Player by Garter

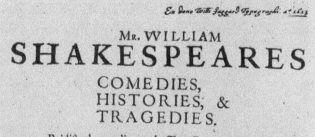

Mʀ. WILLIAM
SHAKESPEARES
COMEDIES,
HISTORIES, &
TRAGEDIES.

Publiſhed according to the True Originall Copies.

LONDON
Printed by Iſaac Iaggard, and Ed. Blount. 1623.

The title-page of the First Folio. This copy was given to the herald Augustine Vincent in 1623 with an inked inscription at the upper right by the printer 'William Jaggard Typographi'. Martin Droeshout was about 22 years old when he engraved Shakespeare's portrait.

Henry Wriothesley, third Earl of Southampton, in a painting, by an unknown artist, in 1600. 'The love I dedicate to your Lordship is without end', Shakespeare told him in the open letter with *Lucrece*.

(*Above, left*) Ferdinando Stanley, Lord Strange, patron of an amalgamated troupe which staged Shakespeare's early dramas.

(*Above, right*) Richard Burbage, who excelled in roles such as Richard III, Hamlet, and King Lear.

(*Below, left*) Ben Jonson, who offered friendship, suggestiveness, and goading rivalry, and (*right*) John Fletcher, with whom Shakespeare wrote three late plays.

Mr John Fletcher

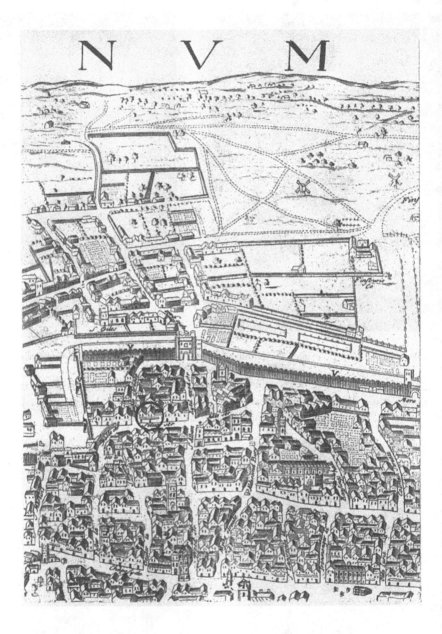

The 'Agas' woodcut map, *Civitatis Londinium*, depicts London as it was in 1553–9. This is from a copy at the Folger Library. The Mountjoys' house, where Shakespeare was living in 1604, appears in conventionalized fashion at the corner of Silver Street and Mugle Street not far from the city's walls, below the left-centre of the picture. To the north lay two useful routes to the Midlands.

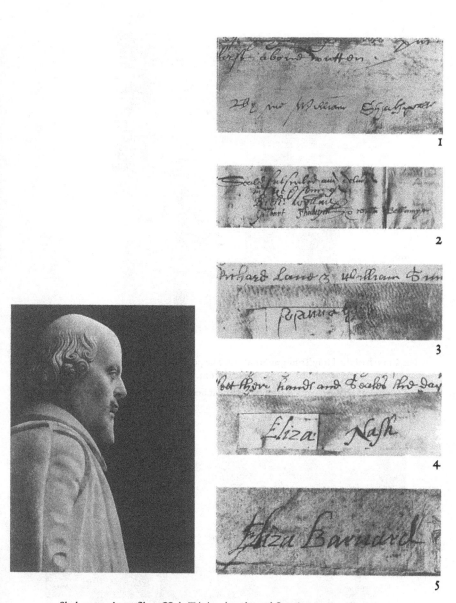

Shakespeare's profile at Holy Trinity church, and five signatures.

(From top to bottom) 1. 'By me William Shakspeare' on the third sheet of his legal will.
2. His brother Gilbert Shakespeare's hand in a neat 'Italian' style.
3. The hand of Shakespeare's elder daughter Susanna Hall, and two signatures of his only
granddaughter: 4. Elizabeth Nash, and 5.Elizabeth Barnard.

The Church of the Holy Trinity at Stratford. The poet's monument in the chancel was in place by 1623.

(*Below*) Shakespeare's Birthplace before it began to be restored in the 1850s.

fused the town's welfare and funds with his own. Neither was on easy, intimate terms with Shakespeare, who treated them with caution.

Should the poet invest in Shottery land? Old Adrian sees no gain to anyone in *that*, and wishes to get him to buy a share in the town's tithes, as Sturley tells Quiney on 24 January. That will bring needed cash to the Corporation and help the poet too, so it is up to Quiney to persuade Shakespeare: 'By the instructions you can give him thereof and by the friends he can make therefore', Sturley writes, 'we think it a fair mark for him to shoot at and not impossible to hit. It obtained would advance him indeed and would do us much good. *Hoc movere et quantum in te est permovere ne negligas* [don't neglect to move in this and, as much as in you lies, move deeply].'[25]

But, probably without seeing Shakespeare, Quiney rushed back to Stratford. Further news in his friend's letter was alarming. The town was in an uproar with citizens 'assembled together in great number' to attack those forcing up grain prices. One man, who had complained to Sir Fulke Greville, said 'he hoped within a week to lead some of them in a halter, meaning the malsters'. A local weaver trusted 'to see them hanged on gibbets at their own doors'.[26] If a mob attacked Quiney's barn they could take torches to New Place, too. Shakespeare's wife and daughters were in jeopardy, and this may be the closest analogue to his showing later, in *Coriolanus*, an intent Roman mob ready to riot over corn.

Stratford's grain survey, a few days after Sturley's letter, may have pacified hot heads, and it shows that excess stocks have magically vanished from barns. In an earlier survey, Sturley was alleged to hold twenty-six quarters of malt and Quiney thirty-two of malt, and forty-seven quarters of barley—all of 632 bushels. But by 4 February, Quiney's hoard on paper has shrunk to a mere fourteen quarters of malt, and Sturley's barn is a place of moral purity and beatitude since his holdings have dropped to only five quarters, half as much as his friend Shakespeare holds![27]

Still, the populace had come close to insurrection and the poet was alarmed, or at any rate his investment plan changed. So far as we know, he invested not a penny at Stratford for the next four years, or until after his father's death and well into 1602. In a time of dearth he had held too much malt, but he may not have been so rash again (it was only after good harvests that he sold twenty bushels to his neighbour Rogers). The Queen's Council called grain speculators 'wolves', and by coincidence Sturley echoed that in a newsy, worried letter: 'Man is a god to man, man is a wolf to man', he told Quiney in Latin.[28] It is only a myth of modern biography that Shakespeare closely befriended either alderman (who can refer to him with distant respect, even as they try to use him), but, then, he may have been amused enough to draw hints from both in his work.

Late in 1598 Quiney was back in London. He and Sturley, over the past few years, had consoled each other, rather as Antonio is consoled in *The Merchant of Venice*, and as profiteering aldermen they had reason to be wary (since their exposure as grain speculators back in 1595). 'Farewell, my dear heart', Sturley salutes his friend this autumn, 'and the Lord increase our loves and comforts one to another.'[29] In fact, both aldermen were then in debt, and Sturley's standing with a moneylender was in peril. In January he had told Quiney that he was 'left I assure you in the greatest need of £30 that possibly may be', for he had borrowed £80 from the moneylender and relied on Quiney to get £40 of the repayment deferred for six months. Now on 16 October, things were worse: a bond for £100 was due for repayment in six weeks, and to meet other creditors Sturley urgently needed £25, which he hoped Quiney's 'good labour' could procure.[30] But Quiney needed money as well, and a few days later at the Bell inn on Carter Lane, he penned a famous letter to Shakespeare.

It is a hurried letter, but Quiney mentions Thomas Bushell, Richard Mytton, and Peter Roswell, who were all in the service of Stratford's lord of the manor, Sir Edward Greville. The poet's brother Gilbert had dealings with two of them, as we recall, and Quiney now proposes Bushell and Mytton as sureties for a loan. 'Loving Countryman', he writes to Shakespeare on 25 October, 'I am bold of you as of a friend, craving your help with £30 upon Mr Bushell's and my security, or Mr Mytton's with me. Mr Roswell is not come to London as yet, and I have especial cause.' Since Quiney was ostensibly in the city on town business, he hoped to get expense money from Sir Edward's agent Roswell, but the agent has not appeared. 'You shall friend me

much in helping me out of all the debts I owe in London', Quiney
assures Shakespeare.

> I thank God & much quiet my mind which would not be indebted. I am now
> towards the Court in hope of answer for the despatch of my business. You
> shall neither lose credit nor money by me the Lord willing, & now but per-
> suade yourself so as I hope, and you shall not need to fear. But with all hearty
> thankfulness I will hold my time & content your friend, & if we bargain
> further you shall be the paymaster yourself.

Probably the poet was not being asked for his own funds, but for help
with a money-dealer who would lend £30, and indeed this is suggested in a note Quiney received a few days later from Sturley, who,
then, was glad to hear that 'our countryman Mr Wm Shak[speare]
would procure us money, which I will like of as I shall hear when,
where, and how'. Moneylending at up to 10 per cent interest was then
permissible, but less than respectable, and risky if not professionally
managed. Still, what is a little odd about Quiney's letter is a dark
undercurrent of inexplicit, half-suppressed worry or anxiety, and he
concludes in a rush:

> My time bids me hasten to an end, and so I commit this [to] your care & hope
> of your help. I fear I shall not be back this night from the Court. Haste. The
> Lord be with you & with us all, Amen. From the Bell in Carter Lane the
> 25 October 1598.
>
> Yours in all kindness
Ryc. Quyney

Quiney folded, sealed, and addressed this 'To my Loving good friend
& countryman Mr Wm Shackespere deliver these'. The letter perhaps
was not sent, unless the poet returned it with a reply, but Quiney made
some contact with him that day. Back at Stratford, his father had got
wind that an approach to the poet was being made, and sent a note to
advise his son to buy knit stockings for resale at home, if 'you bargain
with Wm Sha[kespeare] or receive money there'.[31] The son may have
bought the stockings, but he was disturbed not to see his lord's agent,
Roswell, and he was soon to know the open hostility of the lord of the
manor, Sir Edward Greville—whose men were to crack Quiney's skull.

Lately, Shakespeare's own relations with Stratford had changed. He was a householder, at last, in his mid-thirties, among citizens almost driven to barn-burning or worse. Did his eighty bushels trouble him after February? He was likely to sympathize at first with local maltsters, but a prospect of civic rebellion worried townsmen he knew. One intuits that Shakespeare feared a threat of social dissolution with an increase in violence and a fading of the notion of responsible community. His last series of happy comedies, from *As You Like It* to *Twelfth Night*, might be a good bulwark against his disenchantment; but in view of his own hoarding, in a time of famine and miserable deaths, he perhaps had, on reflection, some very prime, ugly evidence of man's callous, cold social indifference in modern times.

'This is the Forest of Arden'

As You Like It—Shakespeare's happiest play—was composed not long after Richard Quiney had asked for the poet's help in London. Most likely the comedy was written after its author's thirty-fifth birthday, in 1599; it was registered on 4 August 1600. Though it has a relation to problems that involve Quiney, the Grevilles, Stratford, and the Arden forest, the play was not meant to advertise injustice in the English Midlands. As an exuberant comedy it suggests its author's sanguine temperament. Its manner reveals his delight in pastoral romance and in Sidney's nuances of tone in the *Arcadia*, even as its romantic setting flatters the rural nostalgia of Londoners. On a May Day milkmaids paraded in London's streets with pails, and maypoles and morris dancers suggested a yearning for a 'golden' rural world.[32] Aching with love for Orlando, Rosalind dominates her milieu in disguise as the boy Ganymede. She avoids the worst complications of passion, wittily educates a Petrarchan lover (who carves her name on trees), and orchestrates a plot which ends in four marriages and her own Epilogue. The plot nevertheless relates to a malaise of brutality, alienation, and injustice, so that one's enquiries turn after all to the Midlands. To what extent might Quiney's difficulties bear on the poet's attitudes in this play and later?

On the very day he negotiated with Shakespeare, Quiney, in

October 1598, as it appears, was trying to gain benefits for his town. Keeping up that pursuit in the city, he was fretful, but he had word from a loving fellow alderman. Sturley told him in November to give *half* of anything he could get from the Queen's authorities for the Stratford Corporation to Sir Edward Greville, lest 'he shall think it too good for us and procure it himself'.[33] Sir Edward had a sense of his legal, well-protected power, which John Shakespeare, the Quineys, Sturley, and others who served at 'halls' well understood.

For the town, after all, had an odd status. Despite its corporate charter, Elizabethan Stratford had kept a few features of an old manorial borough, subject to a manorial lord; yet no prior lord had had the greed of Sir Edward, who lived south-west of the town at Milcote— which he had inherited after his father, Lodowick, was executed for killing a tenant. Sir Edward's aggression became more overt a few years after *As You Like It* was written, as when he claimed Stratford's toll corn or corn tax, and enclosed the meadowy Bancroft at the River Avon with hedges. (The Bancroft was a common where townsmen grazed cows, sheep, or a few pigs if they were ringed.) Quiney, with others, tore up the lord's hedges in disgust. Sir Edward responded with a lawsuit, and then vowed to win 'by the sword'.

A prophetic claim. Having opposed Quiney's elevation to the baili-wick, Sir Edward relied on bullying tactics with the help of a steward. But it was on a May night, some months after his second election as Stratford's High Bailiff, that Quiney was struck down. Having entered a house full of Sir Edward's men who were taunting its owner in a 'hurly burly' of shouts, the bailiff, as it was noted, 'in his endeav-our to still the brawl had his head grievously broken'.[34] Perhaps his skull was fractured. Richard Quiney certainly made no legal will; the only Stratford bailiff to be killed in office, he died a few weeks later and was buried at Holy Trinity on 31 May 1602. He left behind his widow, and nine children all under the age of 20: Elizabeth, Adrian, Richard, Thomas, Anne, William, Mary, John, and George. (It was his third son, Thomas, who later became a vintner and married Shakespeare's daughter Judith.)

The brutal death of a Stratford bailiff was not lost on Shakespeare, and helps to account for a deepening social pessimism in his writing.

Plays such as *Troilus and Cressida* and *Timon of Athens* are not unin-
fluenced by the violence and anarchy he knew in the town where
Anne, Susanna, and Judith had to live. It is also significant that (as the
Sonnets suggest) he could take his own deficiencies as subject-matter,
and find elements of a community's failures in his own egoism,
obtuseness, or inconsistencies as these appeared to him. It would be
foolish to impose any fancied limit on Shakespeare's reactions to experience, or to say that as a mature artist he learned only or mainly
from books, or to suppose that the two deaths linked with New Place,
or the killing of Quiney, had nothing to do with his attitude to
tragedy. It is not clear that his reactions to individuals were ever
simple; he may not have been horrified even by Sir Edward Greville, as
rapacious as that figure was, and Gilbert Shakespeare's connection
with two of Sir Edward's men is on record. But the disintegration of
order at Stratford would have seemed to Shakespeare, at times, bitter
and irreversible. In the late 1590s, Quiney's problems with a manorial
lord had precedents; the poet's father and old Adrian together once
had tried to wrestle privileges for the town from its former lord, the
Earl of Warwick, and Adrian was aware of his son's efforts and worries
around 1598.

By that year, too, rapaciousness was not limited to Greville's
domain. North of the town was the scrubby, wooded Arden where
Sir Edward's cousin—Sir Fulke Greville—without warrant denuded
large tracts of their trees. This struck at the landless poor, or at squat-
ters depending on wood for fuel, even as landowners enclosed Arden
fields once cultivated by their tenants. Enclosure drove some to
vagrancy, and those left behind faced hunger and destitution. In the
real 'Forest of Arden' there was a high incidence of infant mortality;
and many of its thin, flat-breasted women later stopped ovulating.
Protesters troubled the authorities, of course, but a rebellion against
land enclosures—led by Bartholomew Steer in 1596—had sputtered
out even before its leader was executed.[35]

In a folk-tale context, *As You Like It* does include the bleakest evil.
The usurper Duke Frederick, it seems, after seizing his brother's lands
has driven a good 'Duke Senior' and retinue into exile. Oppressed by
his elder brother Oliver who makes him eat with the hogs, Orlando

asserts his rights, whereupon Oliver arranges with the tyrant's wrestler to have his brother's neck broken. To be sure, Orlando defeats the killer-wrestler and at once falls idealizingly in love with Rosalind, as she does with him.

In her self-confidence and nerve, the heroine steps out of Thomas Lodge's rather gory romance *Rosalynde* or *Euphues Golden Legacy* (1590), the play's main source. Shakespeare softens Lodge's violence, but he develops *Rosalynde*'s theme of the difference between gifts of fortune which do not matter, and gifts of human nature which do. Disguised in the greenwood, Rosalind speaks and acts as a man, while keeping the privilege of feeling as a woman, and the playwright sets psychological realism in tension with a delightful mock-pastoralism which includes sudden love, comic episodes, exuberant rhetoric, and five songs—more songs than in any of his earlier plays. Myths of a 'golden age' are offset not only by Touchstone, but by Jaques, who in his Seven Ages of Man speech saves his very worst for old age. 'Last scene of all', Jaques offers with sombre smartness,

> Is second childishness and mere oblivion,
> Sans teeth, sans eyes, sans taste, sans everything.

(II. vii. 163–6)

That might be a parody of the satiric mode of Jonson and Marston in the late 1590s: and Jaques's cynicism is punctured by the entry of the servant Adam, who, at 80, is defeated only by hunger and knows of 'unregarded age in corners thrown'.

Yet here Shakespeare does not emphasize social issues. Lodge had imagined a 'Forest of Arden', and in the play the dramatist's Forest of Arden is a timeless place of random encounters, mainly happy debates and recollection. The word 'Arden' itself has a relation to the French Ardennes, to the Warwickshire Arden, and perhaps to the author's youth if he once heard folk-tales from the lips of Robert Arden's daughter. In the play's Arden the reality of death is not quite absent, and Touchstone is the first of the playwright's fools to have learned from death. 'But as all is mortal in nature', he tells Rosalind, 'so is all nature in love mortal in folly.' Shakespeare, nevertheless, evokes the dead poet Marlowe diffidently, or, perhaps, as a 'private rite of

memory', as Anne Barton notices. Phoebe the shepherd-girl summons up Marlowe's *Hero and Leander* (which had appeared in two
editions in 1598) when she quotes a line of it—

> Dead shepherd, now I find thy saw of might:
> 'Who ever loved that loved not at first sight?'
>
> (III. V. 82–3)[36]

And Rosalind alludes to the poem's subject (though Marlowe's Leander does not drown) in one of her best anti-romantic comments on
love. 'Troilus had his brains dashed out with a Grecian club', she tells
Orlando,

> yet he did what he could do to die before, and he is one of the patterns of love.
> Leander, he would have lived many a fair year though Hero had turned nun if
> it had not been for a hot midsummer night, for, good youth, he went but
> forth to wash him in the Hellespont and, being taken with the cramp, was
> drowned; and the foolish chroniclers of that age found it was Hero of Sestos.
> But these are all lies. Men have died from time to time, and worms have eaten
> them, but not for love.   (IV. i. 91–101)

Rosalind, as 'Ganymede', has a freedom from fixed personality and
propriety alike in being of both sexes, but retains her vulnerability. In
the green forest, where nature works its subtle change on everyone,
she is the most theatrical of heroines with a mind no less winning
because it resists flattery. 'I was never so berhymed', she says of
Orlando's lyrics, 'since Pythagoras' time that I was an Irish rat, which
I can hardly remember' (III. ii. 172–4). Through her, the author
brightly tests the sensitivity of comedy, as if the comic stage were not
the worst means of postponing any accounting for real loss or distress.
Yet 'The Forest of Arden' is a source of mythical truth as real as dearth,
poverty, injustice, exile, or the blindness of the human spirit. It offers
a romantic setting in which Shakespeare can exhibit an internalization
of values such as fidelity and love, with strong and sharp emphasis on
his lovers' psyches. He exteriorizes their most intimate, evolving feelings and perceptions, and in this respect at least he brings himself to
the edge of the terrible introspections of tragedy.

III

THE MATURITY OF GENIUS

❦

13

SOUTH OF JULIUS CAESAR'S TOWER

Ho no, no, no, no! My meaning in saying he is a good man
is to have you understand me that he is sufficient. Yet his
means are in supposition. He hath an argosy bound to
Tripolis, another to the Indies. I understand moreover
upon the Rialto he hath a third at Mexico, a fourth for
England, and other ventures he hath squandered abroad.
But ships are but boards, sailors but men. There be land
rats and water rats, water thieves and land thieves—I mean
pirates—and then there is the peril of waters, winds, and
rocks. The man is, notwithstanding, sufficient. Three
thousand ducats. I think I may take his bond.

(Shylock, *The Merchant of Venice*)

Ben Jonson's thumb

*L*ate in Elizabeth's reign—on St James's Day, 25 July 1601—two
men of the theatre went to Bricklayers Hall near Aldgate in the capital
to pay dues to one of the city's guilds, the Worshipful Company of
Tilers and Bricklayers. Both workers paid in arrears—2*s.* for the first,
and 3*s.* for the second. The first was Richard Hudson, a building
worker who loyally aided the Burbage family from the 1570s to the
time of the second Globe on Bankside.[1] The other was a gaunt, mus-
cular Londoner who in June 1572 was baptized Benjamin Johnson, but
styled himself 'Ben Jonson'.

No doubt Ben Jonson had learned to hate bricklaying, but he took
it up when in disgrace with fortune and men's eyes. After army service
in the Lowlands he had married, become a strolling actor, and then a

playwright. There is a story (told by Rowe) that he was 'altogether unknown' when one of his scripts came to the Lord Chamberlain's men, who treated it 'carelessly and superciliously' and were about to reject it, 'when *Shakespear* luckily cast his Eye upon it, and found something so well in it as to engage him first to read it through, and afterwards to recommend Mr *Johnson* and his Writings to the Publick'.[2] The story has little to recommend it, since Jonson was not 'unknown' when the troupe first produced one of his *Humour* plays in 1598. A strong demand for new, playable scripts was a fact of life. But whether or not he saved Jonson from a rejection, Shakespeare must have approved the play: he acted in its early version set in Italy; and no doubt also in Jonson's 'Londonized' revision (the one often acted today). A stylish comedy, in which everyone is under the sway of a leading trait, or 'humour', *Every Man in his Humour* pits the brashness of youth against obsessions of age. It is smart, funny, and lifelike: any troupe would have prized it.

Soon after its debut, Jonson displayed a tragic humour of his own. In a duel on 22 September at Shoreditch he killed Gabriel Spencer, an actor who had been in the Marshalsea prison with him the year before as a result of the government's outrage over Jonson's and Nashe's *The Isle of Dogs*. This time, to escape the gallows, Jonson pleaded benefit of clergy: he read his 'neck verse' to prove he knew Latin, and received a brand with a hot iron at the base of his left thumb, 'T', for Tyburn, to identify him if he killed again.

Then he returned to bricklaying—but not for long. In the Induction of his next work for the troupe, *Every Man Out of his Humour*, he mentions his taking 'a good meal among Players' once a fortnight, though living on 'beans and buttermilk' at home.[3] He must have supped with those who acted in his two *Humour* plays, and seen their regular poet. At 26, Jonson was a tall man, thin and scrawny for his height, with no trace yet of a 'mountain belly'. He was said to dress in 'rug' (a coarse woollen fabric) and favour a coat 'with slits under the armpits'. He clearly loomed over Shakespeare, who is not described as tall, and whose normal attire escaped comment, although that may suggest that he wore the predictable, neat silk doublet of an actor–manager. With the oddity of a high, slightly perpendicular forehead if one can trust his portraits, Shakespeare by report was 'a handsome well shap't man: very good company, and of a verie readie and pleasant smooth Witt'.[4] What was vital to Jonson was that the 'well shap't man' was potentially a munificent buyer of scripts, and in his mid-thirties the most famous playwright in London. Shakespeare, at their early meetings, was confronted with a thin, odd, brilliant, voluble scarecrow, and Jonson, if haughtily obsessed with himself, remembered the older poet's naturalness and candour. 'Hee was (indeed) honest', Jonson recalled of his Stratford friend, 'and of an open, and free nature: had an excellent *Phantsie*; brave notions, and gentle expressions'. Such phrases slide vaguely between memories of the man and of his verse; but Jonson claimed in his elegy that the 'father's face lives in his issue', as if Shakespeare's affable manners still lived in his 'well-turnèd and true-filèd lines'.[5]

Nevertheless as Jonson's art matured, he viewed Shakespeare as his principal rival and became by turns awestruck and obsessed, puzzled and dismissive: 'Shakespeare wanted art', he told William Drummond in 1619, and in retrospect he tried to sum up his friend's chief defect. 'I *remember*, the Players have often mentioned it as an honour to *Shakespeare*', noted Jonson, 'that in his writing, (whatsoever he penn'd), hee never blotted out line. My answer hath beene, would he had blotted a thousand. Which they thought a malevolent speech'.[6] He invented, with a little help from his friends, the image of a poorly schooled, naturally gifted Stratford poet who, with 'small Latine and lesse Greeke', had committed silly, egregious faults in a spume of words. *Julius Caesar* irked him for more than two decades, because the play should have been more foolish than it was, to judge from his comments in *The Staple of News* (1626) and in *Discoveries* (probably written after the fire that burned Jonson's papers in November 1623)—yet at his best he judged Shakespeare's merits acutely.

Legends of their 'wit combats' at the Mermaid tavern on Bread Street are unsound,[7] though Jonson was fond of the Mermaid despite its high prices, and Shakespeare knew its landlord William Johnson by 1613. Once at such a tavern, when the two poets were in their cups, Jonson supposedly jotted his mock-epitaph, 'Here lies

Ben Jonson, | That was once one [?one's son]', and Shakespeare obliged by completing it:

> Who while he lived was a slow thing
> And now being dead is no thing.

In another story, the older poet had to be godfather to a Jonson son, and after racking his brains to think of a christening gift came out of a 'deep study' inspired. 'I'll e'en give him a dozen good latten spoons', he told Ben, 'and thou shalt translate them.' (The weak pun is on *latten*, a brass, or brass-like alloy, often used in church utensils.)[8]

The facts suggest that Shakespeare took pains to oblige the tall, intellectual young poet by acting in his *Humour* play and later in his Roman tragedy *Sejanus His Fall*, in 1603. And Jonson's early allusions to his rival are in turn good-natured, neutral, or mildly satirical, with none of the cutting force of his attacks on other poets. Sooner or later Jonson offended every troupe he worked for, but he was a writer the Chamberlain's men tried to please. If the brand on his thumb was a badge of apartness, he was agreeable when he left his beans and buttermilk and sought friends among wild-heads, poetizers, and law students of the Inner Temple: he dedicated his second *Humour* play to the Inns of Court. He knew poets such as John Donne of Lincoln's Inn and Francis Beaumont of the Inner Temple, or Donne's confidant Henry Goodere and the sharp-minded parliamentarian and essayist Francis Bacon of Gray's Inn. He had connections with men who helped to form taste among the gentry. Even younger spirits at the Inns were influential, and the Chamberlain's actors could lose vital prestige if the gentry ever defected.

Furthermore, Jonson not only admired new satirists at the Inns, but expanded on their precedents. He had a friendly enemy in John Marston of the Middle Temple, born in 1576, whose poems in *Scourge of Villainy* set a precedent in snapping at the city's idle, privileged dandies as in 'Cynic Satire' written at 22:

> These are no men, but apparitions,
> Ignes fatui, glowworms, fictions,
> Meteors, rats of Nilus, fantasies,
> Colosses, pictures, shades, resemblances.

Ho, Lynceus!
Seest thou yon gallant in the sumptuous clothes,
How brisk, how spruce, how gorgeously he shows?
Note his French herring-bones: but note no more,
Unless thou spy his fair appendant whore.[9]

Having caught the acid note of classical Latin verse, even as satires were banned in 1599, Marston had begun to bring his sharp talents to play-writing.

Fresh young intellects in these years upset any notion of the merely entertaining play or a quiescent theatre. Shakespeare, for his part, had little to gain from vying openly with *littérateurs*, and might have seemed lacking in competitiveness. It is likely that that aspect of the man struck, if it did not unnerve, the voluble, truculent Jonson. In talk and demeanour, Shakespeare might have seemed unconcerned with his worth, or, at least, been lightly facetious about his real or imaginary detractors. His jokes might suggest that he was troubled by his ease, or facility, or by a demon that let him do anything with words; the difficulty of his projects, even his punning, can look like retorts upon the demon. With joking gravity, he put himself down, as if glad of a delicious chance to do so, as in the implicit view of himself in the Poet of the Sonnets. His Poet is 'tongue-tied' at the notion of a rival, certain that another poet is a 'better spirit', or that his own 'saucy bark' is 'inferior far'.[10] The Poet of Sonnet 78, uneasy among the learned, asks his lovely friend to advance 'as high as learning my rude ignorance'.

One sign that Shakespeare made no claim for his erudition is that Jonson denied he had any, but his friend found the Stratford poet no meek soul. Shakespeare saw himself as a useful, practical poet working up chronicle or story material into new forms for the sake of proficient actors: he was a supplier, leaving within the text of a play broad guidelines for the actors' interpretation of the work, so he neither insisted upon a limited view of his meanings nor abrogated responsibility for what he wrote. Jonson, in contrast, was throwing the onus of interpretation upon an audience, and writing mainly sourceless comedies of social insight while driving at the pride, greed, and chicanery of the age.

Shakespeare was less well attuned to Jonson's self-assertive, cynical audacity than to an imaginative meeting of a troupe's needs. Fashions in play-writing changed, and he tried to stay ahead. Yet Jonson's cutting edge, his free, attacking mind, his trenchant mockery and tireless intellectual zeal for demolition might implicitly have accused the older poet of tameness. Shakespeare was repeating himself in new romantic comedies, doing so with exceptional artistry, but relying on his own older, well-tried situations, on worn devices, and mild versions of often Tarltonesque clowns. It is not that he sedulously imitated Jonson or anyone else, though he plucked twigs off a forest of trees. But his new, lying or boasting railers such as Thersites in *Troilus and Cressida*, Lucio in *Measure for Measure*, or Parolles in *All's Well* have a relation to such a depraved clown as Carlo Buffone in Jonson's *Every Man Out of his Humour*. The intellectual quotient rises, and Jonson's example and influence, among other factors, led Shakespeare to such a difficult, self-trapping, self-challenging exploit as inventing a Prince Hamlet whose mind holds the stage for five acts in which 'revenge' is suspended. Jonson's examples also encouraged a new, hard-edged realism in Shakespeare's so-called 'problem comedies' and other new works ahead.

Anecdotes of their friendship say little of the poets' awarenesses, and Jonson was competitive, restless, nervily ambitious. His *Sejanus* implicitly attacks *Julius Caesar*, and in condemning heroic action and exposing a state's pervasive corruption Jonson's play was surely remembered by the author of *King Lear*. Jonson saved most of his outright criticism of his rival for prologues, prefatory verses, or reminiscences dating from about 1614. In retrospect, he implies that 'three rusty swords' and 'Lancaster's long jars' are not enough to show political realities in *Henry VI*, or that a chorus as in *Henry V* that 'wafts you o'er the seas' is foolishly artificial. As for Shakespeare's stage properties and the imitation of nature an audience needs neither

> rolled bullet heard
> To say, it thunders; nor tempestuous drum
> Rumbles, to tell you when the storm doth come.[11]

For Jonson, *Pericles* is a glib, mouldy tale that wants art. As for *The Winter's Tale* or *The Tempest*, a good neo-classical poet must be

'loath to make Nature afraid in his plays, like those that beget *Tales,*
Tempests, and such like *Drolleries*'.[12] And Jonson is loose enough with
a notion of dates in the *Bartholomew Fair* Induction to show how outmoded his rival is. Those souls who praise *Titus Andronicus* have a
taste which has stood still 'these five and twenty, or thirty years', he
says in 1614.[13] All of this is offset by his critical views in the elegy of
1623, when Shakespeare is judged without an inhibiting sense of the
troubling, creating presence of the living man; there is scant attention
to the man in this intelligent elegy. But in these years Jonson's main
struggle to adjust his own views lay ahead, and in new works the Stratford poet, though by no means oblivious to Jonson and Marston, and
in fact learning from them, sharply impressed and irked a man of
'humours'.

Shylock, the troubled *Merchant of Venice,* and Francis Meres

Just before Hamnet Shakespeare died, Londoners had had bracing
news from the sea. An English attack on Cadiz harbour resulted in the
capture of two opulently laden Spanish galleons. One of them, the
San Andrés—renamed the *Andrew,* becomes a byword for sea-wealth
in *The Merchant of Venice* in Salerio's phrase, 'my wealthy *Andrew*
docks in sand' (I. i. 27).[14] That helps to date the *Merchant,* which
Shakespeare appears to have written after July 1596, when news of the
ship's capture reached London, and before 22 July 1598 when the play
was registered.

In the Midlands this was a period of harvest dearth, famine, and
widespread social unrest; it was also a period in which the poet lost his
only son, and made a large, showy investment in New Place. For all
the claims on his energies and the financial exigencies of his troupe,
one might expect that his mood, at times, was more introverted than
usual in these months. There is a committed inwardness in the *Merchant* with its emphatic moral themes, its pictures of a spiritual
malaise, and its remarkable characterization. The play has compelling
argumentative speeches, but its last act is evasively aestheticized—so
that issues of justice and mercy, raised earlier, are left unresolved.

There is an odd difficulty in the author's treatment of a Jewish villain, a problem no easier for modern directors and audiences after the Holocaust. This is not the only art-work to have been used for a vicious purpose, but if we dismissed all works of art that have appealed to lunatics, we should have little art left. Shylock is radically paradoxical, and—despite his villainy—he can morally shrivel his weary Christian enemies; he is not in dramatic balance with a hazily seen Antonio or with a slightly saccharine, pertly competent Portia.

Lawyers and law students—among others in Elizabethan London—were bound to be riveted by the trial scene in Act IV, when, before Duke and Magnificoes, Antonio bares his breast for the villain's knife, and Portia, in a legal gown as the advocate Bellario, wins Shylock's praise before breaking him. At the play's heart is a conflict between Tudor common law and the mitigating equity of the Chancery courts. Shylock's bond, stipulating a pound of Antonio's flesh, has the rigidity of statute law at its worst, whereas Portia at first represents the fairness of equity. In legal and other aspects, the drama is a folk-tale: no English law permitted anyone to put his or her life in jeopardy, as Antonio has done. The author is not legalistic, but, given his story's bizarre features, he treats them with stunning effect before Act V.

Shakespeare often worked with a large 'given'. In this instance, he used a ready-made medieval tale in Ser Giovanni's *Il Pecorone* (The Dunce) printed at Milan in 1558, in which a merchant of Venice borrows money for his 'godson', Giannetto, from a Jewish lender. The play closely follows this tale's line. In the Italian version, if the debt is not repaid on time, the Jew may take a pound of the merchant's flesh. Giannetto courts a lovely 'Lady of Belmonte'; and the Jew is undone when the lady, having come to Venice in disguise as a lawyer, shows the bond does not permit the Jew to shed one drop of blood or to take more than exactly a pound of flesh. The Jew tears up his bond; the lawyer begs a ring the lady had given to young Giannetto, who, on his return to Belmonte, is accused of having given the ring to a mistress, until his lady reveals her stratagem, the ring is restored, and all ends happily. That story was strong in outline, and Shakespeare developed an active heroine who solves a dilemma, a motif in *Two Gentle-*

men, and later in *All's Well* and *Measure for Measure.* He puts Portia at the mercy of caskets, obnoxious suitors, and her dead father's will at Belmont, before she goes confidently to Venice. Another attraction for him in the Italian tale was its villain-Jew.

No doubt this figure of the Jew as a moneylender touched deep wellsprings in his imagination. Shylock appears in five scenes, but dominates the play. Shakespeare had a good source (not that he closely followed it) in Marlowe's half-comical but villainous hero Barabas in *The Jew of Malta.* Lately, Henslowe had revived the *Jew* in the wake of public feeling about the converted Portuguese Jew, Roderigo or Ruy Lopez, one of the Queen's physicians, found guilty in 1594 of trying to poison her. However, the poet focuses on the stereotype of the Jew as usurer: this is what he found in an Italian tale.

Persecuted, squeezed into ghettos, marked out by unique taxes, beaten, and sometimes killed, European Jews had turned to money-broking as one of the few means permitted for their livelihoods. They were associated with usury, or lending out money at interest—especially at exorbitant, illegal rates—but usury was no longer a moral problem when the *Merchant* was written. Sturley was in debt to a money-broker, and Quiney may have met one through the poet's good offices. Attitudes to usury, however, were evolving. An older communal, theological approach to moneylending was giving way to one that would be defined by economic needs in the Jacobean era.[15] John Shakespeare had been guilty of stiff usury, and his charging 20 per cent interest on two loans might be a feat worthy of the Rialto. Shakespeare had a chance to meet Jewish court musicians, but again the city's Jewish population was very small, and it is only too plain that he had no personal prejudice against Jews or moneylenders. He befriended the wealthy money-broker John Combe, and had dealings with a bolder one in Francis Langley, who at Paris Garden built the Swan playhouse which opened in 1596. Langley is called a 'draper' in Schoenbaum's mainly accurate account of him,[16] but this neglects the fact that Langley had the office of alnager, or sealer and inspector of woollen cloth, in London; he had useful connections and a minor, but potent, civic office; and with broking and other enterprises, he was wealthy enough to buy the manor of Paris Garden in 1589. Seven years later, as Leslie Hotson discovered, William Wayte petitioned '*ob metum mortis*' (for fear of death) in a suit for sureties of the peace against 'Will*elm*um Shakspere', Francis Langley, Dorothy Soer wife of John Soer, and Anne Lee. Hotson's suppositions about these persons have obscured the value of Hotson's facts, and he notes for example that Wayte's stepfather, William Gardiner, was a justice of the peace with jurisdiction over Paris Garden and Southwark. Just why Shakespeare was drawn into the fray is unknown, but he appears in a retaliatory law-suit on the side of an aggressive investor and money-broker.[17]

All of this casts only a small amount of light on the vigour and empathy of his portrayal of the moneylender, Shylock. In an unsentimental production, the villain can seem better than his adversaries, such as his daughter Jessica who lies, steals from him, and squanders the 'turquoise' his dead wife Leah has given him, or worthier than Antonio, who reviles him, or Portia, who defeats him. 'The seeds of sympathy are there', John Gross writes; 'Actors who have portrayed a tragic or sorely misused Shylock may often have gone too far, but it is Shakespeare himself who gave them their opening'.[18] Shylock is given sensitivity, emotional complexity, religious dignity, and incisive speech (as in his remarks to Bassanio at the start of this chapter): it is most unlikely that a Chamberlain's clown often acted him as a simple buffoon with red beard and a foreign accent. He does not speak in dialect, and the play's title-page in 1600 suggests no comic butt: 'The most excellent Historie of the *Merchant of Venice*. With the extreame crueltie of *Shylocke* the Iewe towards the sayd Merchant, in cutting a just pound of his flesh: and the obtayning of *Portia* by the choyse of three chests.'

Antonio—importantly—hates the moneylender partly *because* he is Jewish. A disease of the Christian's mind leads to a despising of the Jew's traits, his whole being: the Jew-as-dog. It is a very comforting notion of critics that Antonio shows religious, not racial, prejudice, but Shakespeare's time was not that simple; the boundary was not so clear. 'You call me misbeliever', Shylock reminds Antonio, and that is unrefuted. 'You called me dog', and the Christian responds:

I am as like to call thee so again,
To spit on thee again, to spurn thee too.

(I. iii. 110–29)

This occurs before Shylock has violated any Venetian law, or threat-ened a life. It is true that, later on, his daughter Jessica is embraced by Shylock's enemies as a Christian, not as a Jew. But by then she has denied her Jewish heritage, the Jewish nation, and stolen her father's jewels; her character might be wholly despicable if her brain were not so inert and empty. In a drama of psychological questioning, Shake-speare depicts a deep malaise of inertia and prejudice. Critics such as Leo Salingar, or Avraham Oz, who edits the Hebrew edition of Shake-speare's works, point to the depth of that malaise, to the inability of merchants and aristocrats to cope with it, and to themes from myth and folklore that complicate it. The director Peter Hall finds that the story shows 'the perils of racism, and how it can poison the persecutor as well as the persecuted'.[19] Shylock's exit in Act IV, in effect, brands his victors, leaving the sets of lovers as obtuse, forgetful, or hypocrit-ical in the muted resolution of Act V. Tensions are hardly smoothed over by the beauty of a magical night, music's harmonies, or the frail comedy of Portia's and Nerissa's rings. 'I live', says the lethargic, self-pitying hero of *Richard II*,

with bread, like you; feel want,
Taste grief, need friends: Subjected thus,
How can you say to me I am a king?

(III. ii. 171–3)

Shylock's humane protest is more powerful than that, as when he evokes the crucified Jew his enemies worship, 'If you prick us, do we not bleed?' He also lusts for his enemy's blood, and here the author reverts to the materialism, prejudice, and self-righteousness that destroy.

Nonetheless there are unreconciled impulses in Shakespeare's treatment of mercantile Venice and romantic Belmont, just as there are in his dramatically evasive and unconvincing handling of the themes of mercy and justice which his characters evoke. Portia's ennui, the tired absurdity of her pretending to obey her father's will, the smugness of Christian aristocrats, Antonio's amorality, and Jessica's shallowness—all of these are out of balance with the faith, integrity, and nerve of Shylock, whose dignity is not lessened even by his maddened bargain for Antonio's flesh. Intentionally or not, the poet appears to subvert his design with figures such as Hotspur, Falstaff, Shylock, and Malvolio, who beat with an intenser life than do their associates. In this case, a revulsion at his affluence in the wake of his son's death seems to have affected Shakespeare's dramaturgy. His outlay for a large Chapel Street house was striking at a time when frightful scarcities and high prices did not allow the poor to buy enough barley, beans, oats, or rye.[20] The attempts of the towns to look after the hungry accused the well-to-do, and Shakespeare highlights the evils of moneylending and turns against materialism. Shylock is thoroughly punished, but the drama's chief interest exits with him— he leaves behind a thematic gap never again filled.

Less paradoxical and on the whole more objectively written, *Much Ado about Nothing* and *Twelfth Night* display a mature wit, pace, and deftness of portraiture developed through Shakespeare's series of romantic comedies, and both plays have an intellectual edge in their attacks on social complacency. The testing of suitors in the *Merchant* has a parallel in the role-playing duels of Beatrice and Benedick. The love plots in *Much Ado* and *Twelfth Night* relate to popular Italian or French tales by writers such as Matteo Bandello and François de Belleforest, and one of Shakespeare's innovations is to impart to the changed, dramatized tale a psychological dimension, so as to use 'love' as a means of exploring a capacity for self-deception. *Twelfth Night*, written soon after *Hamlet*, is deliberately like an overripe plum in its comic scenes; a critic such as Richard Hillman is even oppressed by an entropic, muggy aspect of its imagined Illyria, and by the 'fantasy-ridden self-indulgence of its inhabitants'. Philip Edwards finds the author exposing 'his comedy to questioning at every point'.[21] Implicitly, the authorial self is also in question, and, as different as the stiff, toadying Malvolio is from Shylock, the author again sympathizes excessively with an aggrieved, self-deluding outcast.

❦

His own reputation had been setting Shakespeare apart from all other theatre-poets. A few of his plays had been issued in quarto anonymously before an auspicious change in 1598. Not only were second quartos of *Richard II* and *Richard III* printed with his name that year, but *Love's Labour's Lost* (as 'By W. Shakespere') appeared in its first extant edition. Publication of his love plays whetted interest in their author. John Manningham, a law student at the Middle Temple where *Twelfth Night* was staged in 1602, jots in that same year, in his *Diary*, an anecdote which perhaps fittingly bedevils Shakespeare's biographers to this day. An assumption has been made that Manningham heard it from his room-mate Edward Curle, but the informant's name is too obscurely written to be positively identifiable. One student of the *Diary*'s handwriting plausibly holds that Manningham in all likelihood wrote '(Mr. Towse)' just after this anecdote.[22] William Towes, or Towse, of Hingham, Norfolk, was a member of the Inner Temple, a purveyor of stories about the illustrious, and one of the diarist's chief informants. In its mild scurrilousness and historical allusiveness the story, at any rate, is in tune with wry, fictive anecdotes told at the Inns of Court Christmas revels which lasted into January. Recorded in March 1602, the story is that once, after playing Richard III, Richard Burbage arranged a tryst with a lady besotted by him; but they must have talked too loudly, for Will Shakespeare overheard their talk, reached the lady first, and was 'entertained, and at his game ere Burbidge came'. When a message arrived to say Richard III was at the door, the poet slyly sent word that William the Conqueror had preceded Richard III.[23] Students relished the idea of a poet's outwitting the famous actor Burbage, and the tale was retold, embellished with new details, and printed in Thomas Wilkes's *A General View of the Stage* in 1759, long before Manningham's *Diary* came to light.

More soberly indicative of Shakespeare's fame is a work by an enthusiastic clergyman, Francis Meres, which appeared in 1598 as *Palladis Tamia. Wits Treasury. Being the Second part of Wits Common wealth*. Born a year after Shakespeare and hailing from Lincolnshire, Meres describes himself in this stubby octavo (and also in his first printed sermon, *God's Arithmetic*) as a 'Master of Arts of both Universities'. As a scholar, he is lazy. He lifts his classical allusions mainly from a handbook known as the *Officina* by J. Ravisius Textor, but in a section entitled 'Poetrie' he is keen to show, in a style laden with similitudes, what was felt at the time about living English poets.

Meres's value, for us, lies in his lack of originality and his reflection of popular views. Most of his panegyrics are undiscriminating, and he flatters Michael Drayton with more words and mentions than anyone else. Yet he writes two significant paragraphs, in the first of which an Elizabethan view of Shakespeare's relationship with Ovid is well given. 'As the soule of *Euphorbus* was thought to live in *Pythagoras*', Meres offers with a show of erudition, 'so the sweete wittie soule of Ovid lives in mellifluous & hony-tongued *Shakespeare*, witnes his *Venus* and *Adonis*, his *Lucrece*, his sugred Sonnets among his private friends, &c'.[24] The 'sugred Sonnets', it might be thought, represent a few of the poems printed in the *Sonnets* (1609). So one assumes, although Meres could be referring to some fourteen-line poems and other amatory lyrics by Shakespeare now lost. His second paragraph has other mysteries. 'As *Plautus* and *Seneca* are accounted the best for Comedy and Tragedy among the Latines', he writes,

so *Shakespeare* among ye English is the most excellent in both kinds for the stage; for Comedy, witnes his *Gentlemen of Verona*, his *Errors*, his *Love labors lost*, his *Love labours wonne*, his *Midsummers night dreame*, & his *Merchant of Venice*: for Tragedy his *Richard the 2. Richard the 3. Henry the 4. King John, Titus Andronicus* and his *Romeo and Juliet*.[25]

That list invaluably tells us about dramas which must have existed by 7 September 1598, when Meres's book was registered. He was in London in 1597 and 1598, and his survey is up to date, since he mentions Everard Guilpin's *Skialetheia*, registered eight days after *Palladis Tamia*; but he does not produce exhaustive lists. He omits *Henry VI* for instance, and names six comedies and six 'tragedies' to illustrate Shakespeare's double superiority. If *Much Ado*, then, was not yet acted, could it be the same play Meres calls *Love's Labour's Won*? The latter became less of a ghost in 1953 when a London bookseller found a scrap of paper, used to make a hinge for a volume of sermons, which turned out to show a stationer's notes on books stocked in August 1603. Under '*Love's Labour Lost*' is the manuscript entry, '*Love's Labour Won*'. Meres, then, was not mistaken to list that title, but whether *Love's Labour's Won* describes a missing work, or is an alternative title for an existing drama such as *Taming of the Shrew, Much Ado*, or *All's Well*, is still unknown.

For a poet involved in writing scripts for actors, *Palladis Tamia* was likely to be only a naïve amusing irrelevance. The theatre was concerned with practices of the day and the tastes of contemporary audiences, and very little with supposed literary values. In *Hamlet* Shakespeare may lightly mock the pretensions of *Palladis Tamia*. Meres's verdict, 'Plautus and Seneca are accounted the best for Comedy and Tragedy', seems to be echoed by Polonius just after his fantastic catalogue of the stage-play genres. 'Seneca cannot be too heavy, nor Plautus too light', he weightily instructs Prince Hamlet, as if the latter were a kind of dim grammar-school boy who could hardly tell the difference between dark tragedy and bright comedy.[26]

At all events, the earnest criticism which attends Shakespeare's fame had begun.

Julius Caesar at the Globe

To some extent the successful revival of Marlowe's *The Jew of Malta*—which with Kyd's *The Spanish Tragedy* had been one of Henslowe's two most profitable works at the Rose—would have alerted the Chamberlain's men to the potential of their own *Merchant of Venice*. We lack a diary to tell us how often the latter was played at the Theater or the Curtain but Shylock was a success, and there are signs that the *Merchant* did uncommonly well in a public amphitheatre and at court. Hence it can seem surprising that the Chamberlain's men found themselves in deep trouble by 1597, and that their repertoire did not save them: their survival was in question. The troupe lacked cash, they lacked a secure theatre, they lacked a safe venue, and, facing bankruptcy, they began to sell off their playbooks. The extent of their difficulties by the middle of 1597 has been considerably underestimated.

Ironically it was a far-sighted plan of James Burbage which led to a disaster for Shakespeare's group. A year earlier, the old man had sunk £600 of his reserves in the 'upper frater' chamber of a former priory at Blackfriars. This large room, conveniently near a well-heeled clientele in the city's west would, he hoped, serve as an *indoor* venue. All play-goers, according to Burbage's plan, would have seats, and this would allow for a minimum entry price of 6*d.* with cheap seats in high balconies at the rear, and costlier ones in the pit or stalls, or in boxes flanking the stage (this roughly anticipated the pricing and seating patterns of our modern theatres).[27] In November however, thirty-one residents of Blackfriars petitioned the Privy Council against having a common public theatre in their midst—and signing the petition as if to deserve a reply of 'Et tu, Brute' was the company's new patron, George Carey, the second Lord Hunsdon. The project collapsed.

With his capital sunk in Blackfriars, old Burbage died three months later. Cuthbert and Richard then had to hunt for a new venue, if the company were to survive. The Theater stood on land owned by one Giles Allen—a man of broadly Puritan sympathies—who refused to renew the lease. He played a nasty game, at last agreeing to a lease on inflated terms, and then refusing to sign because he would not accept Richard the actor as surety. While Cuthbert tried, with no success, to get a new lease, the troupe could have used Langley's Swan on Bank-side before their Shoreditch lease expired on 13 April 1597, but they clung mainly to the less than wholesome Curtain while cash ran low and the Theater stood in 'darke silence, and vast solitude'.[28] Money did not flow in. Gatherers waited at theatre doors, without seeing much of it. Just why this happened is after all a little mysterious; but dwindling cash was a worry for any troupe, and the spectre of bored, listless ranks of the gentry defecting, or staying away for any reason, was a nightmare. Actors had to eat; hirelings had to be paid. The poet's fellows valued his scripts as prime assets, and they can only have felt it a hurtful, oppressive loss in 1597 and 1598 when they sold the playbooks of *Richard III, Richard II, 1 Henry IV*, and *Love's Labour's Lost* to Andrew Wise as a cash-raising device.

These were popular works. Sold to Wise, they were printed in quarto, with the result that the first three became the only playbooks by Shakespeare to sell as well as dramas such as Thomas Heywood's *If You Know Not Me, Part 1* (1605), Samuel Daniel's *Philotas* (1605), the anonymous *How a Man May Choose a Good Wife* (1602), or Beaumont and Fletcher's *Philaster* (1620), to judge from the number of times a drama was reprinted in the twenty-five years after it was published. But the release of four of Shakespeare's playscripts to Wise was an act of desperation, and one stresses the point not only because Shakespeare's biographers neglect it but because they have so little to say of his acting company and think of his success as an unbroken phenomenon.

And what did his fame mean? Plays in print advertised his name, but could also signal his troupe's urgent need for cash, or their declining attractiveness. Rival companies left each other's repertories alone; but his fellows clearly believed one of their dramas was stolen, and cannot have been eager to release many of their holdings.[29] If his histories or romantic comedies were well liked on stage, colleagues might want more of the same and he risked repeating himself. On the other hand, if he relied on older forms which he handled well, he could jeopardize his troupe's effort to keep up with new fashions in performance to maintain their prestige. Nothing he had done guaranteed his troupe's solvency.

A doubtfully legal trick saved them. Some of his colleagues lived near the Rose on Bankside, and here the Burbages took out a thirty-one-year lease on a vacant site in December 1598. The winter brought hard frosts, says Stow. The Thames froze at London Bridge before Christmas, and then there was a thaw, followed by icy, cheerless weather on St John's Day, the 27th, and a heavy snowfall on the 28th, when the river 'was againe nigh frozen'.[30] Taking advantage of the snowfall to work undetected, Cuthbert and Richard Burbage, Peter Streete the carpenter, and about a dozen workmen dismantled the old Theater at Shoreditch. Its heavy timbers were piled on wagons, which would have found ice on the streets hazardous. The timbers could not have been dragged over a 'nigh frozen' Thames, so they probably went over London Bridge, before being unloaded at a Southwark site that had been inherited by Nicholas Brend, whose father, Thomas, had bought the land in 1544. Just to the east of the Rose, this was farther back from the river. Here Peter Streete, who pledged to finish in twenty-eight weeks, led his men in building a new theatre to be called the Globe.

There were problems almost at once. Allen sued for trespass, claiming Streete had taken material worth £800 which was rightly Allen's because it stood on his land—and litigation was to last nearly two years. Also, building costs ran high. On 21 February, the Burbages agreed to meet 50 per cent of the costs, and, without precedent, brought in five sharers, each to put up 10 per cent as co-owners or 'housekeepers' in the venture. The five new 'housekeepers' were Shakespeare, John Heminges, Will Kempe, Thomas Pope, and Augustine Phillips: and thus actors (in the path of old James Burbage) became proprietors. Collectively, they had one half-share in the Globe's ground-lease, but in due course Heminges arranged for William Leveson, a mercer, and Thomas Savage, a goldsmith down from Lancashire, to be trustees in a deed which allowed the five to alter their terms to 'tenancy in common'. That enabled an actor to dispose of his share, and so when Kempe quit the troupe at the year's end, his share was taken by the other four.

Thanks to the Brends, on whose land the Globe was built, it is possible to consider for the first time in a biography six documents which, interestingly, mention Shakespeare's name. A modern scholar refers to 'Sir Thomas Brend', but he never had a title, nor was he of gentlemanly rank. In fact he had died in September 1597, and when an inquisition into Brend's heritable assets was at last completed on 16 May 1599, his estate's properties in St Saviour's parish included 'a House [that is, the Globe] newly built with a garden attached' ('una Domo de novo edificata cum gardino') which is then 'in the occupation of William Shakespeare and others' ('in occupatione Willielmi Shakespeare et aliorum'). Significantly, this implies that in May 1599 Shakespeare was thought to be the most prominent Globe tenant, and also that the Globe had a partial existence by that month. The second document comes two years later. When Nicholas Brend—Thomas's son—mortgaged his Southwark properties, including the Globe, to his stepbrother John Bodley, on 7 October 1601, he signed a deed of trust which lists eighteen tenants including 'Richard Burbage and

William Shackspeare, gent.'—and here the troupe's leading actor and its regular dramatist are the Globe's chief tenants. In a third document, they also appear as such on 10 October 1601—when Bodley's control of the property was enhanced just two days before Nicholas Brend died.

The Globe's effective owner for the last fifteen years of Shakespeare's life was John Bodley, but the story is a little involved. Technically, Bodley was a trustee for Nicholas's older son Matthew, and, for a few years, Bodley was obliged to share ownership with two partners. After Bodley's first partner died, the other partner, his uncle John Collet, sold his interest to Bodley in 1608, at which time a deed mentions the 'playhouse' and 'Richard Burbage and William Shakespeare, gentlemen'. Those two are thus linked again as the foremost tenants in a company known, by then, as the King's Servants. Even after his own death, 'William Shakespeare gent' is named as tenant of the playhouse in a decree of 21 February 1622 (since it was common for such descriptions to be repeated for years after a tenant was dead and buried). On 12 March 1624, the deceased friends Burbage and Shakespeare are both listed as tenants with the still-living Cuthbert Burbage and Heminges, and finally, nine years later, on 20 June 1633, the Globe is described as 'now or late in the possession or occupation of John Herminge, Cuthbert Burbage, Richard Burbage and William Shakespeare or any of them, their or any of their leagues or assignes, &c.'[31]

So much, anyway, for legal deeds. Shakespeare as a 'housekeeper' or part-holder of the Globe tenancy benefited from new income and new stimulus in 1599, as a beautiful theatre opened its doors. Yet competition from rivals did not vanish, nor did censorship, Puritan fury, or threats of long closure in plague. What exactly did the Globe look like? To speak of the *first* Globe which lasted until June 1613, the various drawings by Norden, Visscher, Hondius, Delaram, and others show it as either circular, hexagonal, or octagonal, and minus stair turrets. We lack any sketch of its stage or tiring-house. Happily in modern times, or since October 1989, fascinating archaeological data has come from the Globe's site, now mostly under Southwark's Anchor Terrace and Southwark Bridge Road, but the whole site has yet to be exposed. We have more to learn about this theatre. Still, ingenuity can make use of fragmentary clues, and a full-sized replica of Bankside's Globe, opened in 1997, gives one a thrilling sense of what performances may well have been like at 'Shakespeare's factory'.[32]

Streete, at any rate, had set good foundations of chalk rubble around wooden stakes. Using the old Theater's high timber frame, he cut costs as much as he dared, and the Globe rose as a many-sided polygon, roughly a hundred feet in diameter, with sophisticated stair turrets giving access to tiers of galleries.[33] With false economy, the roof was not tiled but thatched, with the result that the whole structure was to burn to the ground in 1613.

As with other theatres, there would be no lavatories, but buckets must have been available to those seeking relief in the galleries: bottled ale sold well. Streete's builders attended to one enemy of Londoners—the sun. It was felt that the sun gave city faces a tanned, peasant look, while fading costly garments. A high gallery roof kept the sun out of nearly everyone's eyes. Actors were sheltered by a colourful 'Heavens', a guttered stage-cover, which served partly as a sounding-board and had painted stars, planets, and other astrological emblems.

Competition soon appeared. In 1600 Streete began to erect the Fortune theatre outside Cripplegate, as Henslowe's and Alleyn's response to the Globe. In worried confusion the Privy Council soon licensed Worcester's men to play at the Boar's Head, and tolerated children's companies as well as other adult troupes in the capital. The Globe must have opened not later than the end of May 1599.

And its bright flag, visible across the river to those watching for it, as well as to watermen carrying over clientele, a trumpeter on the high roof, and clamour and bustle with apprentices and artisans in the crowded yard as the galleries filled up with the élite—must all have seemed very promising to the Chamberlain's Servants. Their poet needed this yellow-topped magnet—in which lavish display seemed natural. Even more vital for him, one suspects, was his troupe's experience over the past five years of hard times, mistakes, disagreements, and experimentalism. His fellow sharers did not see eye to eye, though some of them had lately shown a willingness to work together by pooling their money. Here in the Bankside among bordellos and bear-pits and sharp entrepreneurs, the actors faced a challenge with a new sense of tension. Not since Hunsdon's plan in 1594 had they been free from a threat of bankruptcy, and enemies were near at hand. The vestry of St Saviour's, Southwark, first called for an end of playing and then tried to gain from it by taxing the local theatres. Shakespeare took lodgings in the area for a while, before moving back across the river nearer his friends Heminges and Condell, who were in the parish of St Mary, Aldermanbury.

The sharers needed to go 'up-market' to hold the gentry, and that in itself may have caused friction. After leaving the troupe and undertaking a morris dance from London to Norwich, Will Kempe was to call his enemies 'Shakerags'—perhaps a mild fling at Shakespeare or his hirelings. Vigorous and athletic, Kempe was famous for obscene jigs of a kind not to be repeated on Bankside. Just what led to his quitting a profit-making troupe is still unknown, but his exit may be the tip of an iceberg of after-hours' arguments, debate, and jockeying politics. Even long before Kempe left, the actors' troubles with Blackfriars, with Allen, or with different venues surely caused anxiety. As an artist, what did Shakespeare make of the company's politics? He may not have sketched their debates, but he was familiar with their political behaviour when he wrote *Julius Caesar.*

Thomas Platter, a young doctor from Basle, saw a tragedy about Julius Caesar at a Bankside theatre in the autumn. Visiting England from 18 September to 20 October 1599, Platter reported to his Swiss relatives in a difficult dialect, a peculiar 'form of sixteenth century Alemannic' as Ernest Schanzer calls it, which today can be 'obscure even to German scholars'. But Platter describes London's theatres, and— unless he refers to a rival play—he has seen *Julius Caesar* at the new Globe. 'On the 21st of September, after dinner, at about two o'clock, I went with my party across the water. In the straw-thatched house [streüwine Dachhaus]', as Platter writes,

we saw the tragedy of the first Emperor Julius Caesar, very pleasingly performed, with approximately fifteen characters; at the end of the play they danced together admirably and exceedingly gracefully, according to their custom, two in each group dressed in men's and two in women's apparel.

One suspects that the Swiss doctor paid for excellent, cushioned seats. (He notes of the theatres, 'Yedoch sindt underscheidene gäng unndt ständt da man lustiger unndt basz sitzet' (literally: 'However, there are separate galleries and places, where one sits more pleasantly and better').[34]

And Platter's memory of a cast of about 'fifteen characters' fits *Julius Caesar* pretty well (if one discounts a number of smaller parts), and the graceful dancing at the play's end is an interesting feature. Kempe then had not yet left, so he could have been among the dancers—though Shakespeare's play lacks a good part for a clown. *Julius Caesar* is spare and grave in style, befitting the dignity of Rome and the awe aroused by Caesar's murder, or the chief secular event in the world's history. Often popular in modern classrooms, the tragedy took up a hero whose story was even taught to Elizabethan children. 'Julius Caesar', one reads for example in *The Education of children in learning* (1588), 'the first and greatest Emperour that ever lived, with a most pure stile, set foorth the histories of his times and certayne bookes of Grammar'.[35] Subtle as the tragedy is, Shakespeare might have recited it without a qualm to his own daughters. He mainly avoids sexual puns and any display of petty vices—even Antony's sensuality is kept at a distance—and gives his Globe audiences dignified, heroic Romans who speak in a 'pure' language in keeping with high politics. Also he celebrates the stage's power. Re-enacting Julius Caesar's murder, the actors perpetuate him by making him as interesting as he may have been in life, and the play's effects hinge partly on a careful, tight structure built round the three soliloquies of Cassius, Brutus, and Antony, and the orations over Caesar's corpse by both Brutus and Antony.

Shakespeare's ironies mock his audience. In one sense, Antony's refrain over Caesar's corpse flatters their wit:

> Yet Brutus says he was ambitious,
> And Brutus is an honourable man.

> (III. ii. 94–5)

Yet this also suggests that all city crowds are gullible, though the word 'honourable' might prefigure Antony's lofty praise of the dead Brutus in Act V.

At all events, *Julius Caesar* was popular. Its manner can seem 'plain as a Doric portico', in Arthur Humphreys's phrase.[36] Somewhat less awed by Caesar than by Caesar's Tudor prestige, Shakespeare, in his respect for Roman clarity and Roman simplicity, imposes unusual restraints on his art. By closely following his main guide Plutarch, more closely here than he ever followed Holinshed, he begins to acquire a confidence with Roman topics which will increase with *Coriolanus* and *Antony and Cleopatra*. Plutarch's *Lives* (in North's version) is rather more concerned with political behaviour than with character, but every trait of Shakespeare's Brutus is really traceable to Plutarch's Brutus. Even as Plutarch reductively sketches his Romans, so in this play Cassius is—basically—an austere and sceptical Epicurean, Brutus is an idealizing Stoic, and Mark Antony is a sensual opportunist.

One radical difference in characterization, though, appears in the poet's intuitive method, or in his inventing for each of his heroes a psychology allowing for subtle variations from a norm. For that he had no literary source, though he perhaps had theatrical politics or the internal affairs of his own troupe among other models. As a 'housekeeper' he had motives to attend closely to relationships in his company. Since he did not think in a literal way, one hardly expects to find Will Kempe in Cassius, but, then, this dramatist's mind did not function in an imaginative cocoon in which the 'miracle' of genius alone told him how men interact in crises. Leaning on Plutarch, it is true that he was in some respects all too faithful to his main source. This play lacks an objective commentator, but clearly gives Brutus a vital, plausible intellectual life, and in delicately suggesting the errors in Brutus's thought and feeling Shakespeare most usefully responds to the stimulus of Jonson, especially his neo-classical ideas, and to poets associated with the Inns of Court. With this play, he also prepared himself to write something more intimate, more personally committed and confident, in his next tragedy—for his best 'leap ahead', the largest single advance he made in his career as a dramatist.

14

HAMLET'S QUESTIONS

What a piece of work is a man! How noble in reason, how
infinite in faculty, in form and moving how express and
admirable, in action how like an angel, in apprehension
how like a god—the beauty of the world, the paragon of
animals! And yet to me what is this quintessence of dust?

Was't Hamlet wronged Laertes? Never Hamlet.
If Hamlet from himself be ta'en away,
And when he's not himself does wrong Laertes,
Then Hamlet does it not, Hamlet denies it.
Who does it then?

(Prince Hamlet)

Poets' wars and 'little eyases'

*B*itter, icy weather and deluges of snow appear to have helped
screen the workers who dismantled the Theater, but for actors
intensely cold weather had drawbacks. Thick ice had begun to cover
English rivers in December and January. Alpine glaciers soon crushed
houses near Chamonix, marking the start of colder spells all over
Europe, and winters, as a rule, were to be hard for the rest of Shakespeare's lifetime.[1] There is no sign that he regretted stark winters, but
freezing weather brings no cheer and heralds bleak revelations in his
new play: ''Tis bitter cold, I And I am sick at heart', says Francisco, in
its first scene, and later Hamlet remarks: 'The air bites shrewdly, it is
very cold.'

Inured as they were to the cold, the gentry might not choose to
cross the Thames in biting winds to sit in dark, icy galleries. Moreover,
actors had cause for concern as rivalry sharpened in London, especially
after mere children—skilful boys—began to put on plays again in

indoor theatres. Late in 1599, a tiny hall playhouse reopened at St Paul's grammar school, and its Children of Paul's put on two works by the caustic Marston—his satirical romance *Antonio and Mellida*, and its tragic sequel *Antonio's Revenge*. Marston advertised his theatre's luxury by claiming that here, from about 4 p.m. to 6 p.m. in a room lit by candles, tapers, and torches, one need not fear being 'pasted to the barmy Jacket of a Beer-brewer'.[2] Next year, to get a profit from the cavernous Blackfriars, Richard Burbage leased its room to Henry Evans, a young Welsh scrivener befriended by Sebastian Westcott, a former manager of Paul's Children. Evans revived a second boy's troupe, the Children of the Chapel, who enlisted the help of Ben Jonson—one result was that Marston, Jonson, and Dekker began a slanging match (the Poetomachia, or Poets War) in which the common public stages came under attack.

Bold, warring poets drew the public's attention to two troupes of child actors. How did Shakespeare respond to that rivalry? The boy troupes have a bearing on his sudden, stunning feat of following *Julius Caesar* with *Hamlet*. It has been said (obviously with Greek dramas in mind) that *Hamlet* is the first great tragedy to be written in two thousand years. To quarrel with that view is perhaps only to quarrel with the relative term, 'great'. *Hamlet* is of a higher order of art than any drama before it; and, indeed, arguably only three plays written after it are of its uniquely high order: *King Lear*, *Macbeth*, and *Othello*. (If other plays from any time *are* to be thought their equals one would have to turn, not to Aeschylus or Sophocles, surely, but to Shakespeare.) As remarkable as the first play is, its text is still unsettled. *Hamlet* exists in three contrasting versions—a so-called 'bad quarto' text of 1603, said to be reconstructed from actors' memories of the play; a 'good quarto' of 1604–5 based largely on an authorial manuscript; and the Folio text of 1623 which appears to show revisions. If Shakespeare wrote *Hamlet* around 1599–1600, he may have made 'false starts'. Then or later he revised his work; and scholars mention possible, troubled connections between his likely revisions and his attitudes to Paul's Children or the Children of the Chapel.[3]

Even in the play's First Quarto, Prince Hamlet hears of the plight of touring actors victimized by mere boys. Having lost their regular audience, the actors are forced to tour—

> For the principall publicke audience that
> Came to them, are turned to [patronising] private playes,
> And to the humour of children.
>
> (sig. E3)

That may be a poor version of what Shakespeare actually wrote, but it reflects a real situation. As a novelty in London, Paul's Children sharply competed with the Chamberlain's Servants by 1600, and the passage, with little irony, suggests a poet's bare, uneasy complaint, a worry that may underlie the glancing wit of *Hamlet*. Lately the Globe had revived the finances of the poet's troupe, and Burbage, Heminges, and others had reason for confidence. Yet none of them would have been foolish to worry over child actors. London had not seen expert boy players in ten years, and the new groups were lively, well-trained, bold, and fashionable. Their offerings, in fact, were shrewdly diversified, but Paul's Children, with their clear, innocent, bell-like voices, excelled in giving laughable shocks in plays with modern settings, just as they did in singing.

There is nothing about a children's troupe in the Second Quarto. But *Hamlet*'s Folio text reports on raw, obnoxious imps. Here there is a tranquil, amused reaction to boy actors who would steal audiences. 'Do they grow rusty?' Prince Hamlet asks about the adult actors as they reach Claudius's castle. 'Nay, their endeavour keeps in the wonted pace', replies Rosencrantz with a delicious courtly joke,

But there is, sir, an eyrie of children, little eyases [baby hawks], that cry out on the top of question and are most tyrannically clapped for't. These are now the fashion, and so berattle the common stages—so they call them—that many wearing rapiers are afraid of goose-quills, and dare scarce come thither. (II. ii. 338–45)

This is even funnier if Rosencrantz refers to the Chapel boys at Black-friars who acted under the dizzy height of a vaulted roof thirty-two feet above floor level, or reaching some eighty-five feet at the immense roof-ridge. The boys as 'little eyases' are only wee, scrawny hawks in a high nest or eyrie. Such chirpers and squeakers, noisy nestlings, are applauded at the moment, but are doomed if their rash satire should stir up those 'wearing rapiers'.

In fact, both of London's children's companies at last offended the Privy Council and faced closure. Hamlet himself worries over the little eyases. 'What, are they children?' he asks Rosencrantz, with hunger for theatrical gossip and details,

Who maintains 'em? How are they escoted? Will they pursue the quality no longer than they can sing? Will they not say afterwards, if they should grow themselves to common players—as it is like most will, if their means are not better—their writers do them wrong to make them exclaim against their own succession? (II. ii. 346–52)

Rosencrantz, always *au courant*, remarks that acting companies nowadays only buy plays in which the children's writers and public actors attack one another. 'Is't possible?' asks Hamlet in disbelief, and now both Rosencrantz and Guildenstern are helpful:

GUILDENSTERN. O, there has been much throwing about of brains.
HAMLET.   Do the boys carry it away?
ROSENCRANTZ. Ay, that they do, my lord, Hercules and his load too.

(II. ii. 359–63)

Hercules shouldering the world was the Globe theatre's painted sign. If Shakespeare implies that the boys will carry away the Globe's audience, he leaves it to fated, shallow courtiers to express that worry.

Yet there had been some 'throwing about of brains' in the Poets' War, and there can be no doubt that Shakespeare attended to it with care. Just how did a Poets' War, involving child actors in the late 1590s, come about? Its origins are uncertain, but theatre men were aware of Ben Jonson's prickly combativeness. As early as *Every Man Out of his Humour*, Jonson had mocked a pedantic or fustian excess in Marston's vocabulary. Although Marston's play *Histriomastix* implicitly sides with Jonson in attacking tameness in the public theatres, Jonson, to his horror, saw himself mocked in Marston's inane philosopher Chrisoganus. Both dramas must have been staged by 1600—by which time the war was unstoppable. With Marston's advice or co-authorship, Thomas Dekker next entered the fray with the slap-dash, anti-Jonsonian *Satiromastix*, acted privately by Paul's boys and publicly at the Globe. Jonson, suitably goaded, caricatured his enemies with witty elegance in *Cynthia's Revels* and in *Poetaster*, in the last of which he expresses his views about satire in the wry, long-suffering figure of Horace. Cambridge students, meanwhile, followed the war with glee and noted it in their play The Second Part of *The Returne from Parnassus*: 'O that *Ben Jonson* is a pestilent fellow, he brought up *Horace* giving the Poets a pill, but our fellow *Shakespeare* hath given him a purge that made him beray his credit'.[4] This reference is odd enough to have troubled commentators, who explain it variously. Late in Elizabeth's reign, theatre-goers (and far-away students) might care to know who wrote a drama, but they were better informed about troupes and playhouses. The students perhaps thought that the 'purge' Shakespeare had given Jonson was *Satiromastix*, since it was acted by the Chamberlain's group, unless they confused *Twelfth Night, or What You Will* (one of his two dramas that have subtitles) with Marston's play *What You Will*.

Shakespeare coolly kept out of the Poets' War, at any rate, though he jokingly included a few of Jonson's traits in the Ajax of *Troilus and Cressida*. He was well alert to it, and, indirectly at least, it affected the content and direction of his own writing, if only by throwing him back upon his deeper intellectual and emotional strengths. In one sense the war was trivial and trumped up, with aspects of a publicity campaign welcome to all involved and, indeed, what we sometimes call a 'War of the Theatres' hardly reflected a conflict of repertoires. The boys put on moral plays, love comedies, or works with pastoral, mythological, or contemporary settings just as the adult troupes did.

But implicit from the start, although with earlier roots, and fully developed by the time Jonson created the character of Horace, was a genuine Poets' War, or what Dekker called a 'Poetomachia'—and its underlying issue was art's public responsibility. Jonson, in 'comical satires', appeared to be an independent, patrician critic no matter whom he wrote for; but he was lately using the freedom of a boys' coterie theatre to expose social hypocrisy. George Chapman had shown a fine moral, lofty detachment as early as 1596 in *The Blind*

Beggar of Alexandria, and he, too, began to write for the Chapel Children. Dekker sided with the public theatres, but Marston and Jonson—despite their tiff—saw those theatres as symptoms of modern vapidity and enervation.

Though not under direct attack in the debate, Shakespeare is implicitly a mild if not quite outmoded fixture of the public arena. In nerve and gaiety, the coterie dramatists were appealing to courtly society, to cosmopolitan circles, to the well-educated and sophisticated. The public stages might be viewed as timid—for example in their glorifying of sturdy English citizens, in *The Merry Wives,* or in their endless fuss over patriotism, as in *Henry IV* or *Henry V,* or in their reserved, cautious, but basically uncritical view of legal institutions as in plays from *The Comedy of Errors* through even *The Merchant* to *Much Ado.* What was the yellow-topped Globe, then, but a crowd-pleasing venue for plebeian commonplaces, or the defence of hierarchy and public authority?

Some of the new wits suggested a freer enquiry, a new morality. In Marston's *Antonio's Revenge,* the hero is an aloof, proud stoic of high intellect who with utter indifference to worldly vanities evades death. Here revenge is nearly a good in itself. But coincidentally or not, at about the time of Marston's work, Shakespeare had begun to write with peculiar intent an unusual revenge play of his own.

The Prince's world

In one way *Hamlet* was not a new departure for a poet capable of radically transforming existing dramas. In this case, he was able to draw on a work that was presumably not his own but which the Chamberlain's men performed, or the now-missing *Hamlet*—a revenge play with a ghost—which his colleagues had staged at Burbage's Theater before it apparently went briefly to Newington. It may have been by Kyd, but, again, its author is unknown. It was a noisy if not a tumultuous and ungainly work, conjured up in an allusion in Lodge's *Wit's Misery* (1596) to one who 'looks as pale as the Visard of the ghost which cried so miserably at the Theator like an oister wife, Hamlet, revenge'.[5] Shakespeare had at least one other ready-made play in

279

mind. In Kyd's *The Spanish Tragedy*, he found a kind of kitchen cupboard full of 'revenge' motifs and devices, which must have gathered interest for him after he had discovered in Belleforest's *Histoires tragiques* (1570), the revamped tale of a lively avenger, Amleth, who had earlier appeared in Saxo's twelfth-century *Historiae Danicae*.

Also, his new play relates to the theatrical present. *Hamlet* responds to a mood, noticeable by 1599, entailing the charge that the 'public' stages are crowd-pleasing, unintelligent and lacking in audacity. The tragedy's complex and intelligent hero, its fresh and subtle word-play, brilliantly evoked setting and new treatment of the revenge motif, refined and elegant soliloquies, and philosophical richness all advertise the sophistication of the Globe's public stage. The play has humour to match the satire of new 'wits', and no trace of insular narrowness. The hero is a scholar of Wittenberg—the university of Luther and Faustus—and the action involves not only Denmark and Germany, but Norway, France, England, Poland, even a king's 'Switzers' and (in its atmosphere of intrigue and lechery) a popular notion of Italy. Yet this tragedy is far more than an advertisement for the Globe or a response to a commercial situation.

With its wealth of meanings, ambiguities, high-handed contradictions and supreme and troubling beauty, *Hamlet* is nearly a chaos. It takes enormous risks as a work for the popular theatre and an easily baffled public. *Julius Caesar*—by comparison—is neatly well-mannered, almost timid, and lacking anything like this work's exuberance. The confident writing in *Hamlet* suggests a poet whose best insights and observations are all before him. Suddenly, his whole experience of life is relevant, or the Muses have made it so: indeed Hamlet is often felt to be an all-accommodating, 'personal' expression of its author, and editors point to a few oddities. The Folio and Second Quarto texts together show that Shakespeare wrote too many lines for the work, or enough to keep actors on stage for four or five hours. If the Second Quarto is based on his 'foul papers' (or working MS) as editors believe, the MS may have been a mess of inserts, cross-outs, and badly aligned or missing speech-headings. A compositor in setting the Second Quarto resorted to the inferior but printed First Quarto to make sense of what he saw.

Still, *Hamlet* was meticulously planned. Its ease of style disguises the real intensity of the author's intellectual effort. His sonnet-writing offered one answer, at least, to what has been called the most taxing problem in writing a revenge tragedy, or how to fill in the long interval between the commission of the crime which calls for vengeance, and the carrying out of revenge in Act V. In some sonnets, Shakespeare explores paradoxes almost too refined for the stage, as when he puts morality to the test in Sonnet 121. Is it better to act brutishly, or only to be thought vile by others? ''Tis better to be vile than vile esteemed', he begins in a densely complex lyric, which stands morality on its head. *Hamlet*'s revenge framework gives scope to a hero of sonnet-like nuances of thought and self-awareness, or to a Renaissance man with a 'courtier's, soldier's, scholar's eye, tongue, sword', in Ophelia's view, who is disposed to fully contemplated action.[6] The effect, however, is to displace the revenge theme itself with emphasis on the hero, the Danish court, and issues of power politics.

But if *Hamlet* is activated by a political power-struggle, this is not what sets the work apart. Critics have drawn attention not only to the work's political nature but to how 'interchangeably diversified', as Dr Johnson once put it, the scenes are in content and feeling. 'It would be hard to think of anything less like a classical tragedy', writes one of *Hamlet*'s modern editors, G. R. Hibbard. 'In it the Elizabethan tendency to all-inclusiveness is pushed to the limit by a playwright who is fully conscious that he is doing just that.' One topic impinges upon another, and yet there is a fertile duality in the organized treatment of Elsinore, and that is what most consistently distinguishes Shakespeare's attitude to a Danish milieu. He may not have travelled in Denmark, but his fellow actors Will Kempe, George Bryan, and Thomas Pope had acted in 1585 and 1586 at Elsinore or the Danish Helsingør (which is the name of a township and not of a castle). The medieval castle of Krogen, a damp and ruinous fortress, had then been transformed into the Renaissance palace of Kronborg, full of costly furnishings and graced with colour and light: its renewal was being celebrated.[7] The English actors saw King Frederik II's new, affluent Denmark on the very wave of its emergence from medieval constraints. Denmark's cultural atmosphere, then, was unique, memorable, and not unrelated to the course of English history and Shakespeare's life in the Jacobean age ahead. It was Frederik's daughter Anna who married Scotland's James VI, and, as his consort, later became England's Queen. Her brother King Christian IV did even more than his father to modernize Danish society with an army of builders and painters. At Helsingør, Shakespeare's actors had seen a distinctive example of the northern Renaissance.

What, if anything, he really heard of the actors' visit is unknown. He used in *Hamlet* a report of 'swinish' Danes of dull, drunken excess, which he found in Nashe's *Pierce Penilesse*. Nashe, it is true, fails to note either the grandeur of Kronborg or the enterprise of its master. But *Hamlet*, in taking up the theme of the dual nature of man, implies that this duality is also to be found in a physical locale. One infers that the poet had heard something more than a report of 'swinish' Elsinore, and, in any case, he drew what he could from actors; in some of its aspects, the play might nearly be a veiled tribute to the power of British actors abroad. He designed *Hamlet* in part as a drama about feigning, about acting and theatrical techniques. We do not see Claudius's killing of King Hamlet, but observe such a murder twice performed on a 'stage' in Act III. Hamlet behaves like a stage actor to save himself. Theatre jokes relieve the tragic action, but also anticipate it, as when Polonius avows that he was once thought to be a 'good actor' at university. 'And what did you enact?' asks the Prince.

POLONIUS. I did enact Julius Caesar. I was killed i'th' Capitol. Brutus killed me.
HAMLET. It was a brute part of him to kill so capital a calf there.

(III. ii. 99–102)

The joke seems to be that Heminges has played Caesar and then Polonius, to the Brutus and Hamlet of his colleague Burbage. Killed once by Burbage, poor Heminges will die again. Lunging at the arras, the Prince runs Polonius through—and a mild joke on actors' roles anticipates Hamlet's acting a truly 'brute part'.[8]

Family love is at the play's centre—but what is bizarre mixes with the ordinary. A sensitive son, idealizing his dead father, confronts his usurping and fratricidal uncle and incestuous adulterous mother.

Shakespeare gives the son inwardness and intellect, so the Ghost's return is the more shattering, and adds two more avengers in Fortinbras and Laertes. The Danish court is not excessively evil. Claudius is not horrendous, and his crime is more excusable than the two murders linked with the poet's house at Stratford. Regicide—despite what children heard at school—was little more than an extension of medieval politics. As a villain, Claudius is miserably aware of his guilt, honest with himself, as regretful as he is fearful. Gertrude's sensuality hardly destroys her conscience, and Polonius, Ophelia, and Laertes further establish a sense of domestic ordinariness.

In radically normalizing his materials, the author is able to draw on the complicating pressures of Elizabethan domestic life. He appears to write from inside his own experience of a family's bonding, and pathos arises from his hero's idealization of a prior normalcy. Shakespeare's parents were both alive when he wrote the play, and involved in its 'unrivalled imaginative power' is his ability to show, from within, the pressure of a family's emotional ties. He returned home at long intervals to see his parents, siblings, wife, and children, and carried them off in memory. Tangibly lost to him, they were imaginatively present. *Hamlet* involves an awareness of mortal loss known in every family, but here death freezes the instant of loss, so that the hero has no consolation, nothing he can hope for in Gertrude or Ophelia. Before his interview with the Ghost, he responds to his uncle's words about 'my cousin' and 'my son' in a line that famously typifies him: 'A little more than kin, and less than kind' (I. ii. 65). The puns reflect despair over relationships gone askew. The world he would retain is akin to that of a privileged Tudor child, or of security, promise, and Christian mystery, and it is shadowily evident in Act I. The Ghost returns from purgatory and flees at the cock's crowing, or Marcellus notes the potency of Christ's returns at the season 'wherein our saviour's birth is celebrated' (I. i. 140). Metaphysical reality here impinges on the diurnal, but even in Act I metaphysical truth is obscure and uncertain, and this uncertainty is a keynote in Hamlet's questions.

Fratricide had begun with Cain in Genesis, and the Wittenberg scholar must meet evil and death. But why turn avenger himself?

Crediting filial love as an imperative, Shakespeare suggests a Prince whose past experience might be, after all, wholly that of well-being. News of his father's murder does not make Hamlet a brooding melancholic, but reveals him as mobile, alert, taking on 'antic' behaviour as a player of roles. Like the poet of the Sonnets, Hamlet knows almost too many half-truths; he eschews ideologies and finds his way through humanist grammar-school paradoxes step by step. He offers commonplaces as if no one had ever heard of them, although his soliloquies, in their fresh associative immediacy, enlist Renaissance thought to make it his own. The soliloquies show off his extreme anguish and, importantly, do not transform it, but keep terrible pain and the mind that endures it in view. Astonishingly, universal ideas become the registers of Hamlet's suffering, just as the beauty of his language is an index of his mind. Shakespeare exerts the utmost intellectual pressure here, but what is unusual is that he can project ideas with such intensity within the frame of Hamlet's own obsessions and feelings.

The Prince focuses on the antithesis between the brother kings— his brutal, sensual uncle, and gentle, loving father—and this may be a part of the play's dramatic and moral structure, as Harold Jenkins argues. But Hamlet is concerned with more than mankind's divided nature. Insulting and cruel to Ophelia, he exults in shifting part of the blame for his father's murder to Gertrude. 'Have you eyes?' he demands of his mother in the closet scene in which King Hamlet is a ghostly paragon and Claudius is evoked as a depraved beast,

> Eyes without feeling, feeling without sight,
> Ears without hands or eyes, smelling sans all,
> Or but a sickly part of one true sense
> Could not so mope.[9]

These lines, from the Second Quarto, appear later to have been deleted by the author, as if he had seen an excess in the Prince's railing at Gertrude's organs of sense. That is what is likely; but even if someone else excised them Shakespeare here is artistically faulty, involved, self-indulgent in putting down Gertrude. Far from making dramas out of thin air, he worked out tensions; he responded to closely felt memories, to hard, static, grievous pressures, and even to cold bitterness. Which is to say that he was like the rest of us, given the hopes, regrets, and despairs in every psyche. But *Hamlet* might suggest that Shakespeare's dynamic had much more to do with his mother than his father, and that Mary Shakespeare was involved with his deep under-standing and his artistic faults, his exalting of Juliet or Rosalind, his odd failure with two different Portias, perhaps his blunder with Jes-sica, and with the curious misogyny evident in the Sonnets. Despite his heroines, Shakespeare is very much at ease with feelings that ascribe blame and evil to women. Also in *Hamlet* his belief in psycho-logical interdependence is interesting, for inwardly the hero goes to great lengths to emend his image of his mother to ready himself for death. In the process he awakes to a nightmare of Tudor problems, so far hinted at but barely explored in *Richard II*, and these are almost free of theological bias and have practical concerns at their root. If the medieval outlook is lost, how is one to judge one's existence or rec-oncile conflicts in one's nature? Does sensual appetite condemn the mind? Is it right that conscience should make one endorse a just cause whatever the penalty? Is it worth one's life to oppose social injustice or outlandish personal wrong, and if unusual struggle and strategy are warranted how can one foresee the results of one's actions?

Delving into such corners of modern thought, the Prince exhibits other interests with the players. 'Speak the speech, I pray you, as I pro-nounced it to you—trippingly on the tongue', he says among two or three of the well-tried actors. 'Nor do not saw the air too much with your hand, thus, but use all gently . . .'. Whatever its use to a well-weathered troupe, such advice reflects ironically on its royal speaker's ungentle behaviour. The Prince's most famous speech on acting echoes Ben Jonson's Asper, who in *Every Man Out of his Humour* aims to offer a mirror in which to see 'the time's deformity | Anato-miz'd in every nerve and sinew'. 'Suit the action to the word, the word to the action', Hamlet rephrases that neo-classical wisdom,

with this special observance: that you o'erstep not the modesty of nature. For anything so overdone is from the purpose of playing, whose end, both at the first and now, was and is to hold as 'twere the mirror up to nature, to show virtue her own feature, scorn her own image, and the very age and body of the time his form and pressure.

He adds that all this should not be 'overdone or come tardy off'. Understandably taken aback, the First Player hopes 'we have reformed that indifferently' already in his troupe. 'O', says Hamlet undeterred, 'reform it altogether'.[10]

He is obtuse with the actors, but committed to their craft, and here Shakespeare appears to take a wry view of the contemporary theatre. Holding out for restraint and naturalism, the Prince, in effect, seems to point up skills of the Chamberlain's men, who are more disciplined than the Admiral's, and more lifelike—and life-sized—than boy troupes. Hamlet's advice contrasts with his agony of wavering in killing the king, and one implication may be that his own character is more elusive than the best conventions of acting will show.

Burbage, even so, succeeded in the Prince's great part. *Hamlet* had an immense, lasting success: it established its author as the age's foremost tragedian. The play was heard on land and at sea. Within a few years, Captain Keeling's men on the *Dragon* acted it off the coast of Sierra Leone. Sir Thomas Smith in a mission to Boris Godunov at Moscow compared events there to *Hamlet*, and young John Poulett cited the author when picturing French sports in a letter from Paris to his uncle Sir Francis Vincent: 'men seeme in them as actors in a Tragedye, and my thinkes I could play Shackesbeare in relating'.[11] Nothing supports (and yet nothing contradicts) the First Quarto's claim in 1603 that *Hamlet* was acted 'in the two Universities of Cambridge and Oxford'—it could have been staged, for example, at private houses in these towns.

'The younger sort', wrote Gabriel Harvey gravely, on a blank half-page of his copy of Speght's *Chaucer* around 1601, 'takes much delight in Shakespeares Venus, & Adonis: but his Lucrece, & his tragedie of Hamlet, Prince of Denmarke, have it in them, to please the wiser sort.'[12]

The tragic play that followed this success was *Troilus and Cressida*, though it belongs far less certainly to the genre of tragedy. There is a modern hypothesis that Shakespeare wrote *Troilus* for a law Inn. That chance is reinforced, though weakly, by the claim of two stationers, Richard Bonian and Henry Walley, in 1609, that it was then a 'new play' and 'never clapper-clawed with the palms of the vulgar'. Early that year, they had advertised it as a work already performed for London's public at the Globe.[13] Little else suggests that *Troilus* was meant only for lawyers. By 1602 (when we think it was written) Shakespeare's troupe had cause for anxiety: George Carey, Lord Hunsdon was too ill to attend the Privy Council: they had no patron at Whitehall. On his appointment as Lord Chamberlain in 1597, they had again become the Lord Chamberlain's Servants, but his illness and the Queen's decline put them in jeopardy. Still, none of that accounts for Shakespeare's acid view of the Trojan War, his assault on valour and idealism, or his picturing of a faithless Cressida and a bitterly disillusioned Troilus.

He had, however, steeped himself in a war about which Tudor writers were cynical. In Homer and in Ovid as well as in Robert Henryson's *Testament of Cresseid* and perhaps in Chaucer's *Troilus and Criseyde* among other sources, he had found older versions of the tale. Some three Trojan War plays were staged in the 1590s—and Chettle and Dekker had written a 'Troyelles & cresseda' for Henslowe in 1599. A year before that, George Chapman had dedicated *Seaven Bookes of the Iliades of Homere* to the Earl of Essex, while lauding the Greek hero—Achilles—as one in whose 'unmatched vertues shyne the dignities of the soule, and the whole excellence of royall humanitie'.[14]

Unlikely to have responded to Chapman quite as Keats did, Shakespeare shows Achilles as lazy, corrupt, and murderous, but none of his drama's portraits—not even Ajax's—is 'original' in being free from all Tudor precedent. Its figures had already been judged in legend, and cynicism here is in keeping with recent debate over the *Iliad* and, lately, with the theatre's satiric pessimism. Jonson's *Poetaster* has an armed Prologue, to which *Troilus*'s own Prologue figure responds, since he calls himself:

> A Prologue armed—but not in confidence
> Of author's pen or actor's voice . . .
>
> (lines 23–4)

Shakespeare is less satirical in the play than intrigued by his materials, by war's reality, problems of mixed viewpoints, and history's forcing of roles on its actors.

The situation of the long, futile Trojan War gives him a chance to explore paradoxes of our human faculties—particularly those of intuition and romantic faith on the one hand, and of logic and intellectual reasoning on the other. 'Intelligence here is a primary quality', notes Wilson Knight in *The Wheel of Fire*, in one of the most discerning essays on the play: 'fools are jeered at for their blunt wits, wise men display their prolix wisdom, the lover analyses the metaphysical implications of his love.'[15] The play is freshly analytic, but with long roots in Shakespeare's developing views of history and temperament. As early as *Lucrece* he had referred to 'sly Ulysses', and here Ulysses is at once foxy and flawed. More icily drawn than heroes of the romantic comedies, Troilus is more to blame for love's failure than Cressida, who is not prone to self-deception. The play relates to several of the genres and implies a fine, innovative critique of tragic form—but it is very doubtful that this brilliant experiment was really a particular success in its time on any stage in London, whether private or public.

Investments

In these years there were sad changes at Stratford, where mortality divided the poet a little more from his past. His father had died, and John Shakespeare was laid to rest at Holy Trinity on 8 September 1601. He made no surviving legal will, but his eldest son inherited the two Henley Street houses.

Did the amiable glover—in old age—have a loose tongue? Someone, after all, had spoken to Adrian Quiney of the poet's wish to buy 'some odd yardland or other at Shottery'. That had been a delicate topic, involving, perhaps, no more than a half-formed plan of John Shakespeare's son to invest spare cash. But Sturley and old Adrian had both hoped to persuade John's very affluent son—an actor and theatre-poet with money in his pocket—to forget the Shottery yardlands, and to help himself and the Corporation by buying a share in the tithes. Sturley refers to the poet as an unwitting soul who *can* be guided, but it is not clear that the glover's son was eager to be told what to do with his cash. Having bought New Place, Shakespeare waited four and a half years and until after his father died before making another large outlay—despite his rising profits as a Globe 'housekeeper' and at a time when *Hamlet* (by around 1601) would have been one of the Globe's chief drawing cards.

As he acquired funds, he apparently took pains to guard himself against those too ready to advise; in fact, he did not invest in Shottery, and for a few years bided his time. John Shakespeare's tongue, if it did cause trouble, may have been less embarrassing than the council's kindly fondness for anybody with spare cash. In any case, grief for his father may possibly have outweighed any sense Shakespeare had of the old glover's failings. Grief can elude the Public Record Office, but two poems that he wrote at about this time with their strong elegiac strain may indirectly reflect his sense of loss. It is well to add that their composition dates are unsettled. *A Lover's Complaint*, a narrative in the plaintive vein of Samuel Daniel and the 1590s, may have been written in 1602 or soon after. It takes up themes of seduction and betrayal from the viewpoint of a young woman whose tone is one of elegiac weariness. Her seducer is a clever, interesting version of a young Tarquin bent on self-apology, though the portrait is offset by almost unchanging, leaden effects of her sorrow.

The Phoenix and Turtle, a lyric he never entitled, appeared in the year of his father's death. It was printed along with verses by Jonson, Chapman, and Marston in a collection by Robert Chester, entitled *Love's Martyr: or, Rosalin's Complaint. Allegorically shadowing the Truth of Love, in the constant Fate of the Phoenix and Turtle.* The volume is dedicated to Sir John Salusbury, who in 1586 had married Ursula Halsall, born Stanley, the illegitimate daughter of the fourth Earl of Derby. Ursula and her husband had two children, a daughter Jane born in 1587, and a son Henry in 1589. Using motifs of the Phoenix and the Turtle Dove, Chester's poets appear to celebrate the Salusburys.

Shakespeare writes a requiem on the death of pure love. Alluding to the burial rite, he imagines troops of birds mourning for the Phoenix and Turtle Dove, who had loved ideally:

> Hearts remote yet not asunder,
> Distance and no space was seen
> 'Twixt this turtle and his queen:
> But in them it were a wonder.

(lines 29–32)[16]

Oddly his rhyme 'asunder–wonder' also appears in the light song 'Shall I die?'—which in recent times Gary Taylor, rather unconvincingly and in the face of much disbelief, holds to be Shakespeare's. Here in one stanza, a lady's cleavage is in view:

> Pretty bare, past compare,
> Parts those plots which besots
>   still asunder.
> It is meet naught but sweet
> Should come near that so rare
>   'tis a wonder.
>
> (lines 71–6)

Light love, light verse—and this is only a flying trapeze in rhyme. 'Shall I die?' was first assigned to Shakespeare in a miscellany collected, and donated to the Bodleian, by Richard Rawlinson (1689–1755), in which most of the attributions are reliable. The light song's authorship is in doubt, but further arguments for it might be made, and I think it could very well be by Shakespeare. Missing exercises, not necessarily of any greater weight, must lie behind his most exquisite lyrics, or the 'Threnos' for his Phoenix and Dove:

> Beauty, truth, and rarity,
> Grace in all simplicity,
> Here enclosed in cinders lie.
>
> (lines 53–5)

Investments followed in the year after his father died. In 1602 he made two purchases without being on hand to confirm them. Across from his gardens on the far side of Chapel Lane was land belonging to the manor of Rowington, then held by the dowager Countess of Warwick, lady of the manor. A transfer of copyhold title to the dramatist was arranged; but when her deputy, Walter Getley, came to the manor court on 28 September to surrender the deed, no one was there to be granted it. Four years later, the matter was still irregular. A cottage and garden were on this quarter-acre, and yet a survey of the manor leaves a blank space for the date of the court at which Shakespeare was admitted to tenancy—no record that he had bothered with that formality could be found.[17]

His brother Gilbert helped at another time. On 1 May 1602, Shakespeare bought for £320 from the wealthy Combes, William Combe of Warwick and his nephew John, of Stratford, about 107 acres in open fields north and east of the town in what was then called Old Stratford. Gilbert took receipt of the deed, and Humphrey Mainwaring, Anthony Nash and his brother John, and others witnessed it. The poet's acres lay in nineteen scattered strips of land, or furlongs, which were irregularly shaped. The names of the furlongs and their exact locales were lost when the land was enclosed, but the names interestingly came to light as recently as 1994.*

Why did he buy this land? His motives were unlikely to be as simple or clear-cut as writers have supposed. Land ownership conveyed status, influence, or respectability with local political overtones, and heritable factors were often crucial; moreover, recent evidence in this case is suggestive. A document arising from an inquiry of about 1625 by Simon Archer, lord of Bishopton manor, describes the 107 acres in detail and states rather ambiguously that Shakespeare gave away 'the said land with his daughter in marryage to Mr Hall of Stratford'. If the

---

* The names of Shakespeare's furlongs, lost to us for several centuries, are of more than antiquarian interest; they relate to fields and names he had known since his youth. Some of the furlongs' names are found today in the New Town area of Stratford. In 1602, about a week after he turned 38, Shakespeare acquired in the Old Stratford fields (capitals added): 12 acres at Clopton Nether furlong, and 10 acres more at Clopton Over; 1 acre at Whetegate; 6 acres at Little Rednall; 8 acres at Great Rednall; 2 acres at the Nether Gill Pitt; 6 acres at Lime furlong; 2 acres at the Over Gill [?Pitt]; 4 acres at Homes Crosse; 2 acres at Hole furlong; 4 acres at Stoney furlong; 4 acres at Base Thorne 'shooting into' Clopton Hedge; 4 acres at Nether furlong 'shooting into' the Base Thorne; 4 acres at the upper end of Stoney furlong; 4 acres at the Buttes 'between Welcome Church way and Bryneclose way'; 8 acres 'lying upon the top of Rowley' and 10 'lying under Rowley'; 4 acres 'shooting and lying into' Fordes Greene, and 10 acres of leas ground at 'the Hame'. So much for 105 acres. He also bought about 2 more acres in leas or grassy strips, which are described as 'lying in the Dyngyllis and about Welcome hilles down to Millway and the Procession Bushe'. See Màiri Macdonald, 'A New Discovery about Shakespeare's Estate in Old Stratford', *Shakespeare Quarterly*, 45 (1994), 87–9.

land did figure in his negotiations for Susanna's marriage settlement, in 1607, it would have been the usual or common practice for him to retain a life interest before he bequeathed the estate to Susanna and her husband in his will.[18]

His deep, anxious concern for Susanna is evident. Even by 1602 a new political mood could be felt, so that he would have been obliged to be tactful, far-sighted, and politic in his acquisitions. This mood at Stratford might be called a puritanical one so long as one bears in mind that puritanism had its degrees and shades, not necessarily based on any religious doctrine, and that local crises to come in Shakespeare's lifetime involved other factors, too. But there was a strong rise in local feeling against his own profession. The council did not think less of him because of that—they were to court him urgently enough—although in the parish church he was to be fixed in effigy not as an actor, but as a poet. In these years, he was conspicuous in his absences from New Place. He was a major landowner known to have made money as an actor, and as feeling against play-acting became sharper the aldermen officially echoed it. In December 1602 they passed a measure forbidding all 'plays or interludes' in their Gild hall or other Corporation property, and a fine of 10*s*. (payable by anyone giving 'leave or licence' to contravene that order) was to be raised to a stiff £10.

The council's animus against acting was much more severe, for example, than Sir Edward Coke's 'Charge at Norwich' in 1607 merely against unlicensed, strolling players. The money that bought New Place would not have been thought tainted, but even as his fellows were applauded in London, Shakespeare came back to a town where the corporate council impugned his means of living.[19] In the wake of this a few years later, he thought of the Corporation's tithes.

His last major outlay at Stratford had a politic aspect, since the hard-pressed council, with too many of the poor to care for, depended on returns from tithe leases. The dramatist had more to gain than a tangible reward in this investment. Any share in the tithes could provide a local outlet for his cash, likely profits not for himself, but for his heirs, and a suggestion of his and his family's loyalty to those at 'halls'. Ironically Adrian Quiney's plan thus bore real fruit, after all. On 24 July

1605 from Ralph Hubaud of Ipsley, Shakespeare bought a half-share in the Corporation's tithes for £440. This was his largest outlay of cash, the equivalent of roughly £300,000 or a little more at the end of the twentieth century. His purchase involved the tithes of corn, grain, blade, and hay from Old Stratford, Welcombe, and Bishopton, and tithes of wool, lamb, and other 'smalle and privie tythes' from the whole parish, except that a few tithes of Luddington and Bishopton and certain rights of Lord Carew and Sir Edward Greville were reserved. The tithes—originally a payment to the rector of a parish of a tenth of its produce—had mainly devolved to the Corporation and had been leased out.

How much did his moiety yield? It did entail some continuing costs. For his half-lease he had to pay £5 yearly to John Barker, a sub-tenant, and an annual fee of £17 to the Corporation (as the owner). Shakespeare was never the town's chief tithe-holder, and around 1611 the aggregate value of all of Stratford's tithe estates was given as £293 6s. 8d. The annual value of his own moiety was then £60, or about a fifth of the whole.[20] With fees deducted, he was left with a surplus of about £40, and so in ten or eleven years he might make good his out-lay. His lease had thirty-one years to run when he bought it, so Shake-speare clearly expected his heirs to benefit (as they were indeed to do, before selling most of the half-share back to the Corporation in March 1625). He left the farming of his tithe fields to Anthony Nash, whose father had farmed them for the Hubauds.

With his normal prudence, he put other assets to use. At the Worcester County Record Office, papers which tell us much about the layout of the Birthplace (or the Birthplace and Woolshop together) came to light in the 1990s.[21] One of them is a detailed inventory of ten rooms of the Henley Street premises and of a kitchen, cellar, and brew-house which was made on the death in 1627 of Lewis Hiccox, who had taken a long lease on the property about two decades earlier. At Wood Street, Hiccox's wife, on a modest scale, had brewed malt. Lewis himself acquired a licence to sell ale, but a few years earlier he seems to have tried his hand at the plough, inasmuch as 'Thomas Hiccoxe and Lewes Hiccoxe' are cited—in 1602 in the Combes' deed—as holding tenures 'nowe or late' in the Old Stratford acres.[22]

Soon after John Shakespeare died, the Hiccoxes began to thrive in the Birthplace's eastern wing. Here Lewis and his wife Alice, 'Old Goody Hiccox' who fought with a neighbour, set up an inn, at first called the Maidenhead and later the Swan and Maidenhead. The poet derived a modest, regular rental, and he let his sister Joan Hart stay on in the western wing, where she seems to have been living with her husband in the old glover's days.

15

THE KING'S SERVANTS

These fellows have some soul,
And such a one do I profess myself—for, sir,
It is as sure as you are Roderigo,
Were I the Moor I would not be Iago.
In following him I follow but myself.
Heaven is my judge, not I for love and duty,
But seeming so for my peculiar end.
For when my outward action doth demonstrate
The native act and figure of my heart
In compliment extern, 'tis not long after
But I will wear my heart upon my sleeve
For daws to peck at. I am not what I am.

(Iago, *Othello*)

What, at the wheels of Caesar? Art thou led in triumph?

(Lucio, *Measure for Measure*)

King James's arrival

*H*amlet's success doubtless encouraged Shakespeare, and might have led his troupe to believe their solvency and prestige were assured. Yet their situation offered little ground for optimism in 1602. They had no representative at court, and if the ageing, irritable Queen died they could be closed down once and for all. Their patron was incapacitated (Baron Howard of Walden carried out duties at the Lord Chamberlain's office) and actors were obliged to plan for a dark, worrisome future. A costly Spanish war dragged on, and extremes of wealth and poverty glared in London—where inflation was as relentless as it had been in the 1590s. *Troilus and Cressida* itself suited a public mood of ennui and anxiety, and its somewhat coarse, cynical language of commodity might have indicated a modern time.[1] The troupe's fate depended on much that was far beyond their control, such as the unpredictability of state politics, the unresolved succession, and the whims of England's next monarch: it was clear at any rate that the nobility would not countenance another female on the throne.

Queen Elizabeth's fondness for drama lasted from the Christmas holiday season on through January—altogether she saw eight plays put on by five troupes. Had she ever favoured Shakespeare? She gave little sign that she cared for the man or his work, and distanced herself from Hunsdon and Howard's theatrical plan of 1594, though Lord Hunsdon's daughter, Catherine Carey, could have told her what she needed to know of the public theatres. In February 1603 the unexpected death of Catherine Carey (then Countess of Nottingham) coincided with the physical decline of the Queen. Catherine's widower, the 68-year-old Lord Admiral, soon married an heiress of 19, who was said to have sung on the wedding-night. This prompted debate as to whether the heiress had meant to send her husband to sleep, or had simply tried to keep him awake. The Queen had not credited the Lord Admiral's brains of late, but the death of his Catherine affected her. 'No, Robin, I am not well!' she told Sir Robert Carey in March. She sat up on the floor, until persuaded to her chamber, where her archbishop (says Carey) 'told her plainly what she was, and what she was to come to; and though she had long been a great Queen here upon earth, yet shortly she was to yield an accompt of her stewardship to the King of Kings'. Lord Cecil, her chief minister, had arranged for James VI of Scotland to succeed her, and to this she consented before she died. Upon news of Elizabeth's death on 24 March 1603, Carey rode straight up to Edinburgh, where he arrived with a bloodied head after a fall from his horse to tell James of Scotland that he was King of England.[2]

The new King—whose mother was Mary Queen of Scots—was a sound Protestant with at first a sympathy for Catholics and a partiality for Essex's followers. When still in the north, he released Shakespeare's patron the Earl of Southampton from prison on 5 April and saw him on the 24th. Meanwhile the nation mourned their late

Queen, although Henry Chettle who had been quick to see that Greene's remarks on an 'upstart Crow' and 'Shake-scene' were printed, took care to note this year that Chapman, Jonson, and Shakespeare had forgotten to write elegies upon Elizabeth's death. In Chettle's *England's Mourning Garment*, Shakespeare is a 'silver tongued *Melicert*', who has not loosed 'one sable tear'

> To mourn her death that graced his desert,
> And to his lays opened her Royal ear.
>   Shepherd, remember our *Elizabeth*,
>   And sing her rape, done by that *Tarquin*, Death.[3]

A torrent of verses greeted the new King, who styled himself *rex pacificus* or royal peacemaker. An outbreak of plague kept most Londoners from seeing him in 1603, but the euphoria over his advent appears to be mentioned in Sonnet 107. 'The mortal moon hath her eclipse endured', writes Shakespeare with an allusion to Queen Elizabeth's loss, if the word *endured* can mean 'undergone' or 'suffered',

> And the sad augurs mock their own presage;
> Incertainties now crown themselves assured,
> And peace proclaims olives of endless age.
> Now with the drops of this most balmy time
> My love looks fresh, and death to me subscribes,
> Since spite of him I'll live in this poor rhyme . . .

With echoes of Horace and Ovid, and an allusion in the couplet to 'tyrants', the writer maintains a cool detachment from events. Shakespeare's detachment is worth bearing in mind as we follow him in the new reign.

To most theatre people, the King was as unknown as his rainswept Scotland. Two years younger than Shakespeare, James was an affable, robust figure addicted to hunting, but politically astute, fond of talk about theology, and capable of writing unpedantic books on kingship, demonology, and tobacco. He had two sons, a daughter, and a young wife (known as Queen 'Anna' not 'Anne' at his court) who danced and acted in masques. He was in a difficult position as the King of Scotland and of England. Beneath the keen flattery he met with in the south were fears that the Scots would grab at lands, offices, places in overcrowded universities, and other privileges under English noses. Partly to counter anti-Scottish feeling, he kept the Scots out of office but gave them money, and feeling that he had inherited no loyalties he created allegiances with an 'inflation' of honours (he bestowed 906 knighthoods in four months). James required a court of splendour with art, masques, and stage-plays to hold the devotion of his entourage, beguile domestic enemies, and impress foreign envoys. Ten days after arriving in London he unexpectedly ordered through his secretary that the Keeper of the Privy Seal, *pro tem*—Lord Cecil— issue 'letters patent' to elevate Shakespeare's actors. Drawn up two days later, and dated 19 May 1603, the royal patent (here quoted in modern spelling) has a touch of Polonius's style in authorizing and licensing: 'these our servants Lawrence Fletcher, William Shake- speare, Richard Burbage, Augustine Phillips, John Heminges, Henry Condell, William Sly, Robert Armin, Richard Cowley', and the rest of their acting associates

freely to use and exercise the art and faculty of playing comedies, tragedies, histories, interludes, morals, pastorals, stage plays and such like as they have already studied or hereafter shall use or study, as well for the recreation of our loving subjects, as for our solace and pleasure when we shall think good to see them during our pleasure . . .[4]

Under Queen Elizabeth, actors had noble patronage. In James's reign they had royal patronage, and the patent (renewed in 1619 and again with slight changes after James's death) testifies to the prominence of the troupe henceforth known as the King's Servants, or the King's men or players.

When the epidemic lets up, declares the patent, Shakespeare's troupe may act in their 'usual house called the Globe', or in any city, university town, or borough in the realm. Justices, mayors, and other officers are to 'permit and suffer' them to perform in shows without hindrance, and must allow 'such former courtesies as hath been given to men of their place and quality'. The patent adds that any 'further favour you shall show to these our servants for our sake we shall take kindly at your hands'.[5]

Contrary to what Shakespeare's biographers imply, James delayed before incorporating *other* troupes under royal names, and *his* actors were to be slightly favoured. The King's men would have a 'free gift' of £30 for 'mayntenaunce and releife' in the plague[6] (which kept theatres shut from 19 May 1603 until the following 9 April). Only late in 1603 did Worcester's men become the 'Queen's Players' under the patronage of Queen Anna, who also sponsored the Chapel Children as 'Children of the Queen's Revels' by a patent of 4 February 1604. In turn the Lord Admiral's men became 'Prince Henry's Servants' early in 1604 (though their patent was issued two years later).

A royal patent authorized a troupe to play in town halls—whether or not a council forbade acting. Stratford's council might still bar actors from the Gild hall, but it would have had to appeal to the Privy Council to justify that ban.

For a spendthrift King, the actors, all in all, were a bargain. Despite inflation James paid them just £10 for a performance, exactly what his predecessor had paid. The troupe's gross receipts from his royal court in 1603 through to February 1604 were about £150, a small amount in plague-time if each of a major troupe's actors had been receiving about £1 a week. Whereas Elizabeth had enjoyed plays, King James was not very fond of them, nor did he, nor any of his immediate court so far as is known, find Shakespeare unusual. 'The first holydayes', observed Sir Dudley Carleton at Hampton Court early in 1604, 'we had every night a publicke play in the great halle, at which the King was ever present, and liked or disliked as he saw cause: but it seems he takes no extraordinary pleasure in them. The Queene and Prince were more the players frends, for on other nights they had them privatly.'[7] James was to countermand the decisions of play-licensers, not always to the benefit of a play, while at times tolerating stage satire aimed at himself. If a play struck at an issue about which he felt strongly (such as his plan for a union between Scotland and England), he could be ruthlessly quick to respond.

Shakespeare's troupe played at court far more often than before. They seem to have changed, in a few playbooks, offensive references to the Scots. In new works such as *Measure for Measure, Macbeth, King Lear*, or *Cymbeline*, the poet, in effect, touched his cap to his sovereign. The gesture is clear, firm, distinct, and limited as if obligatory, although his supposed flattery of King James is a delicate and somewhat controversial topic. It is complicated, from time to time, perhaps, by a tendency on Shakespeare's part to find himself in general accord with the views of a Stuart sovereign. That must be set against his clear, matter-of-fact view of his own and his troupe's low status even as royal servants. Unlike Jonson, he kept at a distance from the Stuart court at which he and the actors performed.

Yet the King's men were encouraged. They were optimistic: they took on new shareholders either in June, or, anyway, before the end of the year. But they had no assurance that they could meet rising costs, or maintain their holdings including the Globe in plague-time. In 1603 Bryan had left, and Pope was dying. Kempe had been replaced by the clown Robert Armin, a former goldsmith's apprentice recruited from Lord Chandos's men in Gloucestershire. One of the new sharers was Burbage's protégé, Nicholas Tooley; and another was Alexander Cooke, who must have been Heminges' apprentice. A third was Lawrence Fletcher, who had led a troupe in Scotland in 1595, 1599, and 1601, won King James's favour as a 'comediane to his Majestie', and been granted the freedom of Aberdeen.[8] Though unnamed in the Folio list of actors in Shakespeare's plays, Fletcher was recalled in Augustine Phillips's will in 1605.

The last of the new sharers, John Lowin, was recruited from Worcester's troupe—but probably at first as a hireling who looked forward to early promotion. As a mainstay of the King's men until the outbreak of the Civil War, he resided at St Saviour's parish in Southwark, often 'near the playhouse', and carried memories of Shakespeare down to the closing of the theatres in 1642. From about 1604 or 1605 on, the troupe were usually to have twelve or thirteen shareholders.[9]

King James was crowned before a limited assembly at Westminster Abbey on his saint's day, 25 July, but his grand public entry into the city had to wait for nearly a year because of plague. To avoid what was a severe epidemic the court went on a progress in Surrey to Pyrford, where the poet John Donne—in disgrace over an impolitic marriage—was then languishing; and continued into Hampshire, Berkshire, and Oxfordshire with death nearly at their heels. Close to

Oxford at Woodstock, they received word that Oxford's colleges were closing. Plague was 'daily acquiring greater strength'.[10] But after a voyage to the Isle of Wight, James at last reached Wiltshire for a prolonged stay at Wilton House with the young Earl of Pembroke.

Shakespeare's troupe, not in obvious despair, had already taken to the road, though touring was disliked—and between 1597 and 1603 there was really less of it for actors than at any other time in his life. After about 1605 as a rule, younger men were delegated for touring. In this plague-ridden year wagons of the King's actors rolled north to Coventry and west to Shrewsbury. They also reached Bath, but 3,000 people died in this year at nearby Bristol, and the plague touched towns such as Norwich, Northampton, and Chester. By October the actors had prudently retreated to a small western suburb of London.

This was Mortlake—just beyond Fulham and near Richmond Castle. Augustine Phillips had bought a house at Mortlake near the river, at some point before 1604, and here the troupe appear to have waited for the sickness to lift. Nevertheless late in the autumn they received an order to go from Mortlake to Wilton to meet with their royal patron, and John Heminges later received £30 'for the paynes and expences of himself and the rest of the company in comming from Mortelake in the countie of Surrie unto the courte aforesaid and there p'senting before his ma*jes*tie one playe'.[11] Wilton House was the country seat of the Earls of Pembroke. James had just elevated young Pembroke as a Knight of the Garter. The earl's mother was Sir Philip Sidney's sister, and the house often attracted poets and inspired legends. As late as mid-Victorian times, in August 1865, William Cory, an Eton College master staying over as Greek tutor, jotted an odd report he had just heard from the then Lady Herbert. 'The house is full of interest', Lady Herbert had told Cory, and added, to his surprise: 'above us is Wolsey's room; we have a letter, never printed, from Lady Pembroke to her son, telling him to bring James I from Salisbury to see *As You Like It*; "we have the man Shakespeare with us". She wanted to cajole the King in Raleigh's behalf—he came.'[12]

An attractive story. Cardinal Wolsey died in 1530, so he could not have stayed in a house built after 1544, when the first Earl of Pembroke was granted the abbey and estate of Wilton. Lady Herbert, it may be, called a chamber 'Wolsey's room' because it had a picture of the Cardinal on the wall, but she suffered incurably from 'Shakespeare fantasies'; and a letter about Shakespeare being 'with us' has never been found. In 1996 though, Peter Davison discovered something valid enough in that the Wilton burgesses paid out the sum of £6 5s. 0d., in 'giftes and fees unto the kinges servantes', in 1603[13] (a fair if not a munificent sum for royal actors). If that refers to the King's men, they possibly acted for the local burgesses, but their chief duty was to the King. At Wilton House they put on at least one play, not necessarily *As You Like It*. Also, they learned that they would be needed for the holidays at Hampton Court, and that they might have to offer help, this winter or later, with the amateur court masques beloved by Queen Anna.

After performing for James, Shakespeare's men had no more status at court than low-paid lackeys. Though one acted a king, when a play ended one became subservient or invisible. So it had been in the 1590s, and this amusing metamorphosis, from consequence to nothingness, he had, in effect, pictured in Sly of the *Shrew*, or in Bottom of the *Dream*. But since they were welcome for their skills, his actors were invited back to court for an unprecedented eight shows in this winter, and for eleven in the next; Queen Elizabeth had been less solicitous. In the ten years up to 1613, they were to give at least 138 royal performances. These had more than a tangible monetary value for a Stratford poet who, with his fellows, studied the royal court. And their prestige as the King's Servants did them no harm at the Globe, which offered a source of income that only the terror of plague, or fire, flood, censors, the Stuart King, or diabolic luck were likely to stop.

Pageantry, *Measure for Measure*, and *All's Well That Ends Well*

The relief of Londoners in having crowned a new monarch without bloodshed and a sense of the artful ingenuity that he and Anna might inspire were evident in 1604. With a ruler priding himself on good sense, the changeover was hopeful—at least until faults emerged, in his extravagance, absenteeism, and his somewhat impatient ways. Yet in the first ten years of his reign, works of high art, intelligence, and spiritual strength came into being, and in the Queen's court a fresh atmosphere, a promise, a large-mindedness indirectly affected the theatres—and Shakespeare's own audacity.

For the 'royal entry' into London the playwright and eight of his fellows were each given four and a half yards of cheap red cloth for gowns, since the troupe was a royal organization; from the Crown that was a routine gift. Troupes did not parade in the streets on 15 March, so, it seems, Shakespeare did not march, but, whether or not he wore a scarlet gown of low-grade fabric, he would have been keen to see how royalty was perceived. He was obliged to study his rivals and the public's taste. In this period, there were several kinds of pageantry—including outdoor shows for the sovereign on tours or progresses, the annual Lord Mayor's Show at that officer's inauguration on 29 October, and scenes enacted *en route* during a sovereign's entry into the city.[14] Londoners had not witnessed a great royal entry, with enacted scenes, since Elizabeth's coronation in 1559.

For James's grandiose event, Stephen Harrison had designed tall forms of wood and plaster, the largest of which was ninety feet high and fifty feet wide. With pillars, domes, obelisks, and pyramids, the triumphal arches were overlaid with symbolic ornaments, and had painted cartouches, grotesque caryatids, and flat perches aloft for living actors, as though the city were a public playhouse.

Having slept overnight at the Tower, the King, who disliked crowds, set out in the packed, clamorous ways on 15 March. First along the route was Fenchurch's arch, in the charge of Ben Jonson. At James's approach, a curtain drew back, and a figure clothed as the Genius of the City began a dialogue with the God of the Thames, who poured live fishes out of a pot. Other figures, coming to life, twitched overhead. Supported by Sage Counsel and Warlike Force, the Genius appeared with his daughters—Gladness, Veneration, Promptitude, Vigilance, Affection, and Unanimity. Holding a squirrel and a censer, to suggest nimbleness and the 'perfume of prompt action', Promptitude, for example, 'was attired in a short tuck't garment of flame-colour, wings at her back, her hair bright, and bound up with ribands; her breast open, virago-like'.[15] While the King fidgeted, the Genius

303

told of the nation's ancient Trojans, and brought the story down to their true inheritors, the Stuarts.

The King next moved on to the modest arches of the city's Italian and Dutch communities, then to Thomas Dekker's spectacular 'Nova Arabia Felix' arch at Cheapside. Here King James found himself imaged as a beaming, well-feathered Phoenix, who had given to 'a new Arabia, a new spring'. Music sounded, and two choristers from St Paul's sang in 'ravishing voices'. But, it seems, after a ninety-foot-high New World Arch with a giant globe, royal patience had worn thin. Beyond an arch at Temple Bar, he was stopped by a tailpiece, thrown up at the last moment, in which a rainbow, the sun, moon, and the Pleiades soared between two seventy-foot obelisks, and a human comet, Electra, hailed him as the new Augustus of the British Isles.

Despite inaudible actors and the King's glassy-eyed disgust, the day was hardly a failure. The royal 'entry' into London advertised the skills of writers, actors, and iconographers, and if the courtly pageantry was recondite, it was also profuse, non-literal, and imaginative in trying to picture the truths that lie behind kingship and the ordering of society.

And that boded fairly well for new masques and stage plays. Anna, who was impressed, took on John Florio the translator, and Samuel Daniel the poet, as Grooms of her Privy Chamber, besides employing Jonson and Inigo Jones. Bizarre as it was, the iconography had set a high standard in public entertainment, challenging and appealing to the mind, offering erudition, beauty, and elaborate detail. The gentry, in effect, were being prepared for intelligent, richly allusive dramas, even for the range and grandeur of *King Lear* or *Antony and Cleopatra*. Anna's court became a hothouse of talent, as it drew in men and women from varied social ranks and backgrounds. Her entourage abetted follies, but art and intelligence are not unknown to thrive on gaiety of spirit and some tolerance. The royal consort was Catholic and her husband a Protestant, but James called the Roman Church 'our mother church', and claimed to revere works by St Bernard of Clairvaux and St Augustine. At least at first, he encouraged a climate which favoured poets and Anglican divines in casting a light on the whole spiritual history of Britain. He was to respond harshly to Catholics. He treated his Church's Puritan wing rudely, but he set in motion this year at his Hampton conference the translators who were to produce the King James Version of the Bible. Now and then, he laughed at an entertainment. Perhaps he really approved *The Merchant of Venice*, staged one Shrove Sunday and again, for Prince Henry, on Shrove Tuesday, 'by the 'K's Comm*a*nd'.[16] Anna's appetite was hardly sated by that: 'Burbage is come and says there is no new play the Queen has not seen, but they have revived an old one called *Love's Labour Lost*, which for wit and mirth he says will please her exceedingly', Sir Walter Cope told Lord Cecil. 'And this is to be played tomorrow night at my Lord of Southampton's, unless you send a writ to remove. . . . Burbage is my messenger ready attending your pleasure.'[17] That must have been Cuthbert Burbage, Richard's brother, who had been in Sir Walter's service, and the letter suggests Anna sees more plays than her husband.

Among new works the King's players acted at court were *Measure for Measure* and *All's Well That Ends Well*. Both were generally in accord with James's views in showing potent, natural urges of sexual love, waywardness in men, and illusions of redemption. Both evoke spiritual grace. *Measure for Measure* by one 'Shaxberd' was acted in Whitehall's banqueting hall on St Stephen's night, 26 December 1604.[18]

Its composition date is unknown, but this play alludes to events of 1603. Written in—or close to—its author's fortieth year, it may well be an early product of his troupe's reorganization and expansion when Tooley and Cooke were promoted to the sharers' group, if Shakespeare renegotiated his own arrangements. Either under a contract or by an 'understanding' he had written about two new plays a year, but in the Jacobean era that rate was to be halved: on average he offered one new play a year for the rest of his working life. Stage closures during outbreaks of plague, his actors' needs, or his own convenience would have influenced his rate; also, it cannot be shown that in one year he worked on only one play. He could have begun a complex project such as *King Lear*, put that aside for *Macbeth*, and finished both playbooks at nearly the same time; but to speak of a tendency, he was soon writing less. His handwriting had deteriorated (to compare the writing in *Thomas More*'s early 'Hand D' with *Othello*'s textual problems) and though that need not be a sign of physical debility he was unlikely to have the duties of a '*Johannes fac totum*' any longer.[19] His working life had been hard; profits had accumulated, and, having inherited his father's properties and made new investments, he did not lack money. He was comfortably off. In London, as will be seen, he was in touch with a fascinating network of immigrants and with a few of their descendants, among other people outside the theatre; and he was living in the north of the city, not quite so close to fellow sharers as is generally supposed. If he did not as yet mean to quit London, he evidently welcomed a relief from rehearsals. After acting in Jonson's *Sejanus* (1603), it is likely that he appeared on stage less often, rather than not at all, and that he hoped to compose without tight restraints of time. In the main he had deflected envy, avoided trouble with rivals, and relied on a close, hierarchical fraternity which he tried to abet; it may be that we see his implicit criticism of the fraternity of actors even better in *Othello* than in *Hamlet*. But in any case, his loyalty to his troupe can hardly be questioned. An expansion in personnel is no sign that his own obligation increased; and an elegant script from him each year would have kept up their prestige.

Since the accession, romantic comedies had fallen out of fashion: satires, tragedies and tragicomedies were in vogue. He seldom left a genre quite behind, and *Measure for Measure*, which is more comic than tragic, advances beyond any rival play in its psychological depth. He turns to an Italian novella by Geraldi Cinthio which had been used in George Whetstone's crowded, two-part Elizabethan play *Promos and Cassandra*. Taking details from Cinthio and adapting from Whetstone's comic sub-plot, he imagines modern London in 'Vienna', so that one might be about 200 yards from Bankside's Globe in scene ii. His plays were staged near alleys of enterprise, though the alleys' profits were never sure. 'What with the war', cries poor Mistress Overdone of the bordello trade, 'what with the sweat, what with the gallows, and what with poverty, I am custom-shrunk' (I. ii. 80–2). From what would be a Londoner's viewpoint, she refers to the overseas war, to 'sweat' or the plague, to treason trials at Winchester, and to a shrinking of custom in the almost deserted capital around the autumn of 1603. Shakespeare, in most respects, is less exotic—here and elsewhere—than Middleton, Marston, or Webster tend to be.

In the first act he sketches figures who quickly lead to an impasse—young Claudio, terrified and condemned to death for getting his betrothed lover with child; a correct Angelo, Deputy of Vienna, who succumbs to lust; and a jejune and fiery Isabella, novitiate of the order of St Clare, who craves moral rectitude and rather than sleep with Angelo would let her brother Claudio die. Manœuvring among them all is Vienna's godlike Duke, who absents himself only to return in disguise as a friar, while reminding one sometimes of the monarch of precepts in King James's book *Basilikon Doron* (a source for the play).

Rather like England's Stuart king, the Duke rules by divine right, admits to prior leniency as a governor, and distrusts crowds—'I love the people', he claims,

> But do not like to stage me to their eyes.
> Though it do well, I do not relish well
> Their loud applause and *aves* vehement.

(I. i. 67–70)

So James might have felt on 15 March. But Duke Vincentio of Vienna is oddly vulnerable. He is embarrassed and inconvenienced; he is upset by Lucio's slanders, or again by the murderer Barnardine's unwillingness to be put to death in prison because he has a hangover, with the result that his severed head cannot be sent to Angelo in place of Claudio's head. Such details suggest a playwright dissatisfied with his earlier comic dramaturgy and seeking a better analysis of social malaise. Shakespeare is set apart from other dramatists by his ability to give the utmost eloquence to each person in turn, but also, and just as much, by his special kind of social realism. His characters are marshalled not to satirize human society but to unveil it, and here he ranges over abstract issues of government which appear to involve his attitudes to British towns as well as to London. Angelo's corrupt righteousness might have infected Stratford, where a narrow Puritan clique influenced the council and where, as in other towns, sermons were replacing dramas and other 'obscene' entertainments.[20]

Measure for Measure makes much of the intellectual comedy of repressed feeling, and a spectacular tension is evident in its breathless, twisting plot, in which sexual desire bursts the seams of order. The ending is high-handedly dictated by the Duke himself, who takes Isabella as his bride whether she likes it or not. Is the Duke any better at last than a sexually obsessed Angelo—and is Angelo redeemed? As in the Sonnets, the author represents sexual desire as a force unmanageable, immense, furtive, threatening, if not chiefly degrading, which not even the wise can withstand.

Sexual desire and repulsion mix with a marital theme in *All's Well That Ends Well.* Here the action is based on a story in Boccaccio's *Decameron*, which the playwright found loosely translated in William Painter's *Palace of Pleasure*, first printed in 1566. In Painter's very good rendition of it, one Giletta of Narbonne, a physician's wealthy daughter, heals the ailing French king of a fistula, a long, morbid pipelike ulcer in his body with a narrow orifice. As Giletta's reward for her timely cure, the king agrees that she be given in marriage to a reluctant Beltramo, who stamps off to Florence, where he takes a lover. But Giletta, by a ruse, sleeps with him in place of the new lady, and, after bearing him two healthy sons and otherwise proving herself, she is received back gladly by Beltramo.

While exploiting folk-motifs in that story, Shakespeare develops a remarkable heroine who is poor, of low rank, intelligent, and nervously intense. For reasons purely of rhythm, he calls her both 'Hellen' and 'Helena' in *All's Well*'s Folio text. But he introduces her in scene i as Helena, the name of the third-century saint who in legend, as the daughter of a British prince, wed a Roman emperor and discovered the True Cross. Beltramo in Shakespeare's play becomes an immature, easily led, but not quite unpleasant young Bertram, Count of Roussillon. For his good heart, Bertram is admired by his mother the Countess, the King, Lafeu, and others. The impasse is not sentimental but psychological and sexual. Helena, who is worthy, craves the physical love of Bertram, who, as a ward of the King, feels revulsion in being made to wed her. That carries one back into the author's days of *Venus and Adonis*, and indeed Southampton's career and Shakespeare's Sonnets meet in Bertram's dilemma. As a defiant royal ward, Shakespeare's patron had once yearned for war before becoming the Earl of Essex's General of the Horse in Ireland. The play's hero flees to Italy, where in a pointless war he wins credit as a General of the Horse before his moral decline.

Bertram's psychology is developed realistically, so that his duplicity, vanity, and confusion are apparent even at the end of Act V. All along, he resembles the lovely youth of the Sonnets, admired or adored whatever he does. He is no worse than a rash, unbridled child for the Countess. For the French King he is a 'proud, scornful boy'. For grudging Paroles, he is 'sweetheart' and 'a foolish idle boy' or a 'lascivious young boy'.[21] Certainly, the parallels with a former patron are not very close. Bertram is made to marry as Southampton was not, and the author is not known to have based a portrait, in any poem or drama, on one living model. Nonetheless, the English ward system which victimized Southampton has an approximate counterpart in the French King's command to marry, and Bertram—like the fickle boy in 'A Lover's Complaint'—is probably compounded from imagination and life.

With antecedents in plays dating from *Two Gentlemen* to *Twelfth Night*, Helena has a relation to Henley Street piety. She is the most overtly religious of heroines, despite her wit in bantering over her virginity with bawdy Paroles. The author's values were 'derived from the culture of his Warwickshire ilk and diverged significantly from the received ideas of both city and court', Germaine Greer has argued, and it follows that Shakespeare did not think of 'constancy as a psychosexual characteristic allied to masochism'.[22] No doubt he believed in constancy, whether or not the theatre or his own brothers overwhelmed him with examples of it. In the 'bed trick', which appears in both *Measure for Measure* and *All's Well* (and derives from Boccaccio), a legitimate bed-mate substitutes for a male's fancied lover. So the feckless Bertram sleeps with his Helena, whom he takes to be the virgin Diana. The 'bed trick', of course, underlines lust's reductiveness, and the author uses it with a kind of ironic trust, even with a script writer's relief, as if satisfied that a night in bed might not solve problems in life, but could solve an intractable problem on stage. And it works. Who doubts that? Certainly an audience, watching a

production of *All's Well*, can be made to feel that Bertram needs
Helena, or that, at least, he is ripe for reform. Their marriage need not
be a bleak hell, but then their incompatibility is chiefly dramatized in
five acts. For Shakespeare at about 40, spiritual redemption might be
a dream unrelated to the facts of any complex, realistically seen human
dilemma. But he gives a convincing inwardness to a rough folk-story,
thanks to what Robert Smallwood rather large-heartedly calls the
'infinite care and subtlety'[23] with which he handles his earthy materials. Helena's role has not proved to be easy to act, but she takes one
as close to the ideals of Elizabethan piety as any other figure in the
dramatist's entire works.

The 'plumèd troops'

Lately stage tragedies had helped to fill seats at the Globe, and
Marston's and Thomas Heywood's tragic works were popular. *Hamlet* clearly drew crowds, and Heywood's realistic domestic tragedy
A Woman Killed With Kindness, acted at the rival Rose theatre early in
1603, had a relation to the Globe's own great domestic tragedy about
a black man who murders his wife—*The Moor of Venice*, which we
know today as *Othello*.

Whether Heywood's work preceded or followed *Othello*, the two
dramas were similar enough in kind to compete. Shakespeare's late
'tragic period' had its commercial causes, but the exigencies of commerce nevertheless led to the display of his full intellectual maturity in
Othello as in *Hamlet*. In recent months, the petty, ubiquitous nature
of social evil had not been lost on him in London. He made use of
nearly all of his experience that we know about even as he studied the
public's attitudes. To many Londoners, the optimism over King
James's accession had begun to seem fragile. Thousands of workers
and 'masterless' souls looking for work streamed into a rich, beckon-
ing English capital, but the natural order of things punished the optimistic, liberated self. In *Measure for Measure*, the naïve, the innocent,
or the misled—the 'Dizies' and 'Master Capers' of the day—linger in
prison. Coming into London itself were hundreds of girls and young
women including two, whom we know about, from the poet's own

Stratford-upon-Avon. Elizabeth Evans 'went to a house of ill reporte in Moore lane' and to another 'house in Islington', one finds in London's Bridewell archive today. (These cases were recorded shortly before 1604.) One Joice Cowden said that she had gone with 'the said Elizabeth to schole togither at Stratford uppon haven', and George Pinder, who was born at Stratford, deposed what he knew as follows:

George Pinder borne on Stratford uppon the haven saith that [he] knew her father [of] Stratford uppon haven being a cutler [and] that the saide Elizabeth was borne there. he further saith [that he] hath known the said Elizabeth Evans about this citye three or foure yeares and he hath heard a a verye bad reporte of her and . . . her friendes are verye poore and not of that abilitye to maintain her (1 Feb. 1597/8–7 Nov. 1604, Bridewell prison).²⁴

On Bankside, near the Globe and the Rose, were more than a few Elizabeths and Joices. What relation did *they* have to the new reign's promise? Shakespeare may never have seen Elizabeth or Joice, but it is not so certain that their milieu is absent from *Othello*. The privileged, the gifted, the well-disciplined, and the successful, too, might seem to be at the mercy of hostile, impersonal forces, and the worthiest soul might suffer the most. In comedies, he had sketched modern evils, although the grief, anxiety, and pain in *As You Like It* or *Much Ado About Nothing* are partly assimilated and partly evaded in their comic plots. In *Hamlet* and then in *Othello*, he uses tragic form in an exploratory way to appeal to the deep awarenesses of theatre-goers, involving an audience in what they know of their lives.

At the same time, each of his mature tragedies involves a broader, more general questioning as if to compensate for the artificiality of the play. He is concerned with the possibility of telling valid truth on stage, with testing his medium, even with clearing his head, and his ambiguous feelings about his profession are involved. He adheres to no formula, but relies as in *Othello* upon unusual beauty of form and language, complex designs, and on the illuminations of extreme suffering. Alert to his troupe's needs, he made *Othello* unusually rich in texture and strong in pathos. Arguably it was planned soon after *Hamlet*, in which Ophelia's role was taken by a boy actor who sang well. The same boy, very talented, may also have acted Desdemona who (in *Othello*'s quarto text) sings her Willow Song in Act IV. Observing that Desdemona does not 'sing' in the play's Folio text, one critic takes this as a sign that *Othello* followed *Hamlet* quickly to take advantage of a musical boy before his voice cracked.[25]

Perhaps so. But that is not sufficient evidence to date the play, and many boy actors sang and played the lute. Shakespeare wisely trusted his own 'little eyases'. A boy could shatter an audience even in his silence. Indeed when *Othello* was later taken to Oxford in 1610, a scholar noted in Latin that Desdemona 'in her death moved us even more greatly, when lying in bed she implored the pity of the spectators with her face alone'.[26]

The year 1604 had been busy for the King's players. In the summer they were called to Somerset House to attend the Constable of Castile and his 234 gentlemen who had come over to sign the Spanish Peace. Shakespeare and eleven of his fellows, as low-ranking Grooms of the Chamber, were then made to wait on the party for eighteen days, from 9 to 27 August, and were paid just £21. 12s. 0d. for their pains. Each actor received 2s. *per diem*, or just what the King paid to his ordinary yeomen of the guard. It was only after this unrewarding time that *Othello* was played at court on 1 November 1604. The work may lightly compliment King James in noticing his interest in Venice's war against the Muslim Turks. Shakespeare had been under few illusions about the court's munificence, and he had planned a sharply affecting drama which would last in repertory. He apparently viewed his main source—again a tale by Cinthio—with extreme patience and a lack of self-assertiveness. One suspects that he bided his time so as to put many things to use; but after modifying a given story, drawing amply from his past work and visualizing new scenes, he wrote with that quickness which Ben Jonson, Heminges, and Condell recall. He probably revised his text, but even in the mature tragedies he leaves confused time-schemes, blatant contradictions, changed names, 'ghost' characters who loom up to be forgotten by the author, and other minor faults.

Though based on Cinthio's tale of jealousy, *Othello* is a drama about morality plays, about reputation and male seduction, and, in a subtle way, about an acting troupe. Out of such threads as these its love story, with Iago's defeat of the hero and heroine, is tightly woven. Faults in the weave are not noticeable to an audience, and the play— written with immense assurance and skill—is the most poignant of his tragedies. Critics often forget its action's ugly sordidness, since the whole effect is one of unusual beauty and the story is simple. (One might tell it in two sentences: when Cassio in Venice is promoted to a lieutenancy over an ensign's head, the ensign, Iago, vows an opportunistic revenge against the newly married Othello and the rival. At Cyprus, tricked by Iago into believing that Desdemona and Cassio are lovers, Othello kills first his wife and then himself, but the trickery comes to light so that Cassio is promoted and Iago is left to face trial and torture.)

The simplicity of that action, without a sub-plot, allows Shakespeare to develop the psychological interest of a few main figures. He works up a soldier's milieu, with its interactions, motives, and emotional intensities, even as he dramatizes love's betrayal. Often he draws on older plays, such as Marlowe's *Tamburlaine, Doctor Faustus*, and *The Jew of Malta*. Behind the verbal music of the Moor's talk one is aware of *Tambulaine*'s music, and behind Iago's candour with the audience are comic addresses of the villain in *Jew of Malta*. Even behind the intent, homoerotic exchanges of Othello and Iago, one senses the eerie league between victim and tempter in *Doctor Faustus*.

There are other echoes of more recent dramas. Iago resembles a satirist in a Jonson play, with the difference that he uses his percipience not to mock but to destroy. *Othello* also is made up of rich overlays from the author's own experience in comedy. An officer who woos a lady under her father's nose, weds her in secret, and impresses a Senate before sailing off to be governor of Cyprus might be a romance hero. Even the seas favour Othello by drowning the Muslim Turks. He prospers in all ways until Cassio is cashiered (in Act II, scene iii), and he is then in the dilemma of the *cocu imaginaire*. The cuckold of comedy is a topic of mirth, but here and elsewhere the poet evades this. With care he develops the theme of a villain plotting against a marriage, already used lightly, of course, in Don John's efforts to cross Claudio and Hero in *Much Ado*.

Iago may be like a 'Vice' in a morality play, but what Coleridge called his 'motiveless malignancy' has a realistic beginning. Jacobeans had no difficulty in understanding a grievance over patronage denied. 'Three great ones of the city', Iago tells Roderigo in scene i,

> In personal suit to make me his lieutenant,
> Off-capped to him . . .
> I know my price, I am worth no worse a place.
> But he, as loving his own pride and purposes,
> Evades them
>
> .   .   .   .   .   .
>
>   for 'Certes,' says he,
> 'I have already chose my officer.'
> And what was he?
>
> .   .   .   .
>
> One Michael Cassio
>
> .   .   .   .
>
> That never set a squadron in the field
> Nor the division of a battle knows
>
> .   .   .   .
>
> Mere prattle without practice
>
>   (I. i. 8–25)

This is pellucid and telling, but a good reason for disliking is buried as Iago thinks of other reasons, and his gnawing hatred is epitomized in racial slurs. The Moor's blackness becomes a frame of reference for nearly all that is said of him. Othello is explicitly referred to as 'thick-lips', or as a 'barbary horse', or has a 'sooty bosom', or is 'the lascivious Moor'. Prejudice leaps like an infection to old Brabanzio, the Senator, when Iago shouts that 'an old black ram | Is tupping your white ewe'. Racism even infects a shamed Othello, who declares that his name is 'black As mine own face' (I. i, III. iii. 392–3).

In contrast with its vague role in *The Merchant of Venice*, racist feeling here is treated with a moral lucidity. That allows for indirection and aesthetic effect, and one crucial difference between the *Merchant* and *Othello* is that plays such as *As You Like It* and *Hamlet*, which seem to draw on memories of a domestic past, have come in between. In any case, Shakespeare is better able to use a biblical symbolism which had begun to impress him in youth. What is stunning in *Othello* is that there is no gap, no dividing line of any kind between his aesthetic and moral interests or pressures. Othello is a black Everyman, victimized by light's betrayer, Judas, and there are other biblical strands in the design. A central irony is that low racist slurs, springing from Iago, take for their object a Moor who is dignified, unselfish, and troubled by sensuality in marriage. Prizing what he confusedly calls Desdemona's 'chastity', Othello declares that she saves him from chaos. 'Excellent wretch!' he tells her,

> Perdition catch my soul
> But I do love thee, and when I love thee not,
> Chaos is come again.

(III. iii. 91–3)

Othello's 'Chaos' is a region of lawless passion and anarchy. It is a frame of mind, but it is also a place, even such a city as engulfs Elizabeth and Joice of Stratford and their sisterhood. It is the Shoreditch and Bankside brothels. It has a relation to the city actor and the soldier. The army and the stage after all had much in common. Shakespeare in *Othello* shows us the code-heavy relationships of soldiers on Cyprus who, like actors, have their own rituals, taboos, and male bonding. The army and the stage were both glamorous by 1602, and indeed Burbage had a popular following that might have done credit to Sidney or Essex. In their all-male groups at a slight remove from society, the soldier and young actor were about equally ready to view women as hazards.

Knitting the male troop together is a latent homoerotic feeling, so strong that Iago can allude to it usefully. 'I lay with Cassio lately', says the ensign to confirm the Moor's suspicion of Desdemona's adultery. At night Cassio, supposedly, kissed Iago's lips hard, as if plucking up kisses by the roots, and 'lay his leg o'er my thigh', and sighed, and kissed, and then cried ' "Cursèd fate, I That gave thee to the Moor!" ' (III. iii. 418–30). Enacting a parody of the marriage rite, the hero and villain exchange words fit for a bride and groom.

The Moor's feeling for the tempter is in part disturbingly homoerotic, and at Cyprus, in Iago's presence, the general is implicitly hostile not simply to Desdemona but to the female sex. And yet

315

Othello's talk is natural for the careerist who raises his vocation as a prime standard of value. No dialogue by Shakespeare thus far is more subtle than that between Iago and Othello in Act III, and in the midst of their collusive intimacy the hero degrades his wife. The aural grandeur of his phrases, or the '*Othello* music' as Wilson Knight called it, overrides one's sense of Othello's sick ease in wishing that Desdemona's sweet body had been tasted by the entire camp, pioneers and all, 'so I had nothing known'. What is achingly intense is his need for self-definition. 'O, now for ever', he cries with the air of an actor, extolling painted scenery,

> Farewell the tranquil mind, farewell content,
> Farewell the plumèd troops, and the big wars
> That makes ambition virtue! O, farewell,
> Farewell the neighing steed and the shrill trump,
> The spirit-stirring drum, th'ear-piercing fife,
> The royal banner, and all quality,
> Pride, pomp, and circumstance of glorious war!
>
> (III. iii. 352–9)

That glorification of war might have been felt excessive at any time, but especially in the reign of *rex pacificus.* The Moor's display of his soul need not qualify one's sense of his dignity, nor cause one to admire him less. Shakespeare keeps both hero and heroine at a slight remove, so that an audience does not identify with them but observes and sympathizes. Iago is always closer to us than Othello, and yet the villain despite his banality has a mythical aspect.

What are the author's affinities with his characters? Desdemona is warmly humanized through her minor, calamitous indiscretions, her defiance of Brabanzio, and loving zeal for the Moor, but she remains opaque. One knows her less well than Gertrude or Lady Macbeth, Goneril and Regan, or even Cleopatra. The author might have found hints in his own temperament for his calculating, rational, improvising, and half-comic Iago, as well as for the self-dramatizing Moor, but he sees both objectively. The play has a flawless structure of feeling and yet Othello and Iago, as modern theatre history shows, can be played in many different ways. *Othello* renews itself in productions especially when the blame for the heroine's death is left as ambiguous as it is. The hero's touching integrity appeals to the author at least partly because Othello is undone by the narrow profession he serves. The soldier's vocation is sketched here with a terrible, evocative precision in parallel with the actor's own, and in a tragedy of the highest art. Shakespeare does not condemn actors, but he subjects his calling to an implicitly sharp scrutiny. So he abets his objectivity—he appears to insist on his own inner distance from the theatre, before he turns to the minds of Macbeth or King Lear in the great sequence that he already has under way.

16

THE TRAGIC SUBLIME

All blest secrets,
All you unpublished virtues of the earth,
Spring with my tears

(Cordelia, *King Lear*)

Ein alter Mann ist stets ein König Lear
(An aged man is always a King Lear)

(Goethe)

I'll do, I'll do, and I'll do.

(First Witch, *Macbeth*)

Jennet's guest and Marie's lodger

*I*n King James's reign, Shakespeare was acquainted with a plucky, intelligent, and reputedly beautiful woman known to her family as 'Jennet', who was four years younger than himself. Since the seventeenth century she has been seen in a haze of gossip, but there is no need to romanticize her.

Jennet was baptized at St Margaret's Westminster, on 1 November 1568, as Jane Sheppard. Three Sheppard brothers served the late Tudor Queen before being employed by the Stuart monarch. Her brothers Thomas and Richard were skilled court embroiderers, glovers, and perfumers who served Queen Anna even as the milliner Marie Mountjoy—in whose house Shakespeare lived—pleased Anna by supplying her with hats and headdresses. A third brother, William Sheppard, held an office in the Catery, which procured foodstuffs in bulk for the royal household.

Jennet had married John Davenant who, as a worldly, practical, cultivated man, had been to Merchant Taylors' school before joining his father as a merchant broker and wine-importer. From her house near the church of St James Garlickhithe on Maiden Lane, she could see ships carrying her husband's wine. These often came in from Bordeaux and, with unfurled sails, berthed pale wooden casks which were then ferried upstream by broad-decked lighters to the Three Cranes wharf. Everyone knew of the wine ships. 'There's a whole merchant's venture of Bordeaux stuff in him', as Doll Tearsheet says of Falstaff in 2 *Henry IV*, 'you have not seen a hulk better stuffed in the hold.' Moreover, the Davenants were nearly opposite the Globe across the river and within earshot of the actors' brash trumpets. It is not surprising that the playwright was attracted to a wine-importer with a charming wife; and Davenant—as Anthony à Wood wrote of him in that century—was 'an admirer and lover of plays and play-makers, especially Shakespeare'.[1]

Any friend of this couple, though, would have known of their misfortune. Up to 1600, Jennet had given birth to infants who were stillborn or who quickly died. She had buried five children when in her thirtieth year she gave birth to a sixth, a 'John', who must have died as well, since yet another infant was to have his name. In distress she turned any way she could for help or consolation, perhaps to Shakespeare, and certainly to the eccentric, fashionable astrologer and physician Simon Forman. Nothing compensated her husband for his human losses, and at last to escape the plague-ridden city he threw over his prosperous London life. Around 1601, Davenant took Jennet up to Oxford to run a wine-tavern.

On the east side of Cornmarket on the main street leading up to Stratford, this tavern was then owned by New College. It was not a 'two-storey' edifice as is stated in a documentary life of the poet, but a four-storey building of twenty or more rooms and running back about 120 feet from the Cornmarket. Though reduced and with a modernized front, No. 3 Cornmarket Street still exists near an old inn at No. 5—now the Golden Cross—which has served 'without a break', as Mary Edmond notes, 'for some eight hundred years'.[2] Here up at Oxford Jennet's luck changed, as she was to give birth to seven children, most of whom lived to old age. Her first robust son, Robert, later recalled, as a parson in a small parish, that Shakespeare had once given him as a boy 'a hundred kisses'. Born in 1606, her next boy became the poet and dramatist Sir William Davenant, who was helped by Dryden in an adaptation of *The Tempest*, and there is no reason to doubt the Oxford tradition that Shakespeare was his godfather. According to John Aubrey who knew him, Sir William in later life over a glass of wine would sometimes say to his cronies 'that it seemed to him that he writt with the very spirit that [did] Shakespeare, and was contendended [*sic*] enough to be thought his Son'.[3] This in time—with other rumours—gave rise to stories about William's running to see his famous godfather, when the latter visited Oxford, and being told not to take the name of God in vain. Jennet was 'very beautifull', and so, as people felt, why not believe Stratford's poet had bedded her?

Happily, the room of Shakespeare's supposed dalliance with Jennet at last came to light in 1927, when alterations at No. 3 Cornmarket exposed a painted chamber. It was rapidly guessed that this was the 'best bedroom', an assumption echoed by Schoenbaum, who supposes that if the poet took Jennet to bed, this was the place. 'There the best bedroom had a great fireplace', he tells us; 'the walls were decorated with an interlacing pattern of vines and flowers'. A pretty spot for adultery—but, in fact, a New College inventory of 1594 clearly shows that this and other rooms at the tavern were covered with wainscoting well before the Davenants arrived.[4]

The reality of Shakespeare's visits at Oxford does not quite correspond with myth. John Aubrey, who reported accurately on what he *heard*, was able to consult two of the Davenant sons; he was also acquainted with their daughter Jane (1602–67), who, first with her husband, and then after 1636 on her own, ran the Cornmarket tavern until Restoration days. On his way up to Warwickshire 'once a yeare', Aubrey states, Shakespeare 'did commonly in his journey lye at this house in Oxon: where he was exceedingly respected'.[5] The Wine Act of 1553 had allowed Oxford three wine-taverns, and, unlike an inn, the large building which Shakespeare knew did not offer public accommodation, so if he stayed there at all he stayed as his friends' guest.

The university's system of common rooms had not yet been developed: in Shakespeare's day the Oxford colleges were using wine-taverns as their common rooms, and because as clientele the academic ranks from the colleges often drank and dined separately from one another, the Davenants and their servants had to busy themselves in many chambers. Far from knowing quiet, idyllic rooms painted with vines and flowers, Shakespeare on arriving would have entered a smoky, well-lighted building filled with the din of Masters, Bachelors, and undergraduates. Among her infants Jennet was amenable—'of very good witt' or intelligence, says Aubrey, 'and of conversation extremely agreable'. Her husband was conversant with French, alert to literature and drama, and had civic interests that led him to become Mayor of Oxford.

But his mood contrasted with his wife's. Others confirm that Davenant as Aubrey says, was 'a very grave person'—as if he had given up London for a reason he could not forget. He remembered the deaths of six children there; and one might note that his mood corresponds with an underlying gravity in his visitor's Sonnets—but in any case, having lost his son Hamnet, Shakespeare had something in common with the Davenants. What is unmistakable is that, as a 'respected' guest, he was warmly received, and no doubt he had his reasons for covering their first healthy, surviving son with a storm of 'kisses'.[6]

Shakespeare was very loyal to John and Jennet; they received him over a period of years. As for his choice of London lodgings, he was not especially consistent. Five documents now in the Public Record Office, although they concern his defaulting on taxes, tell us a little more about his London locales and acquaintances than we have already seen. First, a Certificate in the Subsidy Roll of 15 November 1597 lists Shakespeare as one who had failed to pay 'the second payment of the last Subsydye' or 5s., due on goods rated at £5 in St Helen's parish. The next four documents all concern his failure to pay 13s. 4d. (not a large sum, or about half of his basic weekly profit as an actor) on goods again valued at £5 at St Helen's, in an assessment of 1 October 1598. The fact that the last tax was referred to the Bishop of Winchester (for collection in the liberty of the Clink in Surrey) suggests that he had moved south of the river by the winter of 1596-7, or, anyway, not later than 1599. The whole sum of taxes collected by the bishop was within 4d. of what he *had* to collect in 1600-1, so it is probable that Shakespeare paid the 13*s*. 4*d*. tax when he had to, or by the time the authorities caught up with him. It is not known that he ever paid the 5*s*. due, a slight amount; he could have evaded payment (there were many evasions), but the data we have about his taxes is extremely meagre.[7]

At St Helen's he had been living close to—possibly in the same tenement with—Thomas Morley, who was given exactly the same tax assessment.[8] It is amusing to speculate that, if the poet in his St Helen's rooms had quills, ink, and a writing-desk (as is likely), he heard music, some days, as he wrote. His neighbour Morley was obliged to practise: he was a skilled musician, who had trained with a boys' troupe (the Children of Paul's). Also it is interesting to find Shakespeare surrounded by *émigré* families at St Helen's, or by those whose names often suggest France, or the Lowlands, such as 'Meringe', 'de Bewly', 'de Clarke', 'de Boo', 'Varhagen', 'Vandesker', 'Vegleman', 'Vander Stylt'. In fact, an unusual number of those in Shakespeare's circle, whether friends, associates, or casual acquaintances, were of Dutch, Flemish, or French origin. Coincidence does not quite account for this. Apparently, he found himself comfortable with 'strangers', and the respect he had for London's *émigrés* was to be returned. He knew very well Peter Streete, a joiner of Dutch origin, who built the Globe. The printer Richard Field, the poet's Stratford schoolmate, had married his employer's widow Jacqueline Vautrollier of the close-knit French Protestant community. Misconceptions about the Fields are plentiful. They certainly lived in the Blackfriars until about 1610, but at some point before 1615 moved to a new shop, in Great Wood Street in St Michael's parish, so they could not have been living at 'Wood Street, close to the Mountjoy house' when Shakespeare lodged with the Mountjoys, as has been supposed.[9] The Protestant Vautrollier, who dedicated a book to his Catholic patron the Earl of Arundel, and later supplied James VI of Scotland with texts, was no more bigoted in religion than his widow Jacqueline. Her own French Protestant Church tolerated marriages with Catholic *émigrés* more easily than it condoned its members marrying Londoners who were not of French descent. The Fields, inevitably, printed Anglican texts, but held no narrow line, and in fact, in 1599, were among printers listed by the archbishop as all too likely to offend episcopal authority.

Shakespeare also made contacts with *émigrés* through the theatre. Although related to people at Burmington near Stratford, Nicholas Tooley, his fellow actor and shareholder with the King's men, was born in Antwerp to a Flemish mother, whose husband died there in 1583 in the house of Hans Lanquart. Having returned to London, the Flemish mother thereafter was wed to Thomas Gore, whose own mother, Ellen Davenant, was John Davenant's aunt. The Davenants and Gores, in turn, had *émigré* friends among the city's prominent wine traders and brewers. At least one brewer of Dutch descent, the wealthy and unmarried Elias James, who owned a 'great Brewhouse' (as Stow says) near the Blackfriars theatre, is of special interest to us, since this bachelor has been linked with Shakespeare in two ways. We know that Elias's brother's widow married a John Jackson, who seems to be the man of that name who joined Shakespeare in purchasing the Blackfriars gatehouse in 1613.[10] Also a brief epitaph written on the death of Elias James—he died in his early thirties—is attributed in a seventeenth-century MS (now at the Bodleian) to 'W^m: Shakespeare':

> When God was pleas'd, (the world unwilling yet)
> Elias James, to Nature paid his debt,
> And here reposeth: As he liv'd, he died,
> The saying strongly in him verified,
> Such life, such death: then a knowne truth to tell,
> He liv'd a godly life, and died as well.[11]

It is highly probable that the dramatist wrote these lines, which say no more than what an epitaph on an honest brewer ought to say, and that he knew when to write *less* than brilliant verse (as Elsie Duncan-Jones has noted). At any rate, he knew the Blackfriars bachelor, Elias, and his acquaintance with *émigrés* from the Lowlands has a particular importance: this is the matter of what Shakespeare in his late thirties or early forties looked like.

Someone from a Dutch family of artists, or known to them, must have sketched his portrait with care. One's interest focuses on the well-known copper engraving of Shakespeare on the title-page of the

1623 Folio which is signed 'Martin Droeshout sculpsit London'. Baptized on 26 April 1601, Martin Droeshout was only 15 when the poet died (at the age of 52), so the engraving which shows a younger Shakespeare was not made from the life; so far as we can tell it would have been commissioned in 1623 when the artist was 21 or 22. Droeshout belonged to a third generation of Flemish artists residing in London: his grandfather John was a painter from Brussels (then in the South Netherlands); his uncle Martin was a painter, his father Michael an engraver. In most respects the engraving is amateurish, but other experts tend to agree with M. H. Spielmann that Droeshout based his work on a very competent miniature or a limning—a careful drawing showing 'perhaps delicate flat washes of colour'—which was made in Shakespeare's late thirties or early forties.[12] That the engraving of the head is accurate is supported by the bust at Holy Trinity which has comparable skull proportions and the same famous perpendicular forehead. Even if we dismiss Ben Jonson's strong approval of the 1623 engraving (he could have approved it conventionally, perhaps, before seeing it), still, that likeness of Shakespeare's face would have had to satisfy the syndicate which at financial risk published the costly Folio of thirty-six plays.

In popular mythology, Shakespeare is a witty and tavern-haunting poet who writes of famous Dark Ladies whom he takes to bed, and hardly has time for plays. The engraving suggests a different side of him, for which there is plenty of evidence. 'Not a company keeper', as Aubrey heard from the actor son of Shakespeare's fellow player Beeston, 'wouldnt be debauched, and if invited to [be,] writ that he was in paine.'[13] The Poet of the Sonnets regrets he makes of himself 'a motley to the view' on the stage, and none of Pembroke's or Southampton's friends ever reports a sight of him at any locale among *littérateurs*. Droeshout's engraving portrays a thoughtful man with delicate if not fastidious features, an observer who, though 'of an open and free nature', is most unlikely to have impressed anyone as a flamboyant extrovert. If the portrait lacks the 'sparkle' of a witty poet, it suggests the inwardness of a writer of great intelligence, an independent man who is not insensitive to the pain of others, and who could have written *Timon of Athens, Macbeth,* or *King Lear*.

Shakespeare was skilful and natural in his habits of ingratiation and self-preservation: he had learned to protect and save himself among egotists. In his forties he was largely proof against temptation, and his indiscretions—to the extent that we can know of them from Stratford records or the Sonnets—were half-regretted ones of youth or early manhood. He was not ravished by sensual enjoyments, nor is it clear that he was eager to live as long as he could; but he 'loved the surface of the earth and the process of life', as George Orwell has said.[14] He had curiosity. He admired the self-disciplined Davenants, as he did the businesslike Condell, and he could have found few in London more diverse in background or unusual in their viewpoints than the skilled *émigrés*—whose energy and success aroused popular envy.

Plague in the suburbs made Bankside alleys less attractive: and married actors, with children to raise, went north. So did a few others. By 1604 at the latest, he was living in north-west London between St Paul's and Cripplegate. Here, in St Olave's parish, he had taken rooms in a double tenement at the north-east corner of Mugwell (later Monkswell) and Silver Streets; the former street had not taken its name, after all, from monks, but from Algarus de Muchewella, who had held a deed to its land in the twelfth century (the street is 'Mukewellestrate' in 1277, and 'Mugwell streete' as late as the 1570s).[15] The premises here were leased by Christopher Mountjoy, a French Protestant who, with his wife Marie and only daughter Marie or Mary, manufactured ladies' wigs and ornamental headgear. From Crécy where he was born Mountjoy had fled with other Huguenots after the St Bartholomew's Day massacre of 1572; in England he had waited for years before paying a denization fee and becoming naturalized, but had still prospered, not least because the Mountjoys, with apprentices, supplied headwear to the royal court.

Their shop was on the ground floor. Apprentices often roomed in garrets, and it is likely that Shakespeare had ample space (perhaps one flight up) in a double tenement. John Stow refers to 'divers fayre houses' on Silver Street which afforded a respectable neighbourhood; nearby on Monkswell Street were the large, well-built stone and timber premises of Neville's inn and the great Hall of the Barber Surgeons, with Holbein's celebrated painting of Henry VIII granting the barber surgeons a new charter. Farther up the street were almshouses lately founded by a former Lord Mayor, Sir Ambrose Nicholas, whose son Daniel when testifying in a lawsuit, mentioned his talks with the playwright.

That lawsuit reveals Shakespeare's role in a nuptial agreement made when he was lodging with Marie and her husband; it shows us how they regarded him, and also introduces us to the minor playwright George Wilkins. It is rather inaccurately said that Shakespeare lived in a parish 'adjoining' that of his fellows Heminges and Condell: neither was far away, but they lived to the east beyond St Alphage's and St Alban's parishes, at St Mary Aldermanbury's,[16] and other theatre men such as Jonson, Dekker, and Munday at about this time lived to the north, outside the city's walls at St Giles. Shakespeare did not have actors or poets breathing down his neck, but a short walk would have taken him to the watermen for a ride across the river, so he could possibly have reached the Globe in less than half an hour.

In 1604 at any rate his landlady made good use of him. About six years earlier, Marie Mountjoy had welcomed a new apprentice in Stephen Belott, a young man of French descent who seemed personable and competent. Just before that, Marie had worriedly consulted Simon Forman, who diagnosed her as pregnant as a result of indiscretions with the mercer Henry Wood of Swan Alley, but that had proved a false alarm, and a less risky amorous prospect began to appeal. Clearly, her respectable assistant was keen on her daughter Mary, though young Belott hesitated to propose marriage. After consulting with her husband, Marie implored her 40-year-old lodger, Shakespeare, to persuade Stephen Belott to wed Mary with a promise of a sum of money for Belott if he did. No one else, apparently, was trusted with this mission: Christopher Mountjoy also urged Shakespeare to help. As a go-between like his Pandarus, the playwright did his best to move the apprentice to take the Mountjoy girl, with the result that Belott and Mary were wedded at St Olave's church on 19 November 1604.[17]

Christopher Mountjoy, however, fell short of his promises. His relations with his son-in-law soured, and less than eight years later a summons in the Court of Requests (dated 7 May 1612) demanded that

Shakespeare and others give evidence in a civil action of Stephen Belott, plaintiff, *versus* Christopher Mountjoy, defendant.

The key issue in the civil action was whether Mountjoy had ever pledged to give the young man £60 on marrying and also to leave him a legacy of £200, as Belott claimed. None of the witnesses had a remembrance at all of the legacy or an exact memory of the £60, so Shakespeare's failure to remember those sums was not unusual. What was said of the characters of the plaintiff and defendant, however, could be crucial, and in his own comments Shakespeare's even-handedness is truly impressive (possibly this was not the first time he avoided trouble by approving all parties). In his depositions, he rather blandly characterizes the two contenders, finding them both admirable, yet he delicately avoids implying that his own approval of Belott could mean that Mountjoy had felt, or ever said, that the young man was a profitable employee.

The poet has known the plaintiff and defendant, alike, 'for the space of tenne yeres or thereabouts', he gladly admits. Belott, as Shakespeare recalls, 'did well and honestly behave himselfe', and 'was A very good and industrious servant'. On the other hand, to his, perhaps, imperfect remembrance, he 'hath not heard the deffendant [Mountjoy] confesse that he had gott any great proffitt and comodytye by the said service' of this Stephen Belott. And yet for that matter, Mountjoy did 'beare and shew great good will and affecceon towardes' this servant. In fact, at divers and sundry times, Shakespeare has heard the defendant and his wife report that Belott was 'a very honest fellowe'. So far, so good. In another response, Shakespeare conjures up what must have been a rather fraught scene at Silver Street with Marie, then in her late thirties, begging her gentlemanly lodger to persuade Belott to accept the girl, though the legal form of the report is dry enough: Shakespeare 'sayeth that the said deffendantes wyeff [Marie] did sollicitt and entreat [him] to move and perswade the said Complainant to effect the said marriadge and accordingly this deponent did move and perswade the complainant thereunto'.[18]

That scene had occurred in 1604, or about the time he was endorsing the view, in *All's Well* and in *Measure for Measure*, that reluctant bachelors need to be nudged into marriage. It is just possible that

Marie's dilemma gave him ideas for Helena and Duke Vincentio of Vienna, as Ernst Honigmann suggests,[19] but perhaps the important point is only that he had succeeded as a persuader where others might have failed, since that in a small way has a relation to his habits as a dramatist. He projects himself into viewpoints not his own, and here, interestingly, he has not done so without talking over, with his acquaintances, Marie's dilemma and the behaviour and characters of persons. Daniel Nicholas, Sir Ambrose's son, testified for example that he heard

one William Shakespeare saye that the defendant [Mountjoy] did beare A good opinnion of [Belott] and affected him well when he served him. And did move [Belott] by him the said Shakespeare to have a marriadge betweene his daughter Marye Mountjoye [and] the plaintiff . . . as Shakespeare tould him this deponent [Nicholas] which was effected and Solempnized uppon promise of A porcion with her.[20]

Nicholas's phrase, 'make suer' (make sure), indicates that Shakespeare had even brought about a troth-plight between Stephen and Mary in his presence:

And in Regard M[r] Shakespeare hadd tould them [Stephen and Mary] that they should have A some of monney for A porcion from the father they weare made suer by m[r] Shakespeare by gevinge there Consent, and agreed to Marrye, ~~gevinge each others hand to the hande~~ And did Marrye.[21]

Unable to reach a verdict on hearsay evidence, the court, not finding itself vastly clarified on any point by any witness, referred the Belott–Mountjoy suit rather wearily to 'Elders of the french Church', who at last ordered Mountjoy to pay Belott twenty nobles (£6. 13s. 4d.), far less than he had sought, and later excommunicated Mountjoy for 'sa vie desreglée & desbordée'. So the legal part of the wrangle ended. Shakespeare, if one may speculate, perhaps moved out of the house in October 1606 when Marie died, and before the Belotts returned to Silver Street for renewed fighting.

One of the oddest witnesses in the case had been the minor writer George Wilkins, with whom Belott and Mary lived when they left Silver Street. In touch with the underworld and reputedly a brothel-keeper, Wilkins, in his late twenties, clearly had some acquaintance with Shakespeare. He was a troubled young man, bitterly hostile to women. In all of his work he is obsessed with sin and misery as if displaying his guilt. He brutally kicked a pregnant woman in the belly; he beat another woman, and then stamped on her so that she had to be carried home. We know of his behaviour from legal records, and two allusions to the kicking of women occur in Wilkins's plays.[22] His novella *The Painfull Adventures of Pericles, Prince of Tyre* (1608) was not a 'source' for Shakespeare's drama as is assumed in a modern study,[23] but is based on *Pericles*.

Did Wilkins himself write two acts of *Pericles*? If he did, he presumably saw the older poet at Silver Street or in its environs more than once. Living to the south-west of his friend Stephen Belott, Wilkins aspired to respectability in the days before he was arraigned for petty crime. Shakespeare is not to be blamed for the company he kept, and, at any rate, just how well he knew the younger poet is unknown. Wilkins's worst days were ahead of him. But some of his attitudes and habits, including his brutal 'kicking', may have been clear to Shakespeare, who observed what he could of wealthy and of seedy London; we shall meet Wilkins again.

Time's perpetuity: *Macbeth* and *King Lear*

Groups of royal swans, once the delight of Queen Elizabeth, still floated in calm indifference on the river Thames. These creatures could be seen among low, flat-bottomed barges and high-masted vessels on the smooth surface of the water. Many an actor living in the city must have stepped into a waiting, upholstered wherry and crossed within sight of the swans to Bankside—to hear news or gossip at the Rose or Globe. In the late summer of 1605 there was news of the royal patron. King James had reached Oxford on 27 August. He had been made to wait outside St John's College's gates for Matthew Gwinn's brief, pretty welcoming pageant. Three young boys, in the dress of female prophets or Sibyls, had hailed him as a descendant of the Scottish warrior Banquo. 'Nec tibi, Banquo', they told the King of England and of Scotland,

> Not to thee, Banquo! but to thy descendants
> Eternal rule was promised by immortals.

Happily not linked with the bloody usurper Macbeth, the King was next treated to Oxford's learning.[24] For two days he listened to Latin 'disputations' in theology, medicine, law, and other topics. One question debated at the college was, 'An imaginatio possit producere reales effectus?' (Whether imagination can produce actual effects?). The King's players, reaching Oxford on 9 October, may have seen the academic questions which were printed as a broadsheet. The 'imaginatio' one, by coincidence or not, is answered in *Macbeth* when the killer's imagination alone creates a dagger in the air before Duncan's murder.

Oxford's events may not have inspired Shakespeare's play, but they perhaps reminded him of Macbeth and Banquo in Holinshed's *Chronicles*. The new reign's mythology elevated Scottish history, and, by chance, regicide became a topic of talk in November in London. A horrific plan had come to light. Guido or Guy Fawkes, a Yorkshire-born soldier, had carried twenty barrels of gunpowder and many iron bars into a vault under the House of Lords with the aim of blowing up the King, the Queen, Prince Henry, the bishops, nobles, and knights, 'all at one thunderclap'.

Interestingly, Guy Fawkes was attached to a web of conspiracy which led up to the Warwickshire gentry and included Catholics known to the Shakespeares—such as Robert Catesby, whose father had held land in Stratford, Bishopton, and Shottery, and John Grant, a Snitterfield landowner. So many sympathizers and plotters were local men that a board of jurors, including July Shaw—later a witness to the dramatist's will—met at Stratford in February 1606 to investigate the Gunpowder Plot. Like Macbeth in confusing foul and fair, the plotters cannot have seemed very remote to Shakespeare. Trials and hangings meanwhile took place in London. Father Henry Garnet, the Jesuit Superior, was hanged on 3 May. His defence of the right to 'equivocate' at his trial puts one in mind of the Porter in *Macbeth* who thinks of himself at Hell's gate after Duncan is killed: 'Knock, knock. . . . Faith, here's an equivocator that could swear in both scales

330

against either scale, who committed treason enough . . . yet could not equivocate to heaven. O, come in, equivocator' (II. iii. 7–11).

A few public events, then, may be traceable in *Macbeth*, but was the Scottish tragedy played for two kings in the summer of 1606? Or was it written as a 'royal play' for their sakes? In August the bristling, beflagged warship *Tre Kroner* touched Gravesend with King James's brother-in-law Christian IV of Denmark aboard. Having come over mainly to see his sister Anna, he was very well entertained. After all this was the first state visit to England by a foreign ruler in eighty-four years. A tall and almost stout, whitish-blond Dane of 29, Christian IV had an ability to drink most ordinary mortals under the table—his gentle mother is said to have worked her way 'through two gallons of Rhine wine a day'—but he had a weak grasp of his host's language. Anyway, the King's men performed three times for the two jovial monarchs. There is no hint as to which plays were staged, and no sign that *Macbeth* was one of them.[25] (Later, the tipsy shipboard scene on Pompey's yacht in *Antony and Cleopatra* is said to have recalled a shipboard feast of James and Christian, but nowhere else does the author so foolishly risk mocking his patron.)

Nevertheless *Macbeth* was sooner or later acted at James's court, and its relation to the royal patron is fascinating. In Holinshed's *Chronicles*, Shakespeare had found Banquo himself involved in a conspiracy to kill King Duncan, and this he may have changed to avoid implying that James I's ancestor was guilty of treason. Yet to have shown Macbeth and Banquo in league to murder a king would also have been faulty in dramatic terms: he clears Banquo of complicity, so that Macbeth is deprived of any excuse for killing Duncan.

At the same time he refuses to whitewash Banquo, or to give James I an ancestral paragon. Banquo in the play admits to an 'indissoluble tie' with Macbeth, and accepts the latter's accession, though fearing he played 'most foully for't'. He hopes the witches will help *him*, too. 'Why by the verities on thee made good', Banquo says of the Witches' aid,

> May they not be my oracles as well,
> And set me up in hope? But hush, no more.
>
> (III. i. 8–10)

That 'hush, no more' signifies no assault of his robust Scottish conscience, and Banquo is murdered before he can reveal other 'cursed thoughts' about his own or his descendants' prospects. Though innocent of treason he is culpable in condoning Macbeth's rule and guilty in his desire. This aspect of *Macbeth* is biographically interesting in that Shakespeare's dramatic interests, his political realism, his concern for history, psychology, and truth, are really uppermost in his mind. He does not tailor a Scottish play to suit Scottish James; he knows he must take risks, and so he takes them without being foolhardy. Later on, he apparently salutes his patron briefly in Act IV when the Witches offer a vision of Banquo's heirs (who will include James I). Macbeth in horror sees the royal line 'stretch out to th' crack of doom' (IV. i. 133). That echoes a popular notion of Shakespeare's time that James's noble line of descendants would endure to the world's end.

Otherwise *Macbeth* has rather little to do with James I, though his book *Daemonology* (1597) has remarks on witches similar to Banquo's comments. The playwright, no doubt, has read his patron's books. But Shakespeare's Witches are complex, ambiguous creatures who relate to medieval habits of mind. They undermine Macbeth. In one critic's view they become 'heroines' of the play in subverting the evil order which demonizes them,[26] but they are also mysterious and unknowable icons, images of fate, demonic tempters, and malevolent, ugly old hags with living counterparts in the 'wise women', witches, and sorcerers one might consult for a fee at London Bridge, Whitechapel, or Bankside. The author used what he saw and heard at Bankside or in the city. His friend Richard Field, for example, had printed in 1593 the *Sermons* of Henry Smith—Nashe's superb 'Silver-tongued Smith'—whose preaching at St Clement Danes in the Strand includes pungent images which often remind one of the play: 'You are not like hearers, but like ciphers, which supply a place but signify nothing'—or, 'As if we were night-black ravens, which cannot be washed clean with all the soap of the Gospel'—or, 'All his lights are put out at once'—or, our life has been compared to 'a player which speaketh his part upon the stage, and straight he giveth place to another'.[27]

None of this of course proves Shakespeare had known or read Silver-tongued Smith, but habits of his own mind are relevant. For all his originality, the dramatist had an idiosyncrasy which might be ascribed to modesty, to caution, or perhaps to his having been a hireling and then a major actor. He often looked for the grain of sand, or the phrase, the simple authentic remark or known situation uninvented by himself on which his imagination could set to work. He might have found slender hints for Macbeth and Lady Macbeth, idiosyncratic as they are, even in the eager, aspiring, and slightly aloof French *émigrés* whom he knew. Supplying Anna at the royal court, cajoling Shakespeare, and plotting to advance her daughter, Marie of Silver Street is a far cry from Lady Macbeth. But it is after he had begun to know the elder Mountjoys well that Shakespeare created, in part from his whole experience of London, the most horrifying wedded couple in his dramas.

Nothing he had picked up adventitiously, all the same, really accounts for *Macbeth*'s atmosphere, or its enormous suggestiveness, its stunning compression and economy of means, and its complex panoply of images. Involved here is more than its author's prudent husbandry. To a degree this tragedy was made out of his other plays, such as *Richard II* with its state murders or *2 Henry VI* with its equivocating prophecies and witch-scenes. But in a more subtle way the author's emotional conservatism, even his constancy, loyalty, and self-respect are responsible for *Macbeth*: he kept continually in touch with his past. He did not ransack his older plays to make a new one, but had in mind what he had profitably learned about dramaturgy: the channels to his past experience of the theatre were wide open and quick-running. *Macbeth* is the quintessence of his career.

Even for his Scottish usurper, he had one model close at hand, inasmuch as he himself is in all of his heroes, just as he is, in another sense, in none of them. Macbeth's own moral awareness is surprising: he is oddly self-conscious for a rough Scottish field general who, in facing a rebel, 'unseamed him from the nave to th' chops' (I. ii. 22). With mayhem in his sword, he has the imagination and critical self-regard of a model schoolboy, although Macbeth is also that tissue of complexities which his wife helps to illuminate.

'I fear thy nature', Lady Macbeth tells him goadingly. 'It is too full o'th' milk of human kindness' (I. v. 15–16). Not only her sexuality but his own yieldingness abet their role-playing in Act I as they collude to realize themselves. Shakespeare seems to have known such interdependence. Lady Macbeth is at first the more compelling player with her lurid charm, but Macbeth's empathy gives her leave to act out his zealous discontent—which is of a kind which might drive a man to unusual crime, political victory, or success in some nearly impossible double endeavour in a profession. For all her nerve at first, Macbeth's wife is lacking in vanity as if she had little to gain in becoming queen. Her feeling for her husband is nearly that of a mother living almost wholly for her child.

Still, one need not look for developed autobiographical patterns in a drama which so transforms its major materials. Shakespeare subordinated most of the figures to an extent that they barely step out of written sources. But he depicted Macbeth's psyche with such interior pressure that this, and not the usurper's outward action, is what is mainly dramatized. The 'milk' or sensitivity of Macbeth's nature is not annulled by his bloodiness, but feeds his active conscience until he cannot bear his own lucidity. He is, indeed, ground down, torn, and stripped. His crimes annihilate his wife, and part of his punishment is to report on his destruction with an accuracy that complicates one's feelings for him, extends one's knowledge of human life, and gives the text a richness infinitely beyond that of any morality drama even in his casual admissions:

> I have almost forgot the taste of fears.
> The time has been my senses would have cooled
> To hear a night-shriek, and my fell of hair
> Would at a dismal treatise rouse and stir
> As life were in't. I have supped full with horrors.
>
> (V. V. 9–13)

That not Macbeth's but Banquo's heirs will 'get kings' robs him of any consolation, and as the riddling Witches tell him nothing of use he loses his ability to interpret time. Yet his lucidity is unaffected. Macbeth understands his hard, gnawing obsession with Banquo's heirs, and that topic relates indirectly to Shakespeare's personal abiding concern with matters of inheritance.

Among actors such a concern was not unusual. Members of the King's men, for instance, typically named their fellows among their heirs. Augustine Phillips, who died in May 1605, had lately left 30*s.* in gold to Shakespeare, as well as bequests to others in the troupe. The valuable 'share' left by a leading actor could itself provoke hopeful inheritors, cause litigation, and embarrass the company.

But then the poet's concern with inheritance—which links *Macbeth* with *King Lear*—runs unusually deep. He shows in these works 'futures equivocally offered, by prediction and by action, as actual-ities', notes a perceptive critic, 'and the disastrous attempt to impose limited designs upon the time of the world'.[28] That does not quite impute to Shakespeare a moralistic aim, and Macbeth and Lear in turn are involved in nightmares of inheritance, and also in violently disrup-tive engagements, not only with time but with a civic polity and the inner self.

Though it could have been tried out earlier at the Globe, *King Lear* was acted before the court at Whitehall on St Stephen's Night, 26 December 1606. This work pleased its patron, supposedly, by showing King Lear's division of the kingdom to be gross folly. By means of proclamations, coinage, pageantry, and even ships' flags, James's parliaments were being urged to accept Anglo-Scottish union—a matter which in the end required a hundred years—and James styled himself 'KING OF GREAT BRITTAINE'. Yet one doubts that Shakespeare's tragedy includes royal propaganda, and in showing Lear's aim as the opposite of James's the play distances itself from him. Perhaps it had to do so, since *King Lear* was a dangerous work. Its upstarts and courtiers could evoke James's much-detested Scottish favourites, just as its two vicious daughters might be taken for those who with the court's connivance were then snatching at monopolies, and its views of predatory royalty and a decaying order were not bound to delight the Stuart entourage. Censorship or self-censorship could account for some of the extensive revisions in the play's Folio version, as has been suggested.

On stage *King Lear* demanded much. One hears that Burbage so excelled as the hero that old Lear 'lived in him', and the quick, dwarfish, and charmingly ugly Robert Armin had talent to excel as the

Fool.[29] There is no denying their success, but to stress that is probably to mistake Shakespeare's mind. One reason, as directors say, why good (let alone truly outstanding) productions of *King Lear* have been fairly infrequent in modern times is that its title-role is relatively less important than the Prince's in *Hamlet* or the usurper's in *Macbeth*. Peter Brook finds in *King Lear* 'eight or ten independent and eventually equally important strands of narrative' besides the principal one, so that the three-dimensional roles of Edgar, Kent, Goneril, Regan, and others, rather than the storm scenes, are the play's major challenge.[30] Or again what Peter Hall calls *King Lear*'s 'physical marathon' taxes many almost equally.[31] The terrain is very difficult; the runners are in a group; none can afford to stumble. The play distributes its great complexities. In 1605 or 1606, it would seem, Shakespeare relied on two major actors rather less exclusively than is usually supposed, and in writing *Lear* and, later, *The Tempest* he attended the most closely and boldly to a troupe's potential. With *Lear* he is less concerned to sculpt a star part for Burbage than to enlist a group's whole power—and also to explore entirely new kinds of relationships.

For example, the lunatic King in Act III holds a mock-trial in which one of his vicious absent daughters is indicted. 'Arraign her first', cries Lear in extreme torment, '"Tis Goneril. I here take my oath before this honourable assembly she kicked the poor King her father.'

> FOOL. Come hither, mistress. Is your name Goneril?
> LEAR. She cannot deny it.
> FOOL. Cry you mercy, I took you for a joint-stool.
>
> (1608 quarto, xiii. 42–7)

Unencumbered by time, madness of this kind has a double focus. Goneril's crime, in Lear's view, is only that she 'kicked the poor King her father'—and one recalls the poet Wilkins, whose 'kicking' of women was an index of his nature. In reducing his daughter's crime, Lear suggests its specific, painful cruelty, as well as its perpetual meaning as a sign of man's bestiality. And the Fool's impudent proverbial confusion of Goneril with a joint-stool befits a drama concerned with strange relations between the physical and non-physical, as in the force of the storm, or in Lear's speeches over Cordelia's dead body.

Shakespeare prepared for *King Lear* with a studious elaborateness, a range of reading wide and intense even for him. Even in a brief consideration of a few of his sources—which will be the focus of my remarks here—one begins to see the grandeur of his conception. He enriched his outlook and even his vocabulary by reading Florio's vigorous translation of Montaigne (1603), and borrowed a number of Florio's words for the play. Among other versions of the 'King Leir' story he probably knew, he read Holinshed's and the brief, elegant one in Spenser's *Faerie Queene*, Book II and made some initial use of the anonymous *King Leir* published in 1605. Written in stilted couplets, this may be the same 'king leare' play which the Queen's and Sussex troupes, at their last gasp, had put on near the end of the plague outbreak of the 1590s. At its outset, King Leir plans to trick his beloved Cordella into marrying a ruler of Brittany. Alert to his whims, his daughters Gonorill and Ragan both pledge to wed anyone he chooses; but Cordella refuses to flatter and so, without banishing her, Leir divides the kingdom between the evil sisters. Shakespeare condenses seven scenes of that play in writing only a part of his own first scene.

No version of the tale implied that the fated king went mad, but a modern scholarly quest for sources (or is it a wild-goose chase?) has unveiled an odd case about insanity. Around 1603 two sisters, Lady Sandys and Lady Wildgoose, had tried to get their old father, Annesley, a gentleman-pensioner, certified insane. Annesley had a third daughter, Cordell, who urged Lord Cecil to put her father and his estate under care of a benign protector. The Wildgooses contested the old pensioner's will, and at last Cordell Annesley in 1608 was to wed Sir William Harvey, the Earl of Southampton's stepfather—who some would say is 'M^r. W. H.' or the dedicatee of *Shake-speares Sonnets*. A helpful case, but one wonders if the poet needed to know any of it to think of Lear's madness.

Two sources, though, are especially intriguing. From Sidney's prose tale of the Paphlagonian King in the *Arcadia*, Shakespeare derived what has been called 'a perfect parallel to the Lear story' or the underplot in which Gloucester, when tricked by his bastard son Edmund and still blind to Edgar's constancy, has his eyes put out by the fierce Regan and Cornwall.[32] Obtuse when he had eyesight, Gloucester learns to see better when his sockets are clotted with blood. His agony is the outward equivalent of the King's implicit suffering, and here allusions to the Passion are fairly overt. One hand before the other, one foot before the other, were nailed to wood, in the most memorable of all scenes for the Christian West, before a common Roman soldier tried to end the Sufferer's torment. Accordingly between Regan's comment on the gouging of Gloucester's eyes, 'One side will mock another; th' other too', and Cornwall's 'Lest it see more, prevent it', there is a delay in which a common servant tries to save the sufferer and mortally wounds Cornwall; and yet the play is far from being a Christian allegory. Arguably pre-Christian and post-Christian at once, it may be released from all historical time, as R. A. Foakes notices. Lear, after all, 'has no history in spite of his great age. We know nothing of how he came to the throne, of the events of his reign, even how long he has reigned, so that it seems he has been in power for ever. We know nothing of his queen, of her life or death . . .'. Not that we need to know, as Foakes implies, and partly because the play cannot be imagined in a wholly mythical context, *Lear* can always be seen essentially as a contemporary work.[33] The hero watches in most audiences and at all times as Goethe knew, since an aged man is always a King Lear.

One text, which relates to Stratford, had given the dramatist something more than useful hints for tragic form. This was Samuel Harsnett's high-keyed, ironic exposure of Jesuit exorcist practices, *A Declaration of Egregious Popish Impostures*, published anonymously in 1603 and reissued in the next two years. Such an anti-Catholic tract had a special appeal just after the Gunpowder Plot. Having written earlier of a Puritan exorcist, Dr Harsnett as chaplain to the Bishop of London turns to some exorcisms by a group of priests led by William Weston alias Father Edmunds, which had been performed in 1586–7. Three young chambermaids had been exorcized, and Edmunds's priestly cohorts had included Jesuits of the English Midlands, such as Father Robert Debdale of the Shottery Debdales, and Father Thomas Cottam, the brother of the Stratford schoolmaster who had replaced Jenkins in Shakespeare's schooldays.

The priests are only gross feigners sent from France, 'for fire-worke here in England'. Perfidy, as well as perversity, is found in the very names of devils exorcized from the young women's bodies, such as Lustie Dick, Frateretto, Hoberdicut, Maho, Modu, Lustie Huffe-cap (a 'swaggering punie devill'), or Hobberdidaunce who 'could make a lady laugh'.[34] Finding the occult names useful, Shakespeare has Edgar in disguise as the madman Poor Tom tactically use some of them. 'Five fiends have been in Poor Tom at once', Edgar cries to his blind father Gloucester,

as Obidicut of lust, Hobbididence prince of dumbness, Mahu of stealing, Modu of murder, Flibbertigibbet of mocking and mowing, who since possesses chambermaids and waiting-women. So bless thee, master! (1608 quarto, xv. 56–61)

In *The Comedy of Errors* or *Twelfth Night*, Shakespeare had already treated exorcism as a spiritual fraud, and so he does here, except that here Edgar is feigning in order to survive and to save his father. He 'mimes in response to a free-floating, contagious evil more terrible than anything Harsnett would allow', writes a good critic who slightly underestimates Dr Harsnett.[35] Edgar, true to his purposes, tries to purge his father's despair, supposedly at Dover's cliff, and so he, at least, has a redeeming priestly function.

But it may not follow that Shakespeare meant to refute Harsnett, or that he wanted to show his own regard for Shottery Catholics or martyrdom in a schoolmaster's family. The playwright was less doctrinaire than one might think. What is reasonably clear is that a book on exorcism gave Shakespeare some useful language, and perhaps some ideas, for the making of *Lear*, and that its allusions to Stratford names interested him as a man of that parish. Does his own Chapel Street life enter into his work indirectly? It is not too speculative to say that Shakespeare felt profoundly about his own children, or that his elder daughter, Susanna, seemed headstrong or difficult. His own absences from home, as will emerge, were likely to complicate his relations with his two adult daughters. Susanna was hardly his 'model' for Cordelia, but again one cannot impose limits on the range of his sources or his feelings. He drew on what he knew and deeply felt, and after about 1606 the father–daughter bond becomes an almost obsessive theme in his work.

King Lear of course enormously expands upon the initial crisis with Cordelia. Having denied all three of his daughters self-expression, Lear would destroy his kingdom. In opposing that political folly by speaking the truth, Cordelia loses her worldly advantages, though she later proves willing to lay down her life for her father. The vain King recognizes the most crucial of his errors as early as scene iv. 'O most small fault', Lear cries in Goneril's palace,

> How ugly didst thou in Cordelia show,
> Which, like an engine, wrenched my frame of nature
> From the fixed place, drew from my heart all love,
> And added to the gall! O Lear, Lear, Lear!
>
> (I. iv. 245–9)

And yet he must suffer until at last he holds Cordelia dead in his arms. There is no scheme of spiritual development in this entire ordeal, and nothing that Lear learns is of use to himself, to the polity of his country, or to the poor whom he cannot help. This work's political themes anticipate those of Shakespeare's later Roman tragedies, and yet politics is not the central concern. Lear, finally, is divested of most of his illusions, except that he never learns that time is unforgiving, or that pride is inherent in our human condition, or that his folly must result in the death of the only person he really loves.

Classical roots: Egypt, Rome, and Athens

In mornings at Bankside the King's men put their poet's work to the test. A script recited for the troupe, at a vetting in a buzzing tavern, could be different in the cold light of a rehearsal. The stage-management side of a production fell into the hands of the book-holder or book-keeper, who had to be fairly familiar with the whole text of a play. As we have noticed, he had charge of seeing that actors were ready on their cues, and his 'stage-keepers' would have helped to arrange that properties were at hand when needed. Otherwise, as a rule, the actors appear to have been left to their own devices. Practices must have varied, but it is likely that the book-keeper with his senior actors might on occasion cut scenes, rearrange lines, or make up a few, or call for the author or someone else to revise. Shakespeare was much respected, but even his major tragedies were considerably cut and supplemented. Men such as Burbage, Heminges, or Condell might feel that they knew his aims as well as he did himself.

Moreover, his fellows had to care about how he affected segments of the paying public. The gentry, the educated, and the sophisticated at Holborn, in the city's west, and at Westminster were still crucial since they had influence, money, leisure for plays, and a bent for serious themes. Other people might follow the taste of the élite. How did his tragedies relate to the interests and awareness of Londoners? In the suffering of his tragic heroes, he had been articulating a widely felt sense of malaise and had had a chance to seek out areas of feeling not always expressed in pulpits. In the consciousness of the wider public was an awareness of an appalling loss resulting from the English Reformation, which had fractured the Christian Church. In an age in which religion was a crucial factor in nearly everyone's life, the new malaise had lasting consequences. With a weakening in Christianity, one's identity, one's purpose in life, and the meaning of one's activities were thrown in question. Each person was divided from an orientation which medieval faith had given. And even as parliament challenged King James in 1604, the Stuart regime offered little guidance for a public disturbed by momentous changes in politics, social organization, and other aspects of contemporary life.

Shakespeare's outlook was more alleviated by hope than that of his heroes, but he could feel as they did. He was aware of enduring evil, too strong to be self-created by men and women, and yet he does not balance the anxiety implicit in his tragedies with any sign of religious confidence. Each tragedy had been an imaginative hypothesis in which, with his full mastery of rhetoric and dramaturgy, he tested life. But the religious ingredient is withheld. That in itself partly accounts for the affronted speeches of his tragic heroes, as with Lear in the terrible storm. 'Singe my white head', cries the vain, humiliated king,

> and thou all-shaking thunder,
>   Strike flat the thick rotundity o'th' world.
>
> (III. ii. 6–7)

Is Lear's despair ever the author's own? Shakespeare's mind was a complex thoroughfare of contradictions and of extreme feelings. But to a degree he was held in check in the uncertainties, tensions, and tragic endings of his own works. What his actors cared for were receipts at the doors, but this is not to say that they failed to encourage him. And, from time to time, they must have made suggestions for new topics.

Classical subjects, for example, had a wide appeal. After *Julius Caesar* he perhaps had agreed with the sharers that he would write a new play on the triumvirate. This was the *Triumviri reipublicae constituenda* of Lepidus, Octavius, and Mark Antony who, after Ceasar's death, jointly ruled the Roman world.

But if Shakespeare planned that, he put it off. Essex's late revolt, in 1601, affected the stage to the extent that dramas about Romans began to look like jibes at the Crown. Fulke Greville the younger, for example, had penned an 'Antonie and Cleopatra' about lovers who showed 'irregular passions in forsaking Empire to follow sensuality', but had thrown it in the fire. His work had been a closet drama, for private acting, but he felt it would deeply annoy 'the present government'. In the new reign, suspicion predictably touched Ben Jonson. For his Roman *Sejanus*, in which Shakespeare acted, Jonson was hauled before the Privy Council and accused of 'popery and treason' by the old, half-senile Earl of Northampton.[36] Listening to the author's apology (or trying to stay awake), the Council may have realized their vast mistake and let him go. Jonson's trouble, anyway, embarrassed the King's men less than the fact that *Sejanus* was hissed off the stage. In his own late Roman plays, Shakespeare apparently takes hints from Jonson's bold recasting of historical material, as with his own Lepidus, but avoids *Sejanus*'s clotted style, lack of irony, and grinding moral emphasis.

Did a new law prompt his own return to Roman topics? In 1606 a parliamentary Act to Restrain Abuses of Players, which forbade the mention of God, Jesus Christ, or the Holy Trinity except 'in fear and reverence', was taken seriously by the Revels Office. Actors obeyed that ruling, and an increased use of pagan or classical settings resulted. Shakespeare at last offered his fellows *Antony and Cleopatra* around 1606 or in 1607, though records of its early performances are lacking. Its ill-fated lovers had usually been judged in a moral light. However, Chaucer's *Legend of Good Women* and the Countess of Pembroke's *Tragedie of Antonie* (1592), a version of the French of Robert Garnier's *Marc Antoine*, depict Cleopatra as a martyr to love. Samuel Daniel's *Tragedy of Cleopatra* (1594) applauds both lovers and shows even a ruthless Octavius as alert to compassion. A wide range of interpretation was open to Shakespeare, who follows Plutarch's 'Life of Marcus Antonius' in North's version to the extent of borrowing details of phrasing, anecdotes, hints for scenes, and his basic approach to the characters.

His reading of Montaigne's shrewd, self-honouring *Essays*, closely enough, it seems, to borrow ideas, might be taken as a hint of change in Shakespeare's own outlook. This involved an increase in his confidence, a self-restoration with new inwardness, and even a bolder, more questioning attitude to popular values. He was becoming more interested in non-literal truth, in myth, fable, and implicit connections between historical epochs. With thirty-five speaking parts, nearly double his usual number, his new play ranges over three continents in recreating on a wide canvas the events of 41 to 30 BC. In this period, dissension among the triumvirs had finally ended the epoch of republican Rome, with its belief in stern self-discipline, hard service, and anti-absolute civic principles.

Fittingly, the action of *Antony and Cleopatra* opens with a Roman's view of Antony's lapse. 'Look', Philo insists,

> Take but good note, and you shall see in him
> The triple pillar of the world transformed
> Into a strumpet's fool. Behold and see.
>
> (I. i. 11–13)

And so we see. In the famous lovers' quarrels there is a ludicrous contrast between assertion and action, between what they claim and what they do on stage. As in the Sonnets, mutual commitment is lacking or uncertain. Yet Shakespeare so deflates Rome by showing Lepidus's senile weakness, Pompey's futility, or Octavius's hardness that Antony gains in stature through his generosity and latent grace. What we observe of the lovers, peculiarly, becomes less valid or 'true' than what they say,[37] though Cleopatra's exalting words are offset by her lover's homelier reckonings, as in Act IV after a lucky victory:

> CLEOPATRA.   Lord of lords!
>   O infinite virtue, com'st thou smiling from
>   The world's great snare uncaught?
> ANTONY.   My nightingale,
>   We have beat them to their beds. What, girl, though grey
>   Do something mingle with our younger brown . . .
>
> (IV. ix. 16–20)

Antony's 'visible shape' is subject to the breaking of the Roman world. A dizzying pace of brief, dispersed scenes implies the break-up in a recent time with a fracturing of the medieval unity and a loss of a faith that once bound together western Europe. In the deliquescence he shows on stage, Shakespeare evokes a cultural parallel in the Reformation's own chaotic events.

The lovers' suicides complicate *Antony and Cleopatra*'s meanings. Imagining that the Queen has taken her life, Antony bungles his own death. The hoisting of his still-living body within her monument typically occasions puns and comedy. And after he dies, Cleopatra still must endure a diligent Clown—with a basket of asps—who might have had a role in *Much Ado*.

Such comedy suggests play-acting. Nothing has exalted the lovers more than their refusal to let events alter their roles. Cleopatra is stagily linked with Isis's immortality, the Nile's renewals, pyramids, crocodiles while disguising her aims. So long as her sexuality is *acted*, which is to say verbalized, it eludes age. Antony has avoided time's 'strong necessity' by dying, but is he transfigured in life? Can self-discovery or psychological change occur in an arena of almost pure illusion? This mischievous tragedy, happily, shatters its illusions to reveal them, and, in a famous instance, a Jacobean audience is made aware that they are only watching a boy when Egypt's Queen refers to comedians who, one day, may 'stage us', and when her noble, besotted Antony

> Shall be brought drunken forth, and I shall see
> Some squeaking Cleopatra boy my greatness
> I'th' posture of a whore.

(v. ii. 215–17)

Her political acumen saves her from any such fate: in death she outwits Octavius. The author's ironies have not demystified her, but the problem of the worth of her love and of Antony's tragic suffering is left, rather tantalizingly and wonderfully, up in the air.

Coriolanus—which also involves politics and theatricality—belongs partly or wholly to Shakespeare's forty-fourth year. Again he takes his main story from Plutarch, who had coupled the life of the Roman general Caius Martius Coriolanus with that of the Greek Alcibiades. The latter appears in *Timon of Athens*, but Shakespeare prefers as a tragic hero the valiant Roman who had taken part in wars between Rome's infant republic and the neighbouring Volsces, and this gives him leave to explore Rome's nascent politics in light of an English present. Lately at a time of feeble harvests and high prices, new rioting had erupted in the English Midlands, and on a scale not matched in ten years. There were major outbreaks not far from Stratford, at Hill-Morton and Ladbroke.

Coriolanus opens with a plebeian rebellion over Rome's corn-dearth. The First Citizen interestingly echoes Lear's and Gloucester's lesson that a 'superflux' must be shared with the poor: 'If they would yield us but the superfluity while it were wholesome we might guess they relieved us humanely, but they think we are too dear' (I. i. 16–18). And separately, the citizens are reasonable, even though the author models a few of their complaints on a tract of his own county's rebels, *The Diggers of Warwickshire to all Other Diggers* (*c.*1607). Collectively, they are horrendous as they turn from one idol to the next, easily duped, blind to their folly, vicious towards any strange excellence. Revering Coriolanus one moment, they despise him the next.

Coriolanus's mother is especially interesting as a fiercely loving and

managerial figure. Too complex to be a type, she is not entirely different from what is known of Mary Arden (whose managerial talents are
recognized in Robert Arden's will). Volumnia is not unlike other
mothers of genius if one may trust, say, Goethe or Freud, and Coriolanus excels partly to free himself from vulnerability to her. Unfortunately, the Tribunes, as defenders of citizens' rights, exploit his
temperament to turn the plebeians against him, and, denied a consulship, he is in his smarting anger exiled from Rome.

In the Tribunes—Brutus and Sicinius—as well as in the consulship
election, Shakespeare attends somewhat warily to his day. What he
saw in inflation-ridden England was that more people than ever, the
deserving as well as the loose or lucky, were attaining to incomes of
£40 per year which allowed them to vote. There was a new hostile attitude to the King. MPs were emboldened, and after they failed to rat-
ify some of his expenses, James I called his assembled critics 'Tribunes
of the people, whose mouths could not be stopped'. Parliament
counter-attacked with appeals to common law and traditional rights,
and this worked. Among direct results, the election of churchwardens
in the Globe's own parish was confirmed (all parishioners were
allowed to vote), and in 1608 King James further granted London a
new charter. This protected the city against the Crown's encroach-
ment on the right to tax, and extended that to Blackfriars, where the
players were about to open a new theatre.

Coriolanus also glances into the future of British elections. In
Shakespeare's time English candidates were chosen by a few men and
not allowed to canvass, but there were 'disputed' elections in which
voters stubbornly refused to acclaim a candidate. One of the 'dis-
putes', for example, involved Stratford's voters in 1601, when Fulke
Greville, then senior MP for Warwickshire, was not returned until
King James's Council argued he *must* be 'chosen'. Importing the
English system into his drama, the poet has Coriolanus chosen by the
Senate to be Consul. The Roman citizens not only deny him the consulship, but go rather beyond English practice in assuming that candidates need to be approved by majority vote, not just by acclamation.
'But that's no matter, the greater part carries it', says one citizen;
another speaks of the 'honour' of individual choice. English reform-

ers were then urging the popular choice of parliamentary candidates, but that was not instituted until after 1625.[38]

In the play, sophisticated political issues yield to a tragic theme. Rome cannot accept the pride, scorn, and defiance in Coriolanus which have enabled him to save Rome in battle, and his wounds, cherished by Volumnia, emblems of patriotism, avail him nothing. 'Our virtues', says his friend, enemy and eventual killer Aufidius in Act IV,

> Lie in th' interpretation of the time
>
> .   .   .   .
>
> One fire drives out one fire, one nail one nail;
> Rights by rights falter, strengths by strengths do fail.
>
> (IV. vii. 50, 54–5)

The tragedy ends on a muted note in keeping with Aufidius's words, but *Coriolanus* is its author's best analysis of politics, one which displays his subtle use of the politics of his day. There is nothing like 'the *Othello* music' in this tragedy's verse style, but a rough, abrasive lyric music suits its vigorous action. The play's odd phrase 'lurched all swords of the garland'—the word *lurched* means 'robbed all contenders of'—is mocked by Ben Jonson, in his *Epicoene*, around 1609.

Well before then, Shakespeare must have seen Thomas Middleton, who was a city bricklayer's son, nearly as gifted as Jonson. Baptized at St Lawrence Jewry in 1580, Middleton first appears at 22 in Henslowe's stable of gifted hack writers; but he proved an able collaborator and a brilliant playwright, as *Women Beware Women*, *The Changeling* (with William Rowley), and *A Game at Chess* of the 1620s were to show. At some point he added witches' songs and a dance to *Macbeth*, and he may have contributed to, or perhaps tried to revise, Shakespeare's *Timon of Athens*. The exact status of that play remains debatable, though R. V. Holdsworth and others point to Middleton's hand in the text.

Whether or not the Stratford poet saw *Timon of Athens* performed, this tragedy is complete if not polished, and its text is at least better than that for *Pericles*. Timon is shown in prosperity, then adversity, with visits to him by the Poet, Painter, Apemantus, Alcibiades, and others counterpointed in the two parts. The hero is as naïve as if he had stepped out of a ballad. Like Lear, he takes pledges of love at face value: like Coriolanus, he is alienated. Timon regards money in a medieval way as static and sterile, fit to be given away. When his flatterers refuse him credit, he finds that money is a liquid, self-duplicating power which has corrupted the earth. As a colossal hatred for mankind swells, he enjoins the sun:

> O blessèd breeding sun, draw from the earth
> Rotten humidity; below thy sister's orb
> Infect the air.
>
> (IV. iii. 1–3)

Half-crazed and penurious, he discovers gold, which lends irony to his tirades against humanity before he dies. His grave will be washed by the sea, as one learns in the lines beloved by W. B. Yeats:

> Timon hath made his everlasting mansion
> Upon the beachèd verge of the salt flood,
> Who once a day with his embossèd froth
> The turbulent surge shall cover.
>
> (V. ii. 100–3)

This is one of the few works by Shakespeare (wrote Hazlitt when under its spell) in which he 'seems to be in earnest throughout, never to trifle or go out of his way. He does not relax in his effort, nor lose sight of the unity of his design.'[39] *Timon of Athens* reveals that Shylock's view of money as a thing that 'breeds' is, indeed, correct. Jacobeans accepted the view of money as fluid, productive, and self-replicating, which horrifies Timon. King James had begun to be destroyed by money, or by his own spendthrift ways which were firing parliamentary zeal against him. And Shakespeare comments here indirectly on many aspects of the Jacobean money nexus, for example on a new anxiety over patronage, or on suffering caused by unending, sharp price-rises. Mercy might have died with the medieval community. For Shakespeare, money was a mixed blessing: his own earnings as an actor and shareholder, in the 1590s, had tempted Stratford aldermen to try to manipulate him. That, in fact, is what the Sturley–Quiney letters reveal; but they may *suggest* what is worse—that the poet's money, at one point, had been an issue capable of dividing him from his own father, if the two Quineys and Sturley heard about the 'Shottery' investment plan from John Shakespeare's loose lips. After that plan was bruited about, one recalls, the poet (despite his earnings) made no investment at home until his father was dead.

Just when he wrote *Timon* is unknown, but as it derives partly from Plutarch, it may date from about the time he was using Plutarch for his late Roman dramas. In its sketch of an anguished hero betrayed by himself and his ethos, it has thematic interests in common with those tragedies. At what psychological cost had they been written?

After *Coriolanus*, Shakespeare abandoned tight plots and realistic scenes, and, as he wrote no more tragedies, he surely felt he had pursued one line as far as he could. His case was strange: one thinks of Dante, Leonardo, Molière, Bach, and of others, all of them peerless, and yet no one has ever excelled, in art of any kind, over the sheer concentrated immensity, the intellectual and emotional achievement of this poet's late tragedies. He was a man who, for the time being, had exhausted himself; he had run himself dry. He apparently sought a renewal for himself in the theatre, and also in the prospects of a wilful daughter at Stratford's Chapel Street, where he may have arrived sometimes, on horseback, near the Gild chapel, after seeing Jennet and a 'grave' Master Davenant in an old university town.

IV

THE LAST PHASE

17

TALES AND TEMPESTS

Now I want
Spirits to enforce, art to enchant;
And my ending is despair
Unless I be relieved by prayer,
Which pierces so, that it assaults
Mercy itself, and frees all faults.

(Prospero, *The Tempest*)

Sir, she's well restored
And to be married shortly

(Jailer, *The Two Noble Kinsmen*)

Susanna's marriage

*A*n alert traveller riding into Stratford around 1607 would not have found the townspeople invariably sombre or the local trades hopelessly depressed. Puritanical feeling was strong among aldermen who met at 'halls', but old festivals were still honoured. There was jollity enough, and merchants had more to celebrate than in the lean years of the 1590s. Despite fears about the ungodly, some thirty ale-houses were to be allowed at Stratford, along with the three inns—the Crown, Bear, and Swan—all on Bridge Street.

There were tensions in the local council which illuminate the dramatist's late years (as does fresh evidence about his son-in-law). But after leaving dusty London, Shakespeare would have returned to a place of natural beauty. Passing over Clopton's bridge, a rider saw green tillage-lands which ended in high, overgrown earthy banks or meers. Extending by the Avon were rich 'water-furlongs'—where all manner of wild fowl bred and greylag geese fed.

The Gunpowder Plot still cast a long, curious shadow. After he was found with a bag of popish 'relics', George Badger the alderman went to prison; also sent to prison was one William Reynolds, perhaps the same man (a son of Catholic recusants) who was remembered in the poet's will. But, much worse for those at New Place, Shakespeare's elder daughter Susanna broke a new, severe law—the aim of which (in the words of the act) was to penalize 'persons popishly affected'. Among twenty others on 5 May 1606, she was cited in a complaint in the court's act book, which, as it refers back to preceding entries, reads rather drily:

> Officium domini contra
> Susannam Shakespeere   similiter similiter
> dimissa

What this amounts to is that, at the age of 23, Susanna was charged with the fault of not receiving the Anglican sacrament at Easter, 20 April, and so became liable to a stiff fine of between £20 and £60. Along with six others, she increased the fault by ignoring a summons, though cited personally by the apparitor. Hence her penalty was reserved for the next court—when the word 'dimissa', after her entry, indicates that she was discharged.[1]

In his plays Shakespeare minimizes the Protestant–Catholic conflict, and he did not advertise his beliefs. But Susanna's beliefs were likely to be unsettled, and about a year later, at 24, she was wed to John Hall, a church-going physician. It is wrongly supposed that in her mid-twenties a Stratford woman would have been thought a little 'old' for the altar. A modern account represents Anne Hathaway, at her marriage at 26, as 'long in the tooth', and supposes that Shakespeare may have wed to save 'his fading siren of Shottery'. Those are poor male guesses, nothing more. Parish registers are helpful, and a survey based on them shows that the 'mean' age for women at first marriage in twelve parishes (including Alcester near Stratford) during 150 years after Anne's wedding, was just 26. (For a quarter of a century, the age at first marriage for women was even higher in Stratford.)[2] At 24, the elder daughter of the owner of New Place might have had a fair choice among the town's bachelors.

But Susanna accepted Mr Hall—a physician who lacked a doctoral degree. His sister, Sara, had wed a Cambridge scholar of 'physick' who had that degree, but one could practise medicine without a doctorate. Born in 1575 and raised in the rustic village of Carlton, Bedfordshire, in the family of a physician, John Hall had gone thirty miles away to Queen's College, Cambridge; he took his Bachelor's degree in 1593, his Master's in 1597, and then travelled in France. What had brought him to the Midlands? His parish of Carlton was not close to Stratford, but Sir Thomas Lucy had inherited a manor at Carlton. Abraham Sturley had worked for Lucy, and Mr Hall includes a Sturley among his patients. With a few local connections, he set up a practice before marrying Susanna on 5 June 1607.[3]

To judge from his plays, Shakespeare viewed the role of a father at a wedding as of deep sacramental importance. In *Lear, Othello*, or *Romeo and Juliet*, it suggests tragic consequences to come if a father flouts his sacred role, either by 'giving away' his child without her consent, or by withholding it when she marries. And as at Holy Trinity, a country wedding's symbolism would have been important to him. Boys wore sprigs of rosemary tied to their sleeves as symbols of fidelity; bridesmaids carried cakes or garlands of gilded wheat to symbolize fertility. The father accompanied the bride to the altar.

'Who giveth this woman to be married unto this man?' the priest would call out. The father then relinquished the bride, and after that his role in his daughter's life had ended. He watched as the couple plighted troths, and as the groom placed the ring on the bride's finger with these words: 'With this ring I thee wed, with my body I thee worship, and with all my worldly goods I thee endow.'

Yet even for a bride's father, weddings were as hopeful as they are today. John and Susanna might produce children, and at about this time in Act V in *Pericles* Shakespeare wrote one of his most moving testaments of a father's love for a daughter. He also saw the abased side of a father's supposedly blameless love, and symbolized an entwined, difficult, incestuous feeling in paternal love in *Pericles*. His love for Susanna was complex and intense, and one finds signs of it in his legal will and indirectly in his late plays. The recent evidence, coming to light in 1994, implies that John and Susanna knew that they would have the Old Stratford acres he had bought from the Combes, and this may have figured in the marital settlement.[4] The Halls, alert to his good will, probably settled before long not far from New Place, at the street of Old Town, in a timber-framed house known today as Hall's Croft, and Susanna gave birth to her only child, Elizabeth Hall, baptized on 21 February 1608. At 43, Shakespeare was a grandfather.

What did he think of his son-in-law? John Hall's social rank as a physician was not very high, and medical knowledge was more widely diffused then than today. The doctors in the plays so far had been non-descript, or burlesqued as Dr Caius is in *Merry Wives*, but Lord Cerimon in *Pericles*—who restores the hero's wife after her 'burial' at sea—is a selfless practitioner, not unlike Mr John Hall in bringing

> to my aid the blest infusions
> That dwells in vegetives, in metals, stones.
>
> (xii. 32–3)

Mr Hall in fact used 'infusions' which he prepared even with 'Coral' and 'Pearl', and carried his remedies up to forty miles from home. His first casebook is lost, but his second, which begins in 1617, tells us very interestingly of his medical habits. With herbs and 'Pearl', he once treated a Catholic priest, and noted that 'beyond all expectation the Catholick was cured'. ('Blessed be God', Hall noted in Latin, though his pious words for a Roman priest were omitted after Hall's death when his casebook was printed.) Shakespeare knew his son-in-law for nearly a decade, and one gathers that the two were fairly intimate. They appear together in London for example in Thomas Greene's *Diary* (which Stratford's worried town clerk kept from 1614 to 1617 during a local civic crisis), and Hall's notions of curing with coral and pearl were likely to be remembered. 'Of his bones are coral made', wrote the poet for Ariel in *The Tempest*.

> Those are pearls that were his eyes;
> Nothing of him that doth fade
> But doth suffer a sea-change
> Into something rich an strange.
> Sea-nymphs hourly ring his knell.
>
> (I. ii. 401–5)

Hall's cures may not have inspired the song, but to be acquainted with him was to know his strange, transforming liquids and Elizabethan pharmacopoeia. He disliked blood-letting. Some of his ways were superstitious, but he preferred what was mild. He used more than a hundred separate botanical herbs, and Hall's garden, like New Place's gardens, became known for its varieties of plants.

Once when Susanna was 'tormented with the Cholick', he gave her an enema of flowers, and then 'I appointed to inject a Pint of Sack made hot. This brought forth a good deal of Wind, and freed her from all Pain'—and so 'Mrs. Hall of Stratford, my Wife' was cured.

Neuralgia was not unknown to Shakespeare's descendants, and when Elizabeth, as a child, had what he diagnosed as 'Tortura Oris', with pain on her face's left side and then on her right, Hall produced his fullest case-history. The child became worse. But in late stages, when she was weak, he massaged spices into her back, poured almond oil over her head and squeezed it up her nose, until she was 'delivered from Death'.[5]

Asked later to sit on Stratford's council, he twice declined (even as he was to refuse a knighthood). Then he accepted, only to be fined for being absent. When he flared up at that lack of reason, he was expelled from the council. One of Mr Hall's enemies became Daniel Baker, an ultra-Puritan linen-draper of High Street, who as bailiff in 1602 had helped to ensure the banning of plays. Narrow-minded and truculent, he was symptomatic of a new order in Shakespeare's late years: for the town's crafts had all but died out, and retail merchants were in power. There was insecurity among the burgesses partly because Stratford was at once a borough, a manor, and a parish, so boundaries of control overlapped. The haberdashers, mercers, and drapers could be rule-bound, ceremonial, aggressive. Mr Hall was to call them 'forsworne villaines'; they damned him for 'false imputations'.[6] They plotted to get rid of the local vicar (effectively as it turned out) before Shakespeare died, and Hall was to defend the next, well-educated, vicar against the council's wrath.

Even Puritan drapers usually went to Anglican service, and Hall was of Puritan inclination himself; but in these years, class or rank was a contentious factor in the town's life. Local politics had much to do with one's calling, friends, and education—and what helped to divide

Stratford was the contempt of well-educated, professional men such as John Hall for the airs of common tradesmen.

A few months after Elizabeth's birth, the poet's mother had died. Mary Shakespeare was buried on 9 September 1608. Summoned by the vicar's clerk that October, the poet's sister Joan and her husband William Hart appear to have administered her estate.

Mary Shakespeare had used a quill pen deftly, joined her husband in a law suit, and seen more than one of her sons through petty school. From such evidence as exists and from genetic probability, she emerges as an intelligent, quick-minded, eager, and selfless person of use to generations of males, since it is likely that she had helped her father, husband, and eldest son in turn, in a managerial capacity at Arden's farm and Henley Street. Shakespeare had kept his Sonnets out of print while she lived. Eight months after she died they were registered for publication. Their bawdry might have troubled a countrywoman less than some of her son's odd, ironic assertions, which are a gateway to one of the most complex of psyches. The most tangled and contradictory of his relationships, one suspects, was always with his mother. His troubled attitudes to women are too deep to be of anything but early origin. There is no biographical evidence that he abhorred women, but in relation to female sexuality he had become fastidiously self-protective. The Sonnets cast an odd light in their obsession with sexual pollution or contamination, itself a theme in *Hamlet, Measure for Measure,* and *Timon.* The difference between his troubled views of sexuality, and the love he felt for his grown daughters, has a bearing on tensions in his late plays in which he sketches women in a new light and on occasion mocks himself; but it is not so certain, in view of his daughters' eventual problems, that he was confidential or at ease with the daughters he cared for.

We are to see more of Susanna's temperament, but he could not have been luckier in his son-in-law. In December 1607 the doctor's father, William Hall of Acton, made out a will in which the claims of an elder son were overlooked and John Hall as a younger son was named as his father's inheritor and 'sole executor'.[7] The poet too appears to have trusted Hall above other men he knew.

A few of his Sonnets had been in circulation ever since 1598, when Meres noted that 'private friends' had access to them. Some, perhaps, had won admirers. John Weever as a young *littérateur* imitates the form of a Shakespeare sonnet in a lyric called 'Ad Gulielmum Shakespear' published in his *Epigrammes* (1599), but he could have seen the three sonnets in *Romeo and Juliet*. Weever dedicated *Epigrammes* to Sir Richard Hoghton of Hoghton Tower in Lancashire—and there is another vague link between the Sonnets and Lancashire. A manuscript of Sonnet 2 has been found in a collection made either by Sir Edmund Osborne, or by his second wife Anne, whose mother Mary was a sister of the same Sir Richard Hoghton (1570–1630), of Hoghton Tower.[8]

Somewhat less significant is a long poem called *Willobie his Avisa*, licensed on 3 September 1594 and probably written by an undergraduate. Its likely author Henry Willobie had entered St John's College, Oxford, before transferring to Exeter College and taking a degree in 1595. Five years earlier Henry Willobie's elder brother William had married Eleanor Bampfield, whose sister in the same month married Thomas Russell. This is of interest since Shakespeare was to name Russell as an overseer of his will and leave him £5.

The poem, in a leisurely manner, concerns a frustrated lover, one 'Henrico Willobego. Italo-Hispalensis', or 'H.W.', whose 'familiar friend W.S.', recovering from a 'like' passion of his own, is bent on seeing if love will 'sort to a happier end for this new actor, than it did for the old player'. The allusions to 'W.S., new actor, old player' are few, vague, and also tantalizing, though there is nothing in *Avisa* that could not be imagined, perhaps, by a reader of Shakespeare's Ovidian poems who knew that he was also a stage actor. Still, it is silly to be too confident. *Avisa* refers to Shakespeare's *Lucrece*, and, as we learned in recent times, a resident at one of the Inns of Court, a certain 'H. M. of the Middle Temple', links these two poems in a semi-erotic work of his own in 1605:

> We read (*Avisa*) as reports the Writer
> We read that *Lucrece* was persude after:
> *The Strange Fortune of Alerane or My Ladies Toy*.[9]

Every problem with *Avisa*, at any rate, shrinks when one comes to the mystery of the Sonnets' publication. Shakespeare, it is believed, had almost certainly revised his lyrics, and he may have arranged them for a sonnet sequence in the tradition of Samuel Daniel's *Delia* (1592), which had its groups of sonnets, a lightweight interlude, and a 'Complaint of Rosamond'. Months of plague would have given him ample time to order his sonnets in small groups within two main sections, followed by an interlude in Sonnets 153 and 154, and *A Lover's Complaint*.

Certainly, too, Shakespeare's income was reduced by long closures of theatres in 1607 and 1608, and he would have had reason to sell poems of a slightly outmoded fashion while he could. At any rate, a volume of his lyrics was licensed in London on 20 May 1609 and printed by George Eld, for the quality publisher Thomas Thorpe, who since 1600 had brought out works by Jonson, Marston, and Chapman and had contacts with the universities. There is no sign that *Shakespeares Sonnets* was later withdrawn from publication, or that it appeared in irregular circumstances. Thirteen copies still exist, which could mean that a few readers very lovingly saved the volume, or that it was not liked well enough to be read literally to pieces (the highly popular *Venus and Adonis* of 1593 survives in only one copy).

Thorpe, who depended on writers for the theatre, had a fairly creditable record when he issued the Sonnets. His books were respected, and his printer Eld kept to fairly good, if not exceptionally high, standards. In 1611, perhaps as a Jonsonian joke, Thorpe was to issue Coryate's *Odcombian Banquet* without a main text but with its prefatory matter, and in fact he lacked authority for that, although he never printed the *Banquet* itself.[10]

For *Shake-speares Sonnets* he used the impressive, famously obscure dedication which follows. It has become a Riddle of the Sphinx for Shakespeare scholars, who of course have not hesitated to tell us what Thorpe may mean. Supposing 'W.H.' to be a misprint for 'W.SH.', one critic observes that Thorpe elsewhere signs himself, 'T. Th.' or 'TH. TH'. If 'W. H.', then, is a slip for 'W. SH.' or W. Shakespeare, the odd dedication, which is meant to resemble a Latin lapidary inscription, might be nearly intelligible.[11] The phrase 'ever-living poet' might refer to Our Lord, and the metaphor about a 'well-wishing adventurer' could apply to the enterprising volume itself. Even so, the phrasing is remarkably contorted:

TO. THE. ONLIE. BEGETTER. OF.
THESE. INSVING. SONNETS.
M^r. W. H. ALL. HAPPINESSE.
AND. THAT. ETERNITIE.
PROMISED.

BY.

OVR. EVER-LIVING. POET.

WISHETH.

THE. WELL-WISHING.
ADVENTVRER. IN.
SETTING.
FORTH.

T. T.

And, one asks, is it likely that Eld, a competent printer, would let 'W.H.' stand as a glaring misprint? (There are not many misprints elsewhere in the work.) Worried over sales, Thorpe may have hoped to allure sonnet-readers by mystifying them, as publishers did in the 1590s, and changed 'W.SH.' to 'W.H.' himself. That explanation, at least, is not inconsistent with what little is known of Thorpe's character. The 'misprint' theory (first mooted by Brae in 1869) has no small merit in being sane, but attention has focused on a person with the initials 'W.H.' (entailing a little trouble if we favour Henry Wriothesley, Earl of Southampton) who may have been the Sonnets' 'onlie begetter'. The latter word meant 'originator', but it has been taken to mean 'inspirer' or 'procurer', and, so far, the leading contenders for 'M^r. W.H.' are still Sir William Harvey (Southampton's stepfather) and William Herbert, Earl of Pembroke. There was a precedent for addressing a nobleman as 'M^r', but it is unlikely that a publisher in touch with the theatre, or a public actor, in 1609, would refer in print to the great Earl of Pembroke, a patron of the King's men, merely as 'Mʳ.W. H.' Only frail circumstantial evidence supports the attribution to Sir William Harvey, and the dedication remains an alluring enigma—as one suspects Thorpe hoped it would be.

Either the *Shake-speares Sonnets* sold too poorly to be quickly re-issued, or they were withheld from republication during the author's lifetime. But there was a possible tactical advantage, for Shakespeare's actors, in having these elegant lyrics in print in London at a crucial time in 1609.

Lands of 'painful adventure' from *Pericles* to *The Tempest*

At the time of Susanna's marriage to John Hall the city theatres had suffered from repeated closures. The plague hardly relented. Or if it relented for a few weeks, the death-toll, in either cold or warm weather, might subsequently rise unpredictably, forcing the Privy Council to give new orders to the justices of the peace, so that doors again would shut. Weeks passed for acting companies beset by high, inflationary costs, but taking in no money, and yet in this period the King's Servants were helped by their own patron, as when they were allowed to play at court nine days after Lent had begun in 1607. They had good reason to bless King James. In the next year, fifty deaths were recorded in London on 28 July, and more than forty a week thereafter, with up to 102, 124, or 147 dead in three autumn weeks. A long, enforced hiatus had begun—and with the Globe's doors shut for sixteen months, even modest royal gifts were welcome.[12]

The Globe's men, however, had taken a risky step to be in a good position when the sickness lifted. Success would hinge on their pres-tige, authority, and high quality, since they aimed to fulfil a dream by having a theatre inside the city in an élite neighbourhood which had previously rebuffed them. Those who had got up a petition against Burbage and signed their gentlemanly names, such as Harmon Buck-holt, Ascanio de Renialmire, and the like, had complained of 'a com-mon playhouse' in their midst. Twice again such residents were to protest, and, indeed, success for the King's men might depend on their own luck in avoiding *early* complaints while they established themselves in new city quarters. It would have helped to have *Shake-speares Sonnets* in print to testify to their poet's courtly refinement, and Thorpe's edition was thus no calamity in 1609.

The actors were a centre of Shakespeare's observations, though a work such as *The Tempest* suggests that he went well beyond actors' circles for his living sources. Over the years, he can only have heard a good deal about the advantages of a 'winter' hall in the city's west near the Thames. Back in 1596 old Burbage had hatched a plan for a roofed theatre and had purchased the Blackfriars room, but the plan had failed: up to the end of that decade the Upper Frater was empty as a cavern. Then the great hall was leased to the Chapel Children, and when the boy actors got into hot water with satire and political gibes, their leader, impresario, and leaseholder Henry Evans bargained to sell their lease. Finally, when the boy actors had been closed down, Evans made a new, acceptable offer to the troupe, so the Upper Frater came back into the hands of Shakespeare's men in the summer of 1608.

At that juncture, when plague had closed every venue, the Burbages settled on a new 'housekeeper' scheme, and extended this to seven men on 9 August 1608. Pope had died, Phillips lay buried at Mortlake; and their Globe shares meanwhile had gone to William Sly and Henry Condell. Holding back two shares for themselves, Richard and Cuthbert Burbage now brought in Sly and Condell, as well as Hemings and Shakespeare (as survivors of the company's earlier housekeepers), to be equal sharers in the Blackfriars. A seventh share went to an outside financier, Thomas Evans. Sly died when the deal was in progress, and so, when the plague relented, the new housekeepers were six, four of whom were King's players.[13]

Flaunting their supremacy, the actors decided to keep two theatres, although the Globe could easily have been rented or sold. No company had ever been foolish enough to try to maintain two playhouses, each empty as a tomb for half of the year. But from 1609 onwards, the Globe would be used from May to September, then stand empty for the seven colder months, when, with courtiers and lawyers back in town, the company acted in London's affluent west near the river. Indoor hours would be about the same as at the Globe to appeal to idlers or 'afternoon's men' (often the main clientele for a hall theatre), and six shows might be given weekly. A winter stage could be lit partly by daylight, with the help of candles and torches, but whereas the Globe's prices began at a penny, a roofed theatre could charge more. At Blackfriars the cost would be 6*d.* for entry to a gallery, a further 1*s.* for a bench in the pit. A box cost half a crown. As many as ten showy, tobacco-smoking gallants, often in feathered hats, could go through the tiring-house, hire a stool, and sit on the stage itself for a total outlay of 2*s.*

Blackfriars proved ideal for offstage music. The 'little eyases' had capitalized on that, and Shakespeare made increasing use of music and song in works up to *The Tempest.* The Globe's stage balcony, in fact, was rapidly altered so that a consortium of musicians could play there, too, and higher charges were not expected to lead to 'a difference in the plays staged at either place'.[14] Shakespeare had used instrumental effects at times, perhaps, as an artistic crutch to make up for a play's vagueness, confusion, or feeble effects (his poorest work may be lost to us, or expunged from revised texts that exist). Music is sparingly used in the early comedies, but two crucial songs at the end of *Love's Labour's Lost* and a music of enchantment in the *Dream* anticipate a sudden, marvellous development in *As You Like It,* in which instrumental music and song reinforce theme after theme, such as time's passing, the humour of 'holiday', the Forest of Arden's delights, or man's ingratitude. Even so, the late romances are musically his most excitingly innovative works. New facilities at Blackfriars, and then at the Globe, must have led him to experiment, and music in *Cymbeline* or *The Tempest* becomes, in an Elizabethan way, 'an act of faith', reinforcing present but elusive meanings in the work's action.

Even before he had an indoor stage, he had begun the series which includes *Pericles, Cymbeline, The Winter's Tale,* and *The Tempest.* These plays are naïvely presentational, conciliatory in mood, less gestured and less emphatically structured than anything he had done before. They recall Tudor dramatic romances of his youth, as well as the miracle works of late medieval times. Why does he seem to reach back? In avoiding the limits of modern realism, logic, and literalness he might use his art to exploit rich areas of popular romance. But there is something more personal in his aims, if one judges from his insistent return to variations upon only a few themes. From the time of *King Lear*, he appears to have drawn on an effort he was making to set himself right with people he cared for, and perhaps to overcome some aspects of estrangement in his absences from home. Yet if that is so, he also transcends such a need, both intellectually and artistically, and none of his dramatic work correlates exactly with any known outward event in his life. The origin of none of it can be reduced to psychological causes, neuroses, worries, or anything of the kind. Though they differ in form and tone, his late plays are alike in a power of open spiritual enquiry, as also in an expanded focus. With the heightening effects of romance, they seem less concerned with an individual than with what happens to a family over a span of time. A motive such as bitter jealousy splits the family, and causes grievous estrangement, odd outcomes, possible death, and 'painful adventures'.

Again and again, he turned over in his mind the needs of reconciliation, mercy, and forgiveness. These themes permeate even *Henry VIII*, played in 1613, and he looks into the conditions of their existence, such as growth and decay, chance and time's passage, the development of self-awareness, and the effects of one generation upon the other. In *Pericles* and *The Winter's Tale*, a wide gap of years separates two royal generations. Infants grow up; separations have unforeseen results in distant lands. The young aid the regeneration of the old, and heroines have effects which do not depend on the struggle known, say, to a Cordelia or Helena, but rather on their being. Alarmed that his son Florizel loves the supposed shepherd-girl Perdita in *The Winter's Tale*, the King of Bohemia threatens to disfigure her face with briars, but nothing can harm Perdita, nor will the men who lust for Marina in *Pericles'* brothel experience anything but her grace. Evil is sudden, implacable, and ferocious but every evildoer in this series is pardoned, except for the incestuous Antiochus in *Pericles*. Disruption and violence are offset by ceremonial, elaborate endings, and by the recovery of persons supposed lost or dead.

Clearly, though, Shakespeare still catered for upper sections of the play-going market which his troupe needed to hold, and his romances have affinities with Sidney's *Arcadia*, a favourite book for university men and young gallants. The public's taste was turning to courtly fare.

Also he could hope to please London's apprentices and servants, many of whom were female. Psychologically the plays are rooted in the realities of exile and in his view of society's corruption. They show a fascination with strangeness and imaginative disturbance, and what Michael Billington (speaking of *Lear*) calls his awareness 'of the precarious absurdity of human existence'.[15]

It might be appropriate if George Wilkins, a hater of women, did suggest the topic of Pericles. Consorting with leading men of the theatre, Wilkins, unbelievably, was at that time staying out of trouble, neither thumping his whores nor stealing anybody's clothes; most of his crimes were ahead of him. We know that Wilkins had collaborated with John Day and William Rowley on a play about recent and real adventures in the East, *The Travels of the Three English Brothers*, performed in 1607. This work has been compared with *Pericles*, which Wilkins could have begun that year. In some ways *Pericles'* first two acts suggest his style, and Shakespeare may have completed or revised the drama, which was followed in 1608 by Wilkins's prose tale *The Painfull Adventures of Pericles*. This hypothetical view of its authorship, though, is a little weakened by the fact that *Pericles* exists only in an irregular, flawed quarto issued by Henry Gosson in 1609. Most of its passages, however, make perfectly good sense, and we surely have more to learn from Gosson's text. A minor city publisher, Gosson served as a legal guarantor for Wilkins when he nearly killed a woman in 1611. At any rate, the play's first two acts are more banal than anything Shakespeare is known to have written, but with stolid efficiency they fit an unusual scheme.

Strikingly, *Pericles* brings on stage a reincarnation of the fourteenth-century poet John Gower, who in his *Confessio Amantis* had put aside moral concerns to relate over 400 tales about love in a simple, direct style. Gower had included a version of the story of Apollonius of Tyre, upon which *Pericles* is based; and yet Shakespeare also takes details from Lawrence Twine's romance version, *The Patterne of Painefull Adventures*, first issued in 1576. As old Gower, Chaucer's friend, introduces each act of *Pericles* in a crabbed, antique style, the stage action becomes pageant-like, with widely dispersed episodes. Having found the secret of Antiochus's incest with his daughter in Greece, Pericles is melancholy, passive, and victimized despite his goodness, and yet his adventures as a jousting knight or a shipwrecked prince bring him no self-understanding. In the first four acts, he is barely more than an enduring folk-tale hero. In his wanderings and sufferings, in his apparent loss of Thaisa his wife, and then of his daughter Marina, he seems in flight from himself and also from a recognition of the possibility of incest. In Shakespeare's view, the human mind constructs such walls of self-justification that only trials worse than Job's may possibly let in light. When implicitly the hero faces Antiochus's secret at last, he is able to save Marina and then recover his lost wife. In its strong images of female virtue as distinct from female sexuality, the play's view of womanhood is less contradictory than Shakespeare's view could have been, but the work is a powerfully affecting if dreamlike study of guilt and fate.

Much lighter, and yet more complex, *Cymbeline* highlights among other topics British history, a dispersed royal family, and supernatural intervention. The play has a long, threading, inclusive plot which unfolds with a deceptive casualness, even as Shakespeare lightly derides some of his own past works. It is a surprisingly difficult play, and we may still be 'far from having got *Cymbeline* in focus', as Emrys Jones once observed. A critic of modern stage performance notes that the text is fearfully elusive, 'constantly shifting its mood and its ground' and 'apt at any moment to mock itself, to send itself up'.[16]

Not that *Cymbeline*'s themes are wholly parodic or comic. For the nation's chroniclers, as for Spenser in *The Faerie Queene*, the time of the British monarch Cymbeline had been almost uneventful: peace was its mysterious purpose, for near the end of Cymbeline's thirty-five-year reign, which began in 33 BC, Christ was born. The calm of the *pax Romana* had a spiritual meaning; but Spenser adds that, because the island king had refused to pay tribute to Rome, it was in his reign that the struggle for British freedom, culminating with King Arthur, really began. Alert to these sources, Shakespeare contrived a lively story for the public, for wits and lawyers at Blackfriars, and also for the court, in writing *Cymbeline* around 1610.

And it has references which might fit 4 June, when the royal Henry was created Prince of Wales and when James Hay, King James's oldest Scottish friend, was made a Knight of the Bath. Shakespeare turns to Holinshed's *History of Scotland* to bring in the exploits of an earlier Scottish Hay. Sixteen times *Cymbeline* refers to the Welsh port of 'Milford' or 'Milford Haven', which absurdly becomes the nearest embarkation-point for the Continent from London. It is perhaps not enough for critics to tell us that Milford in Wales was a thriving port (which it was), since Kentish ports were also active: the dramatist, who gives Bohemia a sea coast in *The Winter's Tale*, could read a map. Shakespeare's geography is symbolic, and much in his day was being made of the fact that James's great-grandfather Henry VII had landed at Milford Haven in 1485 to conquer a tyrant and win the crown. 'Milford' suggests James's royal line from Henry VII, and a native resistance to tyranny. But if Britain's first resistance hero was Cymbeline, this figure in the play begins as a duped fool wed to a malevolent Queen. When she dies, Cymbeline emerges from mental stupor, and Britons resist the Romans only to make lasting peace.

Such resistance has a parallel in the spiritual freeing of mankind which Christ brings—not that this is made explicit. Disguising his seriousness, the author mocks his own plays and a few of his hoary devices, and, though he has sent up his art in *A Midsummer Night's Dream* and elsewhere, here self-mockery is ubiquitous, permeating the play's situations and texture. Brian Gibbons notes 'the extraordinary frequency with which Shakespeare makes apparent allusions to his own earlier work' in *Cymbeline*, which has references to *Romeo*, *Henry V*, *All's Well*, *Lear*, *Othello*, *Antony and Cleopatra*, and even *Lucrece*.[17] Here, for a final time, the device of turning a 'girl' into a 'boy' is used—as if in ironic apology for a parade of sexual changes feigned by Julia, Jessica, Portia, Nerissa, Rosalind, and Viola. The heroine Imogen (or as some would have her name, Innogen) becomes the boy Fidele, only to wake up in a grave beside her headless, oafish suitor Cloten.[18] Also Shakespeare again takes up just that distrust of female sexuality which appears in his Sonnets, *Measure for Measure*, and several tragedies. Unhistorically, he gives Cymbeline a daughter as well as two sons (thus matching King James's family), but the sons Arviragus and Guiderius are living in a rustic, prehistoric Britain with old Belarius, who has fled the court. At home is the king's daughter Imogen, who is divided from her husband, Posthumus, because he is not of royal blood.

Though far off in Rome, Posthumus is still threatened by Imogen's sexuality: he is unable to respond to love that is sensual as well as spiritual. The author reaches through *Othello* to transfer the problem from the tragic to the ridiculous. Thus the hero takes a wager on Imogen's chastity, virtually wills himself to be a cuckold, and, after believing Iachimo has slept with her, plans to kill Imogen. Hardly a dutiful Desdemona, Imogen shows her mettle, as when the servant Pisanio laments that he has been told to kill her:

> PISANIO. Since I received command to do this business
>   I have not slept one wink.
> IMOGEN.   Do't, and to bed, then.
>
> (III. iv. 99–100)

The plot takes her safely into Wales where she finds her royal brothers. Ever more troubled, Posthumous has thought of her as male property. He would tear her limbs and destroy 'the woman's part in me'; he fears betrayal by all women including his mother, and his phobia leads to disaster before his ultimate regeneration. At the play's centre is a colossal misogyny, too dark and idiosyncratic to suggest any deliberate self-burlesque. Yet there is enough self-mockery in *Cymbeline* to suggest its author's need to be rid of a burden of attitudes he has previously dramatized, and, with the help of folklore elements and a magical view of events, the play is impressionistic and exuberantly fresh in its exploration of history, myth, and male conceit.

Less sprawling and somewhat less topically allusive, *The Winter's Tale* clearly appealed to the wits at Blackfriars and to the Globe's public alike. Its sheep-shearing festival in Act IV and several other scenes so closely evoke Warwickshire that it might well have been penned at New Place. There is an influence from the dance of satyrs in Ben Jonson's *Masque of Oberon*, staged at court, on 1 January 1611, but there are signs that Shakespeare added his own dance of satyrs (in IV. iv) after writing the main text. Simon Forman the astrologer saw *The Winter's Tale* at the Globe on 15 May 1611, and after it was acted at court, in November, it remained in the King's men's repertoire for twenty-nine years.

One has only to read Greene's *Pandosto*, a very popular Tudor romance and the drama's main source, to see how much Shakespeare owes to his former maligner's pattern of contrasts. Not so savage as Pandosto, and not so happy at first in marriage, Leontes flies into a jealous rage at his wife Hermione for her supposed affair with his childhood friend Polixenes. It has been said that Leontes suffers from delusional madness, or from memories of a homoerotic boyhood, but the text carries one quickly on to consequences: he orders his wife's newborn infant, Perdita, to be burned alive, as if Queen Mary's martyr-fires were still alight, but the baby is left on Bohemia's sea coast to be found by a shepherd. Believing that Hermione and the child are dead, Leontes spends the next sixteen years in prayer and repentance, even as Stratford's college of priests had prayed round the year. The burning of a child (which is only threatened) need not evoke martyrs, but the suffering in Greene's *Pandosto* is spiritualized. To be sure, Leontes still doubts Perdita's 'worth' after his ordeal.

A terse, funny link between the wintry opening and the earthy scenes of Bohemia is in the famous stage-direction, 'Exit, pursued by a bear'. Perdita's deliverer Antigonus is eaten by an animal which suggests the Candlemas Bear, the sluggish creature which, in legend, emerged on 2 February, Candlemas Day, to say how long winter still had to run.

But in the subtext, as it were, of this play, Shakespeare emphasizes cruelty, egotism, and blindness. Earlier, when persecuted by her husband, Hermione remarks, 'The Emperor of Russia was my father'. Jacobeans perhaps would have remembered Ivan IV or 'the Terrible' (1530–84) who saw treachery everywhere, killed his son in a fit of rage, and at Moscow released untamed bears on victims.[19] Shakespeare implies that the cruel bear is not far from our lives, and his Bohemian scenes, for all their jollity, suggest his underlying disbelief in redemption. Perdita, though superficially observant, is timid and unresolved until fortune happens to favour her; her lover Florizel boasts of an inheritance he will get at his father's death; and the comic Autolycus (whose namesake in Greek myth is descended from Hermes, god of crooks) knows the stupidity of countryfolk. As a petty thief and conman who pretends to be a mugger's victim, Autolycus takes the sheep-shearing as an event in which pastoral folk are to be 'fleeced'. He delights in his own roguery, sings well, and adds to the play's charm, but Shakespeare's social pessimism did not pass away with this work.

That his indirections, late in his career, are paths to a sharper social realism is perhaps clear in *The Tempest*. This play opens with a famous *coup de théâtre*, rather better suited to stage effects at Blackfriars than at the Globe, in which a ship carrying Prospero's enemies is swept to a rocky isle. Scene i includes nautical orders which a crew might hear, in a storm, to get a ship to veer from rocks dangerously close on the lee side. Books on navigation existed, but the poet had no printed sea-manship manual, though he might have found nautical word-lists in manuscript (as Ralph Crane copied some). He could have talked to 'old salts'; but the scene reflects very up-to-date sailing tactics. What is certain, however, is that he knew the so-called 'Bermuda pamphlets' and some of the men associated with the Virginia Company's enterprise.

In May 1609, nine ships carrying 500 colonists under Sir Thomas Gates and Sir George Summers had set sail to America to reinforce the colony at Jamestown, founded in the spring of 1607. After two years, Virginia's colony was barely surviving—about half of the settlers died each winter. In an unusual storm, Gates and Summers were driven on the Bermudas, before managing to sail to the mainland; and news of their ordeal duly reached London. Shakespeare evidently read an account of the storm, of Jamestown's plight, and of hostile natives in a letter by William Strachey, dated 15 July 1610, then in manuscript. He knew some of Gates's friends, as well as Southampton and Pembroke, both financially interested in Virginia, and he possibly heard from men such as Sir Robert Sidney, Sir Henry Nevile, or even Lord De la Warr, who was to be governor of the colony.

Yet it was not enough for him to seek 'insider information' about ships, American Indians, or the policies and practices of colonial rule, since he had to count on what audiences would know, or on what was being talked about. By 1609, some in London had argued on good evidence that Virginia had been settled by natives who therefore owned the land along the James River, and whom Europeans had no right to supplant. Official Jacobean policy denied this, and in April, for example, two sermons were printed to show that the colonists had truly brought civilization and faith to America's savages. (One sermon, with agile logic, proves degenerate stage actors are the real enemies of Virginia.)[20] *The Tempest* gives both sides of the colonial argument with ironic depth and complication. On the one hand, Shakespeare replies to Montaigne's essay 'Of Cannibals' which exalts the virtuous life of primitives (Caliban is morally stunted, predatory and a would-be rapist); but on the other hand, he includes drunkards and murder-plotters among the suave grandees who reach Prospero's isle. He makes Caliban's claim to the isle sound fairly plausible, and to an extent sympathizes with him. The monster's language is like that of a Stratford glover's son, in being above his worldly station or rank, and he speaks the loveliest blank-verse lines in *The Tempest*. Caliban's final wish to 'seek for grace' (V. i. 299) need not have been construed by audiences as either shallow, feigned, or futile.

The Tempest, however, is set not in the Atlantic but on a Mediterranean isle, and the author sketches an Italian *realpolitik* which he had tested before. Prospero, with nearly Machiavellian sagacity, ensures that his daughter Miranda will wed the son of his worst enemy. A modern critic asks if it is necessary, after all, that we 'run away from the identification of Prospero with Shakespeare?'[21] Probably not. Rather as the dramatist does, the magician assembles and disciplines an almost unmanageable world, heads his people along certain paths, and gives them situations to which they must react. The magician's view of the transience of all things, for example, matches his creator's outlook as often expressed, as when Prospero thinks of the melting of 'the great globe itself' and of our 'insubstantial pageant' which will leave, at last,

> not a rack behind. We are such stuff
> As dreams are made on, and our little life
> Is rounded with a sleep.
>
> (IV. i. 153–8)

This drama—nevertheless—was not Shakespeare's farewell to the stage. He was still to write three more plays. But in its astutely balanced structure, it best shows how in a tragicomic romance he can accommodate a lastingly pertinent and intellectually fresh, ambiguous, and searching view of life. One hears of a performance of *The Tempest* before royalty at Hallowmas, 1 November 1611. About a year and a half later, it was again staged at court around the time of the wedding of the Princess Elizabeth to Prince Frederick—the Elector Palatine—who had come over with his retinue from Heidelberg.

A fire at the Globe

The stage machinery at Blackfriars made Ariel dive, soar up, and circle over the gallants' hats. A boy might hover, sing naturally—ten feet up in the air—and whiz out of sight. Yet despite its magic and enchantment, its beautiful songs, its Edenic lovers in Ferdinand and Miranda, and its bestial, intriguing Caliban, *The Tempest* was only a moderate success— to judge from the number and style of contemporary allusions to it. The troupe profited, but Caliban did not fill seats as Falstaff and Shylock could. Alive or dead, Shakespeare was to be the mainstay of the company until 1642—but a new kind of tragicomedy had come into vogue.

It is doubtful whether Shakespeare believed his fame as a dramatist had much reality, apart from fame shared by his troupe. Yet he knew he was popular. Young poets imitated or parodied him, and by now Londoners had shortened his name to 'Will' and his main rival to 'Ben'—a curtailing later deplored by Thomas Heywood.

> Mellifluous Shakespeare, whose enchanting quill
> Commanded mirth or passion, was but *Will.*[22]

Law students, around 1610, might debate the merits of Ben's *The Alchemist* and Will's *Cymbeline*. Poets opted to be of 'the tribe of Ben', because Ben encouraged disciples; but the older poet had a large following. People had seen him as an actor: 'Some say, good Will, which I, in sport, do sing', wrote John Davies of Hereford late in 1610,

> Hadst thou not played some Kingly parts in sport,
> Thou hadst been a companion for a *King.*[23]

His wit was lauded by the Oxford man Thomas Freeman, who singled out that 'nimble *Mercury* thy brain'. As one sign of Shakespeare's popularity, works not written by him, such as *The London Prodigal* (1605) or *A Yorkshire Tragedy* (1608), were issued under his name, or else coyly with his tell-tale initials, such as *The Puritan* 'by W.S.' in 1607, or *The Troublesome Raigne* 'by W. Sh.' in 1611.

Yet at least three negative accounts of Shakespeare gained ground after *The Tempest*. The first, with antecedents in Greene's and Nashe's remarks, is that he was only an easy, fluent, imperfect writer addicted to 'bombast' or a 'huffing' style, which was simply a 'horrour' in *Macbeth* (as Jonson used to say, according to Dryden's report of the matter). The second charge is that he was unlearned, and this was made by Francis Beaumont about eight years before the remark on Shakespeare's 'small Latine and lesse Greeke'. 'Heere I would let slippe', writes Beaumont to Jonson in a verse-epistle of about 1615,

> (If I had any in mee) schollershippe,
> And from all Learninge keepe these lines as *cl*eere
> as Shakespeares best are . . .

Preachers, as Beaumont adds, will seize upon him as a prime example of 'how farr sometimes a mortall man may goe | by the dimme light of Nature'.[24] There is a suggestion that Stratford's poet is a little dim-brained, or intuitive rather than intelligent. A third charge is that the Midlands man fails to match contemporary fashion, or the refined, best talk of ladies and gentlemen. Dryden echoed this, but it was already implicit in the stunning work of Beaumont and Fletcher.

The King's troupe had gambled on two poets who had failed in the boys' theatres. They were an unlikely pair. Born around 1584 in Leicestershire to a Justice of Common Pleas, and raised partly at the converted nunnery of Grace-Dieu—which was well known to recusants in his family—Francis Beaumont had been up to Oxford in 1597. From there he had gone without a degree to the Inner Temple, where he gave a burlesque grammar lecture, and then wrote two witty, unsuccessful dramas. Also he met John Fletcher, five years his senior, whose father, as Bishop of London, might have scorned the papists at Grace-Dieu; but the old bishop had expired in debt.

Fletcher, at first, also had poor luck. His pastoral play *The Faithful*

Shepherdess failed, as did their jointly written *Cupid's Revenge*, staged by a boys' troupe. But Beaumont and Fletcher went on in 1609 to write *Philaster* for the King's men, and this made them famous. Aubrey later recorded gossip: 'they lived together on the Banke side, not far from the Play-house, both bachelors; lay together—from Sir John Hales, etc.; had one wench in the house between them, which they did so admire; the same cloathes and cloake, &c., betweene them'.[25] In seeming harmony, they wrote about a dozen plays jointly before Francis Beaumont left the theatre, in 1613, for the embraces of a well-to-do heiress.

The art of Beaumont's friend was sprightly, as it is in *The Woman's Prize* which replies to *The Taming of the Shrew*. In Fletcher's amusing script, Maria, a cousin of Shakespeare's Kate who is now deceased, marries Petruchio, but shuts him out on his wedding night and otherwise turns the tables on him. The public's habits had begun to make Beaumont and Fletcher indispensable to the King's men. Play-goers were choosing the kind of playhouse they could afford to attend, and as the open-air Fortune and the Red Bull (where Webster's tragedy *The White Devil* failed in 1612) were becoming 'citizen' theatres, so the Blackfriars and later the small, roofed Cockpit in Drury Lane became gentrified.[26] The King's Servants had begun to feel more secure with élite audiences. Beaumont and Fletcher influenced Shakespeare's work, as he did theirs, but they avoided problems of society and justice, real maladies of the psyche, or any concern with the individual in relation to the state. They cared about notions of honour, emotional dilemmas, polite conduct in politics and love. Fletcher's plays consist of excitement, emotive dialogue and clever plots. His amoral bent pleased the élite, and the King's men capitalized on him.

Why, then, did Shakespeare bother to write plays with Fletcher? All acting companies normally used jointly written dramas, and most of their poets collaborated. A company's needs determined one's work, although Shakespeare, perhaps, was allowed to do what he pleased. He could be in two or three minds about a matter: he was slightly disengaging himself from his troupe, but also testing the winds of fashion. It is most unlikely that he meant to quit London, and in fact he took part in the King's men's new developments by collaborating.

One work he wrote with Fletcher, the now missing *Cardenio*, we know only a little about. This play was acted at court during the winter revels of 1612–13 and again on 8 June 1613. Forty years later Humphrey Moseley, who by then had acquired some of the troupe's scripts, registered a drama called 'The History of Cardenio, by Mr. Fletcher & Shakespeare'. Much later, in 1728, Lewis Theobald published his play *Double Falshood*—based on the romantic fable of Cardenio in *Don Quixote*—and described that as 'Written Originally by W. SHAKESPEARE; And now Revised and Adapted to the Stage By Mr. THEOBALD'. Is the old Jacobean play at all evident in *Falshood*? If so, the old play may have featured a duke's anxiety over the worth of his two sons, a subplot, and a seduction scene—material ripe for Fletcher, perhaps. But it is hard to find Fletcher's famous collaborator in *Falshood* except that words such as 'Imagination', 'Suspicions', and 'Possession', in their older rhythmic uses, may be the ghosts of Shakespeare's lost words.[27]

Fletcher's hand has been found in *Henry VIII* or *All is True*— though there is no external sign that he wrote any part of this. In Cyrus Hoy's linguistic study of *Henry VIII*'s playtext, mainly confirmed by J. Hope's work in 1994, Fletcher emerges as the writer of only a few scenes, and as one who 'touched up' or added very short passages to the work of Shakespeare, who wrote most of the drama.

The topic of the late Queen's father, Henry VIII, was still hazardous in London. The play ironically celebrates King Henry's getting rid of his wife Katherine, and then picking up Anne Bullen and bedding her offstage to give the nation a peerless baby in the future Elizabeth I. When the infant is christened in Act V, there is almost 'group sex' in the streets. The Porter wonders if an 'Indian', over from Virginia perhaps, has not aroused the city's females. 'Bless me', he cries, 'what a fry of fornication is at door! On my Christian conscience, this one christening will beget a thousand. Here will be father, godfather, and all together' (v. iii. 34–6). That bawdry suits Henry's sly, sensual, opportunistic, unforgiving, slightly incoherent character, and the play unfolds as a documentary romance of a new genre. In 1613 Sir Henry Wotton, a sensitive diplomat (and tireless letter-writer), was impressed. This stage-play, he felt, was 'sufficient in truth within a while to make greatness very familiar, if not ridiculous.'[28]

Buckingham, Katherine, and Wolsey—who fall out of Henry's graces—gain in inwardness only when 'divorced' or excluded by the state. Their acts of repentance are moving, but are unlike the reconciliations in *Cymbeline* or *The Winter's Tale*. Here society is not renewed by its spiritual conversions. The author's pessimism is implicit throughout, especially in an acid view of statecraft, though an undercurrent of gloom is balanced by pageantry, lively gossip, and the panegyrics in Act V over Queen Elizabeth's and King James's reigns in time ahead.

Shakespeare's pessimism—as he considers human motives, obsessions, and the will—is even more obvious in a sinister tale about the influence of passion and war over men's minds, which he sketched in *The Two Noble Kinsmen*. His portion of the writing probably included Act I, the bulk of Act V, and one or two of the opening scenes in Acts II and III. He and Fletcher had set about dramatizing Chaucer's descriptive, rather undramatic *The Knight's Tale*—already used lightly in the *Dream*—which focuses in part on the rivalry of the two knights Palamon and Arcite for Emelye's love. Fletcher did his best to follow Chaucer's tale. Departing from it, Shakespeare creates an equivalent, glistening brilliance in his ritualistic Act I, which has some of his finest writing. His talent had not faded in 1612 or 1613, and his collaborate work suggests he might have found a new dialectic of enquiry and new dramatic forms, if his career had lasted. In *Kinsmen*, his verse is powerfully evocative. Theseus, on his way to be married, is stopped by three widowed Queens of Thebes, who tell him that he will never think of their just, urgent need for his help, once he is in Hippolyta's bed.

'Our suit shall be neglected', cries the First Queen, in one of the last set speeches from Shakespeare's pen:

> when her arms,
> Able to lock Jove from a synod, shall
> By warranting moonlight corslet thee! O when
> Her twinning cherries shall their sweetness fall
> Upon thy tasteful lips, what wilt thou think
> Of rotten kings or blubbered queens? What care
> For what thou feel'st not, what thou feel'st being able
> To make Mars spurn his drum? O, if thou couch

> But one night with her, every hour in't will
> Take hostage of thee for a hundred, and
> Thou shalt remember nothing more than what
> That banquet bids thee to.
>
>   (I. i. 174–85)

'To thee no star be dark', the Queens later hail Theseus. 'Both heaven and earth friend thee for ever.'

His collaborator did not try to match that elegance. Fletcher works up Palamon and Arcite's friendship, their *au courant* talk, Emily's bemused love and a sub-plot about madness, infatuation, and sex. His medieval knights become Jacobean courtiers—Palamon, as critics notice, is like the bed-hopping Pharamond in Beaumont and Fletcher's *Philaster*. In the subplot about a Jailer's Daughter whose love for Palamon leads to her madness, Fletcher sets city against the country, exalting an urban aristocracy at the expense of showing rural folk as quaint or naïve, and thus he surely appeals to élite play-goers. His writing in the sub-plot is quick, depthless, and nasty, if not amoral—and thanks to him, this play reflects an absolute ending of the 'Elizabethan compromise', or that vital, social cohesion in audiences which once led dramatists to write for all ranks.[29]

Excluded from the Folio of the older poet's works, *The Two Noble Kinsmen* was printed in a quarto, of 1634, by Thomas Coates as having been

> Written by the memorable Worthies
> of their time;
> $\left\{ \begin{array}{l} \text{M}^r \ \textit{John Fletcher, and} \\ \text{M}^r \ \textit{William Shak}\textbf{\textit{s}}\textit{peare.} \end{array} \right\}$ Gent.

Though it comes first alphabetically, Fletcher's name is probably mentioned first because he had written most of the drama.

🦋

In the spring of 1613, by which time two or three of these plays were finished, Shakespeare bought his first property in London. This was the Blackfriars gatehouse, which as the name suggests stretched over a gate in the thick eastern wall of the priory complex. As a centre of intrigue and a hideaway for priests, it had an almost visible history: 'it hath sundry back-dores and bye-wayes, and many secret vaults and corners', Richard Frith, of the Blackfriars district, had once told the authorities. A priest might handily escape through 'secret passages towards the water'—and only a few paces down St Andrew's Hill, one came to Puddle Wharf, waiting boatmen, and the flowing Thames.

On 10 March 1613, Shakespeare agreed to pay the gatehouse's owner, Henry Walker, a citizen and minstrel of London, £140—or perhaps more than the cost of his New Place. A day later, he put up £80 in cash and signed a mortgage deed, stipulating that the balance would be paid on 29 September (Michaelmas), but the mortgage was still unpaid when he died.

In business deals he could be lax, but he also took peculiar pains here. The title deed shows that he had three co-purchasers, William Johnson, John Jackson, and John Hemmyng, none of whom put up a penny. The latter presumably was his colleague in the King's troupe, Johnson was landlord at the Mermaid, and Jackson perhaps was the man who had wed the sister-in-law of Elias James, the young brewer. One effect of this arrangement was that Anne Shakespeare was denied a dower right in the gatehouse, even if her husband died intestate. In English common law, a widow was barred from a claim on property of which her husband was not the sole proprietor. It is said, in a modern account of the purchase, that this was a speculative investment, 'pure and simple', because the poet had a tenant at the gatehouse.[30] But that badly neglects dates. The tenant, John Robinson, was there in 1616. Three years earlier, Shakespeare possibly had other aims and requirements. He was to stay over in London for weeks, as we know from Greene's *Diary*, and as a *pied-à-terre* the gatehouse would have been on the doorstep of one theatre, and just across the water from the Globe. His troupe's stock of his playbooks was close at hand, and there is no sign that he did not, at first, aim to live and work at Blackfriars.

Still, a disaster may have affected his plans. This occurred less than four months after his new purchase on a day when the Globe was crowded. At the thatched amphitheatre on Tuesday, 29 June 1613, the players had a new drama called *All is True*, 'representing some principal pieces of the reign of Henry VIII', as Sir Henry Wotton wrote on 2 July. The phrase 'a new play' may only mean that *Henry VIII* was then relatively new, since on 4 July Henry Bluett, a young merchant, wrote that the drama 'had been acted not passing 2 or 3 times before'. Wotton, though, best tells us how some thatch caught fire, and flames ran around inside the roof, but fanned by the wind, so that in a short time the whole grand Globe was consumed. The play itself, he writes, 'was set forth with many extraordinary circumstances of pomp and majesty, even to the matting of the stage; the Knights of the Order, with their Georges and garters, the Guards with their embroidered coats and the like'. The garish spectacle, on stage, held nearly every eye.

Now, King Henry making a masque at the Cardinal Wolsey's house, and certain chambers [i.e. pieces of small ordnance] being shot off at his entry, some of the paper, or other stuff, wherewith one of them was stopped, did light on the thatch, where being thought at first but an idle smoke, and their eyes more attentive to the show, it kindled inwardly, and ran round like a train, consuming within less than an hour the whole house to the very grounds.

This was the fatal period of that virtuous fabric, wherein yet nothing did perish but wood and straw, and a few forsaken cloaks; only one man had his breeches set on fire, that would perhaps have broiled him, if he had not by the benefit of a provident wit put it out with bottle ale.[31]

Bluett adds that nobody was hurt in the fire, 'except one man who was scalded . . . by adventuring in to save a child which otherwise had been burnt'.[32] Was he the one whose breeches were doused with bottled ale? Puritans saw God's hand in the 'sudden fearful burning', and a wit produced a ballad on the terrible conflagration:

> Had it begun below, sans doubt,
> Their wives for fear had pissed it out.
> Oh sorrow, pitiful sorrow, and yet all this is true.[33]

Yet almost at once the King's men decided to build a new Globe, on the same site, with a tiled roof. That was to cost approximately £1,400–£1,500, an enormous sum, and each sharer was assessed heavily at £50 or £60, and later more.

The landlord negotiators for the new Globe were Heminges, Condell, and the two Burbages. Heminges had already given up acting, and two other King's sharers—Alexander Cooke and William Ostler—were to die in the next year. Despite his house at Blackfriars, Shakespeare probably felt that it was time to sell his theatre shares. He would thus have avoided paying towards the new Globe, which, with incrementing costs, took a year to build. His shares, at any rate, were sold before he made his will. The limited number of 'housekeepers' who put money into the new Globe may explain why Richard Burbage, then near the end of his days, was worth little more than £300 a year when he died. Shakespeare may have felt that his own new work was of less use to the King's men; and his writing in *Two Noble Kinsmen* is far from Fletcher's mode. That play was staged in 1613— not later than the autumn—and Shakespeare was to be in London again, near his ageing, sweating colleagues. He may not have given up acting, but his writing career was over by the end of the year.

18

A GENTLEMAN'S CHOICES

We make trifles of terrors, ensconcing ourselves into seeming knowledge when we should submit ourselves to an unknown fear.

(Lafeu, in *All's Well That Ends Well*)

Why, thou owest God a death.

(Prince Hal to Falstaff)

We cannot but know [your] dignity greater, than to descend to the reading of these trifles: and, while we name them trifles, we have depriv'd our selves of the defence of our Dedication. But since your *Lordships* have beene pleas'd to thinke these trifles some-thing . . . we hope, that (they out-living [MR. Shakespeare], and he not having the fate, common with some, to be exequutor to his owne writings) you will use the like indulgence toward them.

(John Heminges and Henry Condell, in their dedication of *MR. William Shakespeares Comedies, Histories, & Tragedies* (1623) to the earls of Pembroke and Montgomery)

Stratford friends and family affairs

'*H*e had the good Fortune to gather an Estate equal to his Occasion', wrote Nicholas Rowe in 1709 about Shakespeare, 'and is said to have spent some Years before his Death at his native *Stratford*'.[1] Rowe, one feels, is right in believing that the poet's estate was ample, but the notion of retiring from all useful work was generally speaking not a common one. With energy, health for travel, and an active mind Shakespeare did not spend all of his time at home. He had his reasons no doubt for a long stay in the capital in 1614, at just the time the King's men played at court. He did not hurry home.

Stratford was not a tomb, but there the tempo and scope of his life were reduced, and the exciting and challenging unpredictability as well as the strange illusory grandeur of a calling that had marked him were absent. Public-theatre plays 'were conceived for production on a generous scale before large audiences'—and always there had been 'a need for grand effect and gesture' in chancy, provisional staging.[2] The grandest gestures could fail, no troupe's viability was ever certain, and little had been secure for his fellows in his whole working life.

There were losses for him as he reached his fiftieth birthday in April 1614. His brothers Gilbert and Richard had died almost within a year of each other, and Shakespeare and his sister Joan were the only ones left of the Henley Street family. His Aunt Margaret, the last of his mother's sisters, was to be buried at Snitterfield on 26 August of the present year.

At New Place unfamiliar visitors might see him if only because the house was adjacent to the chapel, and not far from the church. This year a preacher stayed overnight, and to Anne the town allowed 20p. for a quart of sack and a quart of 'clarett' to wet his throat. Preachers arrived to give the foundation sermons—the Oken in September, the Hamlet Smith at Easter, the Perrott at Whitsuntide.

To his immediate neighbours on the north side of his house at Chapel Street, the poet was hardly a stranger. Nearby was Widow Tomlins, whose husband John, a tailor, had once sued the poet's uncle Henry Shakespeare. Close to the widow lived Henry Norman, his wife Joan, and their four children, as well as George Perry the glover. In an odd, stumpy dwelling, its garden bordering on New Place's 'great garden', were the childless Shaws. Later a witness to the poet's will, July or Julyns Shaw had joined the Gunpowder Plot inquiry. He slept upstairs over his hall in a dining-room which served as a bedroom and looked perhaps like the month of July—it had a green rug, a large green carpet, and five green curtains. A shrewd alderman, with funds from malt and wool trading, he rose to the baili-wick in the last year of Shakespeare's life.[3]

Julyns was to prove useful to the poet. Also helpful was Thomas Greene, whose *Diary* this year records scraps of Shakespeare's talk during a crisis over land enclosure, in which Mrs Bess Quiney (the bailiff's widow) and the town's women were defiant. The poet's daughter Judith had helped Mistress Quiney, and the land crisis itself is illuminated by Greene. He and his brother John, who was also active at Stratford, were called to the bar; John was a lawyer of Clements Inn. From the Middle Temple, Greene had been solicitor for the Stratford Corporation, before he served from 1603 to 1617 as borough steward (by patent) and as town clerk. While waiting for a house, he had noted in September 1609, 'I mighte stay another ye*a*re at New Place'.[4] At the time, he and his wife Lettice, of West Meon in Hampshire, and their small children Anne and William, born in 1604 and 1608, were living as Anne Shakespeare's guests, but within a few months they had settled at St Mary's House near Holy Trinity.

Mainly the poet had been an absentee, and local clerks forgot him. That may explain why, at first, his name was omitted from a subscription list in 1611, drawn up to get funds 'towards the charge of prosecuting the bill in parliament for the better repair of the highways'. On a roster, leading men of Stratford are listed in a column of seventy names; against one, the sum of 2*s.* 6*d.* is marked. Far to the right, the name 'm^r William Shackspere' is added, it seems as an afterthought, as if someone had recalled he was still alive.[5]

A year or two later, he was almost too much in the light, and the town's temper was uneasy. His elder daughter had had trouble. In 1613 Susanna Hall had sued John Lane junior, for slander in a case she brought before the consistory court at Worcester cathedral on 15 July. Susanna claimed that Lane 'about 5 weeks past' had reported that she 'had the running of the reins & had been naught with Rafe Smith at John Palmer'. (The 'reins' were the kidneys, or loins. To have 'running of the reins' meant to have gonorrhoea, which did not always denote venereal infection, though that is what is meant in this context.)

Susanna was then 30, with a child of 5; later she is called 'fidessima conjux' (faithful wife) on her husband's gravestone. When Mr Hall travelled, gossip fixed on his wife. Rafe or Ralph Smith, the supposed lover, was a hatter and haberdasher of 35. John Lane himself, only 23, was of an old, respectable, but eccentric family who fittingly had as a coat of arms 'three fireballs, flaming'. His grandfather Nicholas Lane had attacked a man with a crabtree cudgel; and the old man's nephew, another Nicholas, was killed with a cowlstaff by Robert Fisher, who was indicted for murder, but acquitted because he had acted in self-defence. John Lane was rowdy, and the churchwardens once accused him of drunkenness.

But the matter is not so simple. As a leader of the anti-Puritan cause in town, John Lane became one of the five 'gentlemen' who organized a riot against the intellectual incoming Puritan vicar, Thomas Wilson, who was strongly approved by Mr Hall. What is fairly certain is that, even if he also had a personal grudge, Lane—as a leader of anti-Puritan cohorts—had political motives in defaming the church-going, forthright Mr Hall, who had his own Puritan allies. At any rate, Susanna was vindicated. Robert Whatcott, later to witness the poet's will, appeared at the court at Worcester cathedral for the plaintiff. Lane stayed away. Within a fortnight, he was excommunicated.[6]

Susanna herself had defied a church court twice. Unlikely to forget his daughter's troubles whether or not he feared her rashness, Shakespeare was prudent. The times were troubled, and he settled on a policy of strict neutrality in the Welcombe crisis to come. In touch with lawyers and wealthy landowners, he was keenly concerned for his own heritable assets.

The Welcombe crisis, as it turned out, excited most of the town. It was heralded by yet another town fire, which, on 9 July 1614, as Levi Fox notices, involved fifty-four houses and caused £8,000-worth of damage in less than two hours. That very heavily burdened the council, which had to aid those who had lost goods or houses, as well as help about 700 of the poor.

Only a day after the fire, old John Combe the money-broker died; he was said to be the richest soul in town. He left £5 to Shakespeare, who is said to have penned an epitaph on John Combe and his 10 per cent loans—but these lines echo a couplet on usury written by one 'H.P.' nine years earlier:

Ten in the hundred here lies engraved;
A hundred to ten his soul is not saved.
If anyone ask who lies in this tomb,
'O ho!' quoth the devil, ''tis my John-a-Combe.'

Most of the old man's fortune went to his nephew Thomas Combe, to whom Shakespeare was to leave a very personal item, his sword.[7]

It was Thomas's older brother William Combe who hoped to profit by enclosing the open fields in Old Stratford, Bishopton, and Welcombe in 1614. At 28, William Combe was rich, aggressive, and determined, but it was Arthur Mainwaring of Shropshire, steward to Lord Chancellor Ellesmere, who first promoted the scheme with the help of his cousin, William Replingham of Great Harborough. The parish fields, some owned by Mainwaring, had grass for pasture as well as hay for mowing, and if they were enclosed by hedges the arable tracts would all be given over to sheep pasture. Agricultural efficiency might of course result, but Sir Edward Greville had failed with his own hedging plans. There was stubbornly angry resistance to any scheme for enclosing open fields not only because public rights to the 'stubble and harvest aftermath' would end, but because enclosure reduced employment. Sheep husbandry required less work than arable farming (sheep devoured men, as Sir Thomas More put it), and in the eyes of most folk it led to hardship, poverty, and depopulation.

If the plan went ahead, Shakespeare could lose in two ways. The value of his tithe-shares could drop, if pasture yielded less income for the parish. Also, his Old Stratford land was affected (as we learned with explicit details in 1994). For example he held 4 acres 'shooting and lying into Fordes Greene', a furlong to be partly enclosed, and his grasslands in the Dingles and about Welcombe Hills were involved.[8] The tithes and furlongs represented what Shakespeare had earned from a life's work, or a portion of the total estate he meant to leave to his heirs.

On 5 September, Greene as the town's clerk drew up a neat list of freeholders whom the plan would touch, and he described first (though mostly in excluding negatives) the related land-holdings of 'Mʳ Shakspeare':

4. yard Land. noe common nor ground beyond Gospell Bushe, noe grownd in Sandfield, nor none in Slowe Hill field beyond Bishopton nor none in the enclosure beyond Bishopton.[9]

On 23 September Greene next worriedly noted the council's unanimous vote to resist enclosure. As Stratford's executive officer he feared violence, it seems, with himself in the middle. Alerted, Shakespeare on 28 October conferred with Replingham, who agreed to compensate 'William Shackespeare' or his heirs or assigns for any 'loss, detriment and hindrance' with respect to the annual value of the tithes.[10] Greene himself had a tithe-share, so his name was added to the covenant on the advice of Thomas Lucas, the poet's attorney.

With little to lose whether the plan went ahead or not, Shakespeare thus might play a neutral role in any struggle to come. Greene, clearly, was beset by nervous anxiety. Charged to see that the enclosures got nowhere, he had a covenant with Replingham, and might face popular wrath. In this state, Greene kept hectic notes from 15 November 1614 to 19 February 1617—his diary.

In November, he was in London—looking for a more toothy shark even than Mainwaring, namely William Combe. Not finding him, he called upon Shakespeare, who had reached the city with his son-in-law John Hall on the 16th. 'My cousin Shakespeare coming yesterday to town', wrote Greene, 'I went to see him how he did.' The poet was well informed, very precise and specific, but also in an alert, tactfully mollifying mood as the town clerk questioned him. There was nothing for Greene to worry about it seems, as the planners never dreamt of going too far. They had told him, Shakespeare declared, 'they meant to enclose no further than to Gospel Bush, and so up straight, leaving out part of the Dingles to the Field, to the gate in Clopton Hedge and take in Salisbury's piece'.[11]

Such preciseness, it seems, did little for Greene's nerves. Perhaps noticing this, the poet changed his tack. He talked on 17 November in London as if the enclosure crisis were months away (though it would begin in December), and then as if it might never exist. Mr Hall picked up this colourful, changing thread and agreed with his father-in-law. Shakespeare added that 'they mean in April to survey the land, and then to give satisfaction and not before'. One thinks of Goneril reducing Lear's knights, until the threat to herself comes to nothing. Anyway, Mr Hall joined in the reassuring talk. The poet 'and Master Hall', Greene scribbled later, 'say they think there will be nothing done at all'.

But back at Stratford on 10 December, Greene sensed a storm and looked in vain for Replingham, first at the Bear inn, then at New Place. The fact that he hoped to find one of the planners at New Place, in its owner's absence, might suggest that Greene's famous 'cousin' was not so neutral. Shakespeare was close to the Combe family, and, in a crisis of this sort, he may have been tempted to side with men of wealth who had large estates to advance. At Stratford, the planners' cause was at last openly joined by the wilful, ferocious William Combe, to whom the council sent a deputation of six 'to present their loves', and plead with him to desist. Thanking them, Combe would not budge; he might begin, he let it be known, with a thaw, to dig ditches and plant hedges. On 23 December, the council sent letters, signed by 'almost all' of their members, to both Mainwaring and Shakespeare to get their support. 'I also', Greene noted, 'writ of myself to my cousin Shakespeare the copies of all of our oaths made then, also a note of the inconveniences would grow by the enclosure.'

However, on 19 December the frost had broken. Enclosure of the land began. Out near Welcombe, to prepare for hedge-planting, Combe's men dug a trench which soon extended for 'at least fifty perches', 275 yards.

That defied the town. In their response, the council, in the warlike tradition of Quiney who had stormed the Bancroft, made the first violent move while the poet was away. To be sure, this was cautious, or a kind of warlike gesture. Two aldermen would fill in the ditches! They needed spades and good luck—but, first, to be *lawful* in battle, William Walford and William Chandler bought a lease at Welcombe, so they became tenants with rights of common on 6 January 1615. Unluckily, Combe heard that several of 'the better sort' planned to fill his trenches. 'Oh would they durst!' he told the bailiff angrily.

Before they picked up their spades, Greene advised the aldermen to 'go in such private manner as that none might see them go, lest others might follow in Companies & so make a riot or a mutiny'. Out at Welcombe, the two men, as Greene put it, 'endeavoured to hinder the malefactors from their unlawful digging'. The result was ludicrous; the two were cursed by the diggers, and while Combe sat on his horse laughing, were thrown to the ground. So the enclosing party humiliated the council—except they had not reckoned on women. Word, it seems, passed from kitchen to kitchen in the hamlets, as in the town. A small army of women and children came out at night to fill in Combe's and Mainwaring's ditches.

That female protest deeply annoyed Replingham. He found women, in numbers, difficult because they could not be 'thrown down' as Walford and Chandler were. Replingham also had to confront an irate female, since the one woman in town who represented the anti-closure party at a raucous meeting with him on Thursday, 12 January 1615, was Judith Shakespeare's friend Bess Quiney. As the meeting broke up, Greene noticed, Replingham vowed he would give names to the bailiff 'for doing Justice upon the women diggers'.

Despite appeals, threats, and petitions to the justices, the crisis lasted. The Corporation obtained an injunction, on 2 April, against Combe, who did not give up. Far from being stopped, he beat his tenants, imprisoned them, impounded livestock, and depopulated the hamlet of Welcombe, except for his own dwelling.

Back from the city, Shakespeare must have watched developments with interest. In September, Greene made in the diary his most intriguing entry, which seems to hint at Shakespeare's feelings: 'W Shakespeare's telling J. Greene that I was not able to bear the enclosinge of Welcombe'. J. Greene was John, the diarist's brother. Greene started to write 'he', and changed that to the word 'bear'. Why did he bother to jot another person's view of his own feelings? The entry's meaning is still unclear, but it is just possible Greene made no further slip in the pen and used 'bear' in the sense of 'promote' or 'sustain successfully'. Anyway, by the autumn of 1615 Combe had no chance of success, and the poet may have cared little. Even so, Combe was not finally defeated until around 1617.[12]

The Welcombe affair, though, illustrates Shakespeare's wish to seem impartial without being disloyal to friends, and to protect the value of his assets. His daughter Judith's feelings, in the Welcombe crisis, may have been on the opposer's side, though it is not known that she went out with women to fill ditches. As early as 4 December 1611, Judith had witnessed a deed of sale for Bess Quiney,[13] who unmistakably opposed Replingham, with whom the poet had a covenant. If already out of step with her father, Judith was later to alarm him, perhaps more terribly than she knew.

But it need not be true that the poet wanted the enclosure to succeed, or that he cared nothing for the council's troubles, or the jobs of field hands. Shakespeare's neutrality was convincing, and he had earned some rest by 1615. The town did not impugn him because he had stayed above the mêlée in the Welcombe affair, and apart from other concerns, he had the future to consider. That is what his legal will and his late friendships suggest.

Making a will and the struggles of the Harts

With his friends, obviously, Shakespeare might at times be in that alertly relaxed mood in which Greene found him when calling upon him and the selfless, hard-working, outspoken Mʳ Hall in London. The poet did not starve or go thirsty; he enjoyed himself, although with caution and with some purpose. What Aubrey called his 'well-shap't' body cannot—when Shakespeare was 50 or 51—have been what it was at 30. His effigy is not that of an athlete nor of a *bon vivant*, but he put on weight in his late years. That, alone, would not have prevented him from riding. Moreover if he rode between a Midlands town and London, he was perhaps able to ride merely four miles south of Stratford to see his friend Thomas Russell at Alderminster.

This friend was born in 1570. Raised at Bruton in Somerset, Russell was a charming and generous squire (as his gifts, in late life, show) with a fine house in the city. His good nature accompanied him like a benign star, and he had had some luck: in youth he inherited two manors. He had been to The Queen's College, Oxford, then as a widower had courted and wed a lady worth £12,000, Mrs Anne Digges, widow of Thomas Digges the mathematician. Because her house at Philip Lane, Aldermanbury was not very far from Silver Street, the poet perhaps saw Russell in London and met the latter's stepson, Leonard Digges (1558–1635), who wrote two poems about Shakespeare, including memorial verses for the great Folio.[14]

Russell, like Thomas Combe, was a man of some leisure and considerable affluence. Shakespeare enjoyed friends of that stripe, but he also sought out attorneys such as the two Greenes, Thomas Lucas of Gray's Inn, or Francis Collins of Clement's Inn. Lucas lived mainly at Stratford. So did Collins, until (by around 1612) he wrapped up a long, involved law-case for the town and moved out to Warwick.

One suspects Shakespeare's silhouette on horseback was known, at least, at Alderminster. Whether or not his friends often kept him from home in 1615, he had domestic news at the year's end. His daughter Judith was to marry M[rs] Bess Quiney's son Thomas. Even when witnessing a deed for Bess, back in 1611, Judith may perhaps have been betrothed to Thomas Quiney; certainly there are signs of it. The deed, we know, was for the sale of a house in Wood Street which made Quiney independent, and the proceeds seem to have enabled him to take a lease on the Atwood tavern in High Street. It is hard to see why Judith, a young woman in 1611, was called to sign a Quiney deed unless she meant a little to them. At any rate, five years passed before a wedding occurred. On the premises of the Atwood tavern, or nearby, Quiney was to live with Judith after their marriage before taking her to a large, prominent house called The Cage at the corner of High Street and Bridge Street, where he became a vintner and tobacco-seller. He later rose to a few civic offices and became a burgess, constable, and then a town chamberlain who adorned his account (for 1622–3) with a couplet in French from a sixteenth-century romance by Saint-Gelais. Typically, Quiney made a hash of the French verses, which conveyed a pleasant maxim: 'Happy is he who, to become wise, serves his apprenticeship from other men's troubles'.[15] However, Quiney was an apprentice to his own troubles. As a vintner and town servant, he fell from civic grace. He was fined for swearing, then for allowing 'tippell' at forbidden times.[16] Much worse, he and Judith were to have ill luck with their children. Their first son Shakspeare or 'Shaksper' Quiney died in infancy on 8 May 1617, and two boys followed. Richard was christened on 9 February

1618, and Thomas on 23 January 1620. Both sons were to die in 1639, at the ages respectively of 21 and 19.

The difficulties of Judith's life were hardly foreseeable in the winter of 1615–16, yet Shakespeare cannot have been quite free of doubt about his daughter's partner. The myth that he was stunned later by Quiney's behaviour has no relation to the known facts, and it is most unlikely that he was ignorant of the town's view of his future son-in-law. At all events, he was confronted by a situation he could not alter. His daughter Judith was 31, and Quiney 27. They were to be married. Wishing to leave her a marriage portion, Shakespeare called in Francis Collins, his friend and attorney, and sketched out a draft of his will in January 1616. Oddly, the will was not signed and executed in that month.

If planned earlier, the couple's wedding was slightly postponed. The bride and groom both had birthdays in February, but did not choose the month only for that reason. Quiney's problems were grave, and it seems he made a match with Shakespeare's daughter while he could: he married Judith in the parish church on 10 February 1616. Unfortunately, the wedding fell in the Lenten season which began on 28 January (Septuagesima Sunday) and ended on 7 April (the Sunday after Easter), when a special licence was needed from the Bishop of Worcester. The local vicar, John Rogers, claimed the right to issue licences by himself because of the so-called 'Stratford peculiar', or the town's peculiar jurisdictions affirmed by its corporate charter, but the Bishop of Worcester disputed Rogers's right. Hence through no fault of their own, the couple received a summons from the consistory court at Worcester. The summoning official, Walter Nixon, however, was concerned only with the husband. 'The man cited by Nixon did not appear', reads a Latin entry, and either Quiney, or—although this is less likely—he and Judith together, suffered excommunication. So far as the court's main entry is concerned, the excommunication applied only to Thomas.

Clerks, at the time, wrote with bewildering Latin abbreviations, but a marginal note, to the left of the main entry, shows that Judith was cited at Worcester as the offender's wife:

Stratford

officium domini contra
Thomam Quynie
et eius vxorem
excommunicatio
emanatur[17]

That is, the clerk had noted: 'The lord's official against Thomas
Quynie and his wife, excommunication is issued'. This penalty was
soon lifted (the Quineys were able to baptize their first child), but the
incident very possibly affected the bride's father. Shakespeare in his
will left no money for the church, nor a penny for a memorial sermon;
and that coldness may suggest what he thought of clergy who had
struck at least indirectly at his daughter.

It is true, Shakespeare had worse news. Thomas Quiney had taken
a lover in Margaret Wheeler, who died in childbirth and was buried
with her infant on 15 March. Eleven days later, Quiney was called
before Stratford's church court and accused of fornicating or incontinence with the woman who had died ('incontinentia cum quadam
Margareta Wheelar'). At first ordered to stand in a white sheet on
three Sundays at church, he was quickly allowed instead to give 5*s.* to
the poor of the parish, and told to acknowledge his fault in private, 'in
his own clothes', at the chapelry of Bishopton. 'Dimissus', jotted a
clerk,[18] and Quiney, in principle, was scot-free.

The poet may not have dismissed the matter so easily, since Judith
was disgraced by Quiney's scandal. Shakespeare was perhaps angry or
distressed, but that need not have affected him mortally. This spring,
his life did not fall into a neat, unambiguous pattern beloved by popular biographers. For example, he could have had wind of Quiney's
troubles as early as January 1616, when the drawing up of the will was
unaccountably suspended. 'Quiney's trial and disgrace', one reads in
a modern account, 'not only motivated the alterations in the will but
also constituted a shock that hastened Shakespeare's end.'[19] But the
'trial' (a heavy word, perhaps, for a young man's quickly accepting a
light reprimand at the vicar's court) in fact occurred *after* the
dramatist changed his legal will, so it may not have 'motivated the
alterations'.

We know that, by around the third week of March, life had become difficult for those at New Place on Chapel Street. The weather was unseasonably warm, and Shakespeare had fallen ill. Evidence of his illness will be postponed for a little, but it is sufficient to say that he was not at his last gasp, or 'a dying man', by 25 March 1616. On that day, he was capable. Amidst the troubles of the sick room, he was perfectly aware that his legal will drawn up in January had not been signed or executed. To execute the will, he now again called in Francis Collins to whom he dictated so many changes that the attorney had to rewrite the will's first page. 'Collins never got around to having a fair copy of the will made', it has been supposed, 'probably because of haste occasioned by the seriousness of the testator's condition.'[20] But fair copies of wills were then not required, and Collins left other work in the same interlined, more or less scrawled-over state. John Combe's will (made by the lawyer long before Combe died) is in the same condition. E. K. Chambers writes sensibly of the minor changes of 25 March that most of Shakespeare's will's 'interlineations and cancellations are such as might naturally be made either in the process of drafting or on reading over a draft will with a view to a final settlement of its terms. They correct slips, make the legal terminology more precise, or incorporate afterthoughts.'[21]

Shakespeare's will begins with a declaration very similar to openings found in some of the 134 wills, made by other theatre people, which still exist from that time for comparison:

In the name of God Amen. I William Shackspeare of Stratford upon Avon in the county of Warwickshire gent., in perfect health & memory God be praised, do make & ordain this my last will & testament in manner & form following. That is to say first, I commend my Soul into the hands of God my Creator, hoping & assuredly believing through the only merits of Jesus Christ my Saviour to be made partaker of life everlasting. And my body to the earth whereof it is made.[22]

A formulaic phrase, of course, is no sign of the testator's 'perfect health'. Generally, the dramatist's will pictures his estate and a few personal items. Shakespeare has only one sword. He has collected bowls of very fine metals, or accumulated several, such as the 'broad silver & gilt bowl' which he leaves to Judith, though his granddaughter Elizabeth (whom he calls his 'niece') gets the rest of his plate. He does not cite manuscripts or books, as if they did not greatly matter; but they may have been listed in an inventory which has not survived. In contrast as John Barnard of Leeds has shown, one Alexander Cooke, who was also born in 1564, left a will devoted almost exclusively to books. This Cooke, who attended Leeds Grammar School and Brasenose College, Oxford, was a Puritan polemicist.[23] But poets such as Samuel Daniel, John Marston, and James Shirley all fail to mention books or MSS in their wills.

As legatees emerge, Shakespeare reminds one of the Duke in *Measure for Measure*, hoping to control a story that has got out of line. 'Item. I give and bequeath unto my son-in-l[aw]'—hearing those words or copying them from the early draft, his lawyer stopped, and changed 'son-in-law' to read 'daughter Judyth'. Quiney is humiliated by not being mentioned. Other relatives by marriage, too, are ignored. One scholar thinks that Bartholomew's people were then at Shottery, but, for example, Richard Hathaway, a burgess and constable of his town ward in 1614 and a churchwarden at the poet's death, was living at Fore Bridge Street, not far from New Place.[24] For the testator that man is offstage, or does not exist. Shakespeare is fairly hard even on Judith to whom he leaves £150—far less than he gives to her richer sister—and conditions are attached even to Judith's main sum. She is allowed £100 as a marriage portion, but the remaining £50 will be hers only if she renounces a claim to a 'copyhold tenement', or the cottage on Chapel Lane. Judith is left a further £150 if she, or any issue of her body, be living after three years; the annual interest earned, not the principal, will then go to her issue, or to Judith if she is still married. Any 'such husbond' as she then has will be able to claim the sum only on condition that he settles on his wife lands worth £150.

In other wills, theatre men can be worried, mean, vindictive, or even madly eccentric. What is unusual is the urgent extent to which Shakespeare goes in order to guide his estate into the far future. He grants land in tail male, to forestall a division of property in future between daughters and wives, and the main legatee Susanna Hall is left nearly everything. Here, he is as generous as Lear is at first with Goneril—

All my barns, stables, orchards, gardens, lands, tenements & hereditaments whatsoever, situate, lying and being or to be had . . . within the towns and hamlets, villages, fields & grounds of Stratford upon Avon, Old Stratford, Bishopton & Welcombe . . .

All of that, including New Place, the Henley Street tenements and London's Blackfriars gatehouse are to be Susanna's 'to have and to hold'. But he is intent on enumerating her non-existing heirs, who are seen as young males to be born from as yet unborn male bodies. After Susanna enjoys his property for the rest of her natural life, all of it is to go, for example,

to the first son of her body lawfully issuing, and to the heirs males of the body of the said first son . . . [or] second son . . . and for default of such heirs to the third son of the body of the said Susanna lawfully issuing, and of the heirs males of the body of the said third son lawfully issuing. And for default of such issue the same so to be & remain to the fourth son, fifth, sixth, & seventh sons . . .[25]

If these boys are not born, the whole estate is to go to Elizabeth Hall and her theoretical sons, and in default of that to Judith and *her* boys-to-be. Shakespeare, in all this, apparently, feels that his wishes will be challenged, and that Susanna at last can be thwarted. Before listing her many bequests, he adds these words in March, 'for better enabling of her to perform this my will & towards the performance thereof'. For good measure, he makes John Hall her co-executor.

His famous provision has evoked much comment. 'Item. I give unto my wife my second best bed with the furniture' (that is, valence, linens, and hangings, etc.). One writer thinks this must be 'exceptional', but parallels exist in non-theatrical wills. Another says of the bed of marital love, 'And who would gainsay the conjugal affection informing the bequest?'[26] But Richard Wilson's and Margaret Spufford's research, nonetheless, brings a special factor to bear, in that English common law did not always guarantee a widow the dower right of one-third of her husband's estate. A central question is this: *would* Anne, living at Stratford in 1616, be able to get a dower right of one-third of her husband's estate, if we take account of local conditions and Shakespeare's will as we have it? After 1590 in the Vale of Oxford, for example, widows were legally denied the dower right, except on the strict condition they did not remarry. In Stratford and other parts of the Midlands, right of dower may well have been withheld. 'Wills usually provide for the widow with extreme care', Ms Spufford reports; a testator wishing to ensure customary rights for a wife usually expressed her entitlement.[27] (The will of the poet's own lawyer, Francis Collins, does just that.) Shakespeare's 'second best bed', then, may possibly have an indirect purpose, if by acknowledging Anne's existence with a named, specific item, he is able to deny her dower right to one-third of his estate. One purpose of his will, which seems urgent, is to deprive her of power; and this casts no light, of any kind, on his affection for her, or the possible lack of it. He knew the Halls would look after her, but, again, he seems to wish to deny Anne *control* of any portion of his heritable estate.

He adds a few more bequests. His sister Joan Hart is given £20, along with his wearing-apparel, and will be permitted to stay on at Henley Street for 12*d*. a year, a nominal rent. Leaving £5 to each of her three sons, he remembers the names of William and Michael Hart, but forgets that of Thomas. He bequeaths £5 to the obliging Thomas Russell, and £13. 6*s*. 8*d*. to the attorney Francis Collins. Money for memorial rings, at 26*s*. 8*d*. each, is left to his Stratford friends 'Hamlett' Sadler, William Reynolds (the son of Catholic recusants), and the Nash brothers, John and Anthony. Possibly because of recent criticism of his handling of fire-relief funds, the name of 'mr. Richard Tyler the elder', the butcher's son, is now deleted and replaced by that of Sadler. To his 7-year-old godson William Walker, Shakespeare leaves 20*s*. in gold. Not forgetting three actors whom he had known for many years, he stipulates: 'to my fellows John Hemynges, Richard Burbage and Henry Condell xxvi*s*. viii*d*. apiece to buy them rings'.

When the will was completed, he began to sign its third sheet with an emphatic, 'By me William Shakspeare', when energy abruptly failed him. (The first three words are vigorously made.) He signed the other two sheets in a feebler, scrawling hand.

He appointed Thomas Russell and Francis Collins as the will's overseers. His five legal witnesses were Collins, July Shaw, John Robinson, Hamnet Sadler, and Robert Whatcott, but one doubts that all of them crowded into the sick room, and it is probable that Collins, or his clerk, signed two or three of the signatures (which are remarkably similar). Robinson was a labourer, and Whatcott had testified for Susanna in her defamation case. It is said that these two were servants of the Halls or Shakespeares. As an executor of the will, John Hall later had the duty of taking the document to the appropriate church court. Inasmuch as the testator's goods and chattels (*bona notabilia*) were not within one diocese, but in London as well as at Stratford, the executor was obliged to take the will for probate to the archbishop's Prerogative Court of Canterbury in London, where the will was proved on 22 June 1616.[28]

❦

Before returning to the topic of Shakespeare's illness in March, let us look into the consequences of his will and briefly into times ahead. Predictably, the chief legatees to benefit over the years were the Halls. Later Mr Hall fought for an independent-minded vicar against the Stratford council, and gave the church a new, well-carved pulpit, 'which did duty until 1792', says Sir Sidney Lee.

Hall's sympathies hardly extended to irascible aldermen, but he remained popular in the community. When his health deteriorated, he observed his own symptoms with a cool eye. At the age of 60, John Hall died at New Place on 25 November 1635. In the parish register he was described as 'medicus peritissimus' (most expert physician) on the day he was interred in the chancel. His arms, 'Three talbots' heads erased', are impaled with Shakespeare's. Over a Latin epitaph which praises his skill and his wife's strong loyalty, the inscription reads:

> HEERE LYETH Y^E. BODY OF JOHN HALL
> GENT: HEE MARR: SUSANNA, Y^E. DAUGH
>   & coheire
> TER, OF WILL: SHAKESPEARE, GENT. HEE
> DECEASED NOVE^R. 25. A°. 1635, AGED 60.

In a curious incident during the Civil War, Susanna received at her door Dr James Cooke of Warwick, Lord Brooke's surgeon, who asked to see 'the books left by Mr. Hall'. In his preface to Hall's *Select*

Observations on English Bodies (1657), Dr Cooke describes how Mʳˢ Hall showed him those 'books' (unprinted casebooks, no doubt) and said she had others, by a colleague of Hall's, to sell as well. 'She brought them forth, amongst which there was this with another of the author's, both intended for the press', reports Cooke. He was embarrassed, since she did not seem to know Hall's writing. There was tension: 'I being acquainted with Mr. Hall's hand, told her that one or two of them were her husband's, and showed them her; she denied, I affirmed, till I perceived she began to be offended. At last I returned her the money'.²⁹ Susanna possibly did fail to recognize her husband's hand, unless Cooke confused somebody else's writing with John Hall's. Anyway, she 'began to be offended'. The word *offence* had been used twice, long before, to describe Shakespeare's own reactions to verbal injury. This and other allusions suggest that Susanna was not unlike her father, at least in independence of mind, but she apparently lacked his tact, ease, and worldliness.

She did not, however, lack pluck. Her daughter Elizabeth (who for her health had eaten 'Nutmegs often') in 1626 at the age of 18 married a man almost twice her age, Thomas Nash, the son of Anthony Nash whom the poet had remembered in his will with a ring.³⁰ At Lincoln's Inn, Thomas had studied the law, but there is no sign he ever practised it. Inheriting local land as well as the Bear inn, he lived presumably for a time with Elizabeth in the building now called Nash's House, adjacent to New Place. His own will, made on 20 August 1642, about five years before he died, caused much difficulty. It disposed of Mʳˢ Hall's property as if it were his own, and left New Place itself to his cousin, Edward Nash. Taking legal steps, Susanna was to defeat the worst claims of Nash's 'dead hand'.

She had less luck in another matter. Such books and papers as Shakespeare had owned must have gone in the first instance to the Halls, and it is very probable that some were forcibly taken from Susanna. Baldwin Brooks, later to be bailiff, broke into her house in 1637 after failing to collect a judgement against John Hall's estate. This time Susanna's son-in-law was helpful: with Nash, she charged in Chancery that Brooks, with 'men of meane estate', did 'breake open the Doores and studdy of the said howse, and Rashlye [did] seise uppon and take

Divers bookes, boxes, Deskes, moneyes, bonds, bills, and other goods of greate value'.[31] Were these, one asks, ever fully restored to the owner? On that point, the record is silent. 'Witty above her sexe' and 'wise to salvation', reads the epitaph on Mrs Hall's gravestone, and 'Some of Shakespeare was in that.' Susanna died at the age of 66, on 11 July 1649, and was buried beside her husband in Holy Trinity.

The poet's other daughter, Judith Quiney, eked out a fairly penurious existence with her vintner husband, but she led a long life by standards of the time. Somewhat more than a week after her seventy-seventh birthday, Judith was buried on 9 February 1662. 'Judith, uxor Thomas Quiney, Gent.' evidently merited a grave in the churchyard, not the chancel. The latter was getting crowded.

Thomas Nash died in 1647, at the age of 53. Two years later the poet's granddaughter Elizabeth took as her second husband, John Barnard (or Bernard), a widower and country squire of Abington Manor, Northamptonshire who had had eight children by his first wife. The wedding took place at Billesley, four miles west of Stratford, on 5 June 1649. Twelve years later in return for services in the Civil War, King Charles II favoured Barnard with a baronetcy. As the Halls' and the Shakespeares' inheritor, Elizabeth owned New Place and the Birthplace, but the couple chose to live at Abington Manor. Still childless and nearly 62, Lady Barnard died in 1670, and no monument, headstone, or marker from the time survives for her.

The poet had left modest—but not negligible—bequests to his sister Joan, whose husband William Hart, the impecunious hatter, was buried on 17 April 1616. From her famous brother, Joan in all had £20, a life-tenancy at Henley Street for a mere peppercorn rent, plus 'all my wearing apparel', and £5 each for her three sons. Her sons were too young to wear their uncle's clothes. There was also a provisional bequest of £50, depending on Judith Quiney's dying in three years. In that event, Joan Hart would not get the principal, only the interest, but 'after her decease the said £50 shall remain amongst the children of my said sister'.

The lion's share of the Birthplace was occupied by Lewis Hiccox, his busy and quarrelsome wife, and other leaseholders (until 1670 when Lady Barnard left the double house at last to the Harts). While

Joan Hart was alive, the renting innkeepers had ten rooms, as well as a kitchen, cellar and brewhouse, whereas her own share was no more than 'three rooms' (as Jeanne Jones's work has shown) though Joan may have had extra space in outbuildings near the garden.[32] The Maidenhead's lease at last passed from Lewis Hiccox's nephew Henry, to John Rutter, perhaps around 1640. When Joan Hart died in 1646, her boys had settled into the crafts. Her son Thomas's third son, George, who became a tailor, had a son named Shakspeare Hart, who in due course took up plumbing. The Birthplace, meanwhile, was besieged by the curious. The later Hart descendants were helped, not always selflessly, by antiquarians such as William Oldys (1696–1761) as they tried to preserve various beloved 'relics' of Shakespeare. On the whole, they profited very little from their great connection. In recent times, a copy of *Poems on Several Occasions* by Walter Harte (possibly no relation) turned up at the Folger Library in Washington, DC with this inked note on the verso of the last leaf:

A gift from My Dear
Father
Thomas Hart
With manye other items of my
Noble Ancestors [*sic*] Joan Shakespeare
Had it not been for the great
Spirit of kindness of Mr William
Oldys I should not of [*sic*] had the
joy of having in my safe keeping
our great Poets Bible. in the little
Chest with the keys

If genuine, that was probably written by John Hart (1753–1800), a turner and chair-maker in the sixth generation of lineal descendants of Shakespeare's sister.[33] A tiny sketch of a box, or small chest, is drawn under the note. If the box and Bible are ever 'found', they are likely to be hoaxes; and the sad fact is that a lovingly made box, by an eighteenth-century craftsman, could be thought more valuable in later times than an old Bible. The only personal effects of a Tudor actor known to survive today are Edward Alleyn's silver-gilt chalice, seal, and ring. The ring, a gold hoop with a bezel of reddish sardonyx, is two sizes larger than average for the time (equal to size 'P' today); it is hard to believe that Alleyn wore it on his little finger while acting in *Tamburlaine*. As for Shakespeare's relics, they gradually disappeared, and his supposed chair was torn apart to satisfy a souvenir-hunter.

But the Harts, even in poverty, kept the Birthplace. Finally when they sold it in 1806, debts in connection with the house exceeded the sale price (£210), so they received nothing for a historic dwelling they had preserved for nearly two centuries. In 1817, an interview with a direct descendant of Shakespeare's sister was printed in the *Monthly Magazine*. Having sought out William Shakspeare Hart, who was a Tewkesbury chair-maker, the *Monthly*'s editor noted with concern the status of this family. 'In one room of the ground-floor of a wretched hovel lived this man, his wife, and five children', the editor wrote.

In a corner stood a stocking-frame, in which the mother said she worked after her children were in bed. . . . In answer to enquiries about the great bard, Hart said his father and grandfather often talked of the subject, and buoyed themselves with hopes that the family might sometime be remembered; but, for his part, the name had hitherto proved of no other use to him than as furnishing jokes among his companions, by whom he was often annoyed on this account. On the writer presenting him with a guinea, he declared it was the first benefit which had arisen from his being a Shakespeare.[34]

By coincidence, when the Birthplace was bought and vested in trustees in 1847 before its restoration, the Hart family had begun to prosper, and today descendants can be found all over the English-speaking world.

If Shakespeare's legal will fell short of its hopeful aims, he clearly had not displeased his town. He was to be honoured notably with the waist-length effigy or 'bust' in the parish church, which is carved in soft, pale bluish limestone by Gheerart Janssen and set in the north chancel wall. One assumes that the local council, if not the poet's family, approved the effigy's workmanship. Mouth open, Shakespeare stands with a quill in his right hand, a paper under his left, and rests his hands on a cushion. The bust's colours, often retouched in the damp chancel and then painted over with white in 1793, had in all probability shown the buttoned doublet as scarlet, under a black loose gown, the eyes as hazel, and the hair and beard as auburn. Beneath is an inscription which begins in Latin, JUDICIO PYLIUM, GENIO SOCRA-TUM, ARTE MARONEM: | TERRA TEGIT, POPULUS MÆRET, OLYMPUS HABET. (THE EARTH COVERS ONE WHO IS A NESTOR IN JUDGEMENT; THE PEOPLE MOURN FOR A SOCRATES IN GENIUS; OLYMPUS HAS A VIRGIL IN ART.) This legend continues in legible English, although the stone-cutter erringly has carved 'SIEH' FOR 'SITH':

> STAY PASSENGER, WHY GOEST THOU BY SO
> FAST?
> READ IF THOU CANST, WHOM ENVIOUS DEATH
> HATH PLAST,
> WITH IN THIS MONUMENT SHAKSPEARE:
> WITH WHOME,
> QUICK NATURE DIDE: WHOSE NAME DOTH
> DECK Ẏ TOMBE,
> FAR MORE THEN COST: SIEH ALL, Ẏ HE HATH
> WRITT,
> LEAVES LIVING ART, BUT PAGE, TO SERVE HIS
> WITT.
>
> OBIIT AÑO DO[1] 1616
> ÆTATIS · 53 DIE 23 APR.

In addition, a darkly concise legend was cut in the playwright's grave slab, though it was said in the seventeenth century that this was devised by Shakespeare. Nobody has thrown about his bones, anyway:

> GOOD FREND FOR JESUS SAKE FORBEARE,
> TO DIGG THE DUST ENCLOASED HEARE:
> BLESTE BE Ẏ MAN Ẏ SPARES THES STONES,
> AND CURST BE HE Ẏ MOVES MY BONES.

Stratford honoured him, but the tribute paid to him by his fellows was far more remarkable. The book trade had become livelier than ever, and some of the thirty or so bookshops at Paul's Churchyard often stocked foreign offerings. Twice a year a *Catalogus Universalis* listing worthy German and Latin books exhibited at the Frankfurt Fair reached London (such a list, one feels, would have amused Prince

Hamlet and Horatio). In 1622 as it happened, an English reprint of the *Catalogus* with an English supplement listed the following: 'Playes, written by M. *William Shakespeare*, all in one volume, printed by *Isaack Jaggard*, in fol[io].'[35] No such book really existed in 1622, but at the office of old, blind William Jaggard, who once had irritated the dramatist, printers were then at work on the great Folio of thirty-six of Shakespeare's plays. The Folio, issued in November 1623, involved an unusual act of retrieval and restoration on the part of its editors John Heminges and Henry Condell.[36] Eighteen of the poet's dramas were printed here for the first time, and so saved from possible loss. The volume was costly to produce; and its syndicate of publishers, in which the chief spirits were Edward Blount and old Jaggard's son, Isaac, faced a loss. The work was not undertaken chiefly for profit. Nobody knows who proposed it. The typesetting of thirty-six plays, some from printed copy but others from scripts in varying hands and in varying degrees of legibility, for double-columned folio pages, was a colossal task. It may have involved sweat, and we know that it involved urine, which printing-house workers used each night to soak the leather casing of the balls that inked the press. Residual traces of urine and ingredients such as juniper gum, linseed oil, and lampblack are found in the greatest secular book in the English language.

Thrice—in their dedicatory letter in the Folio—Heminges and Condell refer to Shakespeare's plays as 'trifles'. That, it appears, is all that *Hamlet, King Lear, Othello, Twelfth Night, The Winter's Tale, The Tempest* and the ten greatest history plays in the language can be. Three times, thirty-six of the dramas are judged 'trifles'. No word ever applied to the plays tells us more about Shakespeare's life and times perhaps; but, in fact, the editors were theatre men dependent on the goodwill of the earls of Pembroke and of Montgomery, to whom the Folio is dedicated. The word 'trifles' might befit the editors' sense of their own low rank, and the triviality of public plays, in contrast to the glowing worth and stellar rank of the 'most noble and incomparable paire of brethren' whose prestigious names the editors use. The earls were not to be insulted. The first was Lord Chamberlain, and the second was later to hold the same post. They were among the few grandees who aided the King's actors. Plays, so far, had little status or even monetary worth, and few believed that a drama could be artful or literary. Ben Jonson had called a folio of his own plays and poems his *Workes*, in 1616, and people had mocked him by saying he couldn't tell the difference between 'work' and 'play'.

In their preface 'To the great Variety of Readers', Heminges and Condell, however, are much warmer: 'Reade him, therefore; and againe, and againe'. The Folio is also graced by a ten-line poem by Jonson as well as by his elegy 'To the memory of my beloved, The AUTHOR Mr. William Shakespeare: And what he hath left us'. The latter is generous, discerning, and prophetic: 'Soul of the age! | The applause! delight! the wonder of our Stage!' Jonson writes without reserve and adds, 'He was not of an age, but for all time!' If Shakespeare here becomes rather Horatian or a replica of Jonson, he is said as a tragic writer to equal Aeschylus, Sophocles, and Euripides, and in comedy or Jonson's own speciality to eclipse Aristophanes, Terence, and Plautus.

Not the least important memorial poem in the Folio is that by Leonard Digges, who makes it clear, once and for all, that Shakespeare the poet is the same man as William Shakespeare of Stratford-upon-Avon. 'When that stone is rent', Digges writes very instructively in 1623:

> And time dissolves thy Stratford Monument,
> Here we alive shall view thee still.[37]

Such tributes, of course, have wider, more general meanings than one can easily find in Shakespeare's testamentary bequests of 25 March 1616. Nevertheless, when Collins came to see him on that day, Shakespeare had his aims. His will is as open to interpretation as anything from his pen, but it shows his trust in the Halls. He empowered them, with a belief in their ability and perhaps in their generosity. One cannot assume that he forgot his own servants; his will may not express all of his arrangements in March. He tried to see that his estate would not be dispersed, not foolishly wasted in future. He was very specific, in any case. He was not confused on that day, though he was mortally ill.

'For all time'

A Jacobean gentleman who had fallen sick did not wear formal dress. The doublet, in any event, would have been confining and uncomfortable with its high neck, tight sleeves, and a row of close-set buttons. More suitable would have been the long gown, often faced with silk. Shakespeare in his effigy in the church, as one recalls, is seen in a long gown, which hangs open to reveal a doublet with its decorative slashes.

But for gentlemen, there was a very special dress worn 'in sickness or in captivity'. In hot weather, it sufficed by itself. This was the 'night shirt', which was more elaborate than the term suggests, since it had panels or stripes of drawnwork, or beautiful embroidery. Wearing a gown as well, one might receive a visitor or step into one's garden. The poet alertly received Mr Collins on 25 March—but after that he became more feeble.

What caused Shakespeare's suffering as he lingered from March into April? Though one cannot be certain, something other than the plague had struck Stratford in 1616. The year was an extraordinary one with hot weather and a forward spring, and in the strangely warm winter even young people fell ill as the death-rate climbed. On average in the previous five years, about seventy-five deaths had occured annually in Stratford's parish. This year as many as 109 died (if not all of the same cause). One wonders. John Ward as vicar of Stratford later kept a diary and jotted in it, around 1662, that Shakespeare had died of a fever. Ward frequented local taverns, and evidently heard that the fever had been 'contracted' because 'Shakespeare, Drayton, and Ben Jonson, had a merie meeting, and itt seems drank too hard'.[38] Invention runs high in taverns, of course. Michael Drayton was a light drinker, and Jonson is not reported as having been at Stratford. Drunkenness was a topic of jokes—and nothing else confirms that the 'meeting' really took place.

But interestingly Ward was also a physician who, in his enquiries, had some authority for the 'fever' remark. The first editor of Ward's diary, a physician, called this 'low typhoid fever'. E. I. Fripp, an expert on Stratford's records, thought it probable the dramatist had 'typhoid

fever, which killed him'.[39] Typhoid, a so-called 'new disease', was viru-
lent in a forward spring, and it is likely that Shakespeare's New Place
was dangerous because of the fetid stream which ran down beside it to
supply the fullers of cloth near the River Avon. In the nineteenth century, when research into typhoid inspired fieldwork, it was discovered
that the county's small rivulets could be lethal. Dr William Budd (not
trying to explain the poet's disease) followed a small, typhoid-carrying
brook which, he wrote, 'discharges itself into the Avon'.[40] From
March to April, by coincidence or not, Shakespeare's illness lasted
about as long as the normal time it takes for a typhoid victim to die.

His 'fever', by 25 March, no doubt caused alarm. He was made constantly to drink, or he could not have survived into the new month.
Those near him could be infected, and there is evidence that his disease was thought communicable. He was to be interred quickly
enough, only two days after he died. The grave, as William Hall heard
in 1694, was 'full seventeen foot deep'.[41] So close to the river, that is
unlikely, but the report may echo a local memory of contagion.

Townspeople—whatever else they felt about him—took Shakespeare to be financially successful. Few poets had ever had a better
income, and few had been so involved with a highly competitive, commercial enterprise. In the view of some who knew him no doubt, he
simply wrote playscripts after his *Venus* and *Lucrece*. Yet he may have
written less exclusively for the stage than is said even today, and scraps
of 'outside' work have emerged. Did the Sonnets' publisher, Thorpe,
bring out more of Shakespeare's work? On 13 February 1612, Thorpe
had registered 'a Funeral Elegy in the memory of the late virtuous Master William Peter, of Whipton, near Exeter', and this work appeared as
by 'W.S'. Very probably 'W.S.' was a countryman such as Sir William
Strode of Plympton Erle in Devonshire, or the Revd William Sclater,
Rector of Pitminster in Somerset.[42] William Peter had been murdered
in a wrangle over a horse near Exeter. The elegist's style is faintly like
Shakespeare's, but too many linguistic features differ here; no external
evidence links the dramatist with the elegized, and it is only wishful
thinking to suppose Shakespeare wrote the 'Elegy'. Still, it is probable
that more of his occasional verse will be found. His prose may yet
appear in Southampton's or Pembroke's formal letters, if he had a stint

as a lord's secretary, or, of course, we may find his hand in more dramas than the thirty-eight or thirty-nine we allow him.

Why are we lucky enough to have so much of Shakespeare's work? So much written in his time is lost. Of the 175 play titles recorded by Henslowe of the Rose, only thirty-seven plays survive today. The total number of dramas written between 1560 and 1642 must be at least six times the number of plays that survive. Shakespeare's plays have come down to us because he was immensely popular, and, too, he was fortunate. After all, England's population had climbed from about 3 million at his birth, to about 4½ million fifty years later. Despite his actors' many troubles, they could rely, in the long run, on an alert public of ever greater size. Moreover, though his audiences came from all ranks and backgrounds, they included the people Milton praises in the *Areopagitica*, or Londoners who are 'trying all things, assenting to the force of reason and convincement', as the essayist holds, 'disputing, reasoning, inventing, discoursing . . . things not before discoursed or written of'.[43]

London helped Shakespeare to offer the most profound, demanding plays ever given to any city. No doubt, commercial pressures liberated his talent as he worked to supply the needs of actors. But his receptivity and extraordinary insight gave him a unique understanding of human experience, so that all of his works transcend their time. His dramas are inexhaustibly fertile in stimulating new ideas and interpretations—and that they have the power to transform the lives of play-goers and readers testifies not to a 'miracle' but to unique qualities of his artistry and intellect. His intellectual power is felt for example in the strong, subtle, weblike structures of his works, in the enormous variety of his thousand or more portrayals, and even in the upsetting nature of his perceptions and art. His wit and sense of comedy are unsurpassed, but far from soothing an audience, Shakespeare depicts human nature in ways that are at once truthful and deeply troubling. His curiosity about human nature was in a sense remorseless, though it never outran his sympathy for the human predicament. The major changes he makes in using his sources have to do with motive and emotion; he rejects crude simplicities of feeling and of violence, though he ensures that his own stage violence will have the maximum effect. Encouraged by his fellows he gave them what they wanted, and always more in that his dramas brilliantly generate their own renewal and affect people as no other plays have ever done. He challenges the finest skills of a troupe, but it is also true that he amply rewards those who act in his plays. He typically complicates a text by altering the mood, tone, and tempo from line to line, and, in effect, gives an actor a varying inner surface to exploit.

All of this argues his habitual closeness to actors, and probably his need for a group. But his 'myriad-mindedness' arises from his own intellectual and spiritual endeavour, his questing, his hope and dissatisfaction. In the dialectic of his plays he looks for what is valid, worthy, or possible in human nature, and comes at last to a darkening. Henry VIII, as well as Palamon and Arcite in *The Two Noble Kinsmen*, represent the commonness, the banality of our impercipience, faithlessness, and blind, selfish passion, as if humanity's bleak, disappointing past will yield to a bleaker and more tragic future. And yet at the end of *Noble Kinsmen* in Theseus's speeches, Shakespeare perhaps implicitly gives thanks for life itself.

Easter came early in 1616, on 31 March. It might have been that Easter, for all its blessed meaning, had not blessed the month of April. A sufferer with typhoid fever knows incessant headache, lassitude, and sleeplessness, then terrible thirst and discomfort. The features begin to shrivel. Whatever the cause of his own fever, Shakespeare's face in the effigy at Holy Trinity appears to be modelled on a death-mask. His eyes stare, the face is heavy and the nose is small and sharp. Because of the shrinkage of the muscles and possibly of the nostrils, the upper lip is elongated.[44]

It is, on the whole, likely that Shakespeare was so well nursed his miseries lasted little longer than they might have done. But he died on 23 April, and two days later his body was taken into Holy Trinity's chancel, which has ornamental stone knots of foliage, and on the south side, the muzzled bear and ragged staff of the Earl of Warwick. Shakespeare's grave slab was later probably altered, since it is too short. But his sufferings were over, and the speeches of the exiled brothers, Arviragus and Guiderius, in Act IV of *Cymbeline* might well do for his epitaph:

Fear no more the heat o'th' sun,
   Nor the furious winter's rages.
Thou thy worldly task hast done,
   Home art gone and ta'en thy wages.
Golden lads and girls all must,
As chimney-sweepers, come to dust.

Fear no more the frown o'th' great,
   Thou art past the tyrant's stroke.
Care no more to clothe and eat,
   To thee the reed is as the oak.
The sceptre, learning, physic, must
All follow this and come to dust.

Fear no more the lightning flash,
   Nor th' all-dreaded thunder-stone.
Fear not slander, censure rash,
   Thou hast finished joy and moan.
All lovers young, all lovers must
Consign to thee and come to dust.

No exorcisor harm thee,
Nor no witchcraft charm thee.
Ghost unlaid forbear thee.
Nothing ill come near thee.
Quiet consummation have,
And renownèd be thy grave.

THE ARDEN AND SHAKESPEARE FAMILIES

Shakespeare

Richard Shakespeare, of Snitterfield, living 1529, d. c.1560 = wife unknown

John Shakespeare of Henley Street, Stratford, d. Sept. 1601 = Mary Arden, d. Sept. 1608

Children:
- Henry, of Snitterfield and Ingon, farmer, d. 1596 = Margaret, d. 1597
  - Lettice, b. 1582
  - James, 1585–9
- Joan, b. 1558, d. in infancy
- Margaret, 1562–3
- WILLIAM SHAKESPEARE, dramatist, 1564–1616 = 1582 Anne Hathaway, 1555/6–1623
- Gilbert, 1566–1612
- Joan, 1569–1646
- Anne, 1571–9
- Richard, 1574–1613
- Edmund, actor, 1580–1607

Arden

Robert Arden [son of Thomas Arden, of Wilmcote], d. 1556
= (1) wife unknown
= 1548 (2) Agnes [widow of John Hill, and sister of Alexander Webbe, of Bearley], d. 1580

Children:
- Mary Arden, d. Sept. 1608
- Katherine = Thomas Edkins, of Wilmcote
- Elizabeth, d. 1582
- [?] Skarlett, of Newnham, Aston Cantlow
- Agnes = (1) John Hewyns, of Bearley; = (2) Thomas Stringer of Stockton, in Shropshire
- Alice Joyce
- Joan, d. 1593 = Edmund Lambert, of Barton-on-the-Heath
- Margaret, d. Aug. 1614

Alexander Webbe, of Bearley, d. 1573 (1) = Margaret = (2) Edward Cornwell, d. 1624
- Robert Webbe
- Edmund
- Anne
- Elizabeth
- Mary
- Sara

John Skarlett = Joan, of Newnham 1590?

John Lambert, of Barton-on-the-Heath

Hart

William Hart, hatter, d. 1616 = Joan, 1569–1646
- William, 1600–39
- Mary, 1603–7
- Thomas, 1605–61 = Margaret, d. 1682
- Michael, 1608–18

Children of Thomas, 1605–61:
- Michael, b. 1633, no issue
- Thomas, b. 1634, no issue
- George, a tailor of Stratford, 1636–1702 = 1657 Hester Ludiate, 1634–96 → Issue
- Mary, b. 1641

'Edward' b. and d. 1607

Quiney

Thomas Quiney, wine seller, 1589–[still living 1655] = 1616 Judith, 1585–1662
- Shaksper, Nov. 1616–May 1617
- Richard, 1618–39, no issue
- Thomas, 1620–39, no issue

Hall

John Hall, physician, 1575–1635 = 1607 Susanna, 1583–1649
- Elizabeth, 1608–70, no issue = (1) 1626 Thomas Nash, 1593–1647; = (2) 1649 John Barnard, knighted, 1661, d. 1674

Hamnet, 1585–96

DESCENDANTS OF SHAKESPEARE'S NEPHEW THOMAS HART (B. 1605) DOWN TO THE SALE OF THE BIRTHPLACE IN 1806

Michael Hart, b. 1633, no issue

Thomas Hart, b. 1634, no issue. He inherited the Birthplace houses from Shakespeare's granddaughter Lady Barnard in 1670

Shakspeare Hart, a plumber of Stratford, 1666–1747, in turn inherited the Birthplace houses = 1694 Anne Pare, d. 1753

Elizabeth Hart, b. 1658

Jane Hart, b. 1661

Susanna Hart, b. 1663 = 1688 Daniel Smith

George Hart, a tailor of Stratford, 1636–1702 = 1657 Hester Ludiate, 1634–96

Mary Hart, b. 1671 = 1697 Stephen Spencer

George Hart, 1676–1745 = Mary Richardson, of Shottery, d. 1705

Hester Hart = [Mr] Heron

Mary Hart, b. 1641

Thomas Hart, 1673–91, no issue

William Shakspeare Hart, a glazier, 1695–1750 = Mary Southam

Anne Hart, 1700–38

Katherine Hart, b. 1703

Thomas Hart, 1711–46, no issue

Thomas Hart, b. 1698, no issue

Hester Hart, b. 1702 = George Savage

George Hart, 1700–78 = Sarah Mumford, d. 1754

Mary Hart, b. 1705

William Hart, no issue

William Shakspeare Hart, 1743–4

Thomas Hart, 1745–7

Catherine Hart = [Mr] Bradford, no issue

William Hart, 1731–45

George Hart, died young

Mary Hart = ——> eight children William Smith

Frances Hart = William Skinner, a blacksmith of Shottery

Sarah Hart = Joseph M'Laughlin, a tailor of Stratford, no issue

Thomas Hart, a turner, 1729–93; lived at the Birthplace =

Alice Ricketts, d. 1792

Phillis Hart, d. 1742

Anne Hart

Jemima Hart, b. 1745

Jane Hart, b. 1783 = John Iliffe; he lived at Leamington

Mary Hart = [Mr] Clarke

Sarah Hart = Joseph Maule

John Hart, 1753–1800; a chair-maker, who apparently claimed to have Shakespeare's Bible = Mary Richardson, of Tewkesbury, 1765–1835

Frances Hart, 1760–74

Nancy Hart, b. 1767

Samuel Bolt, no issue

Thomas Hart, 1764–1800, a butcher = 1791 Mary Kite, d. 1792

Sarah Hart, 1777–1849 = ——> seven children William Whitehead, 1782–1806, a stocking framework knitter

William Shakspeare Hart, 1778–1834, a turner of Tewkesbury, who in 1806 sold the Birthplace = ——> six children Hannah Potter, 1781–1848

John Hart, d. unmarried, 1821

A NOTE ON THE SHAKESPEARE BIOGRAPHICAL TRADITION AND SOURCES FOR HIS LIFE

It has been said that the year 1616 is an insignificant one in theatrical history. In fact, both Shakespeare and Francis Beaumont died in that year, but the King's men had learned to do without Shakespeare the man while keeping his popular plays in repertoire, and Beaumont, too, had left the theatre earlier. Actors carried on without new dramas from older suppliers, and even the great Folio of Shakespeare's plays broke no trade records in selling possibly 750 copies, or perhaps fewer, inside nine years. Why was curiosity about the Stratford poet at a low ebb for some decades after 1623?

He was not alive to inspire new gossip—and Inns of Court wits (for example) needed to be *au courant* in their enthusiasms. Views similar to Ben Jonson's on his Stratford friend's lack of learning were repeated. That Shakespeare was 'never any Scholar' and that 'his learning was very little' are claimed, by a self-styled 'biographist', in the first formal sketch of him, in Thomas Fuller's *The History of the Worthies of England* (1662); and Fuller's views are echoed in paragraphs about Stratford's poet for the rest of the century.

Furthermore, from about 1660 to the 1730s, with the canons of criticism mainly set against them, Shakespeare's plays were often radically adapted or purged of scenes of bloodshed, of their sensuously strong imagery, and of other assumed faults. As Brian Vickers has written, there is no 'comparable instance of the work of a major artist being altered in such a sweeping fashion' (*Shakespeare: The Critical Heritage*, i, *1623–1692* (1974)). Those who dwelt on his small learning, or his gross diction and imagery, evidently did little to stimulate fresh enquiry into the man.

Useful biographical work really begins with John Aubrey's hectic notes, of about 1661 (but not published until Andrew Clark's edition in 1898), and Nicholas Rowe's short biography which introduces his edition of the plays in 1709.

Aubrey, born in 1626, jotted down what people had told him of the great poet. He knew three members of the Davenant family, as Mary Edmond has shown (*Rare Sir William Davenant* (1987), ch. 2). Stratford 'neighbours' spoke to him of Shakespeare's youthful feats as the son of a 'Butcher'; they were doubtless wrong, but Aubrey also sought out William Beeston (the youngest son of Christopher, the playwright's former colleague in the Chamberlain's Servants), who is the source of the remark that Shakespeare 'understood Latine pretty well: for he had been in his younger yeares a Schoolmaster in the Countrey'. Aubrey twice notes that the poet visited Warwickshire 'once a yeare', and he comments on Shakespeare's personality, appearance, and (it seems) on his not being a 'company keeper', in invaluable notes which today call for unusual caution and tact on the part of critics and biographers. The same might be said of the remarks of Nicholas Rowe, a poet and playwright himself, who in 1709 relied on what Thomas Betterton, the ageing tragedian, had picked up at Stratford, and partly on hearsay, for his 'Some Account of the Life, &c. of Mr. *William Shakespear*', a forty page sketch which remained influential for a century.

By 1709, then, the three main channels for data about Shakespeare's life (through Stratford, Oxford, or London) were being used. Lewis Theobald's biographical sketch in his edition of the plays (1733) acknowledges Rowe, but adds a history of Shakespeare's New Place and discusses for the first time the licence King James I had granted in 1603 to the players. Neither William Oldys nor Edmond Malone completed their lives of Shakespeare. Despite Oldys's interviews with Joan Hart's descendants, and Malone's searches and scholarship, hard facts about Shakespeare's life were slow to emerge. Facts and legends appear in eighteenth-century editions of Shakespeare's plays, or for example in notices by Thomas Tyrwhitt (1730–86) about allusions to the poet in the two Elizabethan works, Greene's *Groats-worth* and Meres's *Palladis Tamia*.

By the end of the eighteenth century, materials for a full, factual biography were accumulating. The known facts hardly exposed the poet's intimate life. But, apparently, the practices of the late Tudor sonnet vogue were forgotten or ignored (as they usually are today), and the notion arose that Shakespeare's Dark Lady and Young Man of the Sonnets were portraits of once living persons. Obviously for some, his anguished private life was on record, though others in the new century doubted that he had sketched in the Sonnets his exact relations with, say, a Tudor bordello-keeper or a lord's mistress. To the notion that the Earl of Pembroke was literally the Young Man of the Sonnets, the Victorian biographer Charles Knight replied in 1841, Would Pembroke suffer 'himself to be . . . represented in these poems as a man of licentious habits, and treacherous in his licentiousness?' But by then not only Pembroke but a real Dark Lady, as Samuel Schoenbaum puts it, had 'sauntered into the best-loved sequence of lyric poems in our language'.

Having unmasked forgeries, edited Shakespeare documents, and studied the order in which the plays were written, Edmond Malone died in 1812. His *Life of Shakespeare* was finished and published by James Boswell's son and namesake in 1821; Malone's fragment is still of interest for its authoritative method and a few, rather cautious, speculations. With much less than Malone's strict sense of fact, Nathan Drake's *Shakspeare and his Times* (1817) and Charles Knight's *William Shakspere: A Biography* (1843) began to explore inspirations the poet may have found in his environment. Malone had given an impetus to genealogical research. George Russell French's *Shakspeareana Genealogica* (1869) was admired for its tables of descent, and more than a century later was praised for establishing the exact 'relationship between Mary Shakespeare's father and Walter Arden [of Park Hall], whose son Sir John was Esquire of the King's body in the reign of Henry VII'. Unfortunately, French, whose pedigrees are flawed, establishes no such thing, and Mark Eccles's statement that 'there is no proof' that Shakespeare was related to the wealthy Ardens of Park Hall, near Birmingham, still holds good, though 'it is possible that Thomas [Arden, Mary's grandfather] may have descended from a younger son of that family' (*Shakespeare in Warwickshire* (1961), 12).

At least two nineteenth-century writers, however, are still useful on Shakespeare's life and locales. The antiquarian Robert Bell Wheler's *History and Antiquities of Stratford-upon-Avon* (1806), which he reissued abridged but with new data as his *A Guide . . .* (1814), as well as

Wheler's thirty-four volumes of MSS now at Stratford's Records Office, have pertinent details. More than an antiquarian, J. O. Halliwell-Phillipps (1820–89) remains the most productive Shakespeare scholar and biographer so far. His 559 printed works, not all of them on the dramatist, are described in Marvin Spevack's useful *James Orchard Halliwell-Phillipps: A Classified Bibliography* (1997). Halliwell also left a sea of scrapbooks, ledgers, letters, and other MSS. Still indispensable is the final version of his *Outlines of the Life of Shakespeare*, issued in expanding editions from 1881 to 1887 and offering, in its vast, crammed appendices, not only some Shakespeare-related documents printed entire, but a description of nearly every contemporary reference to the playwright's father. Halliwell's boxes of MSS and 120 scrapbooks at the Folger, and some of his numerous MSS at Edinburgh University Library, have useful notes on Shakespeare's career, the actors, about thirty-two towns visited by the troupes, play-performances, other shows (including funerals), as well as on plague, harvests, food stocks, prices, and even the weather in the 1590s.

Two late Victorian works anticipate later developments. Edward Dowden's sensitive *Shakspere: A Critical Study of his Mind and Art* (1875) in part looks into the plays for the writer's 'personality' and 'the growth of his intellect and character', but, oddly, neglects the theatre itself. A major biography, Sidney Lee's *A Life of William Shakespeare* (1898), issued in revised versions until 1925, concerns the plays as well as the life; I find the book full, specific, and readable. Yet its commentary is literal or philistine in quality, and, worse, Lee offers suppositions as facts. Guesses become truths. He claims for example that the poet collaborated with Marlowe, and factually errs in his comments on dramas, taxes, and the poet's income. With simpler matters, as in a chapter entitled 'Survivors and Descendants' (in its full 1925 version) Lee is useful, but his work is mainly as badly dated as Joseph Quincy Adams's bland but not eccentric *Life of William Shakespeare* (1923).

Twentieth-century biographers have benefited from the work of their predecessors, and also from a tradition in criticism which has enlisted leading writers in every age since the poet's death. One thinks of remarks upon Shakespeare by Ben Jonson and Milton who were alive in his time, or by Dryden, Pope, Dr Johnson, and Boswell, or in the Romantic age by Wordsworth, Coleridge, Landor, Lamb, De Quincey, Hazlitt, and Keats, or among the Victorians (to name only a few) by Carlyle, Arnold, and Swinburne, by Americans such as Emerson and Hawthorne, or in the twentieth century by Lytton Strachey, T. S. Eliot or, later, Ted Hughes, or in the Irish Renaissance by Shaw, Joyce, Wilde, and Yeats, or by Europeans such as Goethe, Schlegel, Freud, Strindberg, or François Guizot and Victor Hugo. The quality of such diverse commentary has helped to ensure a cultural centrality, and this and the enormous prestige of the dramas have whetted interest in the Stratford man. Victorians displayed biographical hunger, too, but the twentieth century's sheer curiosity about Shakespeare has been incessant and all-permitting. The way has been open for 'pop' lives, *jeux d'esprit* or nutty books about Dark Ladies, or Bacon's or the Earl of Oxford's supposed authorship of the plays, as well as for lightly researched academic works with standard, predictable sections of drama criticism, and for fresher biographies, many specialized studies, works that oppose myths about Shakespeare the man, and for some astute, brilliantly informed syntheses or explorations by writers such as Chambers, Eccles, and Schoenbaum.

The twentieth century opened with three 'vintage' decades for background studies. Charles I. Elton's *Shakespeare: His Family and Friends* (1904) is at least apt and delicate on Stratford's common fields, wider landscape, and the local terms for the countryside used by the poet. Although there are useful later appraisals of the evidence, C. W. Wallace's 'New Shakespeare Discoveries' (in *Harper's Monthly Magazine*, 120 (1910)), is still suggestive on the Belott–Mountjoy case and the playwright's legal depositions, which Wallace and his wife unearthed. Joseph Gray's *Shakespeare's Marriage* (1905) is sane and scrupulous on the marital documents and remains a nearly definitive study of them.

For the spreading contexts of Shakespeare's life at Stratford, Edgar I. Fripp's books are still essential reading. Fripp's four, fairly brief, preliminary volumes, chiefly on Warwickshire persons and locales, are suggestive, although not quite free of factual error: *Master Richard Quyny* (1924), *Shakespeare's Stratford* (1928), *Shakespeare's Haunts Near Stratford* (1929), and *Shakespeare Studies Biographical and Literary* (1930). A graduate of London University, a pious Unitarian, and a tireless student of town records, Edgar Fripp died in 1931. His major biographical opus, which F. C. Wellstood saw through the press, *Shakespeare: Man and Artist* (2 vols., 1938), is sentimental, strongly affected by Fripp's moral and religious beliefs, and full of conjectures (not infrequently persuasive, yet often preceded by 'we may believe . . .' when evidence is lacking); but no one has rivalled Fripp's knowledge of Renaissance Stratford; and the latter work has more factual detail on the poet's local milieu than any other biography. Of basic use, too, for formal records of the town and its council in Shakespeare's time (and just before) are the *Minutes and Accounts of the Corporation of Stratford-upon-Avon and Other Records*, vols. i–iv (1921–30), edited by Richard Savage and E. I. Fripp. These transcribe local records for the years 1553–92; a fifth volume of the *Minutes*, covering the years 1593–8, has been edited by Levi Fox (1990). Other untranscribed MS material on the town, its persons, decrees, landholdings, or other aspects of local history are at Stratford's Records Office. Mark Eccles's *Shakespeare in Warwickshire* does not replace Fripp's studies, but often silently corrects them; Eccles reports on a new Gilbert Shakespeare document and other details and, in a spare style, gives a dense, accurate assembly of facts relating to the poet, his family, and acquaintances. One of Eccles's stated aims (an aim which few in the tradition since Fripp have taken to heart) was to focus upon the poet's 'friends and associates', 'because knowledge of their lives may some day lead to more knowledge of Shakespeare'.

As both Fripp and Eccles illuminate Stratford, so E. K. Chambers (1886–1954) formidably illuminates the theatre in documentary detail up to the year 1616 in *The Elizabethan Stage* (4 vols., 1923). Though by no means superseded in every feature, Chambers's *Stage* has been valuably supplemented by three works of Andrew Gurr, which concern the actors' working conditions, the nature of audiences they tried to please, and the history of the companies to which the actors belonged: *The Shakespearean Stage 1574–1642* (1980; 3rd edn., 1992), *Playgoing in Shakespeare's London* (1987; 2nd edn., 1996), and *The Shakespearian Playing Companies* (1996). Modern comment on the Tudor and Jacobean stage is vast, but M. C. Bradbrook's *The Rise of the Common Player* (1962) and G. E. Bentley's *The Profession of*

Dramatist in Shakespeare's Time, 1590–1642 (1971) and *The Profession of Player in Shakespeare's Time, 1590–1642* (1984) are good introductions to conditions the poet knew; the last two works, with minor corrections, also appear in one volume (1986). A special aspect of his milieu and work is the topic of Kenneth Muir's *Shakespeare as Collaborator* (1960). Among its other features, Richard Dutton's *William Shakespeare: A Literary Life* (1989) has fresh remarks on theatre censorship, and Peter Thomson's *Shakespeare's Professional Career* (1992) offers a chronological and useful, if somewhat distanced, view of the poet's working life and his company's problems.

A scholar cast in the heroic mould of Halliwell, E. K. Chambers, while holding administrative posts on London's Board of Education, had written *The Mediaeval Stage* (2 vols., 1903), then taken twenty years for *The Elizabethan Stage* before writing his authoritative *William Shakespeare: A Study of Facts and Problems* (2 vols., 1930). That this text is still indispensable, despite some faults, is proof of Chambers's quality of mind; the work has a fractured form and a narrative of about eighty-eight pages. (Its index is poor, and a new double *Index* which Beatrice White published separately for this work and for *The Elizabethan Stage* in 1934 is disappointingly incomplete.) Much of volume i of the *Facts and Problems* in its concern with textual matters is obsolete, but volume ii of the *Facts* offers, among other features, precise, succinct entries on the 'Records' of Shakespeare's life, 'Contemporary Allusions' to the man or to his work, and 'The Shakespeare-Mythos', or a listing of hearsay or legends about him from *c.*1625 to 1862.

Equally important in documentary studies has been Samuel Schoenbaum (1927–96), a gifted scholar who taught at midwestern and east-coast universities in the US and served as a trustee of the Folger Library; he takes up the 'Mythos' in *William Shakespeare: A Documentary Life* (1975). With fewer photo-illustrations of MSS but with added data, this appears as *A Compact Documentary Life* (1977; rev. edn., 1987), and remains useful for its astute narrative treatment of the major Shakespeare documents. Especially thin on Stratford and on the theatre, it has questionable remarks (as every study of the life has); for example, it states as a fact that Shakespeare 'chafed at the social inferiority of actors' in the Sonnets; or describes Anne Hathaway at 26 as 'long in the tooth' for marriage, though women in English towns (to cite a mean based on parish records) were often about 26 or 27 when they married; or the book overlooks the fact that Hathaways had settled within a few streets of Shakespeare; or wrongly gives Thomas Brend a title, endorses myths about John Hall and about the Davenants, or includes fiction about the 'Widow Burbage' looking on an event 'approvingly'. Yet its factual lapses are minor, and one adjusts to a format which leaves little scope for actors' lives, or a poet's development. Schoenbaum did not live to write the full-scale biography he intended, but in *Shakespeare's Lives* (1970; rev. edn., 1991), he offered an acidly amused and valuable history of biographical works on Shakespeare (to the early chapters of which the present sketch is indebted). Under 'Pop Biography', shallow works are listed along with M. M. Reese's more careful *Shakespeare: His World and His Work* (1953), but Schoenbaum is typically fair with A. L. Rowse's *William Shakespeare* ('solid middle brow') and other texts. *Shakespeare's Lives* shows each age fashioning a 'Shakespeare' to suit its needs and values. Dispensing with narrative, Schoenbaum's *William Shakespeare: Records and Images* (1981) takes up topics such as 'New Place', 'The Belott–Mountjoy Suit, 1612', or the 'Shakespeare Portraits' in separate, detailed, and well-informed sections.

Several writers bring years of experience, often of a high order, implicitly to bear in critical biographies which do not feature new archival 'finds', but judge the life mainly through comment on the *œuvre*. Books of this kind include M. C. Bradbrook's *Shakespeare: The Poet in his World* (1978), and Philip Edwards's *Shakespeare: A Writer's Progress* (1986), which supplements Edwards's unusual insights into the Sonnets and their writer in *Shakespeare and the Confines of Art* (1968). The recollections of an actor influence Robert Speaight's posthumously published and casually edited *Shakespeare: The Man and his Achievement* (1977). Stanley Wells's work as a play-reviewer, editor, and scholar, and his sense of the ambiguities within the subject, and of those within the beholder, lie behind his *Shakespeare: A Dramatic Life* (1994), reprinted with an added chapter as *Shakespeare: The Poet and his Plays* (1997).

Late in the twentieth century, attitudes to biography and history changed rapidly. Indirectly the ideas of the Annales school of historians in France, as well as works by America's new historicist critics and Britain's cultural materialists, among others, in effect expanded the territory of Renaissance studies. The 'documentary fact' seemed misleading without the social context which was a part of the fact to begin with; it could be argued, then, that Shakespeare's biographers had neglected Tudor and Jacobean society, interpreted documents in a near-vacuum, and neglected the poet's intelligence by explaining him as a 'miracle'. There appeared to be more to take in than formerly, in new editions of the plays (with new dates for them), in fresh and searching performances, or in historical and critical works which impinge on existing knowledge of the life. Bold reappraisals were in order. David Bevington's *Tudor Drama and Politics: A Critical Approach to Topical Meaning* (1968) illuminates Shakespeare's response to politics and society in his day. A radical review of Tudor and Jacobean comments upon him is the topic of E. A. J. Honigmann's *Shakespeare's Impact on his Contemporaries* (1982): 'crucial passages from the records have been misread', states the preface, 'or have been ignored because they clashed with preconceived ideas'. A former pupil of Peter Alexander of Glasgow University, who argued that the dramatist's playwriting began early, Honigmann takes up an 'early start' theory of his own with new, inconclusive evidence of a sojourn among Hoghtons and Heskeths in Lancashire, in *Shakespeare: The 'Lost Years'* (1985; 2nd edn., 1998). In élan and exactness, Honigmann's books remind one of J. S. Smart's earlier biographical studies in *Shakespeare: Truth and Tradition* (1928; 1966). C. L. Barber and Richard Wheeler's *The Whole Journey: Shakespeare's Power of Development* (1986) and Emrys Jones's *The Origins of Shakespeare* (1977) enhance one's understanding of a highly intelligent, psychologically unique poet and his progress. Anne Barton's *Shakespeare and the Idea of the Play* (1962), and M. A. Skura's *Shakespeare the Actor and the Purposes of Playing* (1993) bear on his attitudes to drama and to acting; and, as we apparently become more realistic, it would seem that we can no longer view social facts only as a 'matrix' or 'background' for a biography. A study linking the Shakespeare documents, while filling in with minimal 'background', may not be close enough to the times to explain its own evidence, let alone account for an individual.

Biographies such as Russell Fraser's *Young Shakespeare* (1988) and *Shakespeare: The Later Years* (1992), and Dennis Kay's *Shakespeare: His Life, Work, and Era* (1992) hardly advance our knowledge of contexts, but involve respectable tours through the plays. Jean-Marie and Angela Maguin's *William Shakespeare* (1996)—821 pages in French— lucidly gives theatrical orientation but is slight on the life. Ian Wilson's *Shakespeare: The Evidence* (1993) presses the evidence rather too hard to depict the poet as a crypto-Catholic; but a similar view had been argued in Peter Milward's intelligent *Shakespeare's Religious Background* (1973). Jonathan Bate's *The Genius of Shakespeare* (1997) assesses the origins of the poet's modern reputation with verve and point while asking the reader to imagine, without proof, that Southampton was the Young Man of the Sonnets, and John Florio's wife was the Dark Lady.

Though books compete, Shakespeare biography might be seen as a flawed, co-operative project in which useful works take a modest place in a large tradition starting in 1709 with Rowe's forty pages, and, perhaps, as a project with a fair future. The project values or discards what is offered, without needing to crown or exalt any contributor. Our collective picture of the poet's life is surely best when many people test it, doubt it, discuss it, or contribute to it, and when we are not under the illusion that it is to be finished.

The main repositories of MSS relating to Shakespeare's times are at the Folger, the Huntington, and the Newberry libraries (respectively, in Washington, DC, San Marino, California, and Chicago); at the Public Record Office and the British Library in London, and at the Birthplace Trust Records Office in Stratford. Other county record offices begin to yield new kinds of discoveries. In a sense, the study of Shakespeare in his age is only beginning; relevant material comes to light year by year, or often month by month, and the study of his mind and life is bound to last as long as he is valued.

Three brief guides to MS records of the life, or to what the first Folio tells us, are unusually rewarding. These are: Peter W. M. Blayney's *The First Folio of Shakespeare* (1991); David Thomas's *Shakespeare in the Public Records* (1985) and Robert Bearman's *Shakespeare in the Stratford Records* (1994).

NOTES

Unless otherwise stated, the place of publication is London. In addition to short play-titles, the following abbreviations are used in the notes:

Bearman	Robert Bearman, *Shakespeare in the Stratford Records* (Stratford-upon-Avon, 1994)
Diary	*Henslowe's Diary*, ed. R. A. Foakes and R. T. Rickert (Cambridge, 1961)
EKC, *Facts*	E. K. Chambers, *William Shakespeare: A Study of Facts and Problems*, 2 vols. (Oxford, 1930)
EKC, *Stage*	E. K. Chambers, *The Elizabethan Stage*, 4 vols. (Oxford, 1923)
Gurr, *Companies*	Andrew Gurr, *The Shakespearian Playing Companies* (Oxford, 1996)
Lost Years	E. A. J. Honigmann, *Shakespeare: The 'Lost Years'* (Manchester, 1985)
M&A	*Minutes and Accounts of the Corporation of Stratford-upon-Avon and Other Records 1553–1620*: vols. i–iv, *1553–1592*, ed. Richard Savage and Edgar I. Fripp (Oxford, 1921–30); vol. v, *1593–1598*, ed. Levi Fox (Hertford, 1990)
ME	Mark Eccles, *Shakespeare in Warwickshire* (Madison, Wis., paperback edn., 1963)
MS BL	Manuscripts in the British Library, London
MS Bodleian	Manuscripts in the Bodleian Library, Oxford
MS Edinburgh	Manuscripts in the library of the University of Edinburgh
MS Folger	Manuscripts in the Folger Shakespeare Library, Washington, DC
MS Lancs.	Manuscripts in the Lancashire Record Office, Preston
MS Oxford	Manuscripts in the Oxford City Archives
MS SBTRO	Council-books, wills, and other manuscript records at the Shakespeare Birthplace Trust Records Office, Stratford-upon-Avon
PRO	Public Record Office, London
SR	Stationers' Register
SS, *DL*	S. Schoenbaum, *William Shakespeare: A Compact Documentary Life* (Oxford, rev. edn., 1987)
Worcs.	Worcester County Record Office

1. Birth

1. John Leland, *Itinerary*, ed. Lucy Toulmin Smith (1907–10), ii. 48.
2. The parish and manor had been extensive. In the 13th century the name Old Stratford distinguished the chief manor from its various hamlets such as Shottery, Bishopton, Welcombe, Dodwell, and Drayton. In later times, 'Old Stratford' came to be applied to an area around the church including the street known as Old Town. A document purporting to be a grant by Berhtwulf, King of the Mercians, gives the monastery of Ufera Stretford to the diocesan church of Worcester in AD 845. In 872 Waerferth, Bishop of Worcester, leased land belonging to the monastery partly in order to pay tribute money to the Vikings; W. de Gray Birch, *Cartularium Saxonicum* (1885–93), nos. 450, 533, 534. The last bishop to possess the manor transferred it in 1549 to John Dudley, Earl of Warwick.
3. For Stratford and county history—our knowledge of both improves almost year by year—I have found of special use *M&A* (and other council reports at the Birthplace Records Office), Robert Bearman's *Stratford-upon-Avon: A History of its Streets and Buildings* (Nelson, Lancs., 1988) and *Records* (Stratford-upon-Avon, 1994), the papers of the Dugdale and Stratford-upon-Avon societies, and, among older works, Levi Fox's *The Borough Town of Stratford-upon-Avon* (Stratford-upon-Avon, 1953), Sidney Lee's *Stratford-on-Avon: From the Earliest Times to the Death of William Shakespeare* (1902), and Philip Styles's entry on the borough in *The Victoria History of the County of Warwick* (1904–69), iii. 221–82.
4. Foxe's book, in its first (1563), expanded second (1570), or in a later edition, was often chained in Elizabethan churches. But it was costly and the law did not require every parish to have it.
5. For the will of 'John bretchegyrdle Clercke Vicar of Stretford' (20 June 1565) and inventory, see E. I. Fripp, *Shakespeare Studies Biographical and Literary* (Oxford, 1930), 23–31.
6. Eliz. I, 19 Sept. 1560, and her comments in 1561.
7. See the pulpit evidence cited in R. L. Greaves, *Society and Religion in Elizabethan England* (Minneapolis, 1981).
8. And in other spellings in MS SBTRO, BRU 2/1.
9. *M&A* i. p. xlix.
10. It is probable that she died in 1559 or 1560, when the town's register was badly kept.
11. J. H. Bloom, *Shakespeare's Church* (Stratford-upon-Avon, 1902); and Clifford Davidson, *The Guild Chapel Wall Paintings at Stratford-upon-Avon* (New York, 1988). The old verses are faintly visible; I modernize the couplet's spelling.
12. MS SBTRO, 'Burialls', 14 Mar. 1564.

2. Mother of the Child

1. *M&A* i. 103, 5 Oct. 1560.
2. Ibid. iv. 96.
3. Some Trussells left Billesley; one Thomas Trussell (among several of the same name) did well at the law at Stratford and once drew up an inventory with John Shakespeare (21 Aug. 1592).
4. Citing his 'youngste dowghter Marye' first among his children, in his will of 24 Nov. 1556, Robert Arden leaves her the land at 'Asbyes' in Wilmcote and the crop growing on it. She inherited even more, such as valuable reversionary shares in Snitterfield property.
5. MS SBTRO, ER 30/1–2. She wrote neatly on the deed, but scrawled her mark on the much narrower parchment bond. (The deed measures 57.5 × 30 cm., and the bond 37 × 13.5 cm.)
6. EKC, *Facts*, i. 12–13.
7. Ibid. ii. 1–2.
8. ME 19–22.
9. Hilda Hulme, 'Shakespeare of Stratford', *Review of English Studies*, 10 (1959), 24.
10. *M&A* iii. 25.
11. Leeds Barroll summarizes what has been learned, in an era of microbiology, about forms and symptoms of bubonic and pneumonic plague in modern epidemics, in *Politics, Plague, and Shakespeare's Theater* (Ithaca, NY, 1991), ch. 3.
12. This follows the 'old tale' (*Much Ado*, I. i. 203–4) in Halliwell-Phillipps's version, but variants exist.
13. Cf. *Book of Days*, ed. R. Chambers (2 vols., 1864), i. 332.
14. Phillip Stubbes describes the ideal of courtesy within a household in *A perfect Pathway to Felicitie* (1592), and I have found especially useful on Tudor notions of decorum Lacey Baldwin Smith's ' "Style is the Man" ', in J. F. Andrews (ed.), *Shakespeare*, 3 vols. (New York, 1985), i. 201–14.
15. EKC, *Facts*, ii. 20.
16. MS SBTRO, ER 30/1.
17. Eleven painted cloths are numbered, but only one is assessed (at 26*s.* 8*d.*), at his inventory on 9 Dec. 1556.
18. Richard Mulcaster, *The First Part of the Elementarie which Entreateth . . . of our English tung* (1582; facsimile, Menston, UK, 1970), 25–6.

3. John Shakespeare's Fortunes

1. 'Thaccompt of Willm tylor & Willm Smythe Chamburlens made by John Shakspeyr yᵉ xvᵗ day of february in yᵉ eight yere of . . . lady elyzabeth' (1566; MS at Stratford). This is transcribed in *M&A* i. 148–52, but p. 149 n. 1 is not quite clear as to

the length of his service. The dates matter, if only because his ability to read sums has been questioned. Council elections were held within a few days of St Michael's feast (29 Sept.). Elected as one of the two chamberlains for two years on 3 Oct. 1561, John Shakespeare also served as a director of accounts that were passed in halls on 21 Mar. 1565 (for 1563–4) and on 15 Feb. 1566 (for 1564–5). His senior colleague, John Taylor, supervised the report for 1561–2; even so, John Shakespeare did some chamberlaincy work for at least three years and four months. The council's last recorded debt to him, of 7s. 3d., is marked on 12 Jan. 1568 as paid. The official copies of these reports are in the hand of the town clerk, Richard Symons.

2. MS SBTRO, 3 Sept. 1567.
3. M&A ii. 14 and 41.
4. *Timon*, IV. i.
5. ME 8.
6. See Nora Leyland and J. E. Troughton, *Glovemaking in West Oxfordshire: The Craft and its History* (Woodstock, 1974); I have also found helpful, on the craft in the Midlands, D. C. Lyes, *The Leather Glove Industry of Worcester* (Worcester, 1973), and, for glovers turned wool-dealers, Peter J. Bowden, *The Wool Trade in Tudor and Stuart England* (1962).
7. Cf. W. G. Hoskins, 'Harvest Fluctuations and English Economic History, 1480–1619', *Agricultural History Review*, 12 (1964), 28–46.
8. Act Books for Stratford parish, which are in the Kent County Archives Office; they cover parts of 1590–1616 and 1622–4. See E. R. C. Brinkworth, *Shakespeare and the Bawdy Court* (1972), 121, 128, 134–6, 166.
9. ME 39.
10. M&A ii. p. xxi.
11. *Itinerary* [c.1540].
12. Since Lucy was well known to the borough council, it is of interest that the 'players' sponsored at Charlecote were performing in WS's youth. The Coventry wardens record in 1584 a payment of 10s. to 'Sir Thomas Lucies players' (Coventry Record Office).
13. David Thomas summarizes the evidence, now at the PRO, in *Shakespeare in the Public Records* (1985).
14. Musshem is called 'yoman' and John Shakespeare 'whyttawer' at Easter term 1573 (Common Pleas); M&A ii. 70.
15. Evidently, eleven big-fleeced Midlands sheep yielded a tod (28 lb.) of wool, and Peter Temple, a mid-16th-century sheep farmer at Burton Dassett, paid 21s. for a tod at Stratford. As Roger Pringle points out in 'John Shakespeare: Principal Craft of Glovemaking' (typescript), the Old Shepherd's son seems to reflect these figures in mythical Bohemia: 'Let me see. Every 'leven wether tods [every eleven rams yield a tod], every tod yields pound and odd shilling [or 21s.].' (*Winter's Tale*, IV. iii. 31–2.) Moreover, the shepherds in Act IV appear to be authentic, whereas Greene's pastoral people do not.

16. SS, *DL* 38.

17. The 'Seconde Certificat' of recusancy (*c.* Sept. 1592) rewords the wardens' first text (*c.* Mar. 1592); F. W. Brownlow, 'John Shakespeare's Recusancy: New Light on an Old Document', *Shakespeare Quarterly*, 40 (1989), 186–91. *M&A* iv. 149, 161.

18. Bowden, *The Wool Trade*, 135–6.

19. *M&A* iii. 24.

20. Ibid. 170.

21. EKC, *Facts*, ii. 247.

4. To Grammar School

1. Levi Fox, *The Early History of King Edward VI School, Stratford-upon-Avon*, Dugdale Society Occasional Papers 29 (Oxford, 1984), 16–17; EKC, *Facts*, ii. 264. In formal local records, the King's New School appears for example as 'the free scole' (1565), 'the free schole' (1624), and 'the Kynges ffree Schoole' (1614).

2. MS SBTRO, BRU 7/1. Written in ink (now badly faded) on the flap of the rent roll of 10 Jan. 1561.

3. Bequeathed in 1565.

4. Leicester's school statutes, approved in 1574, are transcribed in M. C. Cross, *The Free Grammar School of Leicester* (Leicester, 1953); see also J. W. Binns, *Intellectual Culture in Elizabethan and Jacobean England: The Latin Writings of the Age* (Leeds, 1990), pp. xvii and 2–4.

5. William Lily, *A Shorte Introduction of Grammar* (1567).

6. 'Of Scholemasters', in *A Booke of certaine Canons* (1571), sig. D1ᵛ.

7. *Sententiae Pueriles . . . per Leonardum Culman* (1639), 1–9; C. G. Smith, *Shakespeare's Proverb Lore* (Cambridge, Mass., 1968), and G. V. Monitto, 'Shakespeare and Culmann's *Sententiae Pueriles*', *Notes and Queries*, 230 (1985), 30–1.

8. Loeb edn.

9. On Shakespeare's schooling I have found of special use T. W. Baldwin's basic *William Shakspere's Small Latine & Lesse Greeke*, 2 vols. (Urbana, Ill., 1944) and four works which, in different ways, expand on Baldwin's research: V. K. Whitaker, *Shakespeare's Use of Learning* (San Marino, Calif., 1953); Emrys Jones, *The Origins of Shakespeare* (Oxford, 1977); A. F. Kinney, *Humanist Poetics* (Amherst, Mass., 1986); and Binns, *Intellectual Culture*.

10. This is to judge from biblical allusions in the plays, a topic illuminated by Richmond Noble's *Shakespeare's Biblical Knowledge and Use of the Book of Common Prayer as Exemplified in the Plays of the First Folio* (1935), as well as by Naseeb Shaheen's *Biblical References in Shakespeare's Tragedies* (Newark, Del., 1987) and *Biblical References in Shakespeare's History Plays* (Newark, Del., 1989).

11. Alexander Nowell, *A Catechisme, or first Instruction and Learning of Christian Religion*, trans. T. Norton (1571), sigs. C4, E3ʳ⁻ᵛ.

12. *A Perambulation of Kent: Conteining the description, Hystorie, and Customes of that Shyre* (1576), sig. ¶4ᵛ (Thomas Wotton's epistle).

13. Raphael Holinshed, *Chronicles of England, Scot-lande, and Ireland*, 3 vols. (1577), i. 243.

14. 'Of Scholemasters', sig. D1ᵛ.

15. If 'Rec. of mʳ hunt towardes the repayringe of the schole wyndowes vijˢ xjᵈ' refers to a 'barring out' (in which the master was locked out and glass was broken) then boys in Hunt's class or their parents would have had to pay the 7s. 11d. (borough account of 17 Feb. 1574, for 1572–3). That sum compares with 5s. 6d. and 10s. collected from Leicester schoolboys for window repairs somewhat later: Cross, *Free Grammar School of Leicester*, 25.

16. ME 56.

17. MS SBTRO, BRU 2/1.

18. *M&A* iii. 150, and iv. 18; Baldwin, *Small Latine & Lesse Greeke*, i. 471.

19. *The xv bookes . . . entytuled Metamorphosis, translated . . . by Arthur Golding* (1567), 'The Eight Booke', sig. o5.

20. See Baldwin, *Small Latine & Lesse Greeke*, ii. 183–4.

21. Camden refers to the year 1574, with respect to this passage in Latin, in his *Annales Rerum Anglicarum* (1616), sig. R7ʳ.

22. W. Raleigh on attire, in *Shakespeare's England*, ed. C. T. Onions (Oxford, 1917), i. 21.

23. Phillip Stubbes, *The Anatomie of Abuses* (1583), ed. F. J. Furnivall (London, 1877–9), 147.

24. At least in Essex, where poaching was incessant; F. G. Emmison, *Elizabethan Life: Disorder* (Chelmsford, 1970), 232–43.

25. *3 Henry VI*, III. i. 6.

26. EKC, *Facts*, ii. 264.

27. ME 108.

28. 'Of Scholemasters's, sig. D1ᵛ.

5. Opportunity and Need

1. MS Bodleian, Arch. F. c. 37.

2. *Lost Years*, 28–9.

3. MS Lancs., WCW 1581. The will was proved 12 Sept. 1581.

4. The possibility that 'William Shakeshafte' was the poet has been discussed often, notably in Oliver Baker's *In Shakespeare's Warwickshire and the Unknown Years* (1937), E. K. Chambers's *Shakespearean Gleanings* (Oxford, 1944), and Robert Stevenson's *Shakespeare's Religious Frontier* (The Hague, 1958), and, with a strong negative answer, by Douglas Hamer in *Review of English Studies*, 21 (1970), 41–8. In 1985 Honigmann, in *Lost Years*, replied to Hamer with fresh research, and in part

focused on Stratford's series of Lancashire-bred schoolmasters in WS's time, in particular on John Cottom in relation to Lancashire recusants such as the Hoghtons. But families of 'Shakeshafte' lived in the north (as the Preston Burgess Rolls show), and the identity with Shakespeare, so far, has not been capable of proof or disproof. Richard Wilson adds a lively essay to the debate (in *TLS*, 19 Dec. 1997, pp. 11–13), but settles nothing.

5. C. Broadbent comments on topographical images in 'Shakespeare and Shakeshaft', *Notes and Queries*, 201 (1956), 154–7.

6. *M&A* iii. 39.

7. See E. I. Fripp, *Shakespeare's Haunts Near Stratford* (Oxford, 1929), 30–1; John Pace, in fact, figures as a creditor (not a 'witness') in Richard Hathaway's will.

8. This occurred on 20 Nov. 1589.

9. J. K. Walton, *Lancashire: A Social History, 1558–1939* (Manchester, 1987), 13; J. J. Bagley, *The Earls of Derby 1485–1985* (1985), 64.

10. 6 Dec. 1571; Ferdinando, Lord Strange was then about 11 or 12; he was born in London in 1559 or 1560.

11. Francis Peck, *Desiderata Curiosa* (1779), 116 (15 Mar. 1582), 141–2 (16 Dec. 1583), and 147 (21 Mar. 1584).

12. Cf. Stevenson, *Shakespeare's Religious Frontier*, 75.

13. Joseph Gillow, *The Haydock Papers* (1888), 3–5; Peter Aughton, *North Meols and Southport: A History* (Preston, 1989), 42–3.

14. MS Lancs., DDHe 11. 93 and DDHe 28. 44. The signatures are in witness to a feoffment of 1591 and to a conveyance of 1608, both with Robert Hesketh, Esq. as recipient.

15. Inventory of 16 Nov. 1620.

16. Cf. Broadbent, 'Shakespeare and Shakeshaft', 155–7.

17. *Lost Years*, 34.

18. Sir Thomas Hesketh (d. 1588), his son and heir Robert, and Ferdinando, Lord Strange appear in household books of the fourth Earl of Derby: 'Sondaye S[r] Tho. Hesketh & his sone'; 'on Wednesday my L. Strandge' (1587); 'Sondaie M[r] Rob[te] Hesketh at dinner and many others'; 'Thursdaie my L. & Lady Strange went to dinner at Rufford' (early in 1589). These social relationships had long antecedents; though often in London, the player–patron Ferdinando was intimate with the Heskeths; *The Stanley Papers*, pt. 11, *The Derby Household Books*, ed. F. R. Raines, Chetham Society xxxi (Manchester, 1853), 47, 75–6.

19. Bagley, *The Earls of Derby*, 74; *Lost Years*, 34–5.

6. Love and Early Marriage

1. W. G. Hoskins, 'Harvest Fluctuations and English Economic History, 1480–1619' *Agricultural History Review*, 12 (1964), 28–46.

2. *M&A* iii. 129.

3. Richard Hathaway's will was made on 1 Sept. 1581; he was buried on the 7th. A pun on 'Hathaway' in Sonnet 145 was first suggested by Andrew Gurr, in 'Shakespeare's First Poem: Sonnet 145', *Essays in Criticism*, 21 (1971), 221–6.

4. *M&A* ii. p. xiii; ME 68.

5. *M&A* iv. 149 and 162.

6. Transcribed and edited by C. J. Sisson, in 'Shakespeare's Friends: Hathaways and Burmans of Shottery', *Shakespeare Survey*, 12 (1959), 95–106, esp. 96–7; ME 78 emends 'Bordon' to 'Baldon Hill' ('Balgandum' in a Saxon charter). Still useful on the Shottery milieu is E. I. Fripp's 'Neighbours of the Hathaways', in his *Shakespeare's Haunts Near Stratford* (Oxford, 1929), in connection with the borough *Minutes and Accounts*.

7. This is so in the probate copy of his will.

8. EKC, *Facts*, ii. 42, 25 Mar. 1601.

9. Whittington, in 1601, leaves 20s. to 'John Pace, of Shottre, the elder, with whom I sojorne', and this seems to be the 'John Pace of Shottery' who had wed Annys Debdale on 20 Oct. 1578.

10. MS SBTRO, 'Baptismes'; ME 69.

11. ME 31.

12. EKC, *Facts*, ii. 44.

13. Legally boys could marry at 14, and girls at 12. Parents could arrange for espousals, but we have no sign that WS's marriage was so arranged.

14. Cited in ME 65. One of the best studies of these events is still J. W. Gray's *Shakespeare's Marriage* (1905), ch. 2, which has a photo-facsimile of the licence with its squeezed, poorly written 'whateley'.

15. Most transcripts of the bond are inaccurate; Gray, *Shakespeare's Marriage*, facing p. 9, offers a facsimile.

16. ME 66.

17. Nicholas Rowe, 'Some Account of the Life, &c. of Mr. *William Shakespear*', in Shakespeare, *Works*, ed. Rowe, 6 vols. (1709), i. iv.

18. Cf. E. I. Fripp, *Shakespeare: Man and Artist*, 2 vols. (Oxford, 1964), i. 193.

19. *Works*, ed. Rowe, i. pp. iv–v. Lewis Theobald, 'The Preface', in Shakespeare, *Works*, ed. Theobald, 7 vols. (1733), i. vi.

20. MS SBTRO, BRU 2/1 (11 Jan. 1584).

21. Surrey, 'A complaint by night', line 10; Spenser, 'October', lines 112–18.

22. Worcs.: *Index to Worcester Wills*, ii. 130, no. 104, Inventory of Lewis Hiccox, 9 July 1627; Jeanne E. Jones, 'Lewis Hiccox and Shakespeare's Birthplace', *Notes and Queries*, 239 (1994), 497–502.

23. EKC, *Stage*, ii. 118–21.

7. To London—and the Amphitheatre Players

1. Urban historians have advanced our knowledge of Tudor and Jacobean London in detail; many former views are no longer tenable. On the capital, I have found especially useful D. M. Palliser, 'London and the Towns' in his *The Age of Elizabeth* (1983); Ian W. Archer, *The Pursuit of Stability: Social Relations in Elizabethan London* (Cambridge, 1991); Jeremy Boulton, *Neighbourhood and Society: A London Suburb in the Seventeenth Century* (Cambridge, 1987); and A. L. Beier and Roger Finlay (eds.), *London 1500–1700* (1986). Despite their datedness, T. F. Ordish's *Shakespeare's London* (2nd edn., 1904) and H. T. Stephenson's *Shakespeare's London* (New York, 1905) are helpful on urban allusions in the plays, as is I. L. Matus's *The Living Record* (Basingstoke, 1991). For Stow's invaluable texts, of 1598 and 1603, I have, as a rule, used John Stow, *A Survey of London*, ed. C. L. Kingsford, 2 vols. (Oxford, 1971).
2. *M&A* iii. 43. Strange's troupe were at Stratford on 11 Feb. 1579.
3. Ibid. 83. This was for a visit late in 1579 or in 1580.
4. MS Bodleian, Arch. F. c. 37. That WS once 'happened to lye' near a main route at Grendon is not improbable, but Aubrey's details are confused.
5. Stow, *Survey*, ii. 34; John Hales, *Essays and Notes* (1882), 1–24; and SS, *DL* 118–19 and 123.
6. For these aspects of the urban populace, see Roger Finlay, *Population and Metropolis* (Cambridge, 1981) and A. L. Beier, *Masterless Men* (1985).
7. I draw on the studies by Lucien Wolf and by Roger Prior, in *Transactions of the Jewish Historical Society of England*, 11 (1928), 1–91, and 31 (1988–90), 137–52.
8. Reavley Gair, *The Children of Paul's* (Cambridge, 1982), 5.
9. Archer, *The Pursuit of Stability*, 11.
10. PRO KB27/1229 m. 30.
11. John Orrell, *The Human Stage* (Cambridge, 1988), 31–4.
12. EKC, *Stage*, ii. 387.
13. Ibid. 384–92.
14. Cf. 'Curtaine *plaudeties*', in John Marston, *The Scourge of Villainy* (1598), sig. G7ᵛ.
15. The liberties of Paris Garden and of the Clink (in which the Rose and later the Globe and the Hope were built) were those of the City of London, but civil jurisdiction in these liberties south of the Thames had passed chiefly to Surrey authorities; even so, there were several levels of civil control. Ecclesiastical jurisdiction was also important. From 1540 to 1670, Southwark had four parishes. The Bankside theatres lay in the parish of St Saviour's, within the deanery of Southwark, a part of the archdeaconry of Surrey, which was in the diocese of Winchester, in the province of Canterbury. London's control of Southwark declined even further in the 17th century; Boulton, *Neighbourhood and Society*, 9–12, 62 n.
16. EKC, *Stage*, ii. 406.
17. *Diary*, 3.

18. *Diary*, 21.

19. John Orrell and Andrew Gurr, in *TLS*, 9 June 1989; M. C. Bradbrook, 'The Rose Theatre', in Murray Biggs *et al.* (eds.), *The Arts of Performance* (Edinburgh, 1991), 200–10.

20. Alan C. Dessen, *Elizabethan Stage Conventions and Modern Interpreters* (Cambridge, 1984), 30–41; John Peter, in *Sunday Times*, 28 May 1989, C7.

21. Dulwich College MS, IX (1617–22), by permission of the Governors of Dulwich College, London.

22. *Documents of the Rose Playhouse*, ed. C. C. Rutter (Manchester, 1984), 66; EKC, *Stage*, ii. 405.

23. *Merchant*, I. i. 19.

24. G. E. Bentley, *The Profession of Player in Shakespeare's Time 1590–1642* (Princeton, NJ, 1984), 53–7; Meredith Anne Skura, *Shakespeare the Actor and the Purposes of Playing* (Chicago, 1993), 35–46.

25. EKC, *Stage*, ii. 119.

26. They were distinct from the 'Quenes Players' who had visited Stratford during John Shakespeare's tenure as bailiff.

27. Cf. P. H. Parry, 'The Boyhood of Shakespeare's Heroines', *Shakespeare Survey*, 42 (1990), 99–109.

28. A. Gurr, 'Theaters and the Dramatic Profession', in J. F. Andrews (ed.), *Shakespeare*, 3 vols. (New York, 1985), I, 107–28. R. L. Knutson, 'The Repertory', in J. D. Cox and D. S. Kastan (eds.), *A New History of Early English Drama* (New York, 1997), 461–80, esp. 465.

29. See Scott McMillin, 'Casting for Pembroke's Men', *Shakespeare Quarterly*, 23 (1972), 151; *Lost Years*, 59. So far, there is little sign of a director for the early stagings, though the book-keeper could fix doubling, props and the entrances and exits, and see that actors were ready on cue. Teamwork by experienced actors was of the essence; see Andrew Gurr, 'Directing Productions', in his *The Shakespearean Stage 1574–1642* (Cambridge, 1980; 3rd edn., 1992), 208–11. For an argument that actors received 'instructions' from the playwright or a directing figure, see Skura, *Shakespeare the Actor*, ch. 2. Both modern Globe companies, in the summer of 1997, agreed that a director is essential.

30. MS Bodleian, Arch. F. c. 37.

31. In *Playes Confuted in five Actions* [1582].

32. From an anonymous letter of 25 Jan. 1587 to Walsingham, cited by EKC, *Stage*, iv. 304. The hostile writer echoes S. Gosson in *The Schoole of Abuse* on hirelings who 'iet under Gentlemens noses in sutes of silke' (2nd edn., 1587), sig. D2; the numbers sound rhetorical.

33. *Midas*, ed. A. B. Lancashire (1970), I. ii. 39–41, 73–87.

34. A. R. Braunmuller, *George Peele* (Boston, 1983), 46–65.

35. Knutson, 'The Repertory', 468.

36. *Documents of the Rose*, ed. Rutter, 128.

37. In his commendatory verses for John Fletcher's *The Faithful Shepherdesse*, *c.*1608–9.

38. Peter W. M. Blayney, 'The Publication of Playbooks', in J. D. Cox and D. S. Kastan (eds.), *A New History of Early English Drama* (New York, 1997), 383–422, esp. 384–8.

39. Cf. S. Wells, *Shakespeare and Revision* (1988), 20. Few scholars doubt that WS revised, but the extent and purposes are at issue; Grace Ioppolo argues a more extreme case for the poet as rewriter in *Revising Shakespeare* (Cambridge, Mass., 1991).

40. George Peele, *The Old Wife's Tale*, ed. Charles Whitworth (1996), lines 868–74.

41. 'The Failure of *The Two Gentlemen of Verona*', *Shakespeare-Jahrbuch*, 99 (1963), 161–73. Yet in the same year Harold Brooks argued for its 'structural parallels', in *Essays and Studies*, 16 (1963), 91–100. Praise of its stageworthiness, from modern actors and directors, is not lacking.

8. Attitudes

1. He had a share (at least) in writing a few plays excluded from the 1623 Folio. E. Sams, in a polemical edition (1985), argues for the heroic *Edmond Ironside* as an apprentice drama by WS, but it perhaps dates from *c.*1593–6; it exists in MS BL Egerton 1994 (fos. 96–118), which suggests that the play's early title was 'A trew Cronicle History called Warr hath made all freindes'.

2. Nashe, *Works*, ed. R. B. McKerrow, 5 vols. (Oxford, 1966), i. 212.

3. John Stow, *A Survey of London*, ed. C. C. Kingsford, 2 vols. (Oxford, 1971), ii. 73–4. EKC, *Stage*, ii. 302, and *Facts*, ii. 252.

4. Stow, *Survey*, ii. 368–9 nn.

5. See EKC, *Facts*, ii. 252.

6. Quoted in T. Dabbs, *Reforming Marlowe* (Lewisburg, Pa., 1991), app. B, 'The Baines Note'.

7. William Gager, *Ulysses Redux* (Oxford, 1592), sig. F5ᵛ. J. W. Binns, *Intellectual Culture in Elizabethan and Jacobean England: The Latin Writings of the Age* (Leeds, 1990), 350.

8. *Diary*, 21.

9. Minute of the Privy Council, 12 Nov. 1589.

10. *Titus Andronicus*, Arden edn., ed. J. Bate (Routledge, 1995), 39–43; G. Ungerer, 'An Unrecorded Elizabethan Performance of *Titus Andronicus*', *Shakespeare Survey*, 14 (1961), 102–9.

11. MS Folger, V. b. 35 (Halliwell-Phillipps's copy). *Titus Andronicus*, ed. E. M. Waith (Oxford, 1990), 4 and 204–7.

12. It is not necessary to assume that WS was at Stratford when the suit was initiated in 1587. His mother's brother-in-law, Edmund Lambert, was buried at Barton that

April. Edmund's son John ('filio et herede') is cited in the Shakespeares' bill of complaint before the Queen's Bench late in 1588 to recover their former Wilmcote holdings; they tried again in the Chancery suit brought against the heir in 1597.

13. EKC, *Facts*, i. 42. A. Gurr, *The Shakespearean Stage, 1574–1642* (Cambridge, 2nd edn., 1985), 38–40.

14. On irony and implied authorial attitudes in *Henry VI*'s episodic structure, see David Bevington, *Tudor Drama and Politics: A Critical Approach to Topical Meaning* (Cambridge, Mass., 1968), and G. K. Hunter, 'Truth and Art in The History Plays', *Shakespeare Survey*, 42 (1990), 15–24.

15. Lois Potter, '"Nobody's Perfect": Actors' Memories and Shakespeare's Plays of the 1590s', *Shakespeare Survey*, 42 (1990), 85–97, esp. 91.

16. Perhaps one less time, if it is not the 'harey' of 16 Mar.; *Diary*, 16–19.

17. Janet Clare, '*Art made tongue-tied by authority*' (Manchester, 1990), ch. 2; *2 Henry VI*, ed. Michael Hattaway (Cambridge, 1991), 232.

9. The City in September

1. Anon., *Ratseis Ghost* (SR, 31 May 1605), sig. A3ᵛ.

2. D. A. Williams, in *Guildhall Miscellany*, 2 (Sept. 1960), 24–8.

3. *Playes Confuted in five Actions* [1582], sig. A1ᵛ.

4. Cf. Jean-Noël Biraben, *Les Hommes et la peste*, 2 vols. (Paris, 1975), i. 15; L. Barroll, *Politics, Plague, and Shakespeare's Theater* (Ithaca, NY, 1991), 98–9.

5. Worcs.: Index to Worcester Wills, ii. 130, no. 104, Inventory of Lewis Hiccox, 9 July 1627.

6. *Diary*, 283–4 (Dulwich College MS, *c*.1592–4).

7. Ibid. 276 (Dulwich College MS, *c*.1 Aug. 1593).

8. Ibid. 277 (Dulwich College MS, *c*. Aug. 1593).

9. Nashe, *Works*, ed. R. B. McKerrow, 5 vols. (Oxford, 1966), i. 212.

10. Ibid. i. 20; iii. 311, 315–16.

11. MS Oxford, A. 5. 6. (Oxford's chamberlains, unlike the keykeepers, ended accounts at Michaelmas, and items for 1592–3 are in order; Strange's troupe were paid on 6 Oct. 1592—not, as has been said, in Oct. '1593'.)

12. 'Polyhmnia', lines 38–40, on the jousts of Nov. 1590.

13. Nashe, *Works*, ed. McKerrow, i. 287–8; Henry Chettle, *Kind-Harts Dreame. Conteining five Apparitions, with Invectives against abuses raigning* (SR, 8 Dec. 1592).

14. Greene, *Works*, ed. A. B. Grosart, 15 vols. (1881–6), vii. 231.

15. Ibid. viii. 132.

16. *Greenes Groats-worth of witte* (1592), sigs. D4ʳ⁻ᵛ, E1, F1ʳ⁻ᵛ. For a contemporary report of Greene's supposed contrition and moral reform, as well as his last evening and death, see *The Repentance of Robert Greene Maister of Artes* (1592), sigs. D1ᵛ–D2.

17. *Groats-worth of witte*, sig. F2ᵛ.

18. Nashe, *Works*, ed. McKerrow, i. 154.

19. J. Rees, 'Shakespeare and "Edward Pudsey's Booke", 1600', *Notes and Queries*, 237 (1992), 330–1.

20. *The Second Part of King Henry VI*, Arden edn., ed. A. S. Cairncross (Methuen, 1985), xliv and 106 n.

21. *Kind-Harts Dreame* (SR, 8 Dec. 1592), sig. A4.

22. Thomas Dekker, *Jests to make you Merie* (1607) in *The Non-Dramatic Works of Dekker*, ed. A. B. Grosart, 5 vols. (1884–6), ii. 352.

23. *Gesta Grayorum: or, The History of the High and Mighty Prince Henry Prince of Purpoole* . . . (1688), ed. D. S. Bland (Liverpool, 1968), 64, 31–2.

24. *Diary*, 19.

25. See Jonathan Bate, 'Ovid and the Sonnets; or, Did Shakespeare Feel the Anxiety of Influence?', *Shakespeare Survey*, 42 (1990), 70.

26. Nashe, *Works*, ed. McKerrow, ii. 182.

10. A Patron, Poems, and Company Work

1. *The Raigne of King Edward the third: As it hath bin sundrie times plaied about the Citie of London* (1596), repr. in *Apocrypha*, ed. C. F. Tucker Brooke (Oxford, 1918), II. i. 449–51.

2. This chronology remains conjectural; the stylistic evidence alone, surely, is too ambiguous to indicate dates of composition. It is not unlikely that *Venus* was completed not long before it was licensed (18 Apr. 1593), and that Munday and 'Hand D', in turn, worked on *More* before the end of 1593; see Scott McMillin, *The Elizabethan Theatre and The Book of Sir Thomas More* (Ithaca, NY, 1987), ch. 3, and the viewpoints in T. H. Howard-Hill (ed.), *Shakespeare and 'Sir Thomas More'* (Cambridge, 1989). An early date for Munday's work on *More*, however, rests mainly on the assumption that he responds to the city's alien crisis, which became acute in 1592. Until the middle of the 20th century, one objection to an early date rested on a plain misreading of Munday's hand. 'The Booke of Sir Thomas Moore' was bound up with Munday's MS 'The Book of John A Kent & John a Cumber' (Huntington Library MS HM 500), which itself is dated 'Decembris 1590', and not '1595' or '1596', as I. A. Shapiro has shown in 'The Significance of a Date', *Shakespeare Survey*, 8 (1955), 101–5.

3. *King John*, ed. L. A. Beaurline (Cambridge, 1990), 185.

4. MS BL Harleian 7368, fo. 9ʳ.

5. Ibid., fo. 3ʳ.

6. MSS Folger Z. c. 39 (7), and Z. c. 9 (144, 150).

7. Ovid, *Amores* I. 15. 35–6.

8. He is 'Willm Shakp', 'William Shakspe', 'Wᵐ Shaksper', 'William Shakspere', 'Willim Shakspere', and 'William Shakspeare' in his six autographs. See Anthony

G. Petti's transcriptions and his remarks on the rapid Elizabethan secretary hand, in *English Literary Hands from Chaucer to Dryden* (Cambridge, Mass., 1977), 86–7, and the comments in EKC, *Facts*, i. 504–6. Variants in the six signatures have less to do with the playwright's psyche than with the age's lax spelling. On the printing of his name, see Margreta de Grazia and Peter Stallybrass, 'The Materiality of the Shakespearean Text', *Shakespeare Quarterly*, 44 (1993), 255–83.

9. Katherine Duncan-Jones, 'Much Ado with Red and White: The Earliest Readers of Shakespeare's *Venus and Adonis* (1593)', *Review of English Studies*, 44 (1993), 479–501.

10. MS Folger, L. b. 338.

11. G. P. V. Akrigg, *Shakespeare and the Earl of Southampton* (1968), 39.

12. MS BL M/485/41.

13. E. E. Duncan-Jones, in *London Review of Books*, 7 Oct. 1993. Legge died in 1607.

14. *Willobie His Avisa*, ed. G. B. Harrison (Edinburgh, 1966), 218; *TLS*, 17 Sept. 1925.

15. Hallett Smith, 'Poems', in J. F. Andrews (ed.), *Shakespeare*, 3 vols. (New York, 1985), ii. 447–9.

16. *Ben Jonson*, ed. C. H. Herford and P. and E. Simpson, 11 vols. (Oxford, 1925–52), i. 142.

17. *Palladis Tamia. Wits Treasury Being the Second part of Wits Commonwealth* (1598), sigs. Oo1ᵛ–Oo2.

18. See M. G. Brennan, 'The Literary Patronage of the Herbert Family, Earls of Pembroke, 1550–1640' (D.Phil., Oxford, 1982).

19. Simon Callow, *Being an Actor* (1985), 127–8.

20. *The Sonnets and A Lover's Complaint*, ed. John Kerrigan (Harmondsworth, 1986), 441–4.

21. See Patricia Fumerton's instructive essay on sonnet practices, ' "Secret" Arts: Elizabethan Miniatures and Sonnets' (in S. Greenblatt (ed.), *Representing the English Renaissance* (Berkeley, Ca., 1988), 93–133), and the dedicatory epistles in sonnet sequences such as Samuel Daniel's *Delia* (1592), William Percy's *Coelia* (1594), and Robert Tofte's *Laura* (1597).

22. *Works*, ed. R. B. McKerrow, 5 vols. (Oxford, 1966), iii. 329.

23. Samuel Daniel, *Poems and a Defence of Ryme*, ed. A. C. Sprague (1950): Sonnet 47 (1594), lines 9–10, and Sonnet 46 (1592), lines 6–8.

24. I. B. [John Benson], 'To the Reader', in *Poems: Written by Wil. Shake-speare, Gent.* (1640).

25. George Gascoigne, *The Posies*, ed. J. W. Cunliffe (Cambridge, 1907), 471–2.

26. Quoted in *Shakespeare's Sonnets*, Arden edn., ed. K. Duncan-Jones (Walton-on-Thames, 1997), 95–6.

27. Helen Vendler, *The Art of Shakespeare's Sonnets* (Cambridge, Mass., 1997), 6.

28. Kenneth Muir, *Shakespeare the Professional* (1973), 233 n. 17.

29. *King John*'s editors carry on a brisk dialogue not only about its composition

date; *King John* has been seen on stage regularly since the Restoration—unlike *Henry VI*.

11. A Servant of the Lord Chamberlain

1. William Fleetwood to Lord Burghley, 18 June 1584; Sir Robert Naunton, *Fragmenta Regalia* (1653), sigs. C6ᵛ–C7.

2. Having wed Lanier, Aemilia Lanyer so styled herself as the author of a poem on Christ's Passion, *Salve Deus Rex Judæorum* (1611), dedicated to nine ladies of the court.

3. M. Eccles, 'Elizabethan Actors', *Notes and Queries*, 235 (1991), 43.

4. See *Diary*, 21–30; EKC, *Stage*, iv. 316. R. L. Knutson, *The Repertory of Shakespeare's Company 1594–1603* (Fayetteville, Ark., 1991), 29.

5. *The Lives of the Noble Grecians and Romanes, compared together by . . . Plutarke of Chaeronea*, trans. Sir Thomas North (1579); Pickering & Chatto, catalogue 658, item 37.

6. Shakespeare Centre Library, SR 93. 2, no. 6223.

7. *Diary*, 88 (modern spelling). *King Henry V*, ed. A. Gurr (Cambridge, 1992), 235.

8. See E. Nungezer's *A Dictionary of Actors* (New York, 1929), and supplementary data on the actors' assets, inheritances, and purchases in M. Eccles, 'Elizabethan Actors' (four parts), *Notes and Queries*, 235–8 (1991–3).

9. See A. H. Nelson, in *Shakespeare Quarterly*, 49 (1998), 74–83.

10. D. W. Foster first described his computer-assisted work to determine WS's acting in *Shakespeare Newsletter*, nos. 209–11 (1991); later he modified his findings; so far, no one can be sure as to the poet's roles in his own, Jonson's, or other plays. EKC, *Facts*, ii. cites the 17th-century reports.

11. EKC, *Stage*, iv. 318.

12. Steve Rappaport, *Worlds within Worlds* (Cambridge, 1989), 295–8.

13. Dekker, *Works*, ed. F. Bowers, 4 vols. (Cambridge, 1953–61), iii. 121–2.

14. MS SBTRO, 10 Jan. 1568–23 Jan. 1577.

15. MS Folger, W. B. 80 (J.O.H.-P. scrapbook): 'Doll Phillips soomtymes . . . callyd the Queene of Fayris . . . was condempnid at Loondon & whippid throughe Loondon for cossonnadge & so let goe' (1595).

16. See T. B. Stroup, in *Shakespeare Quarterly*, 29 (1978), 79–82.

17. *2 Henry IV*, Epilogue, 8–9.

18. John Nichols, *The Progresses, and Public Processions, of Queen Elizabeth*, 4 vols. (1788–1821), ii. 41.

19. EKC, *Facts*, ii. 325. Augustine Phillips was examined, on oath, ten days after Essex's abortive coup of Sunday, 8 Feb. 1601.

20. William Empson, in *Kenyon Review*, 15 (1953), 221; James Laver, *Costume in the Theatre* (1964), 96.

21. John Stow, *A Survey of London*, ed. C. L. Kingsford, 2 vols. (Oxford, 1971), i. 211, 216.

22. Stephen Greenblatt, *Shakespearean Negotiations* (Oxford, 1988), 42.

23. *Henry V*, ed. Gurr, 12–15, 34–7.

24. MS Folger, V. b. 34.

25. Leslie Hotson, *Shakespeare versus Shallow* (1931), 111–22; *The Merry Wives of Windsor*, Arden edn., ed. H. O. Oliver (Methuen, 1971) pp. xlv–xlvi.

26. See the discussion of topical allusions in Barbara Freedman, 'Shakespearean Chronology, Ideological Complicity, and Floating Texts: Something is Rotten in Windsor', *Shakespeare Quarterly*, 45 (1994), 190–210, esp. 199–203.

12. New Place and the Country

1. MS Folger, W. b. 141.

2. Peter Thomson, *Shakespeare's Professional Career* (Cambridge, 1992), 122.

3. MS Oxford, A. 5. 6, 25 Feb. 1595.

4. *M&A* v. 17–18.

5. The joke relates less explicitly to WS's motto than to Nashe's joke in *Pierce Penilesse* about emending a vow to give up salt cod ('not without Mustard, Good Lord, not without Mustard'); *Works*, ed. R. B. McKerrow, 5 vols. (Oxford, 1966), i. 171.

6. College of Arms, Vincent MS 157, Article 24 (20 Oct. 1596).

7. C. W. Scott-Giles, *Shakespeare's Heraldry* (1950), 28–39, esp. 32.

8. EKC, *Stage*, i. 350; SS, *DL* 230; ME 84–6.

9. ME 108.

10. Bearman, 8.

11. B. Roland Lewis, *The Shakespeare documents*, 2 vols. (Stanford, Ca., 1941), i. 156; ME 69–70; E. A. J. Honigmann and Susan Brock, *Playhouse Wills, 1558–1642* (Manchester, 1993), 107.

12. E. I. Fripp, *Shakespeare: Man and Artist*, 2 vols. (Oxford, 1964), ii. 496, 674, 788, 837–8; ME 69.

13. T. Kishi, R. Pringle, and S. Wells (eds.), *Shakespeare and Cultural Traditions* (Newark, Del., 1994), 134–5.

14. Quoted in Keith Wrightson, *English Society 1580–1680* (1982), 95; the spelling of Ann Clifford's words has been modernized.

15. MS SBTRO, 11 Aug. 1596.

16. David Cressy, *Birth, Marriage, and Death: Ritual, Religion, and the Life-Cycle in Tudor and Stuart England* (Oxford, 1997), 393.

17. PRO, SP 12/79.

18. Ibid.

19. EKC, *Facts*, ii. 95.

20. ME 89.

21. For Vertue's comments and sketches in Oct. 1737, see Frank Simpson, 'New Place: The Only Representation of Shakespeare's House from an Unpublished Manuscript', *Shakespeare Survey*, 5 (1952), 55–7; Simpson's own comments on plate 1 are questionable. See also ME 89–90.

22. Fripp, *Shakespeare*, ii. 466; S. Schoenbaum, *William Shakespeare: Records and Images* (1981), 53.

23. ME 91, 98.

24. MS SBTRO, Misc. Doc. i (BRU 15/1), 106 ('The noate of Corne & malte Taken the iiij^th of ffebrwarij' (1598)).

25. MS SBTRO, BRU 15/1/135 (24 Jan. 1598).

26. Ibid.

27. Bearman, 27–8.

28. Quoted in E. I. Fripp, *Master Richard Quyny* (Oxford, 1924), 120 (Nov. 1597).

29. MS SBTRO, BRU 15/1/136 (4 Nov. 1598).

30. Bearman, 33.

31. MSS SBTRO, ER 27/4 (25 Oct. 1598) and BRU 5/1/136 (4 Nov. 1598) and 5/1/131 (Oct. 1598). Throughout, I have modernized Quiney's and Sturley's spelling.

32. Roger Pringle on Stow's *Survey*, in J. F. Andrews (ed.), *Shakespeare*, 3 vols. (New York, 1985), i. 275; François Laroque, *Shakespeare's Festive World*, trans. Janet Lloyd (Cambridge, 1993), esp. ch. 4.

33. MS SBTRO, BRU 15/1/136.

34. It is not clear who (or how many) hit Quiney; but he was threatened by Greville's bailiff, or steward, some days before he was struck down in a room among Greville's men. Cf. Fripp, *Shakespeare*, ii. 542–9, 576–8, and ME 97–8.

35. Richard Wilson, 'Enclosure Riots', *Shakespeare Quarterly*, 43 (1992), 1–19; V. H. T. Skipp, 'Forest of Arden, 1530–1649', *Agricultural History Review*, 18 (1970), 84–111, esp. 95.

36. Anne Barton, *Shakespeare and the Idea of the Play* (1977), 155.

13. South of Julius Caesar's Tower

1. Mary Edmond, 'Hudson and the Burbages', *Notes and Queries*, 239 (1994), 502–3.

2. Nicholas Rowe, 'Some Account of the Life, &c. of Mr. *William Shakespear*', in Shakespeare, *Works*, ed. Rowe, 6 vols. (1709), i. pp. xii–xiii.

3. *Ben Jonson*, ed. C. H. Herford and P. and E. Simpson, 11 vols. (Oxford, 1925–52), iii. 440.

4. MS Bodleian, Arch. F. c. 37 (John Aubrey).

5. *Ben Jonson*, ed. Herford and Simpson, viii. 584, 392.

6. Ibid. i. 133, viii. 583.

7. I. A. Shapiro offers a good analysis of the relevant legends and evidence in 'The "Mermaid Club" ', *Modern Language Review*, 45 (1950), 6–17.

8. For versions of these anecdotes (in 17th-century notes by Sir Nicholas L'Estrange, Nicholas Burgh, and Thomas Plume), see EKC, *Facts*, ii. 243, 246–7.

9. See Satire VII, in *The Scourge of Villainy* (1598).

10. Sonnets 80 and 85.

11. *Ben Jonson*, ed. Herford and Simpson, iii. 303.

12. Ibid. vi. 16.

13. See James Shapiro, *Rival Playwrights: Marlowe, Jonson, Shakespeare* (Cambridge, 1991), 133–70, esp. 154.

14. Thus in Q1600 and F1623.

15. Norman Jones (on the aftermath of the Usury Act of 1571) in *God and the Money-lenders* (Oxford, 1989), esp. 199.

16. Cf. SS, *DL* 137, 198–200.

17. Despite his theories, Leslie Hotson in *Shakespeare versus Shallow* (1931) illuminates Langley, Gardiner, and Wayte; see esp. pp. 9–83.

18. John Gross, *Shylock: Four Hundred Years in the Life of a Legend* (1994), 323. For aspects of Shylock, pertinent supplements to John Gross's survey include the chapter, ' "Ev'ry child hates Shylock" ', in Frank Felsenstein's *Anti-Semitic Stereotypes . . . 1660–1830* (Baltimore, Md., 1995), as well as David Katz's *The Jews in the History of England 1485–1850* (Oxford, 1995), and James Shapiro's *Shakespeare and the Jews* (New York, 1996).

19. Peter Hall, *Making an Exhibition of Myself* (1993), 382–3. Cf. the viewpoints in Leo Salingar, *Dramatic Form in Shakespeare and the Jacobeans* (Cambridge, 1986), and in Avraham Oz, *The Yoke of Love* (Newark, Del., 1995).

20. MS Folger, W. b. 180 has evidence relating to the scarcities; cf. James Bennett, *History of Tewkesbury* (Tewkesbury, 1830), 307–9.

21. Richard Hillman, *Shakespearean Subversions* (1992), 141; Philip Edwards, *Shakespeare and the Confines of Art* (1968), 63.

22. *The Diary of John Manningham of the Middle Temple 1602–1603*, ed. R. P. Sorlien (Hanover, NH, 1976), fo. 29b, pp. 75, 328, Cf. SS, *DL* 205.

23. *Manningham*, fo. 29b. EKC, *Facts*. ii. 212, is useful, but over-confident about the informant's name.

24. Francis Meres, *Palladis Tamia. Wits Treasury. Being the Second part of Wits Common wealth* (1598), sigs. Oo1ʳ–Oo2.

25. Ibid., sig. Oo2.

26. *Hamlet*, II. ii. 401–2.

27. Andrew Gurr, 'Money or Audiences', *Theatre Notebook*, 42 (1988), 3–14.

28. Everard Guilpin, *Skialetheia* (1598), Satire 5.

29. R. L. Knutson, 'The Repertory', in J. D. Cox and D. S. Kastan (eds.), *A New History of Early English Drama* (New York, 1997), 469–71.

30. Stow, *The Annales of England* (1601), 1303; Ann Jennalie Cook, 'John Stow's Storm and the Demolition of the Theatre', *Shakespeare Quarterly*, 40 (1989), 327–8.

31. C. W. Wallace and his wife Hulda originally found but did not publish these

references, which David Kathman assesses in 'Six Biographical Records "Re-Discovered": Some Neglected Contemporary References to Shakespeare', *Shakespeare Newsletter*, 45 (Winter 1995), 73–8.

32. Barry Day's *This Wooden "O": Shakespeare's Globe Reborn* (1997) offers a lively, non-technical history of the modern Globe site.

33. See A. Gurr, R. Mulryne, and M. Shewring, *The Design of the Globe* (1993).

34. *Julius Caesar*, ed. Marvin Spevack (Cambridge, 1988), 3–5. *Thomas Platter's Travels in England 1599*, trans. Clare Williams (1937); and Ernest Schanzer, 'Thomas Platter's Observations on the Elizabethan Stage', *Notes and Queries*, 201 (1956), 465–7. (Some of Platter's meanings are still obscure; I follow Schanzer's translation, and acknowledge Helmuth Joel's advice on the dialect.)

35. K.W., *The Education of children in learning: Declared by the Dignitie, Utilitie, and Method thereof* (1588), sig. D1.

36. *Julius Caesar*, ed. A. Humphreys (Oxford, 1984), 46.

14. Hamlet's Questions

1. H. H. Lamb, *Climate, History and the Modern World* (1982), 201–5, and E. LeRoy Ladurie, *Times of Feast, Times of Famine*, trans. B. Bray (New York, 1988), 312–13.

2. *Jack Drum's Entertainment* (1600), v.

3. See *Hamlet*, ed. G. R. Hibbard (Oxford, 1987), 67–130, citing W. W. Greg; and R. L. Knutson on the 'little eyases', in *Shakespeare Quarterly*, 46 (1995), 1–31.

4. *The Pigrimage to Parnassus*, and the First and Second Parts of *The Returne from Parnassus*, are three anonymous plays written between 1598 and 1602, and acted at St John's College, Cambridge. Edmund Rishton matriculated there and took his BA in 1599, and MA in 1602. He probably owned the extant MS: on its first leaf is the name 'Edmund Rishton, Lancastrensis' (MS Bodleian, Rawlinson D. 398). The quoted lines, from the second *Returne*, are spoken by Kempe to Burbage as they discuss whether to hire Studioso and Philomusus, two recent graduates, as actors in WS's troupe. In the first *Returne*, Gullio, a fool, leaves the reading of Spenser and Chaucer to dunces. He would sleep with *Venus and Adonis* under his pillow. 'O sweet Mr Shakespeare', he rhapsodizes, 'I'll have his picture in my study at the Court'. All three plays either quote or imitate WS; see *The Three Parnassus Plays (1598–1601)* ed. J. B. Leishman (1949), esp. 337, 369–71.

5. Sig. H4ᵛ.

6. *Hamlet*, III. i. 154; cf. *Hamlet*, ed. Hibbard, 32.

7. *Hamlet*, ed. Hibbard, 29; Barbara Everett, *Young Hamlet: Essays on Shakespeare's Tragedies* (Oxford, 1989), 3–8.

8. *Hamlet*, ed. Philip Edwards (Cambridge, 1985), 5.

9. *Hamlet*, Arden edn., ed. Harold Jenkins (Methuen, 1982), 123, 129; *Hamlet*, additional passages, F. 8–11.

10. *Hamlet*, III. ii. 1–5, 17–25, 36–8.

11. Keeling's men acted *Hamlet* at sea in 1607. Sir Thomas Smith cited the play in relation to Godunov's Moscow court in a pamphlet, *Sir T. Smithes voiage and entertainment in Russia* (1605), sig. K1. Poulett wrote from Paris on 10 Oct. 1605: Hilton Kelliher, 'A Shakespeare Allusion', *British Library Journal*, 3 (1977), 7–12.

12. EKC, *Facts*, ii. 197.

13. *Troilus and Cressida*, ed. K. Muir (Oxford, 1984), 193.

14. George Chapman, *Seaven Bookes of the Iliades of Homere* (1598), sig. A4.

15. G. Wilson Knight, 'The Philosophy of *Troilus and Cressida*', in his *The Wheel of Fire: Interpretations of Shakespearian Tragedy* (1961), 47–72, esp. 48.

16. For some of the bearings of religious rite upon the poem, H. Neville Davies, '*The Phoenix and Turtle*: Requiem and Rite', *Review of English Studies*, 46 (1995), 525–30.

17. ME 92; SS, *DL* 246; Bearman, 37–8.

18. Màiri Macdonald, 'A New Discovery about Shakespeare's Estate . . .', *Shakespeare Quarterly*, 45 (1994), 87–9; Bearman, 41.

19. MS SBTRO BRU 2/1, 17 Dec. 1602 and 7 Feb. 1612. E. I. Fripp, *Shakespeare: Man and Artist*, 2 vols. (Oxford, 1964), ii. 845–6.

20. EKC, *Facts*, ii. 119–27.

21. Jeanne E. Jones, 'Lewis Hiccox and Shakespeare's Birthplace', *Notes and Queries*, 239 (1994), 497–502.

22. ME 101.

15. The King's Servants

1. Douglas Bruster, *Drama and Market in the Age of Shakespeare* (Cambridge, 1992), 101–2.

2. *Memoirs of Robert Carey*, ed. F. H. Mares (Oxford, 1972), 58–60. Cf. H. Neville Davies, 'Jacobean *Antony and Cleopatra*', *Shakespeare Studies*, 17 (1985), 146.

3. *Englandes Mourning Garment* (1603), sigs. D2ᵛ–D3.

4. EKC, *Stage*, ii. 208. On the Stuart court itself, I have found especially useful Jenny Wormald, 'James VI and I: Two Kings or One?', *History*, 68 (1983), 187–209; Derek Hirst, *Authority and Conflict: England 1603–1658* (1986); and Graham Parry, *The Golden Age Restor'd: The Culture of the Stuart Court, 1603–42* (Manchester, 1981).

5. EKC, *Stage*, ii. 208–9.

6. Ibid. iv. 168.

7. MS Folger, W. b. 182. *Calendar of State Papers, Domestic, Jac. I*, vi. 21.

8. E. Nungezer, *A Dictionary of Actors* (New York, 1929), 141–2.

9. A. Gurr, *The Shakespearean Stage 1574–1642* (Cambridge, 1985), 46.

10. MS Folger, W. b. 181 (translated from Latin).

11. EKC, *Stage*, iv. 168.

12. M. G. Brennan, ' "We Have the Man Shakespeare With Us": Wilton House and *As You Like It*', *Wiltshire Archaeological and Natural History Magazine*, 80 (1986), 225–7.

13. *The First Quarto of King Richard III*, ed. Peter Davison (Cambridge, 1996), 47. Wilton's burgesses show in their accounts for 1603, 'Paid to mr Sharppe for his layinges out vppon giftes and fees vnto the kinges seruantes £6 = 5 = 0' (Trowbridge Record Office, G25/1/91).

14. David M. Bergeron offers a good overall survey of this topic in *English Civic Pageantry 1558–1642* (Columbia, SC, 1971).

15. Quoted in Parry, *The Golden Age Restor'd*, 6.

16. EKC, *Stage*, iv. 172.

17. *Calendar of MSS of the Marquess of Salisbury* (1883–1976), xvi. 415 (spelling modernized).

18. EKC, *Stage*, iv. 171.

19. E. A. J. Honigmann, *The Texts of 'Othello' and Shakespearian Revision* (1996), 86–8.

20. Patrick Collinson, 'The Church: Religion and its Manifestations', in J. F. Andrews (ed.), *Shakespeare*, 3 vols. (New York, 1985), i. 21–40, esp. 35. For Stratford: MS SBTRO, council-books, 17 Dec. 1602 and 7 Feb. 1611/12; Ann Hughes, 'Religion and Society in Stratford upon Avon, 1619–1638', *Midland History*, 19 (1994), 58–84.

21. *All's Well*, II. iii. 152, 265; IV. iii. 220, 302.

22. Germaine Greer, *Shakespeare* (Oxford, 1986), 109, 113.

23. Robert Smallwood, 'The Design of "All's Well that Ends Well" ', *Shakespeare Survey*, 25 (1972), 45–61.

24. Bridewell archive MS, 1597/8–1604, courtesy of Guildhall Library, London; Laura Wright and Jonathan Hope. On petty offenders in the Duke's 'Vienna', see *Measure*, IV. iii. 1–18.

25. Richmond Noble, 'The Date of *Othello*', *TLS*, 14 Dec. 1935, p. 859; cf. *Othello*, Arden edn., ed. Honigmann (Walton-on-Thames, 1997), 344–50.

26. See G. Tillotson, in *TLS*, 20 July 1933, p. 494.

16. The Tragic Sublime

1. *2 Henry IV*, II. iv. 60–2. *Athenae Oxonienses*, ed. P. Bliss, vol. iii (1817), 802–9.

2. Mary Edmond, *Rare Sir William Davenant* (Manchester, 1987), 18.

3. Ibid. 13.

4. Ibid. 22–3. The errors of fact in Schoenbaum's *Shakespeare's Lives* (Oxford, 1970), 99 (1991 edn.), 61, are repeated in SS, *DL* 224–5.

5. MS Bodleian, Arch. F. c. 37.

6. Ibid.

7. The best analyses of these five documents are still those in EKC, *Facts*, ii. 87–90,

and in M. S. Giuseppi, 'The Exchequer Documents Relative to Shakespeare's Residence in Southwark', in *Transactions of the London and Middlesex Archaeological Society*, NS 5 (1926), 281–8. The summary on taxes in SS, *DL* 220–3 is useful, and so is the background given by B. Roland Lewis in *The Shakespeare Documents*, 2 vols. (Stanford, Ca., 1941), i. 262–71, though transcripts in the latter work are unreliable.

8. The tax assessment for actors and musicians at St Helen's was likely to be a standard one; see PRO, E179/146/369.

9. A. E. M. Kirkwood, 'Richard Field, Printer, 1589–1624', *The Library*, 12 (1931), 1–35: see also the two relevant articles in *Proceedings of the Huguenot Society of London*: W. R. Le Fanu, 'Thomas Vautrollier . . .' (20 (1958–64), 12–25), and Colin Clair, 'Refugee Printers and Publishers in Britain during the Tudor Period' (22 (1970–6), 115–26).

10. Hilton Kelliher, in *London Review of Books*, 22 May 1986, p. 4.

11. MS Bodleian, Rawlinson poet. 160, fo. 41, which gives the spelling 'Helias Iames'.

12. M. H. Spielmann, *The Title-page of the First Folio of Shakespeare's Plays* (1924); S. Schoenbaum, *William Shakespeare: Records and Images* (1981), 168.

13. MS Bodleian, Arch. F. c. 37. Cf. E. A. J. Honigmann, 'Shakespeare and London's Immigrant Community circa 1600', in J. P. Vander Motten (ed.), *Elizabethan and Modern Studies* (Gent, 1985), 143–53, esp. 145–6.

14. George Orwell, 'Lear, Tolstoi and the Fool', in *Shooting an Elephant* (1950), 52.

15. John Stow, *A Survey of London*, ed. C. L. Kingsford, 2 vols. (Oxford, 1971), ii. 339 n.

16. SS, *DL* 260. WS's parish of St Olave, and Heminges' and Condell's parish of St Mary Aldermanbury, were separated by St Alphage's to the north and to the south by St Alban's. See the descriptions in Stow, *Survey*; and Roger Finlay, *Population and Metropolis* (Cambridge, 1981), app. 3.

17. For the twenty-six documents of the Belott–Mountjoy suit unearthed by the Wallaces at the PRO in 1909, C. W. Wallace's 'New Shakespeare Discoveries', *Harper's Monthly Magazine*, 120 (1910), 489–510 is still useful, as are the accounts in EKC, *Facts*, ii. 90–5, and in Schoenbaum, *Records and Images*, 20–39.

18. PRO, Court of Requests, Documents of Shakespearian Interest Req. 4/1 (11 May 1612).

19. In 'Shakespeare and London's Immigrant Community', 149–50.

20. PRO, Court of Requests, Req. 4/1 (11 May 1612).

21. Ibid. (19 June 1612).

22. Roger Prior, 'The Life of George Wilkins', *Shakespeare Survey*, 25 (1972), 137–52, esp. 151–2.

23. Schoenbaum, *Records and Images*, 24.

24. [Matthew Gwinn], *Vertumnus sive Annus Recurrens Oxonii* . . . (1607), 'Ad Regis . . . tres quasi Sibyllae . . .', lines 4–5.

25. Cf. H. N. Paul, *The Royal Play of Macbeth* (New York, 1978); and H. Neville Davies, 'Jacobean *Antony and Cleopatra*', *Shakespeare Studies*, 17 (1985), 123–58.

26. Terry Eagleton, *William Shakespeare* (Oxford, 1986), 2–3.
27. Peter Millward, *Shakespeare's Religious Background* (1973), 127–33.
28. Frank Kermode, *The Sense of an Ending* (Oxford, 1967), 88.
29. E. Nungezer, *A Dictionary of Actors* (New York, 1929), 20, 74. Evidence that Armin played Lear's Fool is only circumstantial; on this actor's roles, looks, and stature (not that dwarfishness is needed for the part), see David Wiles, *Shakespeare's Clown: Actor and Text in the Elizabethan Playhouse* (Cambridge, 1987), 144–63.
30. Peter Brook, *The Shifting Point* (1988), 87.
31. *Peter Hall's Diaries*, ed. John Goodwin (1983), 356.
32. Kenneth Muir, *Shakespeare's Sources*, i. (1957), 145.
33. R. A. Foakes, *Hamlet 'versus' Lear* (Cambridge, 1993), 181.
34. *A Declaration of egregious Popish Impostures* (1603), sigs. G4, H1ᵛ, Q3ᵛ, and Aa2ᵛ.
35. Stephen Greenblatt, *Shakespearean Negotiations* (Oxford, 1988), 127.
36. *Ben Jonson*, ed. C. H. Herford and P. and E. Simpson, 11 vols. (Oxford, 1925–52), i. 141.
37. Janet Adelman, *The Common Liar* (New Haven, 1973), 102–21, repr. in *Antony and Cleopatra*, ed. John Drakakis (Basingstoke, 1994), 56–77.
38. Cf. *Coriolanus*, ed. Brian Parker (Oxford, 1994), 34–43.
39. Hazlitt, *Characters of Shakespeare's Plays* (1817). On *Timon*'s monetary theme in relation to the age, see Coppélia Kahn, on 'Magic of Bounty', *Shakespeare Quarterly*, 38 (1987), 34–57; A. D. Nuttall, *Timon of Athens* (Boston, Mass., 1987); and Michael Chorost, 'Biological Finance', *English Literary Renaissance*, 21 (1991), 349–70.

17. Tales and Tempests

1. Hugh A. Hanley, 'Shakespeare's Family in Stratford Records', *TLS*, 21 May 1964, p. 441. (Act Books, Kent County Archives Office.)
2. Evidence from parish registers as to the ages of women at first marriage is summarized in E. A. Wrigley and R. S. Schofield, *The Population History of England 1541–1871* (1981), 248, 255, and in J. M. Martin's study of Stratford's records in *Midland History*, 7 (1982), 27–31. For Anne Hathaway as 'long in the tooth' see SS, *DL* 82–3.
3. MS Edinburgh, H-P, Coll. 347. Harriet Joseph, *Shakespeare's Son-in-Law: John Hall* (Hamden, Conn., 1964), 1–5. Irvine Gray on John Hall's 'Antecedents', *Genealogist's Magazine*, 7 (1935–7), 344–54. It has been assumed that Hall first came to Stratford 'around 1600'; the earliest record of him in the town is dated 5 June 1607.
4. Màiri Macdonald, 'A New Discovery about Shakespeare's Estate . . .', *Shakespeare Quarterly*, 45 (1994), 87–9.
5. Harriet Joseph, *Shakespeare's Son-in-Law*, 59. John Hall, *Select Observations on English Bodies*, trans. James Cooke (1679), 16, 29, 31–4.

6. Ann Hughes, 'Religion and Society in Stratford upon Avon, 1619–1638', *Midland History*, 19 (1994), 58–84, esp. 69.

7. William Hall's will is dated 12 Dec. 1607; Gray, 'Antecedents', 345–7.

8. G. Taylor, 'Some Manuscripts of Shakespeare's Sonnets', *Bulletin of the John Rylands Library*, 68 (1985–6), 222–3; John Weever, *Epigrammes in the oldest cut, and newest fashion* (1599), sig. E6ʳ.

9. *Willobie his Avisa. Or The true Picture of a modest Maid, and of a chast and constant wife* (1594), sigs. L1ᵛ–L2. See also R. C. Horne, 'Two Unrecorded Contemporary References to Shakespeare', *Notes and Queries*, 229 (1984), 220.

10. K. Duncan-Jones, 'Was the 1609 *Shake-speares Sonnets* really Unauthorized?', *Review of English Studies*, NS 34 (1983), 151–71.

11. D. W. Foster, 'Master W. H., R. I. P', *PMLA* 102 (1987), 42–54. J. M. Nosworthy, in *The Library*, 18 (1963), 294–8.

12. As 'rewarde for their private practice in time of infecction', the Crown granted the King's players £40 (1609) and £30 (in the winter of 1610–11); they also had receipts from touring.

13. Gurr, *Companies*, 294–5.

14. Ibid. 368.

15. *Guardian*, 8 Apr. 1994.

16. Emrys Jones, 'Stuart Cymbeline', *Essays in Criticism*, 11 (1961), 84; R. Smallwood, 'Shakespeare at Stratford-upon-Avon . . .', *Shakespeare Quarterly*, 41 (1990), 104.

17. Brian Gibbons, *Shakespeare and Multiplicity* (Cambridge, 1993), 18–47, esp. 23.

18. For the (unresolved) spelling debate over 'Imogen' or 'Innogen': S. Wells *et al.*, *William Shakespeare: A Textual Companion* (Oxford, 1987), 604; John Pitcher, 'Names in *Cymbeline*', *Essays in Criticism*, 43 (1993), 1–16.

19. Daryl W. Palmer, 'Jacobean Muscovites: Winter, Tyranny, and Knowledge in *The Winter's Tale*', *Shakespeare Quarterly*, 46 (1995), 323–39, esp. 332.

20. Margaret Hotine, 'Contemporary Themes in *The Tempest*', *Notes and Queries*, 232 (1987), 224–6.

21. Philip Edwards, *Shakespeare and the Confines of Art* (1968), 151.

22. EKC, *Facts*, ii. 219.

23. Ibid. 214.

24. Ibid. 211, 224.

25. *Brief Lives*, ed. Andrew Clark, 2 vols. (Oxford, 1898), i. 96.

26. Gurr, *Companies*, 122.

27. John Freehafer, '*Cardenio*, by Shakespeare and Fletcher', *PMLA* 84 (1969), 501–13.

28. Logan Pearsall Smith, *The Life and Letters of Henry Wotton*, 2 vols. (Oxford, 1907), ii. 33.

29. Douglas Bruster, 'The Jailer's Daughter and the Politics of Madwomen's Language', *Shakespeare Quarterly*, 46 (1995), 277–300.

30. S. Schoenbaum, *William Shakespeare: Records and Images* (1981), 47; EKC, *Facts*, ii. 154–69.

31. Pearsall Smith, *Henry Wotton*, ii. 32–3.
32. *King Henry VIII*, ed. John Margeson (Cambridge, 1990), 1–3.
33. 'A Sonnett upon the pittiful burneing of the Globe playhouse in London', lines 40–2. See EKC, *Stage*, ii. 421.

18. A Gentleman's Choices

1. EKC, *Facts*, ii. 268.
2. Russell Jackson, in *Players of Shakespeare 2*, ed. R. Jackson and R. Smallwood (Cambridge, 1988), 10–11.
3. MSS SBTRO, BRU 2/1. E. I. Fripp, *Shakespeare: Man and Artist*, 2 vols. (Oxford, 1964), ii. 798–800.
4. EKC, *Facts*, ii. 96 (9 Sept. 1609).
5. Cf. Bearman, 44–8.
6. Fripp, *Shakespeare*, ii. 813, 839–42; ME 50; SS, *DL* 289.
7. Bearman, 56.
8. Ibid. 52–5.
9. EKC, *Facts*, ii. 141 (capitals added).
10. MS SBTRO, ER 27/3.
11. MS SBTRO, BRU 15/13/26a–29. For transcriptions of Thomas Greene's diary (with commentary), see C. M. Ingleby, *Shakespeare and the Enclosure of Common Fields at Welcombe* (1885); EKC, *Facts*, ii. 141–52; S. Schoenbaum, *William Shakespeare: Records and Images* (1981), 64–91.
12. Bearman, 59, and n. 11 above.
13. ME 132.
14. After taking his BA at University College, Oxford in 1606, Leonard Digges (1588–1635) studied abroad, but returned to be awarded the MA and live at his college. 'To the Memorie of the deceased Authour Maister W. Shakespeare', twenty-two lines long, includes the first known allusion to the poet's monument at Holy Trinity and appears in the 1623 Folio (eighth preliminary leaf). The untitled 'Poets are borne not made . . .', of sixty-eight lines, is a tribute in John Benson's volume of Shakespeare's *Poems* (1640). With very minor typographical changes, Digges's two poems are given in EKC, *Facts*, ii. 231–4.
15. Fripp, *Shakespeare*, ii. 833.
16. MS Edinburgh, H-P Coll. 365.
17. Worcs., 802/BA 2760, Visitation Act Book 1613–17, fo. 27ᵛ. The entry does not concern Judith's absence from the court, only her husband's ('vir cit*atus per* Nixon no*n* comp*aruit*'), and this document itself applies only to Thomas's penalty.
18. H. A. Hanley, 'Shakespeare's Family in Stratford Records', *TLS*, 21 May 1964, p. 441.
19. SS, *DL* 299.

20. SS, *DL* 297.

21. EKC, *Facts*, ii. 174–5.

22. PRO, PROB 1/4 (spelling modernized).

23. John Barnard, 'A Puritan Controversialist and his Books: The Will of Alexander Cooke (1564–1632)', *Papers of the Bibliographical Society of America*, 86 (1992), 82–6.

24. The error is in SS, *DL* 300. See the references to Richard Hathaway in the town council's reports in MSS SBTRO, as well as Fripp, *Shakespeare*, ii. 787–8 and 837.

25. PRO, PROB 1/4.

26. A. L. Rowse, in *TLS*, 25 Nov. 1994, p. 15; SS, *DL* 302.

27. Margaret Spufford, *Contrasting Communities* (Cambridge, 1974), 112; Richard Wilson, *Will Power* (New York, 1993), 210.

28. 'Probate', in *Playhouse Wills, 1558–1642*, ed. E. A. J. Honigmann and Susan Brock (Manchester, 1993), 22–5.

29. John Hall, *Select Observations on English Bodies*, trans. James Cooke (1679), sig. A3^{r-v}.

30. Ibid., sig. D1^r.

31. Frank Marcham, *William Shakespeare and his Daughter Susannah* (1931), 70.

32. See Jeanne E. Jones, 'Lewis Hiccox and Shakespeare's Birthplace', *Notes and Queries*, 41 (1994), 497–502.

33. *Notes and Queries*, 40 (1993), 231–2.

34. *The Tewkesbury Yearly Register and Magazine*, 1 (1840), 213. The interviewer was Sir Richard Phillips.

35. P. W. M. Blayney, *The First Folio of Shakespeare*, Folger Shakespeare Library (Washington, DC, 1991), 7–8.

36. Ibid. 1–2; T. Matheson, 'One Man in his Time', in K. Parsons and P. Mason (eds.), *Shakespeare in Performance* (1995), 8.

37. 'To the Memorie of the deceased Authour Maister W. Shakespeare' (1623), lines 3–5.

38. *Diary of the Rev. John Ward . . . Extending from 1648 to 1679*, ed. Charles Severn (1839), 183.

39. Fripp, *Shakespeare* (1964), ii. 824.

40. William Budd, *Typhoid Fever: Its Nature, Mode of Spreading, and Prevention* (1st edn., 1874; 1931), 76.

41. EKC, *Facts*, ii. 260–1.

42. *A Funerall Elegye*, written for William Peter, was first edited by D. W. Foster in *Elegy by W. S.: A Study in Attribution* (Newark, Del., 1989). The poem's attribution to Shakespeare has evoked a flood of debate: to cite from only one year, 1996, for example in the *TLS* (26 Jan.; 9 and 16 Feb.; 8, 22 and 29 Mar.; 12 Apr.; and 14 June); in the *New York Times* (14 Jan.); in *PMLA* 111, 1086–1105; and in *Studies in English Literature*, 36: 435–60. The poem's author, in fact, is unknown.

43. Gurr, *Companies*, 25–7. Milton's speech *Areopagitica* (in favour of unlicensed printing with remarks on the minds and attitudes of Londoners) was first printed in 1644.

44. Cf. E. I. Fripp, *Shakespeare's Stratford* (Oxford, 1928), 75; S. Wells unhappily notices alterations in the floor of the chancel (*Daily Telegraph*, 22 Apr. 1995).

INDEX

To enhance the usefulness of the index, the spelling of proper names is regularized.

Printed in the USA/Agawam, MA
August 10, 2015

620799.010